Narrative and Freedom

Narrative and Freedom
The Shadows of Time

Gary Saul Morson

Yale University Press

New Haven and London

Designed by James J. Johnson and set in Stemple Garamond type by
Tseng Information Systems, Durham, North Carolina.
Printed in the United States of America by Edwards Brothers, Ann Arbor, Michigan.

Library of Congress Cataloging-in-Publication Data

Morson, Gary Saul, 1948–
Narrative and freedom : the shadows of time / Gary Saul Morson.
p.   cm.
Includes bibliographical references (p.) and index.
ISBN 0–300–05882–9 (alk. paper)
1. Narration (Rhetoric)   2. Time in literature.   3. Literature—History and criticism.
4. Slavic literature—History and criticism.   I. Title.
PN212.M67   1994
809'.9338—dc20   94–7065

A catalogue record for this book is available from the British Library.

10 9 8 7 6 5 4 3 2 1

Everything I do is planned.

—INSPECTOR CLOUSEAU

Contents

Acknowledgments   xi
Note on Punctuation   xii
Abbreviations   xiii

Introduction   1

Part I: The Shape of Narrative and the Shape of Experience
Chapter One. Prelude: Process and Product   17

Time out, 17. Eventness, 20. Creative process, 23. The pun of creativity, 27. Temporal vacuum, 30. Logarithms and sea battles, 33. Double determination, 36. Narrative isomorphism and anisomorphism, 38. Escape from structure, 40.

Chapter Two. Foreshadowing   42

The essential surplus, 43. Foreshadowing, 45. The gathering storm, 47. The future that has happened, 50. Prophetic history, 53. Types of the socialist future, 54. The art of the known future, 57. *Oedipus the King*, 58. Omens, 61. Destiny and determinism, 63. Exemption from inevitability, 66. "The Fatalist," 67. Eluctable destiny, 69. Anna Karenina's omens: Narcissism and stories, 71. Anna: Who is to blame?, 74. Anna: Omens and their causes, 75. Anna: Loose ends, 77. The surplus against itself, 79.

Chapter Three. Interlude: Bakhtin's Indeterminism   82

"The Dilemma of Determinism": Time's "loose play," 82. Novels as forms of thought, 86. The lateness of the author, 88. Bakhtin's second stage: Characters break free, 91. The heteroverse, 94. God subjected to time, 95. Creating freedom by provocation and torture, 97. Strange synchronies, 100. Bakhtin's third stage: Wisdom of the chronotope, 105. "Real historical time," 107. Time in the historical novel, 110. Many realities, and the surplus of humanness, 112.

Part II: Sideshadowing and Its Possibilities

Chapter Four. Sideshadowing   117

The possibility of possibility, and the middle realm, 117. Time as a field, 119. The extraordinary number of facts, if only they are facts, 120. Rumor as hero, 123. The workers rebel, or do they?, 124. Twice *Possessed*, 126. Gaps in the text, 129. The past as "an indistinct abstraction," 132. Pseudo-foreshadowing, 134. *Karamazov:* "Both versions were true," 137. *Karamazov:* Responsibility and the middle realm, 139. Kairova time and processual intentionality, 142. The devil's potentials: The coordinates of the other world, 146. The hunger for possibilities, 148. Paraquels and parodies, 151. Resurrections, 153. Tolstoy and contingency, 155. Aesthetic potentiality, 158. Vortex time, 162. The end of time, 165. After the vortex, 167. Aperture, 169.

Chapter Five. Paralude: Presentness and Its Diseases   173

Sports time, 173. Sports time: Synchronizing public and private, 175. "Longing for the present," 177. Genre painting and memory, 180. Prosaics and the presentness of the past, 183. Present and sequence. The happiest moment and four diseases of presentness, 187. Disease #1, the desiccated present. Epic time and epilogue time, 189. Disease #1, the desiccated present. Epilogue time and the generations, 193. Disease #1, the desiccated present. Eschatology and utopia, 198. Disease #2, the isolated present, 201. Disease #2, the isolated present. Gambling with history, 203. Disease #2, the isolated present. The mutable past, 206. Disease #2, the isolated present. The dialogue of times, and a strange catastrophism, 210. Disease #2, the isolated present. Commemoration, 212. Disease #3, hypothetical time. Edited life, 214. Disease #3, hypothetical time. The impurity of freedom, 222. Disease #3, hypothetical time. Crime and chronicity, 224. Disease #4, Multiple time. The garden of forking paths, 227. Disease #4, multiple time. Multiple-universe determinism, 232.

Chapter Six. Backshadowing   234

Backshadowing defined and characterized, 234. "He should have known": Premises of backshadowing, 235. Retrospection and reciprocity, 238. Whiggism, 241. Time line: The progressive, 244. Arthropodic whiggism: Wonderful life, 245. Two fallacies: Hyperselectionism and inferring history from current utility, 249. Three principles: Anthropic, misanthropic, and brassicic, 251. Looking backward, 255. The single truth and society as artwork, 257. Time and opinion, 260. Vagrant philosophy and the script of time, 262.

Conclusion

Chapter Seven. Opinion and the World of Possibilities   267

Crooked timber, 267. Dialogue and final solutions, 271. The church of Philadelphia, 273. Epilogue . . . , 278. . . . and beyond, 280.

Notes   283

Index   309

Acknowledgments

The notes to this book do not adequately express my debt to Robert Louis Jackson, the best of mentors, who first helped me to sense how rich the theme of freedom and responsibility could be; to Aron Katsenelinboigen, whose example, no less than his ideas, helped me to explore the nature of creativity; to Alfred Rieber, who taught and argued with me about historical narrative; and to Stephen Toulmin, for me the great intellectual resource of Northwestern University and almost a university in himself.

Exchanges with Elizabeth Allen, Barbara Anderson, Carol Avins, Robert Belknap, T. H. Breen, Frances Brent, Sara Burson, Elizabeth Calihan, Neil Carrick, Clare Cavanagh, Frederick Crews, Francis Dunn, Freeman Dyson, Victor Erlich, Robert Fisher, Joseph Frank, Stephen Jay Gould, Susan Harris, Peter Hayes, Marvin Kantor, Aileen Kelly, Richard Kieckhefer, Diane Leonard, Robert Lerner, Amy Mandelker, Thomas Marullo, Hugh McLean, Shannon McLeod, Robin Feuer Miller, Martin Mueller, Barbara Newman, Clara Claiborne Park, Kathleen Parthé, Elizabeth Phillips, Natasha Sankovitch, Irwin Weil, Vivian Weil, Justin Weir, Julie Williams, Meredith Williams, and Michael Williams deepened my sense of important questions and of particular ideas and works. Susanne Fusso, Jean Gurley, and Elliott Mossman, who read papers based on drafts of this study, caught errors and offered valuable suggestions.

Robert Alter, Helena Goscilo, Martin Price, Lori Singer, William Mills Todd III, and Andrew Wachtel read and offered meticulous comments on this manuscript from beginning to end. I benefited and learned a great deal from their suggestions and objections. As always, Caryl Emerson read draft after draft and offered her special mixture of criticism, debate, and encouragement. Jonathan Brent, too, was a superb partner in dialogue as well as a model editor.

As I explain in a note to the introduction, this book was once to have been part of a joint project with Michael André Bernstein. I cannot imagine what this volume would have been like without the stimulation of his thoughtful conversation, the fine-grained wisdom of his literary sensibility, and his infectious appreciation of how valuable it is to maintain dialogue.

Jane Morson, my first and last source of advice on every difficult point and phrase, helped immeasurably with everything important enough to be called prosaic. To my daughter Emily, who already understands life's playful dance, this book is dedicated.

Note on Punctuation

The writers discussed in the present study make frequent use of ellipses. I have indicated ellipses in the original by unspaced dots (...) to distinguish them from my own omissions, which are represented by spaced dots (. . .).

Unless otherwise indicated, all italics are in the original.

Abbreviations

In references to the works of Bakhtin, Dostoevsky, and Tolstoy, I have used the following abbreviations:

Bakhtin

AiG = "Avtor i geroi v esteticheskoi deiatel'nosti" [Author and hero in aesthetic activity], in M. M. Bakhtin, *Estetika slovesnogo tvorchestva*, ed. S. G. Bocharov (Moscow: Iskusstvo, 1979).

A&A = *Art and Answerability: Early Philosophical Essays by M. M. Bakhtin*, ed. Michael Holquist and Vadim Liapunov, trans. Vadim Liapunov, supplement trans. Kenneth Brostrom (Austin: Univ. of Texas Press, 1990).

BSHR = "The *Bildungsroman* and Its Significance in the History of Realism (Toward a Historical Typology of the Novel)," in M. M. Bakhtin, *Speech Genres and Other Late Essays*, ed. Caryl Emerson and Michael Holquist, trans. Vern McGee (Austin: Univ. of Texas Press, 1986).

DiN = "Discourse in the Novel," in *The Dialogic Imagination: Four Essays by M. M. Bakhtin*, ed. Michael Holquist, trans. Caryl Emerson and Michael Holquist (Austin: Univ. of Texas Press, 1981).

EaN = "Epic and Novel," in *The Dialogic Imagination*.

FTC = "Forms of Time and of the Chronotope in the Novel: Notes toward a Historical Poetics," in *The Dialogic Imagination*.

KFP = "K filosofii postupka" [Toward a philosophy of the act], in the 1984–85 issue of *Filosofiia i sotsiologiia nauki i tekhniki*, a yearbook of the Academy of Sciences (Moscow: Nauka, 1986), 80–160.

PDP = *Problems of Dostoevsky's Poetics*, ed. and trans. Caryl Emerson (Minneapolis: Univ. of Minnesota Press, 1984).

PT = "The Problem of the Text in Linguistics, Philology and the Human Sciences: An Experiment in Philosophical Analysis," in *Speech Genres*.

RQ = "Response to a Question from the *Novyi Mir* Editorial Staff," in *Speech Genres.*

TRDB = "Toward a Reworking of the Dostoevsky Book," in PDP (appendix 2).

Dostoevsky

AWD = *A Writer's Diary*, ed. and trans. Kenneth Lantz (Evanston: Northwestern Univ. Press, 1993 [vol. 1] and forthcoming [vol. 2]). References are to month/year, chapter/article (AWD, 1/76, 3.2 = January 1876 issue, chapter 3, article 2).

BK = *The Brothers Karamazov*, trans. Constance Garnett (New York: Random House, 1950).

C&P = *Crime and Punishment*, trans. Constance Garnett (New York: Modern Library, 1950).

G = *The Gambler*, in *The Short Novels of Dostoevsky*, trans. Constance Garnett (New York: Dial, 1945).

I = *The Idiot*, trans. Constance Garnett (New York: Modern Library, 1962).

NFU = *"Notes from Underground" and "The Grand Inquisitor,"* the Garnett translation revised and edited by Ralph Matlaw (New York: Dutton, 1960).

NI = *The Notebooks for "The Idiot,"* ed. Edward Wasiolek, trans. Katharine Strelsky (Chicago: Univ. of Chicago Press, 1967).

NP = *The Notebooks for "The Possessed,"* ed. Edward Wasiolek, trans. Victor Terras (Chicago: Univ. of Chicago Press, 1968).

P = *The Possessed*, trans. Constance Garnett (New York: Modern Library, 1963).

PSS = *Polnoe sobranie sochinenii v tridtsati tomakh* [Complete works in thirty volumes] (Leningrad: Nauka, 1972–90).

RY = *A Raw Youth*, trans. Constance Garnett (New York: Laurel, 1959).

Tolstoy

AK = *Anna Karenina*, the Garnett translation revised by Leonard J. Kent and Nina Berberova (New York: Modern Library, 1965).

Jub = *Polnoe sobranie sochinenii* [Complete works] in ninety volumes, ed. V. G. Chertkov et al. (Moscow: Khudozhestvennaia literatura, 1929–58).

W&P = *War and Peace*, trans. Ann Dunnigan (New York: Signet, 1968).

Narrative and Freedom

Introduction

Time is of the essence. Intellectual models—whether pertaining to the natural or the social world, to history or psychology, to ethics or politics—implicitly or explicitly depend on a specific sense of time. Some of our schools of thought seek to transcend time, others to reveal the temporality of all things, but in one way or another our interest in time is chronic.

A headline on the front page of today's *New York Times* (May 24, 1991) reads, "ETHIOPIANS REJOICE AT FALL OF RULERS / Crowds Celebrate in Capital as Lenin Statue is Felled." Accompanying the story is a picture, three columns wide, showing the toppled monumental Lenin, whose head alone is only slightly smaller than an average person. Crowds of smiling people clamber over and around it. Over the past two and a half years, this scene has been repeated in numerous countries governed by regimes proclaiming that the end of history had been reached. Statues of the man who established the final system, which was sure to reach perfection rapidly and was destined to survive forever, were overthrown in a kind of ritual return to "history." There is no more Leningrad. In Moscow, Prague, Warsaw, and in Petersburg itself, people have voiced appreciation that they have dethroned not just another regime or an ideology, but a supposed inevitability. Like executing the tsar, overturning Lenin was a kind of metahistorical act, in this case asserting the openness of time. For good or ill, the future was no longer guaranteed. After decades of certainty, the possibility of possibility was reborn—or so many people believed.

These events, which seem to reflect on the central experiences of the twentieth century, remind us of the temporal dimension to politics. Images of utopia typically derive not just from a thirst for social justice but also from a hunger for the end of time as we have known it; for the time when (as the Book of Revelation promises) "there shall be time no longer." At the end of history, the anachronizing of beliefs is over. At last, we shall no longer need to fear that our present opinions and values will be outdated; for at the end, what is outdated is outdating itself. Thus, utopian temporality satisfies a hunger for certainty, which the various forms of merely historical time do not.

In our conceptions of human character, temporality also plays a central role. Is personality essentially given from the outset, as it is in Plutarch's *Lives*, or does it change in essential and unpredictable ways, as in many realist novels of the nineteenth century? Does character development resemble the way a seed develops into a plant? Does it merely "unfold" or does it truly "become" (in Mikhail Bakhtin's sense of the word)? Can we make ourselves different or is such change itself prescribed in advance? Biographical time may be closed or open in diverse ways. What connections are there between each of these temporalities and criteria of responsibility? Over the centuries, debates about concepts essential to our sense of being human, such as blame, hope, guilt, and regret, have been closely linked with beliefs about the nature of time. Whether events are determined or fated, on the one hand, or in some way indeterministic or fundamentally contingent, on the other, affects how we think about ourselves and our lives. Each of these possibilities has been connected to conceptions of human freedom, both moral and political.

Thus time is implicated in theology, ethics, psychology, politics, and, of course, history. The same questions that may be asked about individual lives may be asked about societies or about humanity as a whole. Are there laws to history and does it tend to some goal? Or does history admit of many possible directions, the determination of which depends in part on contingency, chance, or human choices? If history has a direction, can it be redirected? Do fundamental social alterations take place because of the gradual accumulation of small changes or by sudden leaps? The many answers that have been given to these questions have been closely linked to fundamental—the Russians would say accursed—questions about the most important ways in which people have assessed the meaning of their lives and actions.

In the sciences, too, time has been a recurrent problem. It would be possible to narrate the history of physics or biology as a history of temporalities.[1] People experience time as *anisotropic*—as having an inescapable directedness from past to future—but many physical laws are written so that time is a mere parameter; they work as well in either direction. On the other hand, some physical laws, like entropy, may (or may not) suggest an essential directedness to time. Is evolution teleological? Does it, for instance, tend to produce more and more complex forms over time, so that there is a tendency for later to be somehow better? Was the universe arranged so as inevitably to produce conscious observers like ourselves who would come to know it? Or is our existence something that might just as easily not have taken place at all? Could evolution have gone in radically different directions, and are we some sort of merely contingent result, a by-product or afterthought? The various answers to these questions have been closely connected with our sense of our dignity, of our place in the cosmos, and of the reliability of our knowledge.[2]

In saying that views of time are closely connected with central questions of human life, I do not mean that these connections are necessarily logical or philosophically defensible. On the contrary, links are often psychological and ad hoc. They may provoke wonder in those who contemplate them from the perspective of another period or culture. Some people might suppose that belief in an ironclad fatalism or predestination would kill initiative, but the example of Calvinism demonstrates that the very opposite may sometimes be the case. Doctrines of inevitability may work as guarantees that effort will be rewarded as readily as they may discourage exertion. Aeneas strives energetically to realize his inevitable destiny. The exploration of a doctrine's connection with other beliefs and with behavior is an immensely interesting topic, and not one that can be resolved by a purely philosophical analysis, however rigorous, of the concepts involved. Sometimes the associations of beliefs are contingent, in the sense that they might just as easily have been different at another time or in another context. And yet certain recurrent sets of associations do tend to repeat themselves.

In considering such questions as determinism or indeterminism, fate or choice, unfolding or becoming, gradual or sudden change, and temporal closedness or openness, people sometimes make global assumptions. They tacitly accept that time must essentially be one sort of thing, so that (let us say) a metaphysical assertion of determinism is applied across disciplines—to psychology, sociology, and history as well as to biology and physics. It may come to affect how people conduct their daily lives. The history of the past few centuries has offered many examples of such broad applications of a doctrine, supposedly proven by a given science, to the rest of culture.

It has often been noted that such doctrines have been misinterpreted or that later scientific developments have essentially qualified them. But apart from finding shortcomings in particular doctrines, we may also question whether it is not misleading to assume a single temporality for all disciplines and all aspects of experience. Might it not be the case that we need multiple concepts of time—multiple "chronotopes," as Bakhtin would say—for diverse purposes and circumstances? The kind of atemporal laws allowing for both prediction and retrodiction that have proven so useful in astronomy may be the wrong sort of thing to seek in evolutionary biology (as Stephen Jay Gould has often pointed out). Some sciences need to make room for contingency, and contingency itself may bear a different meaning from science to science. In social and psychological life, too, it may be helpful to have an array of chronotopes, or conceptions of temporality, at our disposal.

Just as Galileo maintained that the earth was but one of many planets, so it might be useful to assume that there are always a multiplicity of temporalities to consider. Often the hidden problems with a social doctrine concern something it presupposes but does not articulate, its sense of time. If one enunciates that sense, draws out its consequences, and suggests alternatives, one can often deepen an understanding of what the doctrine entails and which other doctrines might be more acceptable. One needs to develop a "Galilean" temporal consciousness.

The present book is, in this sense, a Galilean study. It is committed as well to the idea that the association of temporal models with other aspects of human life may take place on diverse grounds and have quite varied consequences. Above all, it is concerned with the *human* dimension of time. I am interested in the relation of temporalities to how people live and think about their lives. I shall not address a number of important questions arising out of contemporary physics or of technical interest to philosophers. Nor shall I seek to resolve in a rigorous way the thorny nest of questions pertaining to compatibilism (reconciling freedom and determinism).

I am concerned, rather, with exploring the consequences of various positions for issues central to people's lives. In his essay "The Dilemma of Determinism," which I discuss in chapter 3, William James concedes that he cannot prove his belief in indeterminism. "To deepen our theoretic sense of the *difference* between a world with chances in it and a deterministic world is the most I can hope to do," James explains.[3] He goes on to explore the connections (of various sorts) between each view and fundamental human issues, in the hope that we will appreciate what it is we are choosing. I shall be adopting a similar strategy, but with a different set of examples.

Those examples are primarily literary. It seems to me that the heritage of great literature presents us with numerous highly detailed and profound examinations of what specific beliefs entail as well as remarkably rich descriptions of everyday life. Writers explore what it is to live with a particular conception of time, and what consequences, social, historical, and psychological, a commitment to specific temporalities may produce. By comparison, examples drawn from purely philosophical texts seem thin in their sense of human motivation and moral complexity. In this sense, I do not view literary works as applied or sugar-coated or unrigorous philosophy, but as a specific form of philosophic thought in the broad sense. They philosophize not with a hammer but with a feather. And it has always seemed to me that an important purpose of literary criticism is to help us recover the elusive wisdom of great writers who are also great and delicate thinkers. For this reason, the present study alternates discussion of temporal models with analysis of specific works offering a "thick" description of them.

In our time, the greatest critic concerned with examining literary works in this way is, in my view, Bakhtin. A great many of Bakhtin's writings (not only his famous essay "Forms of Time and of the Chronotope") focus on temporality and its connection with ethics, history, and conceptions of personality. In this respect, Bakhtin was responding to the tradition of Russian thought and especially to the Russian novel, which was almost obsessively concerned with temporality. I locate my own work within this same critical tradition. It is therefore Bakhtinian in two senses: it draws on, extends, and (often) disputes his ideas; and it belongs to the same critical genre, in which theory and analysis of specific works serve to raise fundamental human questions.

For Bakhtin, not just individual works but also whole literary genres could profitably be viewed as "forms of thought." Specifically, he maintained that each narrative genre implicitly manifests a specific model of temporality. The several questions about time mentioned above are answered variously in different genres. Some rely on a sense of time as open, others as closed; in some, individual character unfolds, in others it develops; some allow for contingency whereas others are fatalistic. These categories are, of course, far too crude and far too abstract for the highly concrete imagination of people in diverse chronicities offered by great literature. Bakhtin's views on these questions are themselves immensely interesting, and they will be explored in chapter 3. I shall also offer alternative answers to the questions he raised.

I draw the majority of my examples from realistic novels, especially Russian novels of ideas. In part, that is because (for reasons I shall explore) these novels exhibit, and often explicitly advocate, a temporality close to the one I wish to explore and recommend. The selection also reflects the contingent fact that these are the works I know best; and fascination with their ideas about time was one consideration prompting this book in the first place. Above all, it seems to me that, for all the attention paid to Dostoevsky and Tolstoy, their ideas about time and narrative—about how we understand our lives through the kinds of stories we tell—are especially profound in ways usually overlooked. These two writers, therefore, occupy a special place in my meditations.

Because the readers of this book may not be familiar with Russian literature, I have tried to present Russian examples in such a way that they will be accessible to nonspecialists.

Within the plurality of temporalities, I advocate a particular conception of open time that I call *sideshadowing*. I do not want to deny that closed temporalities frequently have value, but I suspect they are often adopted by default, without a deep appreciation of more open alternatives. What those alternatives might be and how they have been represented are key concerns of the present work. It seems to me that people frequently commit themselves to forms of argument, social concepts, or moral doctrines without realizing the consequences entailed and without making a choice among a range of possibilities. That, at least, is what Dostoevsky, Tolstoy, and Bakhtin believed.

The fallacies they pointed out, and the unfortunate moral consequences they hoped to forestall, seem to be all too common today and, one expects, are likely to be so in the future. Thus I hope this book will have contemporary relevance, but at the same time I do not wish to engage in local polemic with current thinkers. For the fallacies are recurrent, and I am more interested in their underlying problems and neglected alternatives than in the specific form they take this year. I am afraid, therefore, that some readers will be disappointed with my bibliography. Not only is the literature on time impossibly large to cover, so that everyone will note the omission of a favorite thinker or school, but the contemporary doctrines corresponding to the fallacies I identify in thinkers or works from previous centuries will go unmentioned. I can only leave this work of application to the reader.

Sideshadowing, the key term of this book and a concept developed by Michael André Bernstein and myself, names both an open sense of temporality and a set of devices used to convey that sense.[4] These devices figure prominently in the novels of Tolstoy and Dostoevsky, who used them to offer an alternative to prevailing deterministic and otherwise closed views of time. For Dostoevsky, sideshadowing offered a concrete image of human freedom and was closely connected with his concept of responsibility. In Tolstoy's hands, it conveyed a sense of the contingency of events, contingency being a central theme of both *War and Peace* and *Anna Karenina.*

In the determinism these writers opposed, events are either actual or were impossible from the outset; our sense that unactualized possibilities could have happened is nothing more than a measure of our ignorance of causes, facts, and laws. By contrast, sideshadowing admits, in addition to actualities and impossibilities, a *middle realm* of real possibilities that could have happened even if they did not. Things could have been different from the way they were, there were real alternatives to the present we know, and the future admits of various paths. By focusing on the middle realm of possibilities, by exploring its relation to actual events, and by attending to the fact that things could have been different, sideshadowing deepens our sense of the openness of time. It has profound implications for our understanding of history and of our own lives while affecting the ways in which we judge our present situation. It also encourages skepticism about our ability to know the future and the wisdom of projecting straight lines from current trends or values.

Sideshadowing reminds us that the presentness we so palpably experience pertained as well to earlier moments and will characterize future ones. In this respect, it calls attention to the ways in which narratives, which often turn earlier presents into mere pasts, tend to create a single line of development out of a multiplicity. Alternatives once visible disappear from view and an anachronistic sense of the past surreptitiously infects our understanding. By restoring the presentness of the past and cultivating a sense that something else might have happened, sideshadowing restores some of the presentness that has been lost. It alters the way we think about earlier events and the narrative models used to describe them.

By contrast, various kinds of *fore*shadowing offer us a world in which time is closed. When foreshadowing is used, certain events take place in a special way. Instead of being caused by prior events, they happen (or also happen) as a consequence of events to come. Foreshadowing, in short, involves backward causation, which means that, in one way or another, the future must already be there, must somehow already exist substantially enough to send signs backward. Thus, if a writer should believe in fatalism, foreshadowing is an ideal way to convey this sense of time. In the *Oedipus*, which relies heavily on foreshadowing, the temporalities of the work and of the world it imagines are perfectly isomorphic (of the same shape), which is one reason the play is so effective.

In life, most of us do not believe we experience backward causation. Foreshadowing therefore appears as the most artificial, and therefore most recognizable, of literary devices. That is perhaps one reason it is taught so often in high school literature courses. And yet it is entirely possible and not that uncommon to believe that real time does resemble the temporality of foreshadowing. One might believe in omens, which can be regarded as foreshadowing outside literature. Some philosophies of history that purport to know its laws and to discern the inevitable future allow its proponents to read current events as signs foreshadowing events to come. The doctrine of types in nineteenth-century Russian radical criticism and its Soviet inheritor ostensibly shows how the future may be read in much the same way as novels. As readers of fiction can often guess what is to come through advance familiarity with works of a given sort, so social critics armed with the right theory can discern patterns in the making.[5]

Even when foreshadowing is not explicitly used, it is implicitly present by virtue of a narrative's reliance on structure and closure. In a well-constructed story, everything points (or will turn out to point) to the ending and to the pattern that will eventually be revealed. When we finish reading such a work, we can see that each detail can be explained not only causally, by what happened before, but also retrospectively in terms of the completed structure. In rereading it, we may take pleasure in contemplating this double explanation of events. For that matter, even before a work is completed for the first time, experienced readers of fiction know that there will be no true irrelevancies and that all loose ends will be tied up in an effective conclusion. Thus some aspects of rereading are possible even during a first reading. In life, most people would regard it as futile to guess one's future by figuring what would make an effective story and would smile at someone who imagined himself invulnerable on a given occasion because otherwise his life would make no sense, but in reading literature this way of thinking is often justified and typically used. For this reason, we sense the artifice of time in narrative literature. In our own lives, most of us know by experience that there is never a point when all loose threads are tied together, at least not until the end of history or the Last Judgment. Real time is an ongoing process without anything resembling literary closure.

Writers who have wanted to represent time as open have therefore sometimes struggled against the demand for structure and closure. And yet for very good reasons, a work without these twin insurers of unity is likely not to be effective at all. It appears that literary structure is not neutral with respect to philosophies of time. Lessing contended that artforms have inherent predispositions, and we may say that narratives, insofar as they rely on structure, are predisposed to convey a sense of fatalism, determinism, or otherwise closed time.[6] It is relatively easy to make a narrative's temporality isomorphic with closed time but, many writers have felt, almost impossible to create isomorphism with open time. That is precisely the task set by Dostoevsky and Tolstoy. The fact that so many readers have been impressed by the uncanny resemblance of Tolstoy's fiction to the feel of real experience—have believed, as Matthew Arnold wrote, that a Tolstoy novel is not a piece of art but a piece of life— testifies to the considerable success he had in escaping the prejudice of structure and closure. He managed to resist what might be called *Lessing's curse.*

For both writers, the effort to represent temporal openness concretely and convincingly was no mere exercise in formal experimentation. They were keenly aware that for their contemporaries among the intelligentsia, determinism was not only true but self-evidently true. For what other view of events was even conceivable, except that they are exhaustively caused by earlier events and explicable by ironclad laws? Our sense of freedom and contingency must therefore be an illusion and an effect of our ignorance. To these arguments, Dostoevsky and Tolstoy sought to respond not only with telling counterarguments (which I shall consider) but also by presenting a concrete image of an alternative view of experience. If they could do so, if they could palpably represent the openness of time, then they would have shown that such a possibility is at least conceivable: for what has been conceived is manifestly conceivable. People would then have to *choose* among visions of experience. Their temporal consciousness would have become Galilean. The predisposition toward determinism, so powerful in nineteenth-century (and later) thought and so strongly reinforced by the structure of fictional narratives, would have been weakened. In this way, the very shape of novels became in their hands a philosophical instrument. Tolstoy in particular was quite explicit about these issues, and Bakhtin's work on Dostoevsky was intended to demonstrate how time could be open. Here again criticism, like fiction, was intended and understood as philosophy by other means.

This book is divided into seven chapters, each of which alternates discussions of temporality and narrative with illustrations drawn from literary works. In part I, The Shape of Narrative and the Shape of Experience, the first chapter, Process and Product, forms a prelude to the main argument. It distinguishes between the sense of life as an open process, in which actions in the present truly matter, and as a finished product, in which the future is already given. If life is product, then the present moment loses its presentness and becomes something resembling the portion of a recording we happen to be watching or the page we are reading in an already written novel. All outcomes are given. Dostoevsky believed that such a view would utterly destroy the meaningfulness of concepts essential to our humanness: choice, responsibility, and creativity. In such a view, creativity becomes mere mechanical discovery, something like (to use the underground man's phrase) "the extraction of square roots." For this reason, Dostoevsky insisted that life must be an open process, and some of the most remarkable passages in his works defend this view. In Bakhtin's terms, we might say that events must have *eventness:* they must not be the utterly predictable outcome of earlier events, but must somehow have something else to them—some "surplus" that endows them with "surprisingness." Otherwise people are transformed into "piano keys or organ stops," as the underground man writes.

It is often overlooked, however, that *Notes from Underground* does not wind up endorsing its hero's views. We learn, for instance, that everything the hero does to make himself unpredictable is itself subject to an iron logic, albeit of a peculiar and spiteful kind. Moreover, his actions are subject to a second kind of predetermination, that of artistic form: in a series of metaliterary reminders, Dostoevsky stresses that all the actions of this philosopher of freedom have already been written and planned by the author. It is as if Dostoevsky the ideologist was at war with Dostoevsky the artist, with the latter taking shrewd advantage of formal opportunities to cast an ironic, deterministic shadow on the former. Dostoevsky apparently discovered how artistic structure lends itself to such irony. The question for him now was, could he create a work whose design conveyed an opposite and open temporality, more in accord with his own indeterministic beliefs?

Chapter 2, Foreshadowing, explores closed temporalities and their representation in literary artifacts. How precisely does literary foreshadowing contradict a sense of open time; what features of open temporality are lost in a narrative with foreshadowing? Or, to ask the question differently, if the world were governed by the temporality of foreshadowing, what would change? How, in fact, have those who believe in closed time understood it? Prefiguration, omens, eternal recurrence, time loops, and substantial philosophies of history allowing for prophecy figure in a discussion of the consequences of temporal beliefs. I argue that those consequences are often less logical than psychological or social. Examples are drawn from the *Oedipus*, from Lermontov's "The Fatalist," and other works.

The chapter concludes with an extended discussion of *Anna Karenina*, whose heroine believes in omens and prophetic dreams and acts as if she were a heroine in a romantic novel. Tolstoy scrutinizes such beliefs, their relation to responsibility, the real alternatives they disable, and (ironically enough) the prior causes leading to acceptance of backward causation. In most novels, identification with the character involves sharing a sense of choice while contemplation of structure reveals inevitability; but in Tolstoy's novel, the reverse is the case. A character who believes in closed time is set in a novel based on open time. In this way, Tolstoy is able to exploit the aesthetic advantages of structure and closure while refuting them. For reasons we shall see, however, this solution to the contradiction between structure and temporal openness did not prove entirely satisfactory.

Chapter 3, Bakhtin's Indeterminism, explores the various solutions he developed for conveying various kinds of temporal openness. Bakhtin's sense of time's loose play, of a universe in which possibilities exceed actualities, resembles William James's defense of indeterminism: James's world "is not a solid block of lawfulness" but one in which law and some kind of lawlessness "rule . . . in motley alternatives."[7] The chapter begins with a discussion of James's essay, the terms of which figure throughout the rest of the present study.

James was content to argue negatively, to show the unfortunate consequences of accepting a deterministic vision, but Bakhtin wanted to argue positively, by showing a concrete image of an indeterministic world. His thought on these questions, which appears to have had a theological dimension, went through three distinct stages. In his earliest writings, he relied on a set of analogies: the relation of the hero of a work to its author is compared with the relations of a person to the world and of an individual to God. Thus, if Bakhtin could show a way in which a hero could be relatively free of the author who created him, he could suggest that individuals have a measure of freedom with respect to God or whatever patterns govern the world.

Unfortunately, Bakhtin's initial model allowed for no such freedom. For the author enjoys "an essential surplus of knowledge" with respect to the hero; he knows the whole of a hero's life in advance, which makes that life subject to an irrevocable "aesthetic necessity" dictating every choice. It was only in the second stage of his thinking that Bakhtin at last found a solution, which he located in the "polyphonic novels" of Dostoevsky. For the first time in literary history, Bakhtin argued, Dostoevsky found a way to make plot isomorphic with human freedom and open time. The position of author to hero changes decisively; a character is truly capable of surprising his creator. In much the same way, Bakhtin seems to suggest, God is a sort of polyphonic author of the world, who deliberately created truly free people whose actions and words cannot be foreseen in advance even by God himself. It is not true (as Leibniz and many others have held) that to the Creator all events are simultaneously present; God himself is subjected to time (as James also believed). The eventness of the world is therefore not illusory.

Dostoevsky found a substitute for structure and the author's advance knowledge by changing his creative process in such a way that we sense him to be somehow simultaneous with his characters. In an extension of this idea, I explore other types of "strange synchronies" and asynchronies that may obtain among reader's, author's, and character's times in diverse literary forms.

The solution of polyphony proved to have its own drawbacks from Bakhtin's point of view. To create it, Dostoevsky relied on a specific kind of temporality—a highly intensified present—that made a rich sense of biographical and historical continuity impossible. For Bakhtin, who believed in the value of tradition, in the historicity of personality, and in the temporal extensiveness of responsibility, Dostoevsky's almost exclusive preoccupation with present moments required correction. In the third period of his thinking about time, Bakhtin set aside the relation of author to hero and concentrated on the varieties of temporality *within* the work. Developing his concept of the chronotope, he sought a world in which freedom and eventness were real but in which the significance of historical and biographical continuity was not obscured. There had to be alternatives, and not just at a few intensified points of time, but at every prosaic moment. He found such a temporality in the chronotope of certain novels, which are based on a sense that "reality . . . is only one of many possible realities," neither arbitrary nor inevitable. But if the chronotope theory resolved the difficulties of polyphony, it did so without solving (as polyphony did) the problem of the author's relation to the hero.

Bakhtin appears to have overlooked the most important devices developed by Dostoevsky and Tolstoy to represent temporal openness: devices of sideshadowing. They are the topic of chapter 4, which explores both narrative techniques and their philosophical implications. In contrast to foreshadowing, which projects onto the present a shadow from the future, sideshadowing projects—from the "side"—the shadow of an alternative present.[8] It allows us to see what might have been and therefore changes our view of what is. In this way, sideshadowing restores our sense of the middle realm of possibility, for time itself becomes a succession not just of points of actuality but also of fields of possibility. A number of examples from Dostoevsky and Tolstoy also clarify the implications of related narrative techniques and temporalities, for example, past sideshadowing, pseudo-foreshadowing, and (most crucial for Dostoevskian psychology) processual intentionality.

Although Dostoevsky and Tolstoy offer the most sophisticated cases of sideshadowing, the device is by no means limited to them. It may be found in popular culture, in religion, and in other forms of low and high literature, such as the form I call the *paraquel* (in which one author continues or fills in the gaps in a well-known classic by another). It may sometimes be detected when an author continues his own apparently completed work (the second part of *Don Quixote*) and in certain series of novels (such as Trollope's Palliser and Barchester novels). In each case, the hunger for other possibilities is satisfied in a distinct way.

The more a work cultivates sideshadowing, the more it seems to "preclude" closure. Thus both Dostoevsky and Tolstoy, in whose great novels sideshadowing is fundamental, faced the problem of creating aesthetically effective artifacts. Dostoevsky solved this problem by combining the open temporality of sideshadowing with an opposite, and closed, temporality that also fascinated him: vortex time. If in sideshadowing apparently simple events ramify into multiple futures, in vortex time an apparent diversity of causes all converge on a single catastrophe. Openness and closure, like freedom and obsession, compete in the Dostoevskian world, and Dostoevsky relies on various combinations of the two to create effective endings that nevertheless do not abolish the essential openness of time. Tolstoy's solutions were rather different. Instead of the vortex, he found a substitute for closure, which I call *aperture*. The chapter concludes with a consideration of this device and the ways it essentially differs from apparently similar and more familiar ones, such as anticlosure.

Chapter 5 (Presentness and Its Diseases) begins by considering the experience of watching live sports, in which the sense that events are happening now, simultaneously with our watching, is so important; witnessing a live sports events is quite different from seeing a recording.[9] I then trace the implications of a debate between Tolstoy and Dostoevsky on the possibility or wisdom of recapturing the presentness of historical events whose product is ourselves. The remainder of this chapter explores four "diseases" of presentness, that is, unwise ways of understanding one's moment in time. In this etiology, one's sense of time may suffer from atrophy or hypertrophy of presentness. The first disease desiccates the present by placing all value on either the past or the future. Either the present is felt to be a mere continuation of a completed sequence or it is regarded as a needlessly prolonged transition to the time that really matters. For example, in epilogue time (examples are taken from Turgenev's *Fathers and Sons* and George Eliot's *Middlemarch*) crucial events are all already over and the present becomes a sort of posthumous life; by contrast, in utopian or eschatological time (propounded by the Russian radical intelligentsia and its Soviet heirs) people of the present are mere raw material for the great time to come.

The second disease, the isolated present, is the opposite of the first. Here the present is felt to be the only time that matters and the only time that is truly real. Dostoevsky points out the immense attractiveness as well as the palpable danger entailed by such a sense of presentness. This is the temporality of the epileptic fit (as Prince Myshkin experiences it in *The Idiot*), of compulsive gambling, and of certain kinds of revolutionism, which gamble with history. In the third disease, hypothetical time, the entire actual sequence of time—past, present, and future—is felt to be somehow unreal, as if it were a mere rough draft for some other time, which may not even exist. This sort of temporality was Chekhov's speciality, and *The Three Sisters* provides the main example. The fourth disease, multiple time, is as interesting as it is rare. Here *all* possibilities are realized in multiple universes, so that whenever two choices or opposing chances appear, both take place in a different universe (as in Borges's story "The Garden of the Forking Paths"). Although at first glance this temporality seems similar to sideshadowing, it is in fact radically different and, somewhat unexpectedly, reintroduces the problems of determinism by a strange new route. Needless to say, this catalogue of "chronic" maladies is not intended as exhaustive.

In addition to foreshadowing and sideshadowing, there is a third "shadow of time," which is discussed in the sixth chapter. *Backshadowing* (Bernstein's neologism) is foreshadowing after the fact: the past is treated as if it had inevitably to lead to the present we know and as if signs of our present should have been visible to our predecessors.[10] Our own time becomes the privileged moment for judging earlier events, and the values of the present are endowed with unique, and unearned, significance. Backshadowing derives from *chronocentrism*, from the natural egotism attendant on taking one's own time as special. This chapter explores the several fallacies about time and our place in it that backshadowing and chronocentrism entail. It also points out the kinds of moral obtuseness usually involved in this sort of judgment.

Some of these fallacies were pointed out by Tolstoy, others by Herbert Butterfield in his once classic, but now too often neglected, study of historical reasoning, *The Whig Interpretation of History*. Still others are examined by Stephen Jay Gould, who demonstrates the ways in which what I call backshadowing sometimes blinds researchers in the sciences. In a way reminiscent of Tolstoy's views of history, Gould rejects the equation of evolution with progress, insists on the effectiveness of contingency, and draws attention to the possibility of alternative paths that could have been taken. No less than culture, nature exhibits sideshadows.

Backshadowing is often practiced by people who would not accept its assumptions about time and history if they were made explicit. But it tends to be most pronounced in the thought of those who believe that they know or have actually reached the end of history. For most utopian thinkers and totalitarian regimes, the pattern of history is fully revealed, and so final judgments about what were once matters of opinion are possible. Official Soviet culture was built upon such backshadowing, which in turn became the target of anti-utopian literature and of Bulgakov's dark but liberating satire *The Master and Margarita*.

By contrast, sideshadowing gives a strong meaning to opinion. Chapter 7, the conclusion of this book, explores the connections among opinion, pluralism, and a world of multiple possibilities. The awareness that the future could follow many distinct paths and that the present could easily have been quite different inclines us to entertain the possibility that events may validate opinions with which we strongly disagree. Thus sideshadowing encourages the sort of intellectual pluralism we find in the thought of Isaiah Berlin, whose insight that there may be no final and utopian solution to conflicting values derives in large part from his meditations on the Russian tradition.

As Tolstoy and others have pointed out, intelligentsias are characteristically prone to various kinds of chronocentrism and backshadowing, which impoverish their sense of other times, cultures, and groups by measuring them dogmatically against the intelligentsia's favored values. But if time is open and final truths are chimerical, then we might benefit from a more dialogic approach to alternative values and perspectives held by people unlike ourselves. The book concludes with a few suggestions about what such enriching dialogues might require.

Each of my earlier books has been, in one way or another, anti-utopian, and the present volume is no exception. We live at the end of a terrible century, one that has witnessed the horrors produced by utopians in power. We have seen the unprecedented tyranny practiced by those who, believing they possess the key to history, imagine their values are final. In their world without loopholes, they admit no sideshadows. I think there has been too little serious reflection about what is wrong with this style of thinking. "There is no *libretto*" to life, wrote Alexander Herzen. "In history, all is improvisation . . . all is *ex tempore* . . . there are no itineraries." [11]

PART ONE

The Shape of Narrative and the Shape of Experience

CHAPTER ONE

Prelude: Process and Product

Time Out

For better or worse, people tend to think of time in spatial terms. We speak of passing through it, of its flow, and of its vast expanse. Events are said to happen at specific points in it. These metaphors are so natural, so common-place, and so widely shared among languages that we often do not reflect upon the fact that they *are* metaphors.

It is possible to survey a great deal of space at a glance, but our direct perception of time is limited to at most a few seconds; beyond that, we consult memory.[1] Perhaps we turn to spatial metaphors of time in order to make up for this deficiency. We do occasionally describe space in terms of time—light-years are a measure of distance, not of duration—but we seem driven to do the opposite. In so doing, we gain the possibility for new insights, but we also risk importing meanings upon which we have not carefully reflected.

After all, time is not a substance that flows; and we do not pass through it as we pass through space. The space ahead of us exists before we get to it, just as the space we occupy exists; but it is not clear that the future exists in the same way as the present does. Space can be directly measured, even remeasured, but time cannot. We can move through space in different directions and at different rates, and we can even remain stationary; but no similar options seem to exist with respect to time. Regardless of our most strenuous efforts, we move through time relentlessly and in only one direction. You can't go home again not because the place is gone but because the time has gone. For all these reasons, we are justified in suspecting that spatial metaphors for time are fraught with dangers for the unwary.

We can map space quite easily. Cartography can, with greater or lesser fineness, indicate whatever features of terrain are of most interest to us. We can therefore cross the same terrain that we or others have crossed before and, consulting a map, know what lies ahead. But we cannot cross the same "expanse" of time again. A map of time would be a very curious thing because time does not in any clear or unmetaphoric way have a shape.

Nevertheless, cultures do imagine time as having a sort of shape. Time may be thought of as a cycle, which repeats as the seasons do; thus the past may be repeated in ritual, or people may be chained to the wheel of fate. This picture is usually opposed to that of time as a directed arrow. In the latter case, time is infinite in both directions. It never repeats and regret is irremediable. Some models are linear—a time line—and may allow for no alternative paths. Others have time ramify, with each moment having many possible future directions, depending on unforeseen contingencies and on countless free choices. Although in such models only one possibility will be actualized in any future instant, many could be. Does time, like an artifact, have a structure, which could in principle be contemplated in a moment? Is it, as some suppose, closed, with only one possibility for each moment? Or is it, as others contend, open?

Inescapably, we live in time, and so, to make sense of our lives, we try to form a picture of it. Just as we seek to understand the place of a detail in a painting, so, too, we may try to identify the proper "place" of an event in our lives or in history. But there is a crucial difference between viewing a picture and "viewing" time. When we contemplate time we do so from within time; but when we contemplate a picture we stand outside it. We look at it, not from within it, because it is framed for us. And so we imagine doing the same thing with time. Literature, philosophy, religion, and mythology are replete with pictures of time that allow for an external vantage point. God and the angels look down on all of history. At the Apocalypse or Last Judgment, we will know the whole story. We will comprehend everything, alpha to omega, in a way that is impossible while the historical "picture" is still incomplete.

But a complete picture of our lives and a vantage point from outside of time are, if unattainable in reality, imaginable in literature and drama, which is one reason we turn to them. Drama may also give us images of such imaginings, and so allow us to reflect on our own desires to grasp the fullness of time. At the end of *Uncle Vanya*, for instance, Sonia consoles her uncle with the promise of this sort of outside vision. Now we live in time, she tells him, but when our lives are over, we shall view them as if we were spectators at a play. At last we will understand the complete pattern and its meaning:

> SONIA: We shall go on living, Uncle Vanya. We shall live through a long, long chain of days and endless evenings; we shall patiently bear the trials fate sends us; we'll work for others, now and in our old age, without ever knowing rest, and when our time comes, we shall die submissively; and there, beyond the grave, we shall say that we have suffered, that we have wept, and have known bitterness, and God shall have pity on us; and you

and I, Uncle, dear Uncle, shall behold a life that is bright, beautiful, and fine. We shall rejoice and look on our present troubles with tenderness, with a smile—and we shall rest. . . . [The watchman taps . . .].[2]

Like so many characters in Chekhov, and so many real people, Sonia contrasts the world of ongoing effort, performed in a position that permits no view of a meaningful whole, with an ultimate vision of life from outside that redeems all. Chekhov notes the hunger for meaning that inspires faith in immortality, which would include a vision of our lives from outside. And he also cautions us against allowing such a seductive hope to alienate us from the possibilities of life within time.

Of course, we, as the play's audience, have been occupying this external position all along. Though not immortal, we are outside Sonia's time, which is indeed framed for us like a picture. And so we can be the redeemers, the forgivers whom she seeks and whom perhaps we all seek. We see the pattern of her life and, as she would wish, we look at her present troubles "with tenderness, with a smile." Art gives us life as life cannot give itself.

Like drama, narrative literature offers special advantages and presents special dangers for an understanding of time. One way in which people explain the world is by telling stories about it, and so to grasp *how* stories explain is to understand our own methods of understanding. In the course of this book, I shall return frequently to the relation of meaning to a narrative's shape.[3] It is worth entertaining the possibility that the variety of story-shapes—of narrative genres—is as great as the variety of worldviews at our disposal.

Narrative comes in many genres, each of which imagines time differently; and so we can choose the shape to match our beliefs or desires—from tragedy to utopia, from almost static pastoral to suspenseful adventure, and from the grand fates of romance to the prosaic choices of realistic fiction. Some genres describe time as the ramification of alternatives, others as the inevitable enactment of a timeless pattern. In some, alternatives are possible only at a few critical moments; time is like a knotted string with deterministic interstices leading to rare and dense moments of choice. In others, choice is entirely absent, and in still others it is constant. Social and historical forces shape individual personality in some kinds of literature but not in others. Some project a series of incidents that brings us back, cyclically, to a starting point; but there are others in which time flows endlessly on, and only through memory can the starting point be recaptured. In explaining the destiny of nations, or the meaning of our lives, we may adopt or adapt these models.

Received narrative forms do not just find the meaning of events, they also— some would say only—smuggle meaning into events, at times cynically but often unawares. Life as it is lived is not storylike, and so we may suspect that whatever story we choose to tell about it will alter it. Lives include all sorts of extraneous details leading nowhere, but good stories do not. Narratives are more successful if they display a structure, which it is hard to find in life. We can stand outside the narratives we read but not outside the lives we live. And stories have real closure, in which all loose ends are tied up; but there is no privileged point in life comparable to the ending of a novel.[4]

Very frequently, narratives and lives are therefore *anisomorphic* (not similar in shape to each other). If we forget this and treat our lives as if they possessed the shape of narratives, we may run into trouble. Such confusion is of course a time-honored theme of novels themselves, from *Don Quixote* to *War and Peace*. And, as we shall see, politicians, especially those with a utopian or other historical end in mind, typically try to persuade us to overlook the differences between our lives and our stories (to treat them as isomorphic). It is easiest to impose a myth on those who are already inclined to think history has a mythic structure.

Another danger of narrative models is that they transform the process of activity into a finished product. Stories are over; they are oriented toward a known ending, and if they are well-made stories, everything tends to that ending. Each moment can be understood in terms of the finished pattern of the whole. But we are always in the *process* of living. We do not know what some future historian will include in the story of our times, and what place the present moment might occupy in relation to those that will soon follow it. And for all we know our own choices may lead to different historians writing different histories. But one thing we can safely anticipate is that this future historian's narrative will be written as part of the process of his or her own times. There are judgments of histories, but no Judgment of History—at least, not until *the* Judgment.

Creativity and ethics, the activity of living and the effort of choosing, are fundamentally processual. To view life as a finished product and the present moment as part of an already determined pattern is to reduce creativity and ethics to mere shadows of themselves. Even those who do see a "product" world usually experience their own lives and exertions more or less processually.

Eventness

Leave us alone without books, and we shall be lost and in confusion at once. . . . We are even oppressed by being men—men with real *individual* body and blood. We are ashamed of it, we think it a disgrace and try to be some sort of impossible generalized man. We are still-born, and for many years we have not been begotten by living fathers, and that suits us better

and better. We are developing a taste for it. Soon we shall somehow contrive
to be born from an idea.
—DOSTOEVSKY, *Notes from Underground*

The most insightful modern student of narrative, the Russian thinker
Mikhail Bakhtin (1895–1975), was deeply concerned with how dominant cultural models close down time by thinking away its processual nature. In so
doing, they leave no real place for creativity or choice. Life comes to resemble a
finished product, in which everything has already been fixed. Bakhtin's cover-
ing term for such models is *theoretism*, which he applied to approaches as diverse
as behaviorism, Freudianism, Marxism, Formalism, and structuralism. What
these schools share is the grounding assumption that to explain a phenomenon is, ideally, to show that it is the consequence of a given set of causal laws
(as in Marxism) or the instantiation of a timeless pattern (as in Formalism or
models indebted to Saussurean linguistics). Typically, the theoretist abstracts
from human action all that is generalizable, then transforms this "transcription" into a set of rules or laws, and, finally, denies that anything of significance
has been left out in the process.[5]

According to Bakhtin, the world of the theoretist consequently consists of
three sorts of things: (1) most important, rules or laws, which are the scholar's
main object of discovery, (2) mere instantiations or consequences of those
rules—that is, concrete events—which are of interest only as confirmation of
the rules, and, perhaps, (3) some residue of phenomena for which rules have
not yet been found or which are too inconsequential to matter.

Such a view leaves time essentially closed. There are no real alternatives, for
everything has already been given in the rules or chain of causes. People act out
patterns or do what the laws have prescribed; their actions instantiate, but never
exceed, rules or pregiven laws. What people do not do is genuinely choose,
even though they might imagine otherwise. History and individual lives merely
unfold in time, and do not make anything that is genuinely surprising. Or as
Bakhtin puts the point, in such models time forges nothing new.

It was evident to Bakhtin that with the loss of choice, ethics also suffers,
for ethics depends on the sense that what I do at this moment truly matters.
Ethics becomes an illusion, as the heroes of so many Russian novels conclude.
Creativity is reduced as well, having been transformed into mere mechanical
discovery of something that, although still unknown, is already there, like the
solution to a mathematical problem with a familiar algorithm. As we shall see,
Bakhtin's long career and many theories may be seen as a series of attempts
to describe time differently, that is, as truly open. Only such a description, he
maintained, would allow for a meaningful sense of ethical choice and creativity.

In his earliest writings, Bakhtin focused on what all theoretical transcriptions (accounts in terms of generalized criteria) leave out, namely, everything that escapes generalization—everything that is irreducibly particular and (to use Bakhtin's term) unrepeatable. He proposed instead to set aside abstract rules and to begin discussion of human action with the concrete act itself and, specifically, with those aspects of it that are not the mere product of earlier situations or timeless patterns. The act *exceeds* the circumstances that occasioned it; this excess or *surplus* [*izbytok*] of the act constitutes its "singular singularity." One reason the surplus exceeds timeless rules or laws is that it is essentially related to the irreducible particularities of the unrepeatable moment in which the act occurred. In this sense, the concrete act, as Bakhtin understood it, is essentially historical. In human action, time is of the essence.

According to Bakhtin, the concrete act "cannot be transcribed in theoretical terms in such a way that it will not lose the very sense of its *eventness,* that precise thing which it knows responsibly and toward which the act is oriented" (KFP, 104). Eventness—a key concept for Bakhtin—is indispensable for real creativity and choice. Without it, the event becomes a mere shadow of itself, and the present moment loses all the qualities that give it special weight.

Obviously, all models of time and behavior allow for events. But those events are not necessarily eventful in Bakhtin's sense. They may not have the weight of an irrevocable decision nor entail the suspense that comes with the need to select one course of action and foreclose others. They may lack the possibility for a surplus. When the present simply actualizes what had to happen, events lack eventness.[6]

For there to be eventness, there must be alternatives. Eventful events are performed in a world in which there are multiple possibilities, in which some things that could happen do not. In such a world, time ramifies and its possibilities multiply; each realized possibility opens new choices while precluding others that once could have been made. The eventful event must also be unrepeatable, that is, its meaning and weight are inextricably linked to the moment in which it is performed. Choice is *momentous.* It involves *presentness.* The same act performed later would not be quite the same act. It is therefore constituted in part by important particularities that no abstract and timeless system could foretell. Above all, the eventful event must produce something genuinely new, something beyond a predictable consequence of earlier events. If eventness is real, no knowledge of the past, no matter how comprehensive, would be sufficient for making a perfectly reliable prediction of the future. Bakhtin viewed all of our choices, however prosaic, as having a measure of eventness, and he rejected all models of the world that did not allow for "surprisingness."

Creative Process

> Men who never think independently have nevertheless the acuteness to dis-
> cover everything, after it has once been shown them, in what was said long
> since, though no one ever saw it there before.
> —IMMANUEL KANT

> Literature, like any other social practice, employs determinate means of pro-
> duction to transform a determinate "raw material" into a specific product.
> —TERRY EAGLETON

In his last writings, Bakhtin approached the problem of eventness in terms of "a new statement of the problem of authorship (the creating individual)" (PT, 119). Bakhtin understood quite well the line of thinking that has since come to be known as "the death of the author"—a phrase that rings rather differently in the Soviet context—and found it unacceptable. For Bakhtin, it is always real people, not disembodied social forces, who act, think, speak, write, and create art.[7] Maintaining that creativity in its strong sense is not an illusion, he stressed that all creative acts, from imaginative responses in everyday situations to the composition of great literary works, always embody "something that never existed before, something absolutely new and unrepeatable" (PT, 119–20).

As it happens, this defining feature of the creative act is precisely what is lost in the usual and most influential accounts of it. Somehow, in explaining creativity, they typically explain it away. Such accounts characteristically reduce the creative act to the conditions and material with which it begins and the rules that govern their transformation. Both the conditions and the rules are *given*. But it is precisely what the most exhaustive conceivable description in such terms leaves out that enables an act to be creative. This surplus turns what is given [*dan*] into what is truly created [*sozdan*].

After all, what is creative about a process if rules given in advance could in principle exhaustively account for it? The creative act then comes to resemble "the extraction of square roots," as the underground man observes. Something unexpected must happen during the creative process: it must be seen as truly momentous and eventful. It is hard to see how an investigation of the creative process can significantly approach its central problems if it focuses precisely on those elements that do *not* make it creative.

In his notes, Bakhtin comments acidly on such received models of the creative process:

> It is much easier to study the *given* in what is created (for example, language, ready-made and general elements of world view, reflected phenomena of reality, and so forth) than to study what is *created*. Frequently the whole

of scientific analysis amounts to a disclosure of everything that has been given, already at hand and ready-made before the work existed (that which is found by the artist and not created by him). . . . [The usual approaches offer] a reduction to that which was previously given and ready-made. An object is ready-made, the linguistic means for its description are ready-made, the artist himself is ready-made, and his world view is ready-made. And here with ready-made means, in light of a ready-made world view, the ready-made poet reflects a ready-made object. But in fact the object is created in the process of creativity, as are the poet himself, his world view, and his means of expression. (PT, 120)

For creativity to be real, it must be a genuine *process* of unpredetermined becoming: it cannot be the mere unfolding of an already completely determined sequence of steps to a ready-made conclusion. Rather, it must be understood as a sequence of eventful events, each of which allows for multiple possibilities. This is what makes it both creative and truly processual.

So conceived, the creative process typically traces not a straight line to a goal but a series of false leads, missed opportunities, new possibilities, improvisations, visions, and revisions. It is constituted by an intention that evolves over time.[8] To be sure, authors typically remove the traces of this process and present their work as if it were the product of a clear plan, known from the outset. By convention, works are usually offered as the expression of an intention that is essentially instantaneous even if it took time to execute and takes time to appreciate. After the work is complete, the authors remove the "scaffolding," as Bakhtin liked to say. But the process of creation is in fact anything but regular.

In Bakhtin's view, any account of creativity that does not describe an eventful process is at best an account of mere mechanical discovery. Understood in this way, the concept of creativity, like freedom defined as the consciousness of necessity, retains nothing but its name. Such an approach is by no means limited to vulgar Marxism; one also encounters what might be called "vulgar formalism," according to which authors merely obey and execute the laws of literary history. In the early years of their movement, the Russian Formalists tried to demystify creativity in just this way. In their view, authors discover, not create, works because the work, even before it appears, is virtually there, wholly given by literary-historical laws. The author produces nothing new in Bakhtin's sense; what seems new was in principle completely predictable in advance. The Formalists concluded that we call an act creative to the extent that we have difficulty in accounting for it; the term tells us not about the act but only about our ignorance.

For all their hostility to Formalism in general, some Marxists have responded appreciatively to this idea; what the two movements share is a concern for demystifying authorship and, so far as possible, abolishing individual agency. Bakhtin, by contrast, sought to preserve and enrich these concepts. Indeed, the controlling metaphor of his early work was the comparison of life itself to acts of individual authorship. He viewed some acts as truly creative in the sense that they could not have been foretold, no matter how much knowledge was available. They produce something not only valuable but also surprising.[9]

The Formalists preferred to speak not of the creation but of the "making" of works. Like more recent Marxists, they were fond of metaphors of industrial production (for example, Victor Shklovsky's *Third Factory*). In their view, all great works of art, no less than minor ones, result from an essentially mechanical fabrication, in which ready-made elements inherited from earlier periods of literary history are combined according to well-chosen principles, which are also historically given. At their most extreme, the Formalists denied the significance not only of the creative process but also of the author who imagines he is engaging in it. Thus, Osip Brik could declare that Formalism "presumes that there are no poets and writers, there are only poetry and literature. . . . Pushkin was not the creator of a school, but only its head. If there were no Pushkin, *Eugene Onegin* would have been written all the same. America would have been discovered even without Columbus."[10] Here the implications of reducing creativity to discovery are explicitly embraced. The laws of literary history would have to be extremely rigid and time especially closed for someone else to have written not just some other romantic poem but, precisely, *Eugene Onegin*. The Formalist universe fits together very tightly; there is no loose play. *Eugene Onegin* was there all along.

In so arguing, the Formalists self-consciously aligned their work with "classical" theories of creativity, which, unlike "romantic" or inspirational approaches, embrace the hard language of rationality to portray creativity as mere craft or industry. And craft is in turn understood (rather questionably) as nothing more than dogged application of received knowledge—an intellectual's (self-justifying) understanding, to be sure. Bakhtin, by contrast, linked literary and prosaic innovation in the opposite way: he maintained that both are eventful and productive of the truly surprising.

The Formalists had special admiration for Poe's debunking description, in "The Philosophy of Composition," of how he wrote "The Raven." Perhaps to parody prevailing romantic theories, Poe exaggerates the traditional arguments of Boileau, Pope, and other theorists of the classical approach. He likens the creation of a poem to the solving of a mathematical puzzle: the poem, like the solution, is already there. And what this means for Poe is that the only alternative to "The Raven" allowed by his material was an inferior version of "The Raven" (an approximate solution). He does not explain how we can be sure that the poem he did write is not an inferior alternative to another poem we do not know.

Poe insists, and the Formalists enthusiastically agreed, that what is true of "The Raven" is true of creativity in general: "It is my design to render manifest that no one point in its composition is referrible either to accident or intuition— that the work proceeded, step by step, to its completion with the precision and rigid consequence of a mathematical problem." [11] *No one point:* there are no leaps, no breaks, no role for contingency, and no moments at all when any alternatives, except mistakes, were available. If we accept his account, Poe did not create but found "The Raven." There is no creative process because nothing is genuinely creative.

One might therefore suppose that Bakhtin would have been more sympathetic to the opposing, inspirational view of creativity, but he was not. According to this alternative tradition, the new comes by revelation to a poet who is essentially passive. "Poetry is not like reasoning, a power to be exerted according to the determination of the will," writes Shelley. "A man cannot say, 'I will compose poetry' . . . for the mind in creation is as a fading coal, which some invisible influence, like an inconstant wind, awakens to transitory brightness." [12] Whether it is an inconstant wind, a muse, the gods, or the subconscious that reveals the poem, the defining moments of its creation according to this school lie outside the poet's agency. If that is not the case, Shelley maintains, the work is not truly poetic at all.

Moreover, the inspiration reveals the work whole. "I appeal to the greatest poets of the present day," Shelley intones, "whether it is not an error to assert that the finest passages of poetry are produced by labor and study. . . . for Milton conceived the *Paradise Lost* as a whole before he executed it in portions" (Shelley, 443). In one or a small series of inspirational bursts, the poem is *given* in its entirety. After that, the poet tries to record the revelation and to provide connecting links where his memory has faded—an endeavor that is never wholly successful. The classical theorists evidently mistake this labor of recording and connecting for the creative act itself. But there is nothing truly creative about this labor: for "when composition begins, inspiration is already on the decline" (Shelley, 443).

No more than Poe does Shelley admit development, alternatives, or unrealized possibilities for something different. In one case, multiple possibilities succumb to hard-edged calculation, in the other, to indivisible intuition. For opposing reasons, then, the two traditions agree that the only alternative to a great poem is another (and probably inferior) version of itself. The time of creativity is closed. As Poe's approach removes the creativity from the creative process, Shelley's removes the process.

Bakhtin was largely correct in sensing that there are very few descriptions of creativity that avoid closing down time. In one way or another, most ultimately reduce creativity to *ex-pression*, the pressing out of something already there. But for Bakhtin, expression was an inaccurate way to describe even the most mundane of utterances.

Like his great contemporary the Russian psycholinguist Lev Vygotsky, Bakhtin was keenly aware that the transformation of a thought from inner speech to outer speech is anything but automatic.[13] It involves a complex series of rapid choices. Inner speech is characteristically abbreviated, and this "extreme, elliptical economy of inner speech" requires expansion so that another can understand it.[14] In one's unspoken thoughts, one assumes a great deal of contextual knowledge, some of which would have to be supplied to an interlocutor. Depending on one's knowledge of the listener and on ongoing reactions to what one is saying, decisions about what assumptions to specify may vary. Indeed, this kind of reflection about interlocutors and about possible misunderstanding may help the speaker become aware of his or her assumptions in the first place, which is one reason that speaking and writing teach us a great deal about our own ideas. Choices must also be made about other aspects of the utterance, including tone, the listener's interests, and how one would react to possible responses.

Each of these specifications allows for alternatives, and, as we know by experience, we frequently make the wrong choices and have to correct ourselves. One reason that we probably believe in choice no matter what some philosophies may say is that we experience it constantly, every time we speak. Creativity is present prosaically. Bakhtin would have agreed with Vygotsky's description of the process of utterance: "The relation of thought to word is not a thing, but a process, a continual movement back and forth from thought to word and from word to thought. In that process the relation of thought to word undergoes changes which themselves may be regarded as development in the functional sense. Thought is not merely expressed in words; it comes into existence through them" (Vygotsky, 125).

For Bakhtin and Vygotsky, it is the ordinary conditions of life, the prosaic daily activities we all know, that provide the best starting point for an account of the more noticeable efforts we have honored with the term *creative*.

The Pun of Creativity

Dostoevsky repeatedly stressed the importance of understanding human activity as an eventful process. In his view, to think away process, as most psychologists have done, is to think away the human. A few examples from his works may deepen our grasp of the concept and its importance.

In Dostoevsky's novel *The Idiot,* Ippolit Terentiev—expressing a view held by the author—offers a famous description of the relation of process to product:

> Oh, you may be sure that Columbus was happy not when he had discovered America, but while he was discovering it. Take my word for it, the highest moment of his happiness was just three days before the discovery of the New World, when the mutinous crew were on the point of returning to Europe in despair. It wasn't the New World that mattered, even if it had fallen to pieces.
>
> Columbus died almost without seeing it; and not really knowing what he had discovered. It's life that matters, nothing but life—the process of discovering, the everlasting and perpetual process, not the discovery itself at all. (I, 375)

Ippolit and Dostoevsky use the thrill of an ongoing project and the sadness that accompanies a completed product to suggest two views of life, two views of time. On the one hand, life may be understood as open and uncertain, as an experience in which what one chooses and does at each moment truly matters. We live in a world of "everlasting and perpetual process," and that process is life itself. On the other hand, one may imagine that the world is a finished product and that the process of events is nothing but an entirely automatic unfolding of a plan given from eternity. Then time is closed, a mere parameter that exerts no shaping power, because the future is in some sense already given. Real process evaporates; innovation becomes an illusion; and a revered genius does nothing but attach his or her name to an inevitability.

A predecessor of Ippolit, Dostoevsky's man from the underground, believes in but resents such a closed world. The underground man's rebellion against determinism and its consequences has become one of the most famous moments in modern thought, and with good reason. As the existentialists never tired of pointing out, the underground man insists on taking the issue personally. All his life, he says, he has been offended by the laws of nature. It is a rather strange sort of reaction because we usually regard only people as capable of giving offense. One cannot be insulted by the weather unless one personifies it, which is surely gratuitous.[15] But if nature reduces even our most willful acts to so many chemical reactions governed by mathematical laws, then it has deprived us of our very selves; and it is this deprivation that insults the man from underground. Or to rephrase this paradox: he takes personally his absence of personhood.[16]

"Twice two makes four is no longer life, gentlemen, but is the beginning of death," the underground man declares (NFU, 30). For life to be meaningful and for work to be more than robotic, there must be something not just un-known but still undecided. And if activity is reducible to "mathematics," that is, to the mechanical execution of predetermined steps, then nothing is unde-cided. "Twice two makes four" contains no potential for a surprise answer; it is not as if the numbers were people, who might some day interact to yield some different result. To hope for such an outcome would be entirely to mis-understand mathematics, and if life resembled mathematics in this way, then freedom, accident, and contingency would be just such senseless hopes. In one of his most remarkable outbursts, the underground man (continuing his para-doxes) personifies this numerical depriver of his free will: "Twice two makes four is a fop standing with arms akimbo barring your path and spitting. I admit that twice two makes four is an excellent thing, but if we are to give everything its due praise, then twice two makes five is sometimes a very charming thing, too" (NFU, 30).

For the underground man, real temporal process—as opposed to an already made product that merely takes time to be revealed—is essential to human-ness. He therefore speculates, with great profundity, as to whether one origin of human destructiveness may be the almost instinctive fear of finished prod-ucts and of goals successfully reached.[17] People love "to engage in engineering; that is, eternally and incessantly, to build new roads, *wherever they may lead*" (NFU, 29), he observes. What they do not like is to finish building or (what amounts to the same thing) to regard their effort as predestined, in effect as already over except for the time that must elapse in any case.

Even the dullest person sometimes dimly understands that

> the road, it would seem, must always lead *somewhere*, and that the destina-tion it leads to is less important than the process of making it, and that the chief thing is to save the well-behaved child from despising engineering. . . . Man likes to create and build roads, that is beyond dispute. But why does he have such a passionate love for destruction and chaos? . . . May it not be that he loves chaos and destruction (after all, he sometimes unquestionably likes it very much, that is surely so) because he is instinctively afraid of attaining his goal and completing the edifice he is constructing? (NFU, 29)

Ants, the underground man continues, are creatures of product; they began with the anthill and will end with the anthill. But "man is a frivolous and in-congruous creature, and perhaps, like a chessplayer, loves only the process of the game and not the end of it" (NFU, 30). One may even suppose that for all our effort to reach goals, the only real goal we cherish is the thrill of process itself. What we most value is to be found "in the incessant process of attaining, or in other words, in life itself, and not particularly in the goal, which of course must always be twice two makes four, that is, a formula" (NFU, 30).

And yet, what sense can a process of attaining have if one knows in advance that one will not want what is attained? There would seem to be some deep-seated contradiction in how we are made.[18] We need to believe in goals in order to strive for them, but we are also dimly aware that it is the striving, not the goals, that matters. What happens if that dim awareness becomes clear? Would not striving disappear along with our belief in their ostensible object? A person "likes the process of attaining, but does not quite like to have attained, and that, of course, is terribly funny. In short, man is a comical creature; there seems to be a sort of pun in it all" (NFU, 30).

This "pun" defines what might be called a *paradox of creativity*. As anyone who has at last finished a long project knows, a peculiar depression overtakes one when there is nothing more to do. One has spent so long developing the frame of mind necessary to experiment, to improvise, and to solve unforeseen problems that it continues by a sort of creative inertia, even when it is no longer wanted. Publishers who warn authors not to rewrite a book when it is in page proofs are aware of this phenomenon. From the perspective of the author, the work isn't over even when it's over.

Temporal Vacuum

To our crepuscular natures, born for the conflict, the Rembrandtesque moral chiaroscuro, [and for] the shifting struggle of the sunbeam in the gloom, such [utopian] pictures of light upon light are vacuous and expressionless, and neither to be enjoyed nor understood.
—WILLIAM JAMES

Dostoevsky never ceased to be haunted by the implications of closed time and by the "pun of creativity." Like so many Russian thinkers, he believed that life can be meaningful only if there is real process, open temporality, and genuine choice, which are threatened by all determinisms and all fatalisms. They are also threatened by utopianism, which is why Dostoevsky and his successors made the decisive contributions to modern anti-utopian literature.

Dostoevsky's profound anti-utopianism reflects his almost underground resentment of its double negation of process. First, he questioned the existence of historical laws, which in most nineteenth-century utopian thought were supposed to lead irrevocably to perfection. Second, he questioned the desirability of "perfection" itself. For perfection is pure product. It would destroy the meaningfulness of effort and, because people place the greatest value on the process of striving, utopia would turn out to be indistinguishable from hell. In calling the goal of utopian socialists an anthill (as he repeatedly did), Dostoevsky meant to suggest that it would be suitable to creatures of product but not to creatures of process.

When everything is perfect, nothing can happen; when the end of history is reached, what shall we do? Certainly there will be no fundamentally unknown truths, potentially at odds with utopian doctrine, left to discover; and sacrifice, no less than regret, will vanish. Utopia is uneventful, as utopian fiction amply demonstrates. All one can do is tour the unchangeable, which is pretty much the only sort of event that ever occurs in utopian fiction. From his arrival in utopia to his departure, the visitor from our time does nothing but learn the solution to social problems and express wonder. In the world of the perfect product, real process—process that entails eventness and uncertainty—is obsolete.

The devil who appears to Ivan Karamazov crafts a peculiar self-justification from the pun of creativity and the human need for obstacles and the unexpected. After all, he inveigles Ivan, obstacles are invented by the devil and so it is the devil, not all those boring angels, who keeps life meaningful. Without me, the devil explains, history would come to a vacuous end: "If everything in the universe were sensible, nothing would happen. There would be no events . . . and there must be events. So against the grain I serve to produce events" (BK, 780). No less than the angels, the devil would like to "sing hosannah"; but, he sadly explains, "they won't allow it" because history must continue: "Before time was, by some decree which I could never make out, I was predestined 'to deny' and yet I am genuinely good-hearted and not at all inclined to negation. 'No, you must go and deny, without denial there's no criticism, and what would a journal be without criticism?'" (BK, 780).

And so the devil sacrifices himself; but people are so ungrateful! They mistake me for Mephistopheles, who willed forever evil but did forever good, he explains. "Well, he can say what he likes, it's quite the opposite with me. I am perhaps the one man in all creation who loves the truth and genuinely desires good" (BK, 787). The devil perpetrates evil "solely from a sense of duty and my social position [that is, the position of "devil"]. . . . Somebody else takes all the credit of what's good for himself, and nothing but nastiness is left for me" (BK, 787).

It is quite characteristic of Dostoevsky to give his favorite ideas to an evil character, in this case to the devil himself. Like so many of Dostoevsky's villains, Ivan's devil is a master at the art of claiming the status of a victim; "I am a slandered man," he insists (BK, 780). In fact, the devil's self-justification has a superficial plausibility to it because it is based on a genuine truth about human nature. *There must be events*—this may be the passage that suggested the term *eventness* to Bakhtin—or else the world would turn into "an endless church service" (BK, 781). It would be holy but insufferably tedious.[19] "And that, of course, would mean the end of everything, even of magazines and newspapers, for who would take them in?" (BK, 787–88).

In a sketch from *A Writer's Diary*, Dostoevsky developed this "demonic" view of events in his own voice. His pretext was the current craze for spiritualism on the part of educated Russians, who claimed to see signs from the other world, from the realm of the devils. Skeptics have objected that these cannot be real devils, Dostoevsky reports, because, in spite of all their supposed otherworldly knowledge, they never tell anyone anything that people do not already know. Real devils (the objection continues) would prove their existence by revealing great inventions enabling us to build a utopia on earth. Then no one could doubt their reality; but nothing of the sort happens. And so, the skeptics conclude, the spiritualists cannot be seeing genuine devils but must be engaged in some sort of trick. This reasoning is completely unsound, Dostoevsky wryly maintains, and only shows that the devils are shrewder politicians than the skeptics. For it may be that these are indeed real devils who are smart enough to realize that however much people claim to want utopia, they would actually hate it and eventually reject anyone who helped build such a gilded prison.

To be sure, Dostoevsky pursues, the devils could provide us with scientific and technological secrets that would end all suffering. But they foresee the likely result. At first, of course, "all the lovers of humanity would cry, 'now when human needs are taken care of, now we will reveal our true potential! There are no more material deprivations, no more corrupting environment, . . . no more ceaseless labor'" (AWD, 1/76, 3.2). Humanity would rejoice—but not for long:

> People would suddenly see that they have no more life left, that they have no freedom of spirit, no will, no personality, that someone has stolen all this from them; they would see that their human image has disappeared. . . . And humanity would begin to decay; people would be covered in sores and begin to bite their tongues in torment, seeing that their lives had been taken away. . . . People would realize that there is no happiness in inactivity, that the mind which does not labor will wither, that it is not possible to love one's neighbor without sacrificing something to him of one's own labor, that it is vile to live at the expense of another, and that *happiness lies not in happiness but only in the attempt to achieve it.* People would be overcome by boredom and sickness of heart: everything has been done and there is nothing more to do; everything has become known and there is nothing more to discover. (AWD, 1/76, 3.2)

Then, Dostoevsky continues, people would rebel, destroy utopia, and return to history, while abandoning the devils forever. Wise as they are, the devils cannot help but anticipate this outcome, and so would never give us fire from heaven. "No, the devils won't make such a grave political error."[20]

Dostoevsky makes the anti-utopian implications of this parable explicit: If it could ever be achieved, the end of history for which socialists have longed will turn out to be a sort of temporal vacuum, with a historical plenum at *both* ends. Given human nature, the end of history would be the prelude to a new beginning, and its finale a mere interim. After product come destruction and renewed process. In utopia, the underground man predicts, there would arise "a gentleman with an ignoble, or rather with a reactionary and ironical, countenance . . . and, putting his arms akimbo, [he would] say to us all: 'What do you think, gentlemen, hadn't we better kick over all this rationalism' . . . but what is most annoying is that after all he would be sure to find followers—such is the nature of man" (NFU, 23).

From this underground prophecy Eugene Zamyatin was to develop the plot of his great anti-utopian novel *We,* which in turn inspired a twentieth-century genre, the story of a *rebellion against utopia.* Given the disastrous results of our century's efforts to create paradise on earth, the popularity of the dystopia— as this new variety of anti-utopia has been called—is not surprising. In Russia and the West, the form has flourished. From *We* to Huxley's *Brave New World,* Orwell's *1984,* Sinyavsky's *Lyubimov,* and countless lesser works, dystopias characteristically describe the rebirth of eventness and process. These devil's advocates narrate the rediscovery of narratability itself. They tell the story of the end of the end of stories.

Logarithms and Sea Battles

> In a world of fixed future, life is an infinite corridor of rooms. . . . We walk from room to room, look into the room that is lit, the present moment, then walk on. We do not know the rooms ahead, but we know we cannot change them. We are spectators of our lives.
> —ALAN LIGHTMAN, *Einstein's Dreams*

It turns out that describing freedom and process is no easy task. Not only has it proven difficult for writers to defend these values philosophically, but there also seems to be something intrinsic to narrative art itself that predisposes it, more or less, to a determinist perspective. Why that should be and how some of the great writers who believed in freedom sought to overcome the resistance offered by artistic structure are questions I shall examine in the next few chapters.

For present purposes, *Notes from Underground* constitutes the most interesting examination of freedom and process. The interest is twofold. First, the explicit polemic against determinism and utopianism in part I contains the most striking metaphors for a world in which time is closed. Second, the futility of the underground man's attempt to assert his freedom raises important questions about how freedom might be represented in narrative. As we shall see, Dostoevsky understood profoundly the difficulty, or perhaps even the near impossibility, of representing freedom in a narrative. As his characters struggle to be free, their author struggles to create them as free.

The underground man's first source of interest is his famous rejection of—or rather resentment against—determinism. Tirelessly and irritably, the underground man argues that if determinism is true, then there can be no genuine alternatives and so choice proves illusory. In such a world it is at least theoretically possible to calculate all of our supposedly free choices in advance. Since ethical responsibility depends on choice, that, too, disappears as soon as we all realize that man

> does not really have caprice or will of his own and that he has never had it, and that he himself is something like a piano key or an organ stop, and that, moreover, laws of nature exist in this world, so that everything he does is not done by his will at all, but is done by itself, according to the laws of nature. Consequently we have only to discover these laws of nature, and man will no longer be responsible for his actions and life will become exceedingly easy for him. All human actions will then, of course, be tabulated according to these laws, mathematically, like tables of logarithms up to 108,000 and entered in a table; or, better still, there would be published certain edifying works like the present encyclopedic lexicons, in which everything will be so clearly calculated and designated that there will be no more incidents or adventures in the world. (NFU, 22)

Logarithmic time, as one may call it, destroys unpredictability and therefore eventness and life. Indeed, even if for some reason we do not succeed in discovering such temporal logarithms, the very fact that they govern our lives all the same destroys the possibility of genuine "incidents or adventures," just as equations requiring logarithms to solve had solutions before we found them. What we call our actions are nothing of the sort; in reality, everything "is done by itself." We are "organ stops," whether or not we can identify the forces that play upon us. There may be actions, of course, but not adventures, if by an adventure we mean an event whose outcome is not just unknown but also still undetermined—a crucial distinction. Bakhtin doubtless had in mind this passage, too, when he distinguished between time that simply unfolds and time that has eventness. The determinist lives in a world of occurrences but not of genuine events.

Philosophers and writers have of course been grappling with this problem since antiquity. The locus classicus of the underground man's problematic is a passage from Aristotle's *On Interpretation*, from which discussion has proceeded ever since. Understanding the present as a moving "now" (as he argues in chapter 4 of the *Physics*), Aristotle insists that the future is genuinely open: that is the meaning of contingency and the basis of freedom. In *On Interpretation* he draws out some logical implications entailed by the existence of real alternatives in the future. Because real alternatives exist, Aristotle reasons, statements about the contingent future cannot be said to have any truth value; only statements about the future that are necessarily true no matter what contingent events take place would have truth value. Thus one might say truly that a sea battle either will or will not take place tomorrow, for one or the other must be the case. But one cannot say, either truly or falsely, that a sea battle will take place tomorrow and one cannot say either truly or falsely that a sea battle will not take place tomorrow. "Since propositions correspond with facts," Aristotle writes, "it is evident that when in future events there is a real alternative, and a potentiality in contrary directions, the corresponding affirmation and denial have the same character."[21] One has to wait until tomorrow for such a proposition to have meaning.

The question is less purely technical than it might seem because, according to Aristotle, if one allows propositions about the future to have truth value, one is willy-nilly driven to a determinist position closing down the future. For if a statement about the future can be true in advance, and if things are so constituted that "a prediction about an event was true, then through all time it was necessary that that prediction should find fulfilment; and with regard to all events, circumstances have always been such that their occurrence is a matter of necessity. For that of which someone has said truly that it will be, cannot fail to take place; and of that which takes place, it was always true to say that it would be" (Aristotle, 47). Aristotle calls these results awkward (Aristotle, 47); and, faced with the choice of adopting some form of determinism or of disallowing propositions about the future, he chooses the latter.

What is important for present purposes is Aristotle's premise: that it is unacceptable to say that "nothing is or takes place fortuitously, either in the present or in the future. . . . that there are no real alternatives, but that all that is or takes place is the outcome of necessity" (Aristotle, 48–49). For Aristotle, such a position contradicts his view of time, which involves both fortuitous events and what we would call free choices, which depend on the reality of alternatives:

for we see that both deliberation and action are causative with regard to the future, and that, to speak more generally, in those things which are not continuously actual there is a potentiality in either direction. Such things may either be or not be; events also therefore may either take place or not take place. . . . It is therefore plain that it is not of necessity that everything is or takes place; but in some instances there are real alternatives. (Aristotle, 47–48)

Aristotle's model leads to an image of time as a tree, with many (perhaps an infinite number of) branches extending into the ever-ramifying future. Such a model of time was for Aristotle insurance against fatalism.[22] It is the sort of insurance that might easily be sold at a premium to the underground man. For if time does genuinely resemble an infinitely ramifying tree, then there can be no table of logarithms, even in principle. In such a world there is no possibility of finding "a mathematical formula" of the sort that would reveal that only a single branch was ever possible. We are once again not organ stops but musicians.

Double Determination

The underground man's second source of interest derives from the failure of his rebellion against a determinist world. That failure, as we shall see, has multiple causes, some of which are philosophical and psychological, while others pertain to the nature of narrative and to the very fact that he is a character in a written artifact.

Dostoevsky gives us a good deal of evidence that the very actions devised by the underground man to make himself unpredictable in fact conform to an iron logic of their own. After a while, we recognize that we can guess his actions in advance. For all his desire to surprise, the underground man can be counted on to do the most spiteful and self-destructive thing. Thus he avoids the rationalist formulas of the "gentlemen in their crystal palace" only to be governed by another formula, which is perhaps more complex but no less rigid. As one astute critic has observed, the underground man, "contrary to all his intentions . . . puts a fatal order into the episodic plot of his life; he creates his own tragic necessity."[23] Intensely self-conscious, the underground man himself understands the futile method of his madness: if you have been reading carefully, he tells the reader, you already know what I did next.

But it is Dostoevsky who establishes the hero's lack of freedom most conclusively. In his role as "editor" of the underground man's text, Dostoevsky appends an "explanation" to the title of part I, "Underground." The underground man claims full freedom to define himself or to leave himself altogether undefined, but he does not have the first word. Before we hear the underground man's self-characterization, we hear him characterized by another, who is inaccessible to him: "The author of these notes and the 'Notes' themselves are, of course, imaginary. Nevertheless, such persons as the writer of these notes, *not only may, but positively must*, exist in our society, considering those circumstances under which our society was in general formed" (NFU, 3; italics mine). Ironically enough, it would seem that the underground man's very polemic on behalf of freedom was inevitable.

We are left to imagine the underground man's sense of profound insult should he read this note. But of course he cannot read it because he is imaginary, entirely the product of another's will, a character in someone else's fiction.

Here Dostoevsky makes shrewd use of metaliterary devices. For all of his struggles to be free, the underground man is doubly determined, not only from within the narrative world but also from without; not only by the iron logic of spite governing his actions but also by the fact that he is the creation of someone who has plotted all his actions in advance. His world is not just deterministic but overdeterministic. What Dostoevsky has done here is to make the very fact that the story is a story, that it has a structure and *has already been written*, a sign of failed choice and futile self-assertion.

At the story's famous end, the author returns to this device. He interrupts his character's now thoroughly repetitive arguments:

But enough; I don't want to write more from "underground" ...

- - - - - - -

The "notes" of this paradoxalist do not end here, however. He could not resist and continued them. But it also seems to me that we may stop here. (NFU, 115; ellipsis in original)

Just as he has the first word, the author also has the last. Dostoevsky suggests that the underground man's further notes endlessly repeat what we already know; they are predictable in substance and in expression; and so the three dots indicate more than mere ellipsis. In a sort of punctuational pun, they also assume something like their mathematical status, as when they are used to indicate an endlessly repeating decimal or sequence of decimals ($\frac{1}{3} = .333 \ldots$; $2/11 = .1818 \ldots$). They graphically echo the underground man's earlier mathematically metaphoric comment that he refuses to be appeased by "an endlessly recurring zero" [*ne uspokoius' . . . na bespreryvnom periodicheskom nule*] (NFU, 32). Given the underground man's own use of mathematics as a sign of determinism, this peculiar punning on the author's part conveys special irony.

The text's final words remind us that it is the author, not the character, who determines when the work concludes, when there is nothing more to be said, and when we have reached an Aristotelian ending (an event that requires something before it but allows for nothing after it). That is always the case, of course: the privilege of closure necessarily comes from outside the frame, from the author and reader. "For the event of lived life as a *whole* is without any ultimate issue out of itself," as Bakhtin observes. "An ultimate issue out of life is not *immanent* to a lived life: it descends upon a life-lived-from-within as a gift from the self-activity of another . . . from *outside* its bounds" (A&A, 79).

Life as it is experienced does not have closure or an Aristotelian ending, a point at which continuation is unthinkable and at which all loose ends are tied up. Lives end but they are not completed. Closure and structure mark the difference between life as it is lived and as it is read about; and real people live without the benefit of an outside perspective on which both closure and structure depend. Bakhtin put the point quite dramatically: one's death cannot be an event in one's life. The point is almost tautological, but its implications are far-reaching. My death can be an event only in the lives of others; I can never see my whole life. In Bakhtin's terms, that is because "finalization" (the sense of a completed whole) demands radical "outsideness": an end requires an external standpoint. Only in that way can process become finished product. Thus Dostoevsky, who sought above all to be true to his characters' own perspective, "never depicts death from within. Final agony and death are observed by others. Death cannot be a fact of consciousness itself" (TRDB, 290). We may experience our own dying, but not our own death; for we are always living into the future.

Closure and structure belong to the author and testify to the artifact. They mark the difference between the shape of narrative and the shape of experience, between the product of narrative art and the process of living. If that is so, how then can narrative art faithfully represent the openness of real temporality?

Narrative Isomorphism and Anisomorphism

To those who believe that time is open, the shape of narrative fiction seems most artificial whenever it reminds us of its status as an artifice with structure and closure. If time is open, our lives lack inherent structure and allow for multiple possibilities. The possibilities that were realized were not necessarily the most fitting, and we have no right to expect that the incidents of the future will make sense of all past contingencies. Unlike art, life does not subject contingencies to a pattern and thereby turn accidents into a meaningful inevitability.

Narrative structure therefore falsifies in several distinct but closely related ways. It violates the continuity of experience by imposing a beginning and an ending; it reduces the plurality of wills and purposes to a single pattern; it makes everything fit, whereas in life there are always loose ends; and it closes down time by conferring a spurious sense of inevitability on the sequence actually realized. The very possibility of possibility is ultimately eliminated. Whenever structure is present, there is no truly eventful process, only the execution of a pregiven plan.

For all of these reasons, then, the temporality of narrative history or fiction, however truthful or realistic it may aspire to be, differs radically from the open temporality of our real experience. In that sense, realistic literature and the world it describes are *anisomorphic* (different in shape) with respect to time. The shape of narrative and the shape of real, lived time are not congruent.

These statements presume the openness of time, but what if time is not open? What if it were governed by deterministic laws, fated to a given end, or haunted by an implacable destiny, as many different people and cultures have believed? In that case, narrative structure could readily represent the structure of real time; the two would then be *isomorphic* (identical in shape). Congruency would be attainable because narrative requires, and art fabricates, endings. If history had a plot and if real events were prestructured to arrive at a predetermined goal, then there could be a perfect symmetry of world and story. Utopian literature of the past two centuries, which characteristically draws on one or another "discovery" of history's inner pattern, typically displays such symmetry. Thus, the problem of escaping structure in order to represent time as eventful process, a problem that so concerned Tolstoy, Dostoevsky, and Chekhov, never arose for the authors of utopias. They believed themselves to be rendering history's own hidden structure, which was destined to lead, as utopian fiction inevitably does, to a fixed and happy ending. In utopia everything fits.

The end of the utopian narrative matches and is always a symbol for the end of history, which in the utopian view can be known as surely as if it had already happened. It is as though we could stand outside flux and see the pattern whole; the lesson—better, the conceit—of utopian fiction is that we actually can. As the reader can stand outside a completed story, so he can stand outside history and contemplate it in all its progressive splendor. This analogy between the reader's view of the work and the recommended view of the real world describes the basic principle shaping utopian literature as a genre. As we shall see, the revelation of how history ends allows the reader of utopian literature to understand his own time and to judge any earlier stretch of time from an absolutely privileged position. No longer does the fact that the reader lives within the flux of time impose any epistemological limitations.

The conceit, in short, is that the reader has made the same journey to utopia as the hero. Both have traveled to the future, and both have come to regard the present quite differently. They have *arrived at* the truth, one by traveling through time and the other by imagining and reading about such a journey. Having learned the whole pattern, the hero and the reader come to possess an Archimedean point. They learn that whatever is present and local, and whatever present experience by itself suggests, is distorted because from within time one does not see the pattern as it appears from outside. Where others see only process, the convinced reader of utopian fiction discerns the part of a product; where others see fortuitous events, he or she sees an unfolding pattern. A key purpose of utopian literature is to encourage this kind of "Archimedean" thinking, to foster a disengagement with present and prosaic concerns for the sake of a larger view—in fact, the largest conceivable view. Socialist realist fiction was explicitly designed with this very purpose. Like utopia, it exploits the isomorphism of generically given structure and revealed historical pattern. It is the true artifice of eternity.

Echoing various utopianisms from Buckle's philosophy of history to Chernyshevsky's utopia *What Is to Be Done?*, the underground man's antagonists share such historically and aesthetically comforting beliefs. In their view, ironclad laws of history mandate progress and lead to the utopian end of history knowable from within the historical "process." A supreme rationality shapes time, and time is as artful as a well-made story.

Escape from Structure

In some of his most brilliant diatribes, the underground man presents both empirical and logical objections to such historical rationality. He insists that process is real and product a fanciful projection. "One may say anything at all about the history of the world—anything that might enter the most disordered imagination," he remarks. "The only thing one cannot say is that it is rational" (NFU, 27). And yet, as we have seen, the underground man's own arguments, though powerful, are themselves both governed by an iron logic and integral to the author's well-crafted structure. For all the underground man's refusal to state a final word, the work in which he has been placed exhibits strong closure.

In short, freedom is defended within the narrative, but the narrative itself inscribes the opposite view. Thus a radical divergence is established between the perspective of the character and the shape of the work. Inner and outer, character and author, are at odds. It would seem that in all such disputes, the author is bound to win, even when (as in this case) the author is sympathetic to the character's defense of freedom. Many of Dostoevsky's own articles on history and human nature refute liberal and radical utopianism in terms, and sometimes in tones, similar to the underground man's. But his activity as author, as the maker of a structure, seems to draw him in the opposite direction. What philosophy gives, genre takes away. Dostoevsky was well aware of the problem. In *Notes from Underground,* Dostoevsky the ideologist struggles with Dostoevsky the artist, and it is the latter who successfully exploits an inherent advantage.

Dostoevsky's ending to this novella illustrates how the formal desiderata of narrative—structure, advance planning, and closure—make it a superb way to illustrate determinism or to describe life as perfectly ordered. No matter how much a character might struggle to be free—and surely no one struggles for freedom more explicitly and desperately than the man from underground—he remains a character in someone else's already written story. Each supposedly unpredictable act, like each rebellion of Milton's Satan, helps to realize the predetermined structure of time. Closure itself tacitly refutes the character.

Here then is a problem posed by the anisomorphism of realistic narrative: is there any escape from structure? If an author wants to represent freedom, can he escape the determinations of his own design and ending? A belief in temporal closure accommodates narrative isomorphism; is there any way for a narrative designed to affirm the openness of time to be anything but anisomorphic? Freedom is assertable, but narrative anisomorphism seems to make it unnarratable.

Dostoevsky uses the very fact of structure to defeat the underground man's tangled defense of freedom. But could he—or anyone—have done the opposite? For Dostoevsky, who deeply believed in freedom, this question seems to have arisen quite often, and some of his most interesting innovations in the novel apparently derived from his attempts to avoid the unavoidable fatalism—the inevitable inevitability—of narrative. As we shall see, Bakhtin suggested that Dostoevsky solved this problem by creating "the polyphonic novel." Tolstoy worked out a different answer. I shall argue that what I call sideshadowing represents their most successful solution.

In each of their innovative models, the temporality of lived experience triumphs—more or less—over the temporality of completed structure. We sense, not just are told to believe in, freedom, contingency, and openness. The picture resolves the frame. To our surprise, and with the author's blessing, the characters or incidents contend on at least equal terms with their maker.

Jacob wrestles with the angel and wins.

CHAPTER TWO

Foreshadowing

To some great nineteenth-century writers, the novel must have seemed a place of refuge. Faced with a culture in which determinism seemed validated by science itself, they recognized that life could be meaningful in human terms only if time is open. For choice to matter, for the present moment to have real weight, and for creative effort to be more than "the extraction of square roots," the world had to be imagined as an eventful process capable of leading to many diverse futures. Such a vision could be most readily projected, if it could be projected at all, in the novel.

Thus the novel became a peculiar sort of philosophical vehicle, or substitute philosophical vehicle. Many novels do palpably represent a world in which choice matters and creativity is real. Reading George Eliot, Jane Austen, and Turgenev, we sense, as we do in life, the presentness of the present and the multiplicity of possible futures. We experience suspense, a sign of our belief in alternative possibilities, and judge actions that, it seems evident, might have been different. Even if philosophy or science should instruct otherwise, readers and authors of many nineteenth-century novels presumed that time must be understood as open for experience to make sense at all.

Some writers went further and argued that the time we experience—cultural, historical, and psychological time—is genuinely open and that novels offer a truer picture of social life than determinist science or philosophy. Tolstoy and Dostoevsky, among others, deeply believed in this "novelistic truth" about time. They also maintained that the human dimension of time is less successfully captured by abstract systems (which typically eliminate the density of experience) than by thick novelistic description (which tends to preserve life's unsystematic richness). Generalizing from his favorite writers, Bakhtin accepted and defended this position. He recognized that even in philosophical novels concerned with time, it was important to attend not only to explicit arguments but also to the very temporality in which the novel's action takes place. Plot is concrete philosophy. And so Bakhtin tried to analyze and paraphrase the novelistic sense of time.

Perhaps, then, if we are truly to deepen our sense of what it means to say that time is open, processual, and eventful, it would be helpful to examine time in literary, and more specifically novelistic, terms. From such an examination I hope to clarify the particular version of open temporality that I wish to defend.

The Essential Surplus

I maintained in chapter 1 that formidable obstacles confront the writer who wishes not only to assert that time is open, contingency irreducible, and characters partially free but also to represent such freedom, contingency, and openness. The need for a literary work to possess structure and closure works against the project of representing freedom. Because structure itself imposes a pattern, any structured description of freedom may be tacitly self-contradictory. The shapes of the work and of the world it represents are likely to differ, thereby creating temporal anisomorphism and the constant threat of unwanted irony.

Determinists and fatalists often argue that even though people may sense themselves as free, these sensations themselves are entirely controlled by unseen forces; no matter how much people might imagine they have alternatives, their choices are, in principle, as predictable as so many entries in a logarithmic table.[1] Might it not also be true that no matter how much a novelist may wish to represent temporal openness, novelistic structure and closure are bound to illustrate the determinist's or fatalist's point? After all, every experienced reader understands that however ardently a character may believe himself to be free, however deeply a hero or heroine may agonize over choices, and however strongly the reader may identify with the character's agonies of decision, all these choices, along with their outcomes, have been planned in advance. Known to the author, they are dictated by the demands of a structure of which the character is entirely unaware but which readers keep in mind. Much as real people may be utterly controlled by the laws of nature or the unseen dictates of fate, so literary characters are compelled by a structure beyond their ken. Readers cannot help suspecting as much because they typically guess what a character may do not only by seeing events from the character's perspective but also by guessing at what good literary structure would demand. Freedom and structure would seem to be fundamentally in conflict.

Readers of literary narrative have a double experience: they both identify with characters and contemplate structure. Alternating between internal and external views, they not only project themselves into the character's horizon but also view the character's entire world as a completed aesthetic artifact. One perspective gives them process, the other product; one an open future, the other a future that has long since been determined. It is therefore possible, indeed easy, to read literary narratives as emblems of utterly closed time in which characters falsely believe they are free, just as we mistakenly sense our own freedom, which is a mirage if determinism or fatalism is true. In theological terms, the work could be said to embody the double perspective of limited people and of an omniscient God, the former experiencing time as an eventful process and the latter contemplating it in its completed entirety. Given this implicit *bias of the artifact,* it is understandable that some novelists who wanted to represent time as truly open were led to rethink the very nature of artistic structure. Perhaps they could find a way to create a work whose shape did not belie freedom, a work that managed to be isomorphic with open time. In that case, they might at least show that such a vision of experience was conceivable and coherent.

Bakhtin refers to the information unavailable to a character as the author's "essential surplus" of knowledge. Readers are aware that authors can know things about their characters that characters cannot know about themselves or each other. Most obviously, the author can know what will happen to a character. In life, we do not have that information about others any more than we have it about ourselves. When we have something resembling it, such as secret knowledge that an unwitting person faces disaster, we may experience a heady but morally troubling feeling because we occupy a position analogous to a god's. And even then, we are simply predicting and, therefore, subject to error. But in literature the author does have godlike power; the future is part of his image of a character. The author normally knows a character's destiny for certain and beyond the possibility of revision by the character. For the author, the character's life is in effect already over before it has begun. Closure has been silently there all along. Therefore the significance of each event is accessible to the author, as it could not be to the character or to anyone within the flux of time.

The author's experience of a character is consequently quite different from his experience of anyone in the real world. Real people anticipate possible futures but do not know actual ones, as authors do. Readers participate in the author's essential surplus. Even on a first reading, when they do not know what will happen to a character, readers are at least aware that the author (or an earlier reader) knows; though readers do not know the character's fate, they know that it is already known. Indeed, practiced readers of literature confidently assume that part of the reading experience consists in identifying the structure that contains the character unawares. They also take for granted that they will be able to reread the story, whereas characters, like real people, may not relive their lives. In fact, every act of reading is shaped by the possibility of rereading, whether or not that rereading ever takes place.

The author and rereader have access to the whole of a character's life, which cannot be experienced from within. From outside the process, the most eventful and suspenseful life is revealed as a product; from within, the best the character can do is project what that product might turn out to be and then, throughout life, continually amend those projections, as all of us do with respect to our own lives. People may guess at the future and imagine what story might someday be told about them, but so long as they live they may well be wrong, as Greek literature never tires of reminding us. Count no man's life happy until he is dead, as Herodotus repeats. No life is ever free from the possibility of unanticipated irony, because it has not been plotted in advance.

Whenever the reader senses the author's surplus of knowledge, he or she will be palpably reminded of the work's status as artful product. The reader will mark the difference between time as it is lived and time as it is read about. Perhaps the most dramatic sign of the essential surplus is *foreshadowing*. Foreshadowing is a literary device immediately recognizable as such. For in life we do not experience foreshadowing; and we may perhaps understand better our own experience of time if we inquire why we do not. Of course, many people have believed in something like foreshadowing in real life, and so it would also be instructive to consider what such a belief implies about the temporality of life as it is lived.

We would expect that authors who believe in open time would avoid foreshadowing; or if they used it, would do so self-consciously, in some way parodically, so as to invite readers to contemplate its very artifice. The double perspective of narrative art—process and product, internal and external—allows for numerous ways in which open and closed temporalities may be made to confront each other. We will see how authors who believe in freedom have drawn on the possibilities for such conflict to create a convincing vision of a world in which the future can be many different things.

Foreshadowing

My boyhood, indeed, which no longer is, belongs to past time, which no longer is. However, when I recall it and talk about it, I perceive its image at the present time, because it still is in my memory. Whether there may be a like cause of predicting future events as well, namely, that actually existent images of things which as yet do not exist are perceived first, I confess, O my God, I do not know.
—AUGUSTINE, *Confessions*

Why is foreshadowing absent from life? We may ascribe this absence to the asymmetry of time, which we experience as having a direction, as *anisotropic* (not the same in both directions).[2] Space is isotropic: it has no inherent direction, and we can move backward as well as forward. What we call backward and forward is relative to our desires. But that is not the case with time. As a word processing program allows us to amend only that part of the text where the cursor is, so we can act only in the present moment; but in contrast to a cursor, which can be moved in any direction, the present goes only one way. Because of this directedness in time, action taken to affect the past is senseless, whereas we feel that action taken to affect the future is, if uncertain in result, at least not absurd in principle. We make the effort.

The past is over and has left its traces, but the time to come has not yet had a chance to do so. As a result, we are aware that one consequence of the anisotropy (directedness) of time is an *asymmetry in knowledge:* we know a lot more about the past than about the future. To be sure, some future events may be known with impressive certainty: the position of Halley's comet in the next millennium may be predicted as easily as its past positions may be retrodicted. But on the whole, we know the past a lot better than the future because we know the past as already accomplished, whereas we anticipate a future still being shaped.

No one sells insurance against accidents that have already happened. Kidnappers can prove their victim is alive by photographing the victim holding a copy of today's newspaper because no one could have tomorrow's paper even though everyone could have yesterday's. Evidence of this sort is singularly convincing.

We have ways of recording the past or inferring with tolerable accuracy what happened in times gone by. To do so, we rely on numerous natural and invented recording devices of the most diverse kinds, including memory, photographs, tape recorders, phonographs, fossils, written records, paintings, and footprints in the sand. But we have no such comparably reliable *pre*recording devices and, we suspect, we could not have them. Prerecording devices would be possible only if time were symmetrical with respect to knowledge. Footprints in the sand are traces of the past, but we have no equivalent traces of the future. Whatever we may fear, anticipate, or imagine, we do not remember forward.

Paul Horwich has described these features as consequences of a "fork asymmetry" in time (Horwich, 97–98). If two improbable events are correlated in their occurrence, we may infer (though not with absolute certainty) that we may find an earlier event, that is, a prior cause, to account for the correlation. We may draw a V-shaped diagram in which A and B are linked to earlier event C.

What we do not find is an inverted V, in which A and B are linked not to a prior but to a subsequent event, E. We do not account for correlated events by discovering an effect that they will both produce or by saying that they are

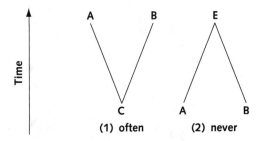

A and B, two improbable events, occur together (1) because they are effects of a prior cause (often) and (2) because they are leading to a subsequent event (never).

both the effect of a cause that follows them. The V goes only one way, which is why it—and knowledge—is asymmetrical with respect to time.

But when a literary work uses foreshadowing, none of these strictures apply, at least as far as the reader is concerned. The character may experience time as anisotropic and asymmetrical with respect to knowledge, just as we do in life, but foreshadowing gives the reader a sign indicating what *will* happen. Of course, it is the fact that the story is already written and the structure already determined that makes such a sign possible, and so foreshadowing is an infallible reminder of the author's essential surplus. It establishes the merely illusory nature of what the character experiences as open temporality.

The Gathering Storm

In what space, then, do we measure passing time?
—AUGUSTINE, *Confessions*

Let us suppose that a character is happy, confident of the future, and celebrating a victory that promises still greater success. Obstacles are melting ever faster. But although he does not know it, a thunderstorm, which the author describes in some detail, is approaching. Even if the hero did know of the storm, it would indicate to him nothing more than rain; but the reader recognizes it as foreshadowing, the sign of a reversal of fortune. In life, people rarely imagine that a change in the weather indicates an alteration in prospects having nothing to do with weather. But for the reader of fiction, such a conclusion is often entirely warranted.

The storm happens *because* something else *is going to happen*. It is caused by a subsequent event, and that is why it is an instance of foreshadowing. If the reverse were the case, if somehow the storm were itself the prior cause of the misfortune (say, of a literal shipwreck), we would not have a case of foreshadowing but of a cause revealed to the reader before it is perceived by the

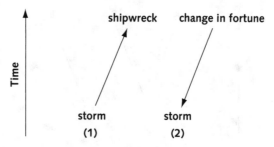

(1) Storm as the cause of a later event (shipwreck); (2) storm as foreshadowing of a later event (change in fortune).

character. In foreshadowing, the storm itself does not cause anything; rather, it indicates that something is coming. The causation, so to speak, works backward.

The very term *foreshadowing* indicates backward causality. A spatial metaphor for a temporal phenomenon, it is a shadow cast in advance of an object; its temporal analog is an event that indicates (is the shadow of) another event to come. The spatial image contains nothing unfamiliar. An object in our path may cast a shadow backward, so that we reach the shadow before reaching the object casting it; and from experience, we may know to expect the object when we encounter the shadow. The shadow does not cause the object ahead but is caused by it, even though we encounter the shadow first. A temporal foreshadow works the same way. The storm is there because the catastrophe follows; it is an effect of that future catastrophe visible in temporal advance, much as the shadow of an object may be visible in spatial advance.

As we have seen, spatial metaphors of time have proven singularly tempting to philosophers and in everyday life, probably for as long as temporality has been discussed. It is inscribed deeply in language in countless expressions based on movement through time or on time's flow. Such metaphors may be both helpful and misleading; in any case, they are very difficult to avoid. So far as foreshadowing is concerned, the consequences of the spatial metaphor are quite dramatic. In space, we often come across effects in advance of their causes: moving windshield wipers on cars in the opposite lane indicate rain ahead of cars going in our direction. But (I think) we have experienced no temporal equivalent. We know nothing of effects preceding their causes and thereby serving as signs of what will cause them. In the world of foreshadowing we do: in this world, there is a fork *symmetry,* and the V diagram may be drawn both ways. Causes may come prior to or after effects. Foreshadowing makes time symmetrical with respect to knowledge. It is a prerecording device.

Forward and backward causation may be used together. An event may be caused both ways. In using foreshadowing, the author may also indicate some prior cause of the sign foreshadowing the future. The storm need not come out of nowhere; he may give some meteorological information. The author may even include prior causation to create irony: perceiving the storm, the hero, who can detect only prior causes, draws false conclusions, whereas the reader, who recognizes foreshadowing, correctly attributes the significant event to future as well as to past causes. In the process, the reader marks the difference between his knowledge and the hero's. But neither such irony nor the existence of prior causes is necessary. When foreshadowing is used, prior causation is optional and is not what constitutes the event *as* foreshadowing.

Foreshadowing seems utterly to preclude the possibility of options. Choice becomes illusory. If the future branched and if many possibilities could happen, then how could any single future affect the present? For that future would have no actuality, only possibility; and how could the mere possibility of something be substantial enough to have an effect in any direction? In space, foreshadows are not cast by objects that might be ahead of us, but only by those that *are* ahead of us, and the same would seem to be true of time.

Foreshadowing normally makes the ramification of time merely apparent. Time must be utterly linear (a single, nonbranching line). But that is not all, for time could be linear without the possibility of foreshadowing, as in many deterministic models. One may easily be a determinist without believing in signs of the future. Foreshadowing makes the future not just an inevitability but a substantial actuality. It is invisible but there, both virtually (in its effect) and actually. In a sense, it has already happened, and we are in its shadow.

Theologically, we might say that the future is there in the mind of God, for whom there is no past and future because to him all things are present. "Thus also the divine mind contemplates everything in one altogether simple act at once and without succession, that is, without the difference between the past, present and future; to Him all things are present," wrote Giordano Bruno, whose view was by no means unique. God contemplates history the way we view a painting or think about a novel we have finished. Leibniz observed that someone with sufficient insight "would see the future in the present as in a mirror."[3] Such a person might be seeing the future events themselves or he might be seeing the eternal pattern, which all events instantiate. Either way, he would have prerecording or preregistering devices; he could see the footprints left by the future or, as we might say, read history as one would read a novel with foreshadowing.

In a novel the future in fact is there, already written; we need only skip a few pages. It has the full substantiality of a past event. Novels that do not rely on foreshadowing allow us more easily to suspend this knowledge and so come closer to representing open temporality; novels that use foreshadowing call our attention to the already written nature of narrative time. In so doing, they may either foreground the artifice of fictional narrative or, quite the contrary, may indicate a Leibnizian appreciation of real-world time.

In life (as I understand it), only prior causation is possible. (Today most people are usually uncomfortable with the notion of teleology, except as a sort of convenient, but potentially misleading, shorthand.)[4] But in a world of foreshadowing, events are not only pushed but *pulled*.

The Future That Has Happened

> When the present comes into being from the future, does it proceed from some hidden source?
> —AUGUSTINE, *Confessions*

When foreshadowing is used in a realistic novel, it inevitably marks a radical difference between the character and the reader. Whatever allows us to *identify* with a character, it is not foreshadowing, which places us in a temporality radically different from that of the character. Even if we believe in a future already written, we have no access to it and, on the whole, do not experience time that way. To the extent that identification with a character is to take place, it requires that readers share essential features of the character's experience. But the character in realistic fiction experiences time as open. Everything that makes foreshadowing possible is not available to the character.

Foreshadowing directs our attention not to the experience of the character but to the design of the author, whose structure is entirely responsible for foreshadowing. Of course, identification and foreshadowing may both be present, which means that the reader's experience of the work involves an overlap of distinct temporalities. If a work has a compelling hero, the reader's experience will consist of a pull in two directions, toward "losing himself" or herself within the world and simultaneously contemplating it from an external position.

Even without explicit foreshadowing, this experience of antithetical times is always present in literature to some extent. We never entirely forget that we are reading an artifact; few mistake realism for documentary, much less for actual reality. But foreshadowing, one might say, foregrounds the inevitable divergence between the world within and the world without. By marking the essential surplus, it forces a break in identifying with a character for the sake of contemplating the whole.[5]

If life had foreshadowing, what would it be like? We may imagine, for instance, that history has foreshadowing if we believe that it tends toward a fated end. For Soviet Marxists, as an example, communism in the future was woven into the temporal fabric of the universe; in other belief systems, nations may be governed by an implacable fate or a benevolent destiny. The end may be impossible to detect from within time, and we may be fated (as part of the plan) to mistake causes for signs and to misread whatever real signs are apparent. But it is also sometimes held that the end may be known not only to God but also to those people who have discovered God's plan, the eternal archetypes, or history's laws. Mysticism and certain forms of socialism provide abundant examples.

For someone who accepts such beliefs, foreshadowing might well be evident to a potential reader of history. History would be an already finished artifact. The believer might imagine a divine reader; or he might picture a human one either looking down from the other world or, having been present at the Apocalypse and Last Judgment, looking back after history is over. And perhaps a preview of the fatal book would be possible, a glance at its index or table of contents? If that book could be read, then foreshadowing in the reader's own time would probably be apparent. Contemplating the whole, such a reader would have made life a form of rereading. He or she would be able to draw connections irrespective of temporal sequence, could read a pattern. To such a reader all things would indeed be present. If history resembled a novel, then the present would resemble the page that happens to be open; but the whole would be there.

In principle, one might believe that history is novelistic in this way even if one denied the possibility of knowing outcomes. For instance, one might argue that to attain such knowledge, one would have to step outside history, which is impossible. This view, though less obviously disturbing than the one that supposes such a step is possible, might prove unwelcome enough in its consequences. For it still makes open temporality an illusion and our experience of openness a misleading epiphenomenon. As the moral equivalent of characters in a novel, people alive today would lose their claim to any special attention and concern. Their lives would truly be already over and would have always been already over. Their choices would be illusory, for they would have already been made. Those aware of this depressing fact would then not so much live their lives as *live out* their already-plotted lives.

The same would be true if one believed in eternal recurrence, as some Pythagoreans and Stoics did. According to Eudemius of Rhodes, "Everything will return in the self-same numerical order, and I shall converse with you staff in hand, and you will sit as you are sitting now, and so it will be in everything else, and it is reasonable to assume that time too will be the same."[6] Nemesius described Stoics as believing that "again there will be Socrates and Plato and each one of mankind with the same friends and fellow citizens; they will suffer the same things and they will encounter the same things, and put their hand to the same things. . . . The gods who are not subject to destruction . . . know . . . everything that is going to be in the next periods. For . . . everything will be just the same and discernible down to the smallest details."[7]

It is possible to find this view comforting, especially if the world that repeats itself is the best possible one, but it may also be regarded as deeply disturbing if the world is evil or if one values unpredictable choice. In *The Brothers Karamazov*, the devil taunts Ivan with the image of endlessly repeating identical cycles of events. "Why, you keep thinking of our present earth!" he remarks.

> But our present earth may have been repeated a billion times. Why, it's become extinct, been frozen; cracked, broken to bits, disintegrated into its elements, again "the water above the firmament," then again a comet, again a sun, again from the sun it becomes earth—and the same sequence may have been repeated endlessly, and exactly the same to every detail, most unseemly and insufferably tedious ... (BK, 783)

In such a model, time is symmetrical because it is perfectly circular. The future has already been completely decided because it has already happened in another cycle; and the past that we remember is yet to be in a subsequent cycle. This temporal pattern makes succession entirely relative, since everything happens both before and after everything else.[8]

If we remember that everything the devil says repeats Ivan's observations on some earlier occasion, we may recognize this chapter itself as a sort of recurrence, in which Ivan's undeniable torments of conscience are mocked by his own theories. And if we are *re*reading the book, we may recognize that Dostoevsky here makes a particularly shrewd use of the metaliterary devices that so appealed to him: novels also go through an exact cycle of repetition, down to the last detail, every time they are read. Everything returns in the self-same order.

The devil suggests and Ivan understands that a vision of eternal recurrence makes nonsense of all human choice and all moral responsibility. If everything has already happened and is still about to happen, then the sentiment of regret (which torments Dmitri), the experience of guilt (which Ivan feels throughout this scene), and the agony of choice (the theme of his Grand Inquisitor legend) are all pointless, if not utterly farcical. Such a sense of pointlessness accompanies the belief in eternal recurrence even if one does not imagine one can know what has happened in a previous cycle and therefore what will happen later in the present one.[9]

Prophetic History

It is possible to imagine that some foreshadowing is detectable from within history: as if, to return to our hypothetical example, someone could tell that this storm was unlike all others, that it is a shadow cast by catastrophe in the making. However odd this view may seem to some, it is in fact quite common, not only as applied to individual lives but also with respect to history. It is routinely shared, to varying degrees and on different grounds, by totalitarian ideologies. As ours has been the century most given to such thinking, it would perhaps be wise not to discount its appeal.

In his *Analytical Philosophy of History*, Arthur Danto accuses what he calls substantive philosophies of history, such as Marxism, of accepting something very close to the novelistic picture of the historical process.[10] In Danto's view, such philosophies claim to be able to judge events in terms of the whole of history, much as a literary critic can judge an event in a novel in terms of the whole.[11]

But the whole of history is never available, Danto argues. Even if we somehow possessed documentary evidence of everything that had ever happened, and even if we had access to some great cosmic recorder that has been running for all of human history, we would still not have the whole of history, but only the whole of the past. And the past is certainly not the whole story, for future events may change the story's shape and significance. Major crises may turn into mere prologues and disasters into preparations for triumph or, perhaps, into mere local color. In general, the future has the power to transform, not past facts but their significance, which depends in part on what they lead to later. Insignificant thinkers, neglected in their time or ours, may have been both the predecessors and remote inspirers of the celebrated geniuses to come. To know the significance of present and past events would entail knowing the shape of things to come, for which we would require not just a cosmic recorder but something approaching a cosmic prerecorder, registering the future while it was still future. Substantive philosophers of history claim to be able to assign such significance in advance because they know the outcome of the story.

If communism is destined, if standards of progressiveness and reaction may be measured in terms of that final goal, then judgments about the significance of recent events cease to be speculative. In Danto's view, they become prophetic:

> It is, I think, instructive to recognize that Marx and Engels, although they were materialists and explicit atheists, were nevertheless inclined to regard history through essentially theological spectacles, as though they could perceive a divine plan, but not a divine being whose plan it was. Whatever the case, the substantive philosophies of history . . . are clearly concerned with

what I shall term *prophecy*. A prophecy is not a mere statement about the future, for a prediction is a statement about the future. It is a certain *kind* of statement about the future . . . an *historical* statement about the future. The prophet is one who speaks about the future in a manner which is appropriate only to the past, or who speaks of the present in the light of a future treated as a *fait accompli*. A prophet treats the present in a perspective ordinarily available only to future historians, to whom present events are past, and for whom the meaning of present events is discernible.[12]

This characterization seems essentially correct, except for the last sentence, which does not quite follow from Danto's argument. No *merely* future historian could be in a position to evaluate significance as some prophets and substantive philosophies claim to do—in terms of the whole—because the future historian will himself be limited by his own historical position. He will still be within history. After all, there will be a future that he does not yet know, and that future may change the significance of the events he evaluates; unlike the historical prophet or substantive philosopher, he does not know the whole story. Only a historian at the end of history, a historian beyond revision and superannuation, could be equal to such a prophet.

For those inclined to believe both that the whole future is already there and that signs of it may at times be detected, historical experience becomes to that extent forward-looking and prospective—even annunciatory ("Unto you a Savior is born") and revelatory of the whole ("I am alpha and omega"). We live toward omega. What religion figures as divine revelation, Soviet Marxism claimed by the discovery of scientific laws, which in principle make the future of society no more unknowable than the future positions of Halley's comet. Danto captures the strangeness of this annunciatory view and its difference from lived experience when he imagines it outside a sacred context.[13] It is as if somebody could have said to Madame Diderot in labor, "Unto you an encyclopedist is born" (Danto, 12).

Types of the Socialist Future

The citations to be found under "foreshadowing" in the *Oxford English Dictionary* may deepen our understanding of this concept: "The ceremonies in the law did foreshadow Christ" (1577); "Our Savior's death . . . was by manifold types fore-shadowed." These citations make foreshadowing a virtual synonym for "prefiguration," defined as "representation beforehand by a figure or type." The quotations under this entry are similar: "Many of the ancient Fathers . . . thought likewise their sacraments to be but prefigurations of that which ours in present do exhibit" (1600); "The personages and events of the Old Testament were, for the most part, regarded as prefigurations of those of the New" (1851). These terms, which of course reflect a long tradition of Christian biblical interpretation, figure earlier events as signs of later ones. In this reading, the preferred explanation of events in the Old Testament is their foreshadowing or prefiguration of events to come. Jonah's three days in the belly of the whale are to be understood as prefiguring the time between the Crucifixion and Resurrection, when Jesus harrowed hell. As God made Eve from the sleeping Adam's rib, so the dead Christ's side was pierced; Adam's sleep figures Christ's death sleep, and the creation of the mother of humanity foreshadows the birth of the Church, the mother of people in spirit, from Christ's blood. As Erich Auerbach observes, such interpretation reflects the nature of the divine intelligence: "In God there is no distinction of times since for him everything is simultaneously present, so that—as Augustine once put it—he does not possess foreknowledge but simply knowledge."[14] The One for whom all events are present establishes connections without respect to what humans know as time's directedness.

This view of the Old Testament, of course, cannot be accepted by Jews. If the events in their sacred book prefigure anything, it cannot be the sacred book of another religion. Such a view destroys the integrity of those earlier books; it is incompatible, for example, with the special status accorded by Jews to the Torah. For Jews, the meaning of the Torah is to be established by first accepting its uniqueness and priority; it is not simply a sign of something to come or commentary in advance on a more important but still unwritten book. There is therefore all the difference in the world between speaking of the Old Testament and of the Hebrew Bible.

Prefiguration is one way in which a later book may supersede an earlier one and vitiate its integrity while claiming to preserve its sacred status. One may also supply a key to the Scriptures, as various religions and mystical sects have done. By so doing, one does not just interpret but in effect supplants. Religions are defined by the *latest* book they acknowledge as sacred. A straight line drawn between an earlier and a later testament or key eliminates readings that lead in other directions. Among other things, Christian prefiguration destroys the possibility of seeing events in the Hebrew Bible as prefiguring events in Jewish history, which in its own turn overwrites possibilities imaginable at the time the books were written.

That great iconoclast Tolstoy rejected out of hand the meaningfulness of interpretation by prefiguration. He believed rather in the radical integrity of each present moment and each story. In *Anna Karenina*, Karenin's son Seryozha senses deeply the power of Old Testament narratives but cannot apply the required deadening interpretation:

Seryozha recounted the events themselves well enough, but when he had to answer questions as to what certain events prefigured, he knew nothing, though he had already been punished for this lesson. The passage at which he was utterly unable to say anything, and began fidgeting and cutting the table and swinging his chair, was the one about the patriarchs before the Flood. He did not know one of them except Enoch, who had been taken up alive to heaven . . . chiefly because Enoch was the character he liked best in the whole of the Old Testament, and Enoch's being taken to heaven was connected in his mind with the whole long train of thought, in which he became absorbed now while he gazed with fascinated eyes at his father's watch chain and a half-unbuttoned button on his vest. (AK, 552)

Enoch's ascent to heaven provides Seryozha with proof that death is not, or does not have to be, real and therefore somehow also offers evidence that his mother has not died, as he has been told. In his childish way, Seryozha responds directly to the story, whereas his father's questions invite him to dispense with any immediate experience of it.

When in subsequent decades Tolstoy formulated what he took to be the true Christian faith and offered a corrected Bible of his own editing, he sought to eliminate anything that could distract from, overwrite, allegorize away, or otherwise soften the *presence* of Jesus's words. Prefigural interpretation was banished by eliminating the entire Old Testament; and by casting out what he called "the insane ravings of the Apocalypse," which invited a sort of *postfigural* interpretation of the Gospels, Tolstoy precluded seeing simple moral injunctions as signs of extrahistorical events to come.

In rejecting the hermeneutics of prefiguration, Tolstoy was also responding to its secular equivalents in Russian thought at the time, which cultivated the interpretation of current human events by means of *types*. This term, which was central to aesthetic debates surrounding nineteenth-century Russian literature, carried various meanings for different groups. As used by the radical "democrats," it increasingly took on a prophetic interpretation. Invoking a sort of clairvoyance ostensibly derived from knowledge or intuition of history's laws, a writer was expected to describe representatives of social trends who did not yet exist but were destined to exist. As Dobrolyubov wrote, the writer was to reveal to the people "what, as yet, lives in them, vaguely and indefinitely." [15] He was to be a historian of the future. Chernyshevsky's *What Is to Be Done?: From Stories about New People* claimed and was taken to be just such divination of the new kinds of people to come—not only the next heroic group that was soon to appear but also the one after that, which would be as superior to the first group as the first group was to be to Chernyshevsky's contemporaries.

In such formulations, "typicality" and the "type" come remarkably close to their traditional religious sense: "that by which something is symbolized or figured . . . specifically in theology, a person, object, or event of Old Testament history, prefiguring some person or thing revealed in the new dispensation." As has often been noted, the resurgence of this kind of thinking in the radical democrats is hardly surprising when one recalls how many of them, including the most influential ones from Chernyshevsky to Stalin, either were trained in Russian Orthodox seminaries or were sons of priests. Generations of Russian revolutionaries took Chernyshevsky's heroes as models for their own lives; and after 1917, the radical democrats were themselves honored as, in effect, types of their victorious successors.

The Art of the Known Future

In our time, the artform most committed to the doctrine that the future is both historical and knowable has been socialist realism. The strangeness of these works for the Western reader derives in large part from their embodiment of a temporality alien to most of the great novels, whether Russian or Western, with which we are familiar. They therefore provide excellent examples of what it is like to think about life and the historical process in terms of types and foreshadowing.

When the doctrine of socialist realism was codified, the idea of the type as an image of the destined future gained unprecedented importance. As every student of the subject knows, socialist realism was defined at the First All-Union Congress of Soviet Writers (1934) as "the basic method of Soviet literature and literary criticism. It demands of the artist the truthful, historically concrete representation of reality in its revolutionary development. Moreover, the truthfulness and historical concreteness of the artistic representation of reality must be linked with the task of ideological transformation and education of workers in the spirit of socialism." [16] By "reality in its revolutionary development" is meant the known future. As L. I. Timofeev's classic text on the subject observes, "The artist sees today in the light of tomorrow" (cited Mathewson, 43n). That is, the Soviet writer must represent the future's traces on the present and describe the future both *historically* and *concretely*. Such a prescription presumes that the future has already been ascertained through the application of Marxist-Leninist science, which enables literature to become a sort of prerecording mechanism.

In his classic essay on the subject, Andrei Sinyavsky paraphrases the official contrast between such earlier "critical realists" as Tolstoy, Balzac, and Chekhov and the later socialist realists. The difference is primarily one of temporal knowledge. Sinyavsky writes, "Not having been instructed in the genius and teachings of Marx, they [the critical realists] could not foresee the future victories of socialism, and they certainly did not know the real and concrete roads to these victories" (OSR, 149). But the socialist realist writer, "while representing the present . . . listens to the march of history and looks toward the future. He sees the 'visible traits of Communism,' invisible to the ordinary eye" (OSR, 149). Whereas critical realists could detect only prior causes, socialist realists identify future ones; they can sense not just the push but the pull of history. "Our art, like our culture and our society, is teleological through and through," observes Sinyavsky (OSR, 150), because it presumes that communism, as "the inevitable logical outcome of all human history, inevitably pulls us forward" (OSR, 201).

It followed that the hero of socialist realist fiction would be *typical of the future*. Thus was established the doctrine of the "positive hero," who seems superhuman and (to a Western reader shaped by critical realism) implausible precisely because he reflects a different time and a superior temporality. The Soviet novelist Leonid Leonov called the positive hero "a peak of humanity from whose height the future can be seen" (cited OSR, 172).

Sinyavsky attributed the utter artistic failure of the socialist realist novel to its crude yoking of two alien artistic methods, utopian fantasy and Tolstoyan realism, either one of which taken by itself might have produced better results. The combination produced a "loathsome literary salad" in which characters first "torment themselves though not quite as Dostoevsky's do" and then, "suddenly becoming aware of the time they are living in, scream at the reader the copybook slogans which they read in Soviet newspapers" (OSR, 215). What Sinyavsky describes as the combination of incompatible methods might also be seen as the yoking of contradictory temporalities. The hero exists, successively or simultaneously, in two kinds of time. This temporal contradiction is not to be confused with the anisomorphism of the realist novels, in which the open temporality of the characters conflicts with the closed temporality of structure and closure. The contradictory elements of socialist realism pertain to the world of the characters themselves.

Oedipus the King

> Chance is my mother.
> —OEDIPUS

The best-known and most successful work to embody the idea that the future is already given is probably Sophocles' *Oedipus the King*. In this tragedy, and in others like it, foreshadowing is no mere artistic device. Whereas in most realist novels, foreshadowing marks the work's artifice, in the *Oedipus* it conveys the temporality that is supposed to govern the real world. Not fate but temporal openness proves to be the mirage, as time is shown to be essentially oracular.

In the *Oedipus* the future is never in question. In part because knowledge of the myth is presumed, the audience is aware from the beginning of the story's outcome. Even a first viewing (or reading) of the play therefore exhibits some characteristics of rereading.[17] Traces of the future are everywhere present.

The play's distinctive effect depends on foreshadowing and the dramatic irony it enables. The meaning of what Oedipus "chooses" at each moment is given by our appreciation of the story's end, which he does not know. We detect a radical divergence between the audience and the hero, and that divergence pertains not only to knowledge but also to ways of knowing. Tieresias, however, knows what we do and as we do because he has access in advance to the whole story. We are told that the man who solved the riddle of the Sphinx can draw inferences from past and present events better than any living person. But he scorns the signs of the future, those detected by the seer and by the audience.

"I came, know-nothing Oedipus, I stopped the Sphinx. I answered the riddle with my own intelligence—the birds had nothing to teach me."[18] Oedipus's frequently noted similarity to a modern detective reflects his extraordinary capacity for making reasoned deductions from traces of the past. But the play's irony depends on traces of the future, on foreshadows cast back by the terrible ending Oedipus does not see. He responds to the past, but these very responses are themselves shaped by the end that must happen.

Thus, Oedipus repeatedly asks and answers questions about the past, but his words resonate for us in terms of the future they adumbrate. As he responds to the present he unwittingly describes the future because he is in the grip of a temporality inverse to the one he imagines. His past and present are composed of hidden prophecy. "For whoever killed Laius might decide to raise his hand against me. So, acting on behalf of Laius, I benefit myself, also" (Sophocles, 359). "Laius and I would be closely connected by children from the same wife. . . . So I shall fight for him as if he were my own father" (Sophocles, 361). Of course, Oedipus will suffer the lengthy and terrible curse he calls down on Laius's killer.

In the course of the play, this sort of dramatic irony is almost always present. Words are doubly determined by the past and by the future, by causes and destinies; they are shaped both internally and externally, by the character and by the structure of the whole. Oedipus lives by one temporality and senses the other too late; but we and Tieresias have known it all along. Tieresias sees the present pulled forward to its prescribed destiny.[19]

When Oedipus talks with Tieresias, the two opposite temporalities collide. The one in which the future shapes the present proves more powerful. It would have to because that is the temporality of the gods and of the drama as a whole. For all his intelligence, Oedipus does not know, cannot know, the most essential facts about himself.

Oedipus's assertion that "the birds had nothing to teach me" is delivered as a taunt to Tieresias, who claims to see the future but (as Oedipus reminds him) could do nothing to rescue the town from the Sphinx. For that, plans based on the past were needed. By invoking the past, and judgments based on it, Oedipus duels with time: past-based reasoning challenges the value of revelation from the future. But the outcome of that duel is itself ordained.

Later, Jocasta will observe that Oedipus is unlike himself, for he "is distracted with sorrows of all kinds. He does not act like a man in control of his reason, judging the present by the past" (Sophocles, 374). She does not know what she is saying; but we recognize the change in Oedipus as his growing awareness of another and harsher chronicity. Jocasta insists that "there is no human being born that is endowed with prophetic power" (Sophocles, 370) and that "life is governed by the operations of chance. Nothing can be foreseen" (Sophocles, 375). But in this play life is governed not by chance but by a future already decided. Causal reasoning is nothing more than our poor substitute for revelation, which is not usually available. Signs of the future may be rare and difficult to interpret, but they are nonetheless infallible. Tieresias answers Oedipus's insults by telling him what will happen, sure in the knowledge that even such a disclosure cannot threaten the very specific predictions he has made.

Perfectly symmetrical, the *Oedipus* establishes a precise fit between its temporality and its structure. Events are given in advance by fate and by the structure of the play. And so the plot becomes the apt vehicle for a temporality driven by an outside pattern to which events must conform. As fate directs the character to a predestined catastrophe, authorial design propels the play relentlessly toward closure. The already familiar myth, the play already written, and the audience's knowledge that the author has already shaped everything, all correspond to the end-determined temporality that governs within the play and is its theme.[20]

In short, the temporalities of the structure and of the characters could not be more isomorphic. In advance, "Zeus and Apollo, it is true, understand and know in full the events of man's life" (Sophocles, 366–67); in the same way, the author and audience know in advance the events of the hero's life. As we have seen, such perfect isomorphism would not be easy to achieve in a represented world in which freedom is real. In such cases, the reader's awareness that all events have already been recorded would detract from the sense that the character is in the process of choosing. To the extent that the reader is reminded of structure, drama fades into a shadow of itself. Product threatens process; and so metaliterary allusions to the work as an artifact characteristically lead, if unintended, to a jarring effect and, if designed, to a species of self-referential wit. Such devices need have no such effect in works representing a fatal chronicity. Structure favors isomorphic fatalism but works against isomorphic freedom.

Foreshadowing in *Oedipus* is thus the necessary sign of its temporality. The device does not appear in the least gratuitous or artificial, which is one reason it works so powerfully. The play is enacted in a world in which time obeys a logic of prophecy. In that world, there can be—and is—one person, Tieresias, "in whom truth is inborn" (Sophocles, 362) and who can therefore speak the pattern known to the gods and the audience.

The audience recognizes this temporality while retaining the sense of past-based temporality as well. On the one hand, we contemplate the structure of the whole, and we see the signs of it as the action unfolds. On the other, we also identify with Oedipus and his experience, which, like our own, is lived without knowledge of the future. Lacking such identification with the hero, we would probably lose interest in the play.

Our experience of time in *Oedipus* is therefore double: we can imagine what each act of the hero feels like, and we also see what it "really" is. The disjuncture between these two temporalities produces the drama's peculiar and intense fear and pity. Thus the meeting of the two times in Oedipus's dialogue with Tieresias encapsulates our own experience, which is another reason the scene is so moving. One character speaks from within the story and one from outside it, and we as audience are constantly aware of both perspectives.

Omens

Even in our own time, it is not all that rare to encounter people who believe in a world partly shaped by the future. Such people may, for instance, believe in omens and therefore treat life as if it resembled an already written narrative. Omens are signs of the future, traces "left" by events to come. They are instances of foreshadowing discernible from within ongoing experience.

The concept of omens is worth clarifying, since one may distinguish among different senses of the term. *Omen* is defined by the *Oxford English Dictionary* as "any phenomenon or circumstance supposed to portend good or evil; a token significant of the nature of a future event; a prophetic sign, prognostic, augury." The ancient Roman augur was supposed to divine the future on the basis of the flight of birds, the entrails of sacrifices, celestial phenomena, and other omens or portents. In this (stricter) sense, the term seems to involve some form of backward causation. But *omen* is also used in a looser sense, as when we call an incident "ominous." We shall be concerned here with elucidating the temporality of omens in the stricter sense.

If someone believes that his arthritic knee forecasts rain or that his dreams indicate events to come, he does not necessarily believe in omens in the stricter sense. For he may believe that whatever causes rain also causes the sensation in his knee; and he may suppose that his subconscious, which shapes dreams, registers otherwise overlooked indications of future occurrences. From experience, he may trust his knee or his dreams because he believes that they somehow are one early effect of a cause that also tends to produce another shortly after.

Seeing the barometer fall, one waits for rain; but in so doing, one supposes neither that barometers cause rain nor that rain destined to come causes barometers to fall. Rather, one supposes that something causing the barometer to fall is also likely to cause rain. The death of canaries in mines neither causes future mine explosions nor is caused by them. In short, belief in advance indicators does not necessarily imply belief in backward causation or in a future pulling events forward.

If an insurance company should notice a statistical correlation between two disparate events, neither one of which could conceivably cause the other, it might still be wise to adjust its rates (or cancel a policy) when one of them occurs. In so doing, it would not be treating the former event as an omen because there might well be an undetected causal correlation of both events. The insurance company, one may suppose, "frames no hypotheses"; it just raises its rates.

In these cases, we have an example of the usual fork asymmetry in which two subsequent events, one of which precedes the other, result from a common cause prior to both. One's knee, one's dreams, and countless similar phenomena behave like barometers, and barometers are not omens. Those familiar with such debunking publications as *The Skeptical Inquirer* will be aware that omens (like ESP and other alleged phenomena attributed to backward causation) are in fact typically explained away by interpreting them as registers of otherwise unnoticed causes.

A genuine omen, if there are any, is to be accounted for in terms of the event it foretells. It happens *because* a future event is going to happen: it results from backward causation or teleological pulling. In Lermontov's "The Fatalist" (a story in *A Hero of Our Time*), the hero, Pechorin, believes that it is possible to read "the seal of death" on the face of a person about to die in a few hours. The sign will be there no matter how bizarre or otherwise unforeseeable the chain of events leading to death might be; fatality is registered even if the cause of death has nothing to do with the doomed man and even when there is no possibility that an unconscious death wish may be involved. In so characterizing the seal, Pechorin means to rule out the much less interesting possibility that it is a sort

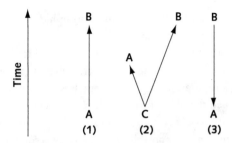

(1) A causes B; (2) A is a barometer for B: both are caused at different times by C; (3) A is an omen for B (A happens because B *will* happen).

of barometer. As the story's title implies, he is concerned with real fatalism, not advance indicators, and he tries to understand the seal as an omen.

"I have observed, and many old soldiers have confirmed the observation, that frequently the face of a person who is to die in a few hours' time bears some strange mark of his inevitable fate which a practiced eye can scarcely fail to detect," Pechorin remarks, and he is speaking of fate with due care.[21] The face with the seal becomes a prerecording device. To be sure, someone might try to explain an impressive ability to predict someone's death in this way by insisting on an undetected cause; and this sort of explanation is in fact proposed by several characters. But it is also clear to them that if the seal exists as an omen, what that means is that it is to be accounted for by the future operating through backward causation. The story turns on attempts to test which sort of relation obtains in such circumstances.

For those who believe in omens, the future leaves its mark on the present, much as a thunderstorm in a novel may occur *in order to* indicate a catastrophe to come. If the event caused by the future is detectable only by the reader, we speak of foreshadowing. If it is recognized as a sign by the character, he will have discovered an omen. Conversely, those people in real life who believe in omens are implicitly treating real time the way we would treat time in a narrative. For good reason, the already written book or scroll is a standard metaphor for fatalism.

Destiny and Determinism

What does a belief in omens and in the sort of oracular temporality that makes omens possible do to the sense of responsibility? We may be inclined to think that such beliefs eliminate a sense of responsibility, and sometimes they do. But the issue is rather more complicated. For one thing, we know that religious groups who have accepted predestination (as in Calvinism) are often anything but passive. For another, various philosophies that reject choice often have quite different effects on the people who believe them. The differences may reflect the specific tenets of the given philosophy. But they may also reflect psychological or cultural factors that associate beliefs with behavior in a way that, while not strictly logical, may be nonetheless compelling.

Many have argued that if the future ineluctably dictates all events leading to it, then responsibility would seem to be illusory. For choice then becomes only apparent, and there is no responsibility in the absence of choice among genuine alternatives. But alternatives also disappear if the *past* ineluctably dictates each later event, as the underground man insistently argues. Whether events are pushed or pulled, the multiplicity of options collapses to singularity if time is (to use Dostoevsky's term) "rectilinear." The sense of such multiplicity becomes analogous to an optical illusion. It would be a *temporal illusion*, falsely indicating mirages of only apparent possibilities.

It would seem that total prior causation and total future destination amount to the same thing, and yet people often feel quite differently about determinism and fatalism, about being pushed and being pulled. Sometimes liberals or skeptics may be more willing to accept the former, and utopian believers the latter. Various temperaments may react in diverse ways. But why should there be any difference at all?

One reason for difference is that fate more strongly suggests purpose and meaning, although a deterministic process may be meaningful and a fatalistic one meaningless in human terms. Another, less obvious reason is that determinism, as it is usually advocated, admits of no exceptions. One chance instance disrupts the model. But destiny or fate often does allow for temporal patterns other than a straight line; and it may allow for a considerable measure of free will. The diagram on page 65 may be helpful.

When an oracle or omen predicts a given inevitable outcome, it does not necessarily specify the path leading to it. Rather, it suggests that whatever path is chosen and whatever choices are made the omen will be fulfilled. But different paths may still make an important difference to the people who follow them. So Juno reasons when, despairing of preventing Aeneas's destined marriage to Lavinia, she nevertheless intensifies her hostile efforts:

> . . . if I cannot
> Bend Heaven, I can raise Hell.
> It will not be permitted me—so be it—
> To keep the man from rule in Italy;
> By changeless fate Lavinia waits, his bride.
> And yet to drag it out, to pile delay

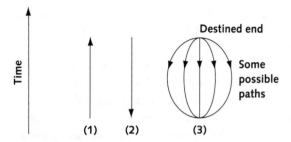

(1) Determinism as a straight line, with no alternative paths; (2) fate as a straight line; (3) fate or destiny as a vortex, with multiple paths to an ineluctable end.

> Upon delay in those great matters—that
> I can do: to destroy both countries' people,
> That I can do.[22]

Destiny or Fate specifies the end point, not the intermediate ones.

The temporality of destiny is something like a vortex. The further one is from the center, the more freedom of movement one experiences. But the closer one comes, the more one's movement is constrained by the future pulling one in. At some point near the center of the vortex, all moves have the same immediate result.

Thus, it is futile to struggle against an ineluctable destiny, but the concept makes sense; whereas it is nonsense to struggle against determinism. The concept of such a struggle is incoherent. (One may struggle against the theory of determinism, but not against determinism itself—a distinction that the underground man sometimes fails to draw.) Fate would appear to be the vaguer term: it may specify the outcome alone or it may specify all events without exception.

If destiny or fate is personified, as it sometimes is, we may imagine it as supremely confident—confident enough to show its hand and issue challenges. It plays cat-and-mouse with its victim. For even the revelation of fate and all strenuous efforts to avoid it will not change the outcome, though it may affect the intermediate steps.

Thus, stories about fate often seem to be based on an unexpected way of arriving at the confirmation. Fate handicaps itself, sets itself impossible challenges, reveals all to an intelligent opponent—to Oedipus, the smartest man in the world—but it does not matter. Fate always wins, and we know that in advance.

In the Russian primary chronicle, a seer tells Prince Oleg that he will die because of his horse, and so he sends his horse out to the field to graze. Years later, Oleg remembers the prophecy, asks about the horse, and is told the animal died long ago. Oleg laughs at having outwitted the oracle and asks to see the remains of the horse; but a viper slithers from its skull, bites the prince, and kills him.

Even though the outcome of such stories is known in advance, their plots may generate considerable suspense because it is not known how the oracle will be fulfilled. Suspense and wit are generated by the unexpected route. Narratives of this kind resemble those detective stories in which we learn the murderer's identity and method at the beginning but must wait to see how the detective arrives at the truth we already know. Our interest is sustained by the imaginative way in which the crime is solved.

Exemption from Inevitability

Even when fate and determinism work the same way, neither seems to have the psychological effects that we might expect from a purely logical analysis of the concepts. We know from experience that it is entirely possible to accept either fatalism or causal determinism and yet believe in responsibility, however irrational such a deduction might appear. Indeed, the promise of certain success, whether from ironclad causal laws or a teleology built into history, is often used to motivate people. Like Aeneas, they strive to realize their destiny. Such a promise may also serve as an excuse for otherwise unacceptable behavior. It is notoriously true that myths of historical inevitability or the guarantee of a splendid future are widespread among politically committed people who *urge us to action,* a position that one might deem a contradiction.

Critics of the Russian revolutionary intelligentsia tirelessly pointed out such contradictions. "The intelligentsia asserts that the personality is *wholly* a product of the environment, and at the same time suggests to it that it improve its surroundings, like Baron Munchausen pulling himself out of the swamp by his own hair," Sergei Bulgakov objected in vain.[23] He provoked the response that such arguments were *bound* to be made by scared liberals at a revolutionary moment.

This response illustrates one reason that myths of inevitability often do not lead to paralysis or indifference: they are characteristically applied to *other people.* One does not have to answer the "objectively" reactionary arguments that are predictably made by class enemies. Myths of inevitability are also characteristically applied to *other times;* we in the present are treated as somehow exempt. In causal models, contradiction is not felt because it is the *past* that is treated as inevitable. The present *will* turn out to *have been* inevitable, too, of course, and whatever happens our political theorist will show why nothing else could have; but in the meantime, things depend on us. The inevitability of the present—that's for later. Now there is work to be done! An essentially similar scenario can be constructed from teleological models. And it is not uncommon for one theory—Marxism, for example—to invoke both, as necessary.

"The Fatalist"

> Are these then necessities?
> Then let us meet them like necessities.
> And that same word even now cries out to us.
> —SHAKESPEARE, *Henry IV, Part Two*

> He breathes the moist air and feels oddly free to do as he pleases, free in a world without freedom.
> —ALAN LIGHTMAN, *Einstein's Dreams*

Ironically enough, then, both fatalism and determinism allow for an array of consequences. Let us return to a literary example illustrating some of them. In "The Fatalist," a group of officers playing games of chance debate "the Moslem belief" in fatalism and cite instances given "on reliable authority" that are said to confirm this belief (Lermontov, 164). Nonsense, someone objects. "Where is the reliable authority who has seen the scroll on which our mortal hour is written? And if there is such a thing as predestination, why have we been given will and reason? Why are we held accountable for our actions?" (Lermontov, 165). The events that follow contain what are described as four tests of fate. First, one officer, Vulich, offers to try to shoot himself in the head: if he fails, it will prove that his predestined hour has not yet come and therefore that fate exists. Wagers are placed, with the narrator, Pechorin, betting that Vulich will die because he sees "the seal of death" on his face. It would therefore appear that Pechorin himself is relying on fate to win his bet against fate.

As it happens, Vulich's gun misfires, he collects his winnings, and, for those who accept Vulich's reasoning, fate is vindicated. But in a purely fortuitous chain of accidents, Vulich is killed a half hour later by a drunken Cossack. Thus, the seal of death proves an accurate omen, which is taken to mean that fate is again vindicated, and even more impressively. Moreover, someone tells the murderous Cossack that he is fated to be captured, which also proves true. And Pechorin, in a repeat of Vulich's experiment, tests whether his own hour has come by undertaking the unequal attempt to capture the Cossack, which he does. Thus, the story offers four tests of fate, all of which seem to establish its existence.

Immediately after these experiences, Pechorin asks, "How could one possibly *avoid* becoming a fatalist?" (Lermontov, 173; italics mine); but this very sentence, of course, suggests the possibility of self-referential paradox. Are we ordained to fatalism, or do we choose it?

Pechorin confesses to the reader that although at the time he found the proofs of fate striking, he now doubts. The story suggests a number of reasons why. Such tests of fate appear fallacious. For one thing, any apparent proof of fate may really establish an unknown causation. In the story's final scene, Pechorin's prosaically wise friend Maxim Maximych observes that "these Asiatic pistols" often misfire when they are not properly oiled. For another, the result of any test that seems to establish freedom may itself be fated; by the same token, any proof of fate may be accidental.

In short, such tests of fate are structured as attempted *interruptions* of the course of events. That is why their success or failure is supposed to indicate whether that course can be changed, much as the attempt to divert a projectile might indicate whether it is divertible. Such tests presume a position external to the course of events, which means they presume freedom. They tacitly accept that there is at least the freedom to test; but a test is meaningful only if more than one outcome is possible, which is precisely what is to be proved. There is no reason that fate, if it exists, could not operate through our own apparently free choices, including our choices to interfere with fate's workings—as the Oedipus story and numerous other tales of predestination indicate.

Lermontov does not develop these objections in explicit detail because his story seems more concerned with the psychological effects of fatalism or skepticism. And here again, the issue is left murky. In a famous passage shortly after the first test of fate, Pechorin muses that the naive ancients, who believed that the gods preordained the events of human life, consequently drew immense strength from the sense of their own importance in the universe;

> whereas we, their wretched descendants, who roam the earth without convictions or pride, without joys or fears other than the nameless dread that constricts the heart at the thought of the inevitable end, we are no longer capable of great sacrifices either for the good of mankind or even for our personal happiness since we know that happiness is impossible; and we pass indifferently from one doubt to another just as our forebears floundered from one delusion to another, without the hopes they had and without even that vague but potent sense of joy the soul derives from any struggle with men or destiny ... (Lermontov, 169)

Here, belief in fatalism, far from leading to paralyzing indifference, enables great action; whereas indifference is the consequence of doubt. Evidently, fatalism or doubt influences us not in isolation but as a component of a larger picture of the universe.

At the end of the story, however, the consequences of fatalism and doubt are reversed. Doubt, after all, may suggest not meaninglessness but freedom, and fatalism may signify the futility of our efforts. Where there is doubt, Pechorin reasons, there is adventure, which may itself be a motivation for action. "I prefer to doubt everything," he concludes; "such a disposition does not preclude a resolute character; on the contrary, as far as I am concerned, I always advance more boldly when I do not know what is awaiting me" (Lermontov, 173). Psychologically, if not logically, neither fatalism nor skepticism has any necessary consequences.

But there is yet another twist to the story's psychology. Curiously, Pechorin, though he doubts, also suffers the paralyzing effects of fatalism. Having been a dreamer, he explains, he imagined life in advance to the extent that it all seemed repetitive when it happened: *déjà vécu*. In vivid anticipations "I exhausted the warmth of soul and the constancy of will which are essential to an active life; when I embarked on that life, I had already lived it through in my thoughts, and hence it has become as boring and repulsive to me as a travesty of a long-familiar book" (Lermontov, 169). He experiences everything as if it had already been written down. Like so many Russian superfluous men to follow, Pechorin lives his life as if he were living it over. It is in this odd sense that he is truly the fatalist of the story's title. Lermontov's story solves neither the philosophical nor the psychological questions it poses, but it deepens our sense of their difference and their complexity.

Eluctable Destiny

What happens to responsibility if the fated future is *not quite* inevitable? After all, it is possible to regard omens and prophetic dreams not as signs of what will necessarily happen—what in a sense has already happened though we have not yet experienced it—but as warnings about what is likely to happen *if* preventive action is not taken. There is a difference between premonition—an advance warning—and precognition. One may consult an augur to determine if the signs are favorable for a risky enterprise and postpone it if they are not. In Greek literature, dreams are often premonitory in this way. Indeed, even in the *Oedipus*, the plot depends on the evidently accepted (but in this play false) view of oracles as issuers not of inevitabilities but of warnings. Presumably, that is why Laius and Jocasta attempt to escape catastrophe by sending their child to an apparently certain death and why Oedipus abandons his supposed parents in Corinth. Much as causality may be seen as offering constraints that limit but do not eliminate choice, so omens may suggest that a new course of action is warranted (say, to propitiate an angry god).

Although belief in omens as warnings rather than as signs of an already certain future may seem more comforting, it is even more paradoxical. Even the spatial metaphor becomes fraught with problems. How can a shadow be cast backward by something that only *may* exist? If the future catastrophe is averted, where did the foreshadow or omen come from? What this weaker concept of omens seems to involve is a sense that even possibilities, if they are likely enough to occur, may have a substantiality of their own. The spatial metaphor seems to be one of avoidance: if one is moving rapidly toward an unseen obstacle but notices its shadow in advance, one may be able to swerve around it. Translating such a swerve into temporal terms produces strange results, for it suggests that the obstacle exists in some real but unrealized time, much as the object avoided exists in a space we avoid passing through. Time seems to continue by some sort of chronic inertia on a given path unless, by extraordinary effort, a detour can be made.

It is one thing to imagine the future as branching forward from the present, as in Aristotle's model, with no future existing before it happens. It is quite another to see the future as a multiplicity of already "existing" outcomes, only one of which comes to "be." It is very hard to describe this conceptualization in rigorous language. And yet it is not all that difficult to visualize.

Science fiction, for example, often exploits such images in variations of the time-loop plot. In the *Back to the Future* films, for example, a journey to the past allows for action that will make the existing present cease to be, though we know it has "already happened." If a journey to the future shows a bad enough outcome, one may go back to the future's past and try to change it; or one may even have to change the changes that some other time traveler has made.

All these changes take place in the *Back to the Future* series. The palpable image of a future already there is represented by newspapers brought back from a (the choice of article is important) future. When action in an earlier time forces that particular future out of existence, the headlines and text on the newspaper fade away and are replaced by their counterparts from the future that has come into being. Photographs of the future also change; the image held in one's hands alters because of events that will happen—or we might better say, that have happened—later. In each sequence extending forward from every moment, the future is already there and ineluctable; but somehow the sequence itself is not ineluctable, providing one can travel through time.

Augustine asks, "If future and past times exist, I wish to know where they are."[24] In science fiction stories of this kind, both past and future seem to be "always" existing, even if they are not the "real" time. If multiple changes are made by different time travelers, which one prevails? The latest? According to which sequence? Such views of time seem to point necessarily to some concept of hypertime (or metatime), in which there would be only one time "at a time." Or must we allow for a hyper-hypertime, ad infinitum?[25]

To return to more ordinary omens-as-warnings, in one respect they are like causes or barometers, for they allow for preventive action. Nevertheless, belief in omens as warnings usually has an effect quite different from belief in prior causes. Psychologically, it does tend to diminish responsibility to a much greater extent. There are several reasons that this should be so.

To begin with, people who believe in omens also accept the efficacy of prior causes, but the reverse is not usually true. One believes either in causes and in omens or only in causes. If one chooses to believe in both, it is often precisely because the association of omens with fatalism may diminish responsibility. Guilt may be eased or contemplated actions known to be immoral may be excused in advance, as fated.

Moreover, since omens do not happen to everyone, they create a sense of exceptionality and importance for those to whom they are directed. They indicate that a certain sort of known story is happening to the believer; and that story is often appealing, exalting, or romantic. A familiar plot confers a secure meaning. One becomes a tragic hero or heroine or assumes the role of a "fatal" person with a meaningful destiny. Pechorin claims to experience such reliving as repulsive and boring, but it is quite possible to find it consoling and interesting. In the shadow of destiny, events otherwise contingent and meaningless acquire significance, and so a hunger for meaning is satisfied. For such satisfaction even catastrophe and loss of freedom may seem a small price to pay.

Anna Karenina's Omens: Narcissism and Stories

Tolstoy's *Anna Karenina* offers a psychologically complex exploration of belief in omens. To explore these complexities, let us consider this novel in some detail.

Anna Karenina believes in omens and indulges in fatalism. From the time she meets Vronsky and proclaims the death of the trainman "an evil omen," we see her thinking repeatedly in terms of living out stories that are already told, prepared in advance, and governed by an attractive if implacable fate. Her stories lead to catastrophe but ensure significance.

As her friend Liza Merkalova observes, Anna imagines that she is "a real heroine out of a [romantic] novel" (AK, 315). For Anna, everything seems to fit a melodramatic plot centering on a grand passion; there are neither accidents nor choices. That is why she so often seems to resemble Greta Garbo *playing* Anna Karenina. She lives a story whose shape is already given and for which not just anyone could have been destined. The Garbo film, in fact, captures quite well the story of Anna *as she tells it to herself.* But Tolstoy has told a different story—not of a fated heroine, but of a woman who imagines that she is one.[26]

Fatalism plays a complex role in Anna's thinking. In part, it turns all obstacles into aggravations of passion, as Vronsky, who learns this story from her, correctly observes:

> "So it had to be," he said. "So long as we live, it must be so. I know it now."
>
> "That's true," she said. . . . "Still, there is something terrible in it after all that has happened."
>
> "It will all pass, it will all pass; we shall soon be happy. Our love, if it *could* be stronger, will be strengthened because there is something terrible in it." (AK, 456)

Tolstoy means us to understand this as a particular and false view of love, by no means the only way in which love can be understood or valued. It is, in fact, an ideology, according to which true life is lived when it is most intense, when it is most heavily plotted, when it most resembles a romance, and when it is farthest of all from ordinary happiness or daily routine.

Tolstoy's view is the precise opposite: real life is lived in the small and ordinary moments. It is both prosaic and undramatic and is lived best when there is no story to tell. The reason that all happy families resemble each other whereas each unhappy family is unhappy in its own way is that unhappy families, like unhappy lives, are dramatic; they have a story and each story is different. But happy families and happy lives, filled with undramatic incidents, do not make a good story; and it is in this sense that they all resemble each other. In his notebooks and letters of the period, Tolstoy at least twice quotes a French proverb farthest of all from Anna's romantic ethos: "Happy people have no history." Plot, especially when known in advance, is an index of error.

Tolstoy would have largely agreed with the central point of Denis de Rougement's analysis of this plot and of the terrible role fate plays in it:

> Love and death, a fatal love—in these phrases is summed up, if not the whole of poetry, at least whatever is popular, whatever is universally moving in European literature. . . . Happy love has no history. Romance only comes into existence where love is fatal, frowned upon, and doomed by life itself. What stirs lyrical poets to their finest flights is neither the delight of the senses nor the fruitful contentment of the settled couple; not the satisfaction of love, but its *passion.*[27]

Tolstoy therefore gives us a double plot in which one love is based on passion (Anna and Vronsky) and the other on prosaics (Levin and Kitty).

Each love has its orientation toward temporality. Prosaic love thrives on the everyday and is therefore shown in moments that have almost no plot significance, for example, the jam-making scene, Kitty's embroidering, or Dolly's little dramas with her children. The ability to live in this prosaic way forms a special temporal zone of happiness that is called "the Shcherbatsky element" because it constitutes the essence of that family's way of living. Levin, who began by loving this family as a whole before he came to love Kitty in particular, tries to learn its largely unarticulated but powerfully felt wisdom.

Levin and Kitty enjoy the small cares of daily life, the work that is, as Levin says, "incontestably necessary." Their focus is on the immediate and the present. By contrast, we find Anna dreaming of other times and other kinds of time. She displays, as romantic love does by its nature, a refusal or an "inability to enjoy the present without imagining it as absent" (de Rougement, 285). Not presence, but absence; the fatal events to come structure life.

Thus Anna can at times even take pleasure at the loss of her son, for it fits the tragic plot. Abroad, she tells herself that she is suffering from her separation from her son, and she finds in these reflections comfort and self-justification. They are nonetheless false. "But, however sincerely Anna had meant to suffer, she was not suffering" (AK, 487), Tolstoy drily notes.

Readers often wonder why Anna so idealizes Seryozha, who is Karenin's child, and neglects the daughter of the man she loves, though one might expect the opposite. Tolstoy suggests a number of reasons but one of the most important is the romantic tendency to cultivate obstacles and idealize what is absent. Before she has run off with Vronsky, she idealizes him so much when he is absent that she is shocked by the contrast when he is present, because her imaginary picture is "infinitely superior, impossible in reality" (AK, 377). When she does live with Vronsky, she can never adjust to daily routine without high drama, and so she is always manufacturing scenes, fabricating crises, sending urgent telegrams, and indulging in jealous fits in which she herself does not believe. In much the same way, Anna loves the child she cannot have and neglects her present child, whose needs are prosaic and unromantic.

Romantic destiny, the sense that one has been chosen for a special and tragic story, feeds narcissism. This is another reason that the Garbo film, precisely because it leaves out all the Levin scenes that have nothing to do with Anna, is so eerily true to Anna's *Anna*. Her sense of a fatal plot governing her life places her in the center of all the stories around her, which is one reason that, almost as soon as she meets Vronsky, she becomes such a poor parent. We sense, as she occasionally realizes, that her love for Seryozha is a role; and we recognize that his importance to her derives almost entirely from what he and his loss mean *to her*. He figures in her thoughts as the one person who would not condemn her. We do not see her worrying about him in respects that have nothing to do with her.

As if to illustrate the moral problems with such a self-image, Tolstoy has the young Kitty briefly indulge it. Kitty imagines that the day on which she hopes that Vronsky will propose (and on which Levin does propose) is somehow fated to be a turning point: she knows this "for certain." These men are part of her story. But when Levin, in all his painful self-doubt and sincere love, awkwardly proposes, she suddenly places herself in his position. Knowing that she will refuse him, she forgets her role and sees the world through his eyes. This scene is one of many in which Tolstoy indicates what is wrong with placing oneself at the center of stories. As Kitty learns, first here and then when helping people at the spa, morality involves the opposite, including the ability to make oneself *the minor character in someone else's story*. Moreover, the day that Kitty regards as fated to decide everything does no such thing. Levin will propose again and be accepted.

Anna: Who Is to Blame?

For Anna, fatalism also serves to relieve her guilt. When Dolly comes to visit her, Anna repeats a speech she has evidently often made to herself:

> "Yes, yes," said Anna, turning out of the open window. "But I was not to blame. And who is to blame? What's the meaning of being to blame? Could it have been otherwise? What do you think? Could it possibly have happened that you didn't become the wife of Stiva?"
> "Really, I don't know...." (AK, 664)

If everything is fated, no one is responsible, she reasons.

But this way of thinking exacts a price. Focusing on fate, she neglects causes; she forgoes decisions and trusts to inevitability. Alternative, prosaic ameliorations, which do not fit the shape of the story she condemns herself to live, seem pointless to her. So do major choices. Vronsky finds it almost impossible to get her to think practically about her situation, and she does not allow herself to think about it. Before leaving Karenin, "she had not the least idea what would settle the situation, but she firmly believed that something would turn up" (AK, 372). Contrast this view with Levin's: faced with daily farm work, he assumes that problems left alone usually get worse, and therefore he continually improvises.

As the story develops, Anna's refusal to examine causes and make appropriate decisions—to take responsibility—grows. Vronsky asks Dolly to get her to face reality and seek a divorce, but Anna refuses. Dolly notices her new habit of averting her eyes when important questions are raised. "Just as though she half shut her eyes to her own life, so as not to see everything," Dolly thinks (AK, 656).

Anna has once refused a divorce when she could have had one, and now she refuses to consider it or any other practical step. "You say I take too gloomy a view of things," she tells Dolly. "I try not to take any view at all. . . . You tell me to marry Alexey, and say I don't think about it. I don't think about it!" (AK, 668). She sees only two conceivable endings to her story, one utopian and the other catastrophic, and the utopian one is impossible:

> "It is only these two beings [Vronsky and Seryozha] that I love, and one excludes the other. I can't have them together, and that's the only thing I want. And since I can't have that, I don't care about the rest. I don't care about anything, anything. And it will end one way or another, and so I can't. I don't like to talk of it. So don't blame me, don't judge me for anything." (AK, 669)

Anna's stories are told from the ending, and nothing else, nothing middle or present, matters. As so often happens, she seems to forget here that she has a daughter. When Tolstoy gives us the lengthy stream of thoughts that leads to Anna's suicide, we may remark that one thing she never thinks of is Annie, who has no role to play in this tragic plot.

Anna: Omens and Their Causes

Anna is not just uttering a phrase when she refers to the trainman's death as an omen. She is in fact as superstitious as she is fatalistic. Indeed, the two qualities often go together, inasmuch as they both construct explanations that elude causality and foreclose choice. Anna believes in prophetic dreams as well.

In one remarkable passage, Anna has her recurrent nightmare about a strange peasant with a sack who says in French that one must beat the iron; and she wakes from that dream into another. In that second dream, she asks the meaning of the first and is told it indicates that she will die in childbirth. The outer dream frames the inner one and gives its meaning; the two dreams together become a self-interpreting omen, and when Anna wakes, she believes in her fated death from childbirth. This belief shapes her behavior. Told that the present state of affairs cannot continue, she thinks not of alternatives but of the omen. " 'Soon, very soon, it will end anyway,' she said; and again, at the thought of death near at hand and now desired, tears came into her eyes" (AK,

384). In the childbirth scene, her feverish thoughts, suffused with the sense of certain death, shape her reactions to both Vronsky and Karenin and so the belief in destiny exerts considerable causal force.

But of course the omen proves false; she survives the birth. This disconfirmation seems to escape her notice, however, and does not affect her acceptance of omens or prophetic dreams. But it does indicate to the reader that the temporality of the novel (and the real world) is not what she imagines. The reader may recall that Levin has explicitly rejected a whole range of superstitions, from omens to the faddish spiritualism of the upper classes.

Anna sees a world in which plots are already written from the future and in which responsibility has no meaning; Tolstoy describes the causes that lead to these beliefs and the real alternatives they disable. In the *Oedipus*, as we have seen, identification with the hero involves a sense of choice, but contemplation of the structure reveals the inevitable outcome shaping all prior events. *Anna Karenina* works in the opposite way: when Tolstoy allows us to identify with the heroine, readers see her as she sees herself, as a foredoomed tragic heroine. But the novel subjects that self-image to scrutiny and discovers in fatalism a self-indulgent and self-destructive choice.

Tolstoy allows us to see why, to a person inclined to tragic plots, the dream might well appear to be an omen. It has all the characteristic marks of a sign from the future: its sense of mystery, the strange images that seem to demand interpretation, its frequent recurrence, the terror it inspires, and, at one point, the fact that Vronsky has a quite similar dream. But Tolstoy also suggests causal explanations for these apparent marks of futurity. For Tolstoy, it is what we have done and what we do that shape both the future and our various anticipations of it. But our attention does not always focus on those shaping events, and so, in the inability to detect causes, we ascribe destinies.

Each element of Anna's dream has occurred either during the scene when Vronsky first meets and flirts with her or during her subsequent train ride home, when the flirtation has progressed quite far. But Anna has not necessarily noticed them. Let us take just one example, the strange peasant. The train for which Vronsky and Stiva have been waiting and on which Anna has been traveling with Vronsky's mother arrives at the station and the passengers disembark:

The engine rolled up, with the lever of the middle wheel rhythmically moving up and down, and the stooped, muffled figure of the engine driver covered with frost. Behind the tender, setting the platform more and more slowly swaying, came the luggage van with a dog whining in it. At last the passenger cars rolled in, jolting as they came to a standstill.

A dashing guard jumped out, giving a whistle, and after him one by one the impatient passengers began to get down: an officer of the guards, holding himself erect and looking severely about him; a nimble little merchant with a satchel, smiling gaily; a peasant with a sack over his shoulder.

Vronsky, standing beside Oblonsky, watched the carriages and the passengers, totally oblivious of his mother. What he had just heard about Kitty excited and delighted him. (AK, 66)

Tolstoy gives no special emphasis to the peasant with a sack, perhaps no more than any observer on the scene would give. After all, peasants and people with sacks were common sights at Russian train stations. Throughout the novel, Tolstoy often notes how people stare at things without taking conscious note they are seeing them, and that is evidently what is happening here. Vronsky is thinking of Kitty, and Anna, most likely, of meeting Vronsky, about whom she has just heard so much. Rereaders of the novel may or may not notice this peasant, but its original readers, and current ones who do not know its story in detail, will likely miss him. The image will register, as it presumably registers with Vronsky and Anna, at the periphery of attention.

So will numerous other elements of this scene and of Anna's train ride home with Vronsky in pursuit. When dreamed, the peasant, like the engine driver, appears muffled and stooped. Dozing off and thinking of Vronsky, Anna half perceives and half transforms into dream material, a thin peasant who "seemed to be gnawing at something on the wall," "a fearful shrieking and banging, as though someone was being torn to pieces," and "the voice of a man muffled up" (AK, 108). When the train stops, she goes onto the platform, hears "sounds of a hammer on iron," and encounters Vronsky following her. "At that moment the wind, as if surmounting all obstacles, sent the snow flying from the carriage roofs, and clanked some sheet of iron it had torn off. . . . All the awfulness of the storm seemed to her more splendid now. He said what her soul longed to hear, though she feared it with her reason" (AK, 109). The emotional charge of these two scenes, the initial thrill and the guilt that grows over time, fuses its barely perceived images into a dream, where they seem arbitrary and therefore prophetic. Anna imagines fate and tragedy where Tolstoy gives us causes and conditions largely outside her notice.

Anna: Loose Ends

By definition, no one can focus on what happens at the periphery of one's attention. Tolstoy uses his essential surplus to describe key facts about his characters that they themselves could not know. Anna imagines that life is structured like a novel, but this novelist's essential surplus indicates that she is mistaken. In this case, authorial omniscience is used to discover those aspects of experience—undetectable from within experience itself—that make it utterly *un*like art.

Life as Tolstoy imagines it does not fit a pattern, as art does. Our lives tend to no goal; neither are they destined to be shaped into a story. They are filled with chance events that nevertheless have lasting effects and are shaped by incidental causes that need not have happened. Events filled with promise lead nowhere. Everything that the essential surplus provides in art—structure, closure, the assurance of significance—is usually absent from life. But people sometimes imagine that life is more or less like novels in this respect. Tolstoy's paradoxical method is to use the essential surplus to make us aware of its pure artifice.

The plot of *Anna Karenina* is exemplary in this respect. In those last moments leading to her suicide, Anna's various false and novelistic beliefs about time and about her life interact. Her growing narcissism and paranoia lead her to eliminate contingency from her world. "In that new glaring light in which she was seeing everything" (AK, 792), nothing is accidental and everything has a meaning. She discovers significance in every chance word of every passerby; "Tiutkin, coiffeur" and every other shop sign. All is hateful or false: a man crosses himself, and, looking at him angrily, Anna thinks, "It would be interesting to ask him what meaning he attaches to that" (AK, 796).

And in this frame of mind the common images of train stations have been accumulating. While she is still in the carriage, "a deformed peasant covered with dirt, in a cap from which his tousled hair stuck out, passed by that window, stooping down to the carriage wheels. 'There's something familiar about that hideous peasant,' thought Anna. And remembering her dream, she moved away to the opposite door, shaking with terror" (AK, 795). Shortly after, standing on the platform, she feels it sway, as it did when she first arrived in Moscow,

and she imagined that she was in the train again.

All at once she thought of the man crushed by the train the day she first met Vronsky, and she understood what she had to do. With a rapid, light step she went down the steps that led from the water tank to the rails and stopped close to the approaching train. (AK, 798)

"She understood"—she grasped the solution to a riddle—"what she had to do" (*chto ei nado delat'*). Anna identifies the path marked out for her, how the omen will be fulfilled. As her love began with death by a train, so it must end. To her the repeating images are signals of a completed pattern. Time is symmetrical.

It is important to notice here that these are Anna's beliefs, not the author's. Tolstoy has not created a world in which omens are fulfilled; rather, Anna has chosen to fulfill what she takes to be an omen.

In what is perhaps the cruelest passage of the book, Tolstoy indicates what is wrong with her closed temporality. As Anna is preparing to jump, "a feeling such as she had known when about to take the first plunge in bathing came upon her, and she crossed herself" (AK, 798); she performs the very gesture that she has just declared meaningless. But it now suggests a great deal that her system of interpretation has left out: "That familiar gesture brought back into her soul a whole series of memories of her childhood and girlhood, and suddenly the darkness that had covered everything for her was torn apart, and life rose up before her for an instant with all its bright past joys. But she did not take her eyes from the wheels of the second car" (AK, 798).

These memories evoke what her story—the tragic story that leads to suicide—has omitted. They begin long before that story, long before she has met Vronsky or even Karenin; and they offer the image of *other possibilities*, other sources of meaning that she has experienced but not brought to mind. They challenge her story's closure, which is her death, with the possibility of alternative plots that have been and might still be. They are, in spite of everything, the loose ends the story does not resolve; they are the signs of her failed authorship of her life, grounds for hope that make one despair. They come just too late, even though she has not jumped yet: for the momentum of her decision carries her forward. Anna does not focus on her childhood memories, which remain at the periphery of her attention, but concentrates instead on the difficult task of timing her jump.

But after Anna has jumped, while she is lying on the tracks and there is nothing more to do, her attention does shift to the other line of thought: and she suddenly recognizes the mistake, now beyond repair, of obsessively neglected other possibilities. Her recognition of these possibilities creates the true terror of her final seconds, as "the light of the candle by which she had read the book filled with troubles, falsehood, sorrow, and evil flared up more brightly than ever before, lighted up for her all that had been shrouded in darkness, flickered, began to grown dim, and was quenched for ever" (AK, 799). In this context, what would otherwise be the hackneyed image of a book creates a deep if understated irony because it bespeaks the danger of living as if one's life were already written.

The Surplus against Itself

Tolstoy deeply distrusted not only conventional plots but also plotting per se because they both impose closure and structure on a world that is fundamentally innocent of both. And yet he also was aware that novels must have some structure and something like a coherent plot if they are to be readable at all.

Therefore, he gives the structuring impulse to his character. In so doing, Tolstoy has it both ways: the story gains a structure that the author rejects. The novel relies on a temporality it negates. Tolstoy's fundamental solution to the problem of escaping plot and the lie of the essential surplus was to develop various forms of negative narration.

And yet, it is not clear that this solution entirely succeeds. More often than not, readers have interpreted *Anna Karenina* as if it, and not its heroine, relied on omens and foreshadowing. They have displaced the locus of structuring to the wrong agent.

Why should this have happened? For one thing, readers have so identified with Anna that they have usually adopted her point of view. Because Tolstoy describes Anna's psychology not only convincingly but also from within her perspective, readers assume that he approves of it. The readers join her story and accept her perspective even when counterevidence is readily available.

One often hears versions of the following scenario: Tolstoy might at first have meant to write a novel condemning Anna's values and behavior, but in the course of writing and in the process of giving her a realistic psychology he necessarily came to sympathize with her unawares; and so his moralistic tract was transformed into a great novel essentially against his will. To understand is to forgive.

There is some plausibility to this argument because, as Tolstoy himself noted, the process of writing often does reshape the product, and intentions thereby evolve and shift.[28] The problems with this argument lie elsewhere. For one thing, it is by no means the case that the act of describing someone from within necessarily leads to sympathy, much less to exoneration. One does not have to be Dostoevsky to recognize that very often the better one knows someone, the more one *dis*likes him, as divorce rates and Balkan history attest. When one investigates the circumstances leading to a morally reprehensible act, one often sees that the mentality leading to it could, under different circumstances, lead to much *worse*. The notion that understanding is forgiveness, like the related notion of knowledge as a sure antidote to intolerance, would seem to be a sentimentality.

To understand is not necessarily to forgive, and why should it be? What people usually have in mind is that once one appreciates all the circumstances that led to behavior of a given kind, one will recognize that no other choices could have been made.[29] As knowledge increases, alternatives decrease and disappear until they are revealed as only apparent; and one does not blame where there are no real alternatives. There is, in short, a concealed determinism in the argument which, if accepted, would make all moral judgments a mere function of ignorance. Tolstoy and this novel endorse neither determinism nor an ineluctable moral neutrality.

Readers may also read the novel in terms of foreshadowing because that plot is so conventional. Or they may be sympathetic with Anna's ideology of romantic love, which they may take to be not an ideology but what love truly is. Such readers tend to be especially hostile to Karenin and neglectful of Dolly. A novel unsympathetic to Anna would conflict with our culture's fundamental mythology, including our assumption that truly great writers necessarily challenge, not reaffirm, such bourgeois norms as marriage and the family. Readers' expectations are shaped by both thematic and formal presuppositions, and it is extremely difficult to overturn them, especially in the direction opposite to avant-garde beliefs.

Tolstoy tried to retain the essential surplus while turning it against its tacit implications, but it seems that the essential surplus resists negative use. As we shall see in the next chapter, Bakhtin described Dostoevsky as having made a quite different choice: to renounce that surplus altogether.

CHAPTER THREE

Interlude: Bakhtin's Indeterminism

Bakhtin must surely be regarded as the most remarkable modern thinker to examine time in narrative. In his hands, literary theory became a vehicle for understanding the possible existence of human freedom and ethical responsibility. If God created a universe in which these qualities are real, then what sort of creator was he, and what sort of time did he make for us? Could God create people, and an author create characters, who are, in a meaningful sense, free, and what would be the nature of such freedom? For Bakhtin, who took seriously the analogy between a literary work and the real world, the problem of whether in fiction there might be an artifice of true freedom necessarily pertained to the most fundamental questions of life. In light of these informing questions, his work may be read as a series of meditations in which aesthetic, ethical, and theological issues are intricately woven together.

In the officially atheist Soviet Union, the theological dimension of Bakhtin's work of course remained largely implicit. And it remains unclear whether Bakhtin was truly a believer or simply someone steeped in an intellectual culture in which theology provided an especially convenient framework for examining ultimate questions. In either case, it would be helpful for us to begin with a digression about another thinker who wrestled with similar issues (and whose terms will figure prominently in subsequent chapters). We may then turn to Bakhtin's sequence of three solutions—one negative, and two partially positive—to the dilemma of freedom in narrative and the world.

"The Dilemma of Determinism": Time's "Loose Play"

In his essay "The Dilemma of Determinism," William James begins by taking issue with the idea that all the juice has somehow been squeezed out of the debate on free will. He regrets that a "soft determinism," or reconciliationism, seems to hold sway. In this view, ironclad laws do indeed govern the world, but freedom, understood as compatible with such determinism, is also real. For James, this position constitutes "a quagmire of evasion under which the real issue of fact has been entirely smothered" (DD, 149).

In James's view, such evasive formulations reflect the desire of every camp to claim the honorific word "free." As a result, the term has gradually lost its meaning. With even determinists claiming to believe in some sort of freedom, it seems to many that the debate is over. Apparently, "freedom" has won in word and determinism in fact. In this way, real understanding has been sacrificed to an essentially rhetorical move. James therefore prefers to avoid the word "freedom" altogether and to cast the argument as one between determinism and *in*determinism.

For James, the real issue at stake concerns the nature of time. For the determinist, the universe is all of a piece, which means that the future can be one and only one thing. Determinism professes

that those parts of the universe already laid down absolutely appoint and decree what the other parts shall be. The future has no ambiguous possibilities hidden in its womb: the part we call the present is compatible with only one totality. Any other future complement than the one fixed from eternity is impossible. The whole is in each and every part, and welds it with the rest into an absolute unity, an iron block, in which there can be no equivocation or shadow of turning. (DD, 150)

By contrast, the indeterminist sees a world in which the fit between parts and whole is not perfect. There is "loose play" among the parts, so that "the laying down of one of them does not necessarily determine what the others shall be" (DD, 150). As a result, "possibilities may be in excess of actualities" (DD, 150). Of two or more conceivable futures, both may really be possible, even if only one is eventually realized. In James's opinion, indeterminism corresponds closely with "our ordinary, unsophisticated view of things," according to which "actualities seem to float in a wider sea of possibilities from out of which they are chosen; and *somewhere*, indeterminism says, such possibilities exist and form part of the truth" (DD, 151). Even if not "actual," they are real.

The heart of the question, then, is *whether there are more possibilities than actualities* and whether it therefore makes sense to speak of unrealized but genuinely possible futures (or presents or pasts). For the determinist as James describes him, unrealized possibilities are pure illusions, merely measures of our ignorance.[1] If knowledge were perfect, we would see no unrealized possibilities, and we would recognize the future as virtually and unalterably there. But for the indeterminist, no single future is there because many are possible. For James, this difference constitutes the real dispute, and he contends that all the ways in which reconciliationists have resolved it miss what is really at stake. The determinist asks us to accept a singular world, the indeterminist a world in which there is "a certain pluralism"—what James calls an excess, and Bakhtin a surplus, of possibilities.[2]

James hopes to persuade his audience to accept the *in*determinist view, but not because it can be proved. On the contrary, he says, no facts and no science could ever adjudicate between these positions, even though determinists often speak as if they had such proof. They typically cite an impressive array of causal connections in the world, but the existence of *some* causal links is compatible with both positions, for indeterminists do not presume that the world is sheer chaos. They envisage not pure randomness, just some loose play. James also points out that though we often discover connections between one part of the world and *an*other, we never find them between one part and *all* others. Such connections as we do discover could of course be part of a world in which everything is a solid block of lawfulness, but they could also testify to a world in which "law and lawlessness rule the world in motley alternatives."[3] Moreover, science draws conclusions from what has actually happened, "but how can any amount of assurance that something actually happened give us the least grain of information as to whether another thing might or might not have happened in its place?" (DD, 152). Almost by definition, unrealized possibilities, even if they exist, leave no traces.

It therefore cannot be science or evidence that leads some of us to find one view or another convincing. "What divides us into possibility men and anti-possibility men is different faiths or postulates,—postulates of rationality" (DD, 152). For those of one faith, the world seems more rational with possibilities included, and for those of the other with possibilities excluded. Both sides appeal to evidence, but "what makes us monists or pluralists, determinists or indeterminists, is at bottom always some sentiment like this" (DD, 153).

People usually become determinists, James suggests, because they cannot imagine a world that would make sense if there were such a thing as chance. For them, the determinist picture exhibits coherence, and it seems indubitable to them that if chance is allowed—is even once allowed—then we live not in a universe but a "nulliverse" (DD, 155). What is to prevent the whole fabric from unraveling, the stars from being extinguished, and chaos from taking over? The determinist is guided above all by a sentiment that no other coherent picture of the world capable of securing order is even conceivable. This then is the division among people: indeterminists accept what James, with rather complex irony, calls an "ordinary and unsophisticated view" based on the everyday experience of chance and choice; determinists, who are often sophisticated intellectual folk, are persuaded by the lack of any other model that would make sense of the whole and all its parts.

Because no proof could decide between these visions, James tries to convince us of indeterminism in a different way. He hopes to make our deliberation more informed by showing us in greater detail what each position, and especially determinism, entails: "to deepen our theoretic sense of the *difference* between a world with chances in it and a deterministic world is the most I can hope to do" (DD, 159). James cagily suggests that this procedure at least has the advantage of allowing our choice for or against determinism to be a free one.

What, then, is the consequence of a deterministic, monistic universe, in which each moment could not be other than what it turned out to be? According to James, belief in this picture immediately banishes the sentiment of regret as an absurdity, for regret makes no sense if things could not have been otherwise. Contemplating a recent heinous murder, the determinist could not regret it, for the murder must have been necessary from eternity. To call something bad means to wish that something else were in its place, James reasons, but determinism makes such a wish incoherent. And yet, we cannot help feeling that the crime, "although a perfect mechanical fit to the rest of the universe . . . is a bad moral fit, and that something else would really have been better in its place" (DD, 161). In these passages, James begins to sound increasingly Dostoevskian, especially when, like Ivan Karamazov, he returns his ticket to such harmony. If the murder was not regrettable, he writes, then "I deliberately refuse to keep on terms of loyalty with the universe" (DD, 177).

Because evil exists, it must, to a determinist, be without alternatives, and so one response to this view has been a thoroughgoing pessimism. The determinist, James points out, cannot regret particular incidents, he could only regret the whole universe. Alternatively, the determinist might disallow even that kind of regret, and so wind up in a Pangloss-style optimism, in which all must be for the best because nothing else could have been. James also outlines a third common response to determinism, a form of subjectivism that makes not events but our awareness of them important. In this view, nothing is regrettable but fortunately things are knowable. "Not the doing either of good or evil is what nature cares for, but the knowing of them. . . . The world is neither an optimism nor a pessimism, but a *gnosticism*" (DD, 165). Of course, this is an intellectual's vision, beyond "the stupid virtues of the philistine herd" (DD, 172); and yet somehow those philistine virtues seem increasingly preferable to the baneful sophistication of intellectuals.[4] If ordinary virtues "do not then come in and save society from the influence of the children of light, a sort of inward putrefaction becomes its inevitable doom" (DD, 172).

The moral consequences of the gnostic vision are truly appalling, James maintains. The world becomes one long Zola novel, "a 'roman experimental' on an infinite scale" (DD, 173). Crime becomes just another datum to contemplate. Such gnosticism "makes the goose-flesh the murder excites in me a sufficient reason for the perpetration of the crime. It transforms life from a tragic reality into an insincere melodramatic exhibition" (DD, 178). If we contrast this stance toward crime with the instinctive horror of the unsophisticated, then, James allows, "there are *some* instinctive reactions which I, for one, will not tamper with" (DD, 177–78).

The ordinary person responds to this gnosticism by stressing that neither sensibility nor knowledge but conduct "is the ultimate fact for our recognition" (DD, 174). That person will therefore imagine the world as a place in which it makes sense for conduct to be judged good or bad. His world will be one in which actions, once taken, cannot be changed—they have real consequences—but also one in which, until actions are taken, choice is possible. The past cannot be changed, but the present and future are open; that is what an emphasis on conduct requires and what ordinary experience teaches. Moreover, the world of conduct is one in which our behavior, though it has some effect, cannot determine everything. Many powers, not just our own actions, affect outcomes. It follows that we must do what is right because we have some effect, but we must also accept the unforeseen. Such is a world based on conduct and in which moral choice makes sense.

The world of conduct, James concludes, is indeterministic. Life so viewed "belongs to a plurality of semi-independent forces, each one of which may help or hinder, and be helped or hindered by, the operation of the rest" (DD, 175). If we behave badly, this world is above all "vulnerable." Not only do possibilities exist but the choice among them matters. James urges us to accept this "pluralistic, restless universe, in which no single point of view can ever take in the whole scene," although, he concedes, "to a mind possessed of the love of unity at any cost, it will, no doubt, remain forever inacceptable" (DD, 177).

As James's essay proceeds, it becomes more and more explicitly theological. "The theological form of all these disputes," James maintains, "is the simplest and deepest, the form from which there is the least escape," if only because the question of evil is central to it (DD, 164). Whether or not one accepts God, theology, in some loose sense, provides a language and a framework for such issues. It is in this sense, at least, that Bakhtin's works on time and freedom are also theological.

Novels as Forms of Thought

Those familiar with the fundamental moral problems informing Bakhtin's thought will recognize in James's essay a cogent statement of a position with which Bakhtin began. Ethics formed the core of Bakhtin's early work, and the topic remained central throughout his career.[5] Like James, Bakhtin was concerned to describe a universe in which moral choice—responsibility, to use the word Bakhtin preferred—would be real. Bakhtin, too, saw that responsibility requires an indeterministic world, a "pluralistic, restless universe, in which no single point of view can ever take in the whole scene." And, again like James, he saw the choice between determinism and indeterminism as one in which the best guide would be a deeper understanding of each vision. Unlike James, however, he soon found purely philosophical argument too thin.

From Bakhtin's perspective, determinism seemed to have the rhetorical advantage of being easily imaginable, especially for intellectuals. After all, the determinist, "monologic" vision has dominated scientific and philosophical thought for a few hundred years, according to Bakhtin. When we are asked to choose *in*determinism, we often feel that it is hard to imagine concretely just what such a world would be like. James argued negatively, contenting himself with pointing out the unfortunate consequences of not accepting indeterminism, but Bakhtin hoped to argue positively. He wanted to show that concrete visions of an indeterministic world are actually available, if we only knew where to look and how to see. Indeed, they are plentiful and much more richly detailed than the models of the monologic philosophers. Therefore we truly have a choice among visions of the world. Finely wrought pictures of open time are to be found in certain kinds of literature—not so much in their explicit assertions as in the way they represent human action. Read this way, the plots of certain literary works possess great philosophical importance.

For Bakhtin, the history of narrative literature constituted an encyclopedia of concretely realized worldviews. In his view, philosophers and intellectual historians who overlook that history necessarily miss a crucial part of human thought. Looking for explicit statements in tracts or essays, they do not consider that some of the greatest discoveries of world thought have taken place first, and sometimes exclusively, in the visualization of artistic *form*. It is especially common, Bakhtin argued, for insights about temporality to be achieved first in narrative form; these insights are later "transcribed" (often with considerable loss) into discursive philosophy. Finally, an intellectual historian attributes the discoveries to philosophers or other transcribers. In so doing, the historian not only misunderstands the development of ideas but also often reduces their complexity.

Bakhtin's favorite example of this erroneous way of thinking is the truism that Enlightenment thought is preeminently ahistorical, a view that withstands scrutiny only so long as literature is excluded. Before Herder and Hegel turned to the problem of development, the novelists were imagining and exploring it in rich new ways. "In general," Bakhtin observes, "the whole notion of the notorious lack of historicity during the Enlightenment should be radically revised" by considering such phenomena as the development of the bildungs-roman and other literary experiments directed toward a new understanding of time. "This process of preparing for the disclosure of historical time took place more rapidly, completely, and profoundly in *literary creativity* than in the abstract philosophical and strictly historical, ideological views of Enlightenment thinkers" (BSHR, 26).

In short, Bakhtin came to view narrative forms as "artistic models" of time, and he worked out methods for grasping, so far as possible, the precise characteristics of each genre. He was of course primarily interested in the forms that embodied an indeterministic world, but he soon realized that the distinction between determinism and indeterminism was too rudimentary. Open time may be conceived in many ways, and to understand it many qualities need to be considered. And in fact many have been considered in the European literary tradition, which has in effect conducted complex experiments to understand the shape of lives and the flow of history.

Eventually, Bakhtin discovered the genre he regarded as having the richest and most convincing sense of time: the novel (by which he meant not all prose fiction but works resembling such realist masterpieces as *Anna Karenina, Middlemarch,* and *Eugénie Grandet*).[6] He hoped that by pointing out explicitly what readers concretely experienced when reading novels he could make their choice between the worlds of determinism and of indeterminism, between the closed time of strict causality or fate and the open time of novels, a more informed one.

The Lateness of the Author

> And if God did exist, it would be necessary to abolish him.
> —BAKUNIN

One may identify three stages in Bakhtin's thinking about these questions. In his early writings, Bakhtin used the relation of the hero of a work to its author as a figure for the relation of a person to the world and of the individual to God. Because literature offers remarkably thick descriptions, this set of analogies had the potential advantage of offering a concrete image of an indeterministic world, should Bakhtin have been able to locate a literary form based on indeterminacy. But as Bakhtin first formulated the comparison, it had the notable disadvantage of making such a discovery almost impossible.

As we have seen, the author of a literary work enjoys what Bakhtin was later to call an essential surplus with respect to the characters. The author knows everything about them and about the world in which they live. He knows their destiny before it happens, their choices before they are made, and the outcome of their actions before they are even considered—the sort of information that is forever and in principle inaccessible to the characters themselves. How then can heroes or heroines be free, and how can their time be open? If God has the same knowledge with respect to us, then we, too, live in a world of closed temporality in which our lives are already written and virtually already lived.

Thus, Bakhtin's model at this stage of his thought seemed to make the very fact of authorship an obstacle to freedom. Apparently, we can be free, and the heroes of fiction can live in an open time, only if the world is unauthored, but for art, at least, that is impossible. In thinking through this problem, Bakhtin offered a number of fascinating illustrations to clarify it, and one or two are worth considering here.

It will be recalled that Freud explored the nature of art through a comparison with dreams and fantasy.[7] Freud contrasts all three to reality. By contrast, and somewhat surprisingly, Bakhtin groups reality together with dreams and fantasy, all of which are, in one crucial respect, opposed to art. That crucial respect is authorship. Because heroes and heroines are authored, they are *located in* a created world and are seen fully within that world. But in reality as I experience it, I *enter into* the world. Instead of being located in "surroundings," I am aware of my "field of vision," which emanates from, but does not include, my own act of looking. Others appear in my field of vision, but I do not. I develop "finalized" images of them, but not of myself. To me they may resemble novelistic heroes or people in paintings, but I do not sense myself in the same way.

Similarly, I do not and can not sense myself as finished, as I can sense another person. Rather, I experience myself as "unfinalized," as able to make choices that will render untrue previous definitions of myself. The same is true in dreams or fantasy: I see others, I act with respect to them, I live into the "yet-to-come" world, but I myself am not visualized as concretely embodied. In my dream, I exist on a different plane from others. I sense myself in the process of acting and making choices. I cannot be a mere character in my own dream.

But everything changes when the dream is over and I describe it to another. Then the I of my dream does become the hero of my story, and that hero becomes, like all heroes in narrative, an embodied, authored being. That I is *located in* the narrated world; the I who is *entering into* the world becomes the present I who is in the unfinished process of telling the story. As author of the story, I am freely shaping it, but as character I am now on the same plane as other characters, as I was not while experiencing the dream. Narrative art resembles not a dream but a story about a dream. It depends on the author's "outsideness," which confers on him an essential surplus that removes from the hero all the openness of ongoing present activity. Openness cannot belong to both author and hero simultaneously, Bakhtin concluded; when there is an author, openness belongs to him alone.

It would appear that the presence of an author (or a reader, who is also "located outside" the narrated world) changes everything. For the author "always encompasses the whole temporally, he is always *later*, not only in time but in *meaning* as well" (AiG, 104). That is, the author exists in a different kind of time, one that makes the *whole* of the character's life subject to contemplation as it could never be in the character's own time. Once there is such a whole, then each moment of my life figures in advance in an already written story; once there is "story-line weight," my actions lose their "eventness."

Life in an artwork, but not life as we experience it in reality, possesses what Bakhtin calls "rhythm." In a poem, rhythm testifies to the author's controlling presence at every moment. By extension, there is something resembling rhythm even in prose or drama. In understanding and planning a story, the author discovers the rhythm of the whole from its beginning to its end, the patterning that ensures closure and dictates the significance of everything along the way. In Bakhtin's terminology, rhythm therefore becomes the opposite of "loophole," the capacity for genuine surprise. In life we have a loophole because (or insofar as) life has no preplanned rhythm. But in literature, rhythm closes the loophole, even if the author should wish to leave it open.

Once there is an author and rhythm, the "risk-laden" and plural future of possibilities becomes a mere illusion. To be sure, the character may envision the future as if it had real alternatives, but the reader knows better. Bakhtin therefore speaks of art as ensuring "a certain hopelessness with respect to meaning" (AiG, 103)—hopelessness not in the sense that the hero is doomed to misery (which is of course not always the case) but in the sense that genuine surprise, required for hope to be meaningful, disappears. In Bakhtin's terms, the life of the hero is accompanied throughout by "the tones of a requiem" (AiG, 115) that he does not hear. In the machine we call art, the requiem is the music of the gears. Bakhtin's tragic phraseology evidently alludes to the possibility that our own sense of freedom may be as illusory as that of the artistic hero.

In short, art appears to allow for nothing but a chimerical freedom. "The aesthetic embodiment of the inner human being anticipates from the beginning the hero's hopelessness as far as meaning is concerned; artistic visualization gives us the *whole* hero, enumerated and measured to the full extent; there must not be for us any meaning-related secrets to him, our faith and our hope must be silent" (AiG, 115). To use Bakhtin's vocabulary, art gives us a "soul"—a finalized image of a person—but not "spirit," the active energy experienced from within as each of us enters a world that is open, yet-to-come, and unfinalizable. Unfinalizability is apparently banished from art, and therefore art would seem incapable of providing a concrete image of an unfinalizable world. This is what Bakhtin apparently means when he writes, "Ethical freedom (the so-called freedom of the will) is not only freedom from cognitive (causal) necessity, but also freedom from aesthetic necessity" (AiG, 105). And aesthetic necessity seems to be essential to art.

Bakhtin's Second Stage: Characters Break Free

In the second stage of his thinking about this problem, Bakhtin at last found a solution. He discovered a writer—Dostoevsky—who he thought had found a way to represent indeterminacy and to populate his works with "spirit" rather than with "souls": "Dostoevsky made spirit, that is, the ultimate semantic position of the personality, the object of contemplation, he was able to *see* spirit in a way in which previously only the body and soul of man could be seen" (TRDB, 288). Such an unprecedented portrayal of spirit, of a surprising self sensed from within, had seemed impossible for any artwork, but what has been done is manifestly possible. In this achievement lies the greatness of Dostoevsky. Dostoevsky invented a whole new genre—a radically different way of perceiving the world—which Bakhtin called "the polyphonic novel."

The concept of polyphony is so often misunderstood, and so often used as if it meant a mere plurality of voices, that some clarification would be helpful from the outset.[8] As Bakhtin coined the term, a polyphonic novel is one in which a special relation obtains between author and hero. That relation allows the hero to be truly free, capable of surprising not only other characters but also the author. In some crucial respects, the polyphonic author—not just the narrator—resembles just another character. Strange as it may seem, the Dostoevskian hero is not wholly the author's product; once created, he has a life of his own. (For the moment, I follow Bakhtin's paradoxical formulations.)

According to Bakhtin, the peculiar excitement that Dostoevsky's novels have provoked in readers derives primarily from this ability of characters partly to escape the author's control. Sensing a character's relative independence, readers often find themselves relating to him or her in ways usually reserved for real people. Thus we witness the odd phenomenon that generations of highly sophisticated critics who would not think of arguing with the ideological heroes of Turgenev or Joseph Conrad have directly polemicized with Raskolnikov and Ivan Karamazov. Bakhtin finds this fact of critical history important enough to begin his first chapter by remarking on it at length:

> Any acquaintance with the voluminous literature on Dostoevsky leaves the impression that one is dealing not with a *single* author-artist who wrote novels and stories, but with a number of philosophical statements by *several* author-thinkers—Raskolnikov, Myshkin, Stavrogin, Ivan Karamazov, the Grand Inquisitor, and others. For the purposes of critical thought, Dostoevsky's work has been broken down into a series of disparate, contradictory philosophical stances, each defended by one or another character. Among these also figure, but in far from first place, the philosophical views of the author himself. (PDP, 5)

Some critics have found themselves attacking the views of one or another character, others defending them, and still others extending them into finished philosophical systems. As a rule, "the character is treated as ideologically authoritative and independent; he is perceived as the author of a fully weighted ideological conception of his own, and not as the [mere] object of Dostoevsky's finalizing artistic vision" (PDP, 5). The same critics who argue with Tolstoy for the way he portrays a character bypass Dostoevsky entirely to confront his characters almost as if there were no author. In short, the views of Dostoevsky's characters have called forth, time and again, "an unmediated response—as if the character were not an object of authorial discourse, but rather a fully valid, autonomous carrier of his own individual word" (PDP, 5).

Bakhtin cites several earlier critics who have remarked on this feature of Dostoevsky criticism. Julius Meier-Graefe, for one, asked, "Would it ever occur to anyone to participate in any of the numerous conversations in *L'Education sentimentale?* But we do enter into discussions with Raskolnikov, and not only with him, but with every bit-player as well" (cited PDP, 6). Of course, Meier-Graefe exaggerates: we do not argue with every bit player, and some critics do argue with the ideologists of other novelists. But with Dostoevsky's novels such argumentation takes place so frequently and so passionately—and is found in the responses of so many critics who confine this approach only to these novels—that Dostoevsky criticism really does seem to be a thing apart. Bakhtin proposes to take this reader response seriously. The critics are reacting to something particular about Dostoevsky, to a "basic structural feature" of his works (PDP, 6).

According to Bakhtin, Dostoevsky criticism reflects the fact that major characters somehow seem capable of an unexpected answer, not only in the novels but even beyond them. It feels as if one might mentally try to wrest new ideas from them. Living somehow beyond the text, they seem to invite new questions, and so readers find themselves continuing the novel's dialogues— both those among the characters and those that must have taken place between each character and the author.

Of course, readers still recognize that each character is fictitious. Nevertheless, they sense in Dostoevsky's heroes and heroines a quality they normally find only in living people: their "inner unfinalizability, their capacity to outgrow, as it were, from within, and to render *untrue* any externalizing and finalizing definition of them," whether imposed by another character or even by the author. Readers unmistakably sense the basic premise of Dostoevsky's artistic world: "As long as a person is alive he lives by the fact that he is not yet finalized, that he has not yet uttered his ultimate word" (PDP, 59). Or as Bakhtin also explains his point, readers sense, so palpably as to be thrilling, the hero's "noncoincidence":

A man never coincides with himself. One cannot apply to him the formula of identity A≡A. In Dostoevsky's artistic thinking, the genuine life of the personality takes place at the point of non-coincidence between a man and himself, at his point of departure beyond the limits of all that he is as a material being, a being that can be spied on, defined, predicted apart from its own will, "at second hand." (PDP, 59)

To be sure, Bakhtin exaggerates; not all characters in Dostoevsky manifest noncoincidence. Readers feel drawn into discussion with Raskolnikov or Ivan Karamazov but not, say, with Luzhin (in *Crime and Punishment*) or Miusov (in *Karamazov*), even though these characters, too, carry an ideology. Luzhin voices a version of Raskolnikov's ideas, but no one wants to argue with him; he has said all he is going to say.

To extend Bakhtin's thought: Only those characters we are prone to think of as "major" seem capable of uttering something surprising. Or rather, it is this quality, rather than mere presence over a large number of pages or importance to the plot, that in Dostoevsky's novels *defines* a character as major. Bakhtin does not explicitly discuss the distinction between major and minor characters, but his ideas may suggest that for each author or each genre this distinction will be made on different grounds, depending on the character's connection with the work's essential purposes or defining qualities. Thus readers tend to feel that Platon Karataev is a major character in *War and Peace*, even though he does not appear until page 1100 and dies soon after. The same might be said of Ippolit Terentiev in *The Idiot*. In Dostoevsky's works, characters are sensed as major when they manifest a palpable unfinalizability.

The interaction of unfinalizable characters in Dostoevsky makes the *world* of his novels an open one. Many things can happen, and time allows for multiple paths. In addition to the dialogues we have, we sense that the material could sustain many others. It is as if there were more still to come, though they have not been recorded. In one of his most famous sentences, Bakhtin paraphrases the central belief that informs the very shape of Dostoevsky's novels: "Nothing conclusive has yet taken place in the world, the ultimate word of the world and about the world has not yet been spoken, the world is open and free, everything is still in the future and will always be in the future" (PDP, 166).

Bakhtin also puts the point this way: readers of Dostoevsky sense his works not as a completed structure but as "a concrete event" that somehow seems to take place before our eyes *as* we read (PDP, 93). In Bakhtin's view, poetic theory does not possess the tools or terms to describe such novels because poetics developed in response to earlier works based on structure rather than on eventness.

The Heteroverse

One would normally be inclined to dismiss the response of readers who argue directly with characters as impossibly naive, and for most writers that dismissal would be justified, in Bakhtin's view. But we must allow that sometimes readers are wiser than theorists. What sort of account would theorists formulate if, instead of trying to instruct readers, they tried to generalize from readers' practices?

Bakhtin observes that we usually engage with a literary work as a whole and with the characters only indirectly, through their participation in that whole. As Bakhtin phrases this point, there is normally only one "ultimate semantic authority," the author (more accurately, our image of the author). A reader senses and may wish to argue with the author's ideas; but the ideas of heroes become mere "characterological traits." They do not "mean directly," but, like other traits, serve to exhibit the hero's psychology or social position. In this way, they figure in the work's overall plan, which mediates their meaning. Readers measure the hero's or heroine's ideology primarily against the overall import of the work. Neither does the author engage his character in dialogue because the two exist on fundamentally different planes. One serves the purposes of the other. The author makes the world, a character dwells in it. Like readers, and unlike characters, the author is located outside that world, and so it is with him that readers engage. He alone can mean directly.

But Dostoevsky (as Bakhtin describes him) found a way for the author and characters to exist more or less on the same plane. In his works, characters emerge as "not only objects of authorial discourse but also subjects of their own directly signifying discourse" (PDP, 7). Readers intuit that Dostoevsky's heroes also retain the power to mean directly. *It is as if each major character could be the organizing point for the novel.* In a sense, the work seems to oscillate between several possible novels, each somehow intended by a different character. It is this peculiar plurality that creates that special sense of palpitating contradictoriness we recognize as quintessentially Dostoevskian.

This contradictoriness must not be confused with mere ambiguity of the sort that might be maintained by any author with a particularly rich and complex vision. No, it is rather an alteration of such visions themselves. We sense the novel's material as inviting diverse unities and yet not reliably sustaining any single one of them, if only because so many compete. To use Bakhtin's analogy, we leave the Ptolemaic universe, in which the author, like the Ptolemaic earth, is indisputably at the center and enter a Copernican cosmos, in which there are as many possible authors as there are planets.

Our theories have no way of describing this phenomenon, which therefore seems paradoxical or impossible. Bakhtin explicitly links the modern versions of these literary theories to what he calls the "whole ideological climate" of the past few hundred years. Poetics parallels ideology. In Bakhtin's view, structuralism, Russian Formalism, and Marxism (among other forms of modern poetics) all reflect the same basic approach that has elsewhere given us the picture of a deterministic universe governed by a unified set of "logarithmic" laws. Bakhtin therefore refers to such systems of poetics as Newtonian, and (somewhat implausibly) he imagines Dostoevsky's achievement as somehow Einsteinian, if for no other reason than that Einstein's universe demands many systems of measurement irreducible to one another. Or as we might say, Bakhtin's Dostoevsky places humanity not in a *uni*verse but a *pluri*verse or a *hetero*verse.

God Subjected to Time

In theological terms, traditional poetics with its single ultimate semantic authority and modern ideology with its "Newtonian" unity correspond to a particular understanding of the monotheistic God who is both omnipotent and omniscient. In particular, poetics and determinism correspond to the God for whom all time is present and for whom temporality is therefore either an illusion or an empty form. This is the God who can see the pattern of the whole picture, much as a poet can contemplate in an instant the pattern of his poem. In neither case is surprise conceivable for the one ultimate semantic authority.

Bakhtin was by no means unique in seeing the theological and ethical difficulties of this view, which seems to turn freedom, chance, and surprise into mirages. Those who have sought to picture an indeterministic world have often felt compelled to picture a different sort of God; for him, time cannot be all present because many things could happen at a given moment. Such a God must wait until the moment to know which possibility will be actualized. James, for instance, explicitly chooses such a theology, which limits the Creator by making him subject to time. Like some others, he hypothesizes that this limitation may itself have been the result of God's decision to make people free and the world truly historical.[9] "Time and chance happeneth to them all."

James therefore imagines God deciding in advance to make time a real force. "Suppose him to say, I will lead things to a certain end, but I will not *now* decide on all the steps thereto. At various points, ambiguous possibilities shall be left open, *either* of which, at a given instant, may become actual" (DD, 181–82). To the word "now" James appends the following remarkable footnote:

This of course leaves the creative mind [God] subject to the law of time. And to any one who insists on the timelessness of that mind I have no reply to make. A mind to whom all time is simultaneously present must see all things under the form of actuality. . . . So that none of his mental judgments can possibly be called hypothetical, and his world is one from which chance is excluded. Is not, however, the timeless mind rather a gratuitous fiction? And is not the notion of eternity being given at a stroke to omniscience only just another way of whacking upon us the block-universe, and of denying that possibilities exist?—just the point to be proved. To say that time is an illusory appearance is only a roundabout manner of saying there is no real plurality, and that the frame of things is an absolute unit. Admit plurality and time may be its form. (DD, 181 n1)

Properly conceived, *time is the form of plurality;* and freedom can exist only if time is so understood. If God created us free, he created the world so that time matters.

This same complex of ideas dominates Bakhtin's many writings on time. Even his Soviet context did not prevent him from hinting at the theological dimensions of his theories. In one passage, he uses the "time-honored" technique of speaking not about actual Christianity but about a literary image of paganism. Bakhtin observes that "Dostoevsky, like Goethe's Prometheus, creates not voiceless slaves (as does Zeus), but *free* people, capable of standing *alongside* their creator, capable of not agreeing with him and even of rebelling against him" (PDP, 6).

In the first edition of the Dostoevsky book, Bakhtin also refers briefly to the influence of the Book of Job on Dostoevsky. In this passage, he is ostensibly writing about purely formal problems (the use of dialogue), but something more vital may be at stake. For in demanding a dialogue with God, Job challenges his Creator to come down and argue with him "in the same plane": "Then summon me, and I will answer; or I will speak first, and do thou answer me" (New English Bible, 13:22). Job also imagines a kind of court in which God and man may confront each other as equals and despairs that God "is not a man, as I am, that I can answer him or that we can confront one another in court" (Job 9:32). This imagined confrontation is surely one of the boldest paradoxes in the Hebrew Bible. Bakhtin believed that an analogous confrontation between author and heroes takes place in Dostoevsky's novels.

And we might add that Job does indeed seem to enjoy "relative independence" with respect to God. After all, God engages in a bet with the devil about whether an unjustly punished Job would rebel, and betting by its very nature presupposes uncertainty. Perhaps Dostoevsky sought to reproduce this sort of uncertainty, in which creatures may surprise their creator.

In his private notes "Toward a Reworking of the Dostoevsky Book," Bakhtin extends the theological parallel. The polyphonic novelist, and God as Bakhtin imagines him, address people dialogically and with the expectation of being surprised: "Dostoevsky frequently interrupts, but he never drowns out the other's voice, never finishes it off 'from himself'. . . . This is, so to speak, the activity of God in His relation to man, a relation allowing man to reveal himself utterly (in his immanent development), to judge himself, to refute himself. This is activity [on the part of author and God] of a higher quality" (TRDB, 285). Two ideas of God, two kinds of authorship: for "it is one thing to be active in relation to a dead thing, to voiceless material that can be molded and formed as one wishes, and another thing to be active *in relation to someone else's living autonomous consciousness*" (TRDB, 285).

Creating Freedom by Provocation and Torture

> Dostoevsky himself was perhaps interested, extremely and intensely interested, to discover the ultimate outcome of this ideological and ethical conflict between the imaginary persons he had created (or, more precisely, who had created themselves in him).
> —ANATOLY LUNACHARSKY

This, then, is the theology and poetics of indeterminism: Bakhtin's Dostoevsky confronts his characters "on the same plane" and engages them in dialogues the outcome of which he cannot foresee. Readers sense this unfinalizability of the characters and respond to the genuine eventness of the narrative. Dostoevsky's novels do not just unfold in time but happen temporally; the author does not plan what his characters will say or do but responds to them as they say or do it. For James, "the timeless mind [of God] is a gratuitous fiction"; in Dostoevsky's novels as Bakhtin reads them, the timeless mind of the author is no less gratuitous.

The mind of God is not one for whom "all time is simultaneously present." The equivalent principle in aesthetics and authorship *banishes structure* in the usual sense. Read polyphonically, Dostoevsky's novels cannot, without significant distortion, be contemplated as a synchronic whole or grasped as a pattern displayed to the mind in an instant. Such contemplation, demanded by most other works and presumed as the starting point of poetics, necessarily abolishes time and destroys eventness. In Dostoevsky's novels, as in the world of Bakhtin's God, time continuously "forges the new" in unforeseeable ways.

As God at the Creation has renounced such foreknowledge, so Dostoevsky has renounced the essential surplus, especially his knowledge of what characters will say or do in advance. Instead, Dostoevsky maintains merely "that indispensable minimum of pragmatic, purely *information-bearing* 'surplus' necessary to carry forward the story" (PDP, 73). He creates situations for the characters and brings them together, but he then allows them to respond as they will. Often he includes a character who defends the political or philosophical views of Dostoevsky himself, but this character must debate without assistance from the author, and he may (often does) lose the debate. Prince Myshkin's failures (in *The Idiot*) constitute only the most dramatic example.[10]

Polyphony, then, is above all a *theory of the creative process*. The polyphonic novel requires a distinctive kind of authorial activity—one that is both special and perceived as special by the reader. Unlike the forms of creativity I examined in chapter 1 (epitomized by Poe and the Formalists on the one hand and by Shelley and Freud on the other), polyphonic creation is truly *processual*. Bakhtin's is a theory of the *middle* of the process.

When a work is created polyphonically, the eventness it conveys partakes of the real eventness happening during the creative process, when the characters surprise the author. Dostoevsky wrote so as to capture in the final text the thrill of that exciting process.

To be sure, other authors are also often surprised by their characters, whose inner logic may invalidate an earlier plan. It is not unusual for an author to discover that a character "refuses to do" what the author has destined for him; that is, the author recognizes that the outcome he or she has in mind would be perceived as false and forced. But in such cases most authors revise so that their surprise is not visible to readers. They may rewrite earlier sections so that the desired outcome does not appear forced or they may recast the novel so that what turned out to be the better outcome is prepared for all along. In either case the surprise that altered the original plan is masked.[11]

Still more important, the surprise experienced by other authors is not vital to the success of their work, according to Bakhtin. But in polyphonic works surprise *is itself planned*—not any specific surprise (for then it would not be surprising) but the likelihood that there will be many surprises. For Bakhtin, Dostoevsky's creative process is designed specifically to provoke unexpected events or ideas, and the process would be a failure if it did *not* produce them. In the same way, Bakhtin's God designed a world in which people would be truly free to do genuinely surprising things. This paradox of planned surprise is essential both to the polyphonic work and to the real world.

Thus, Bakhtin stresses that Dostoevsky's "creative process, as reflected in rough drafts, differs sharply from that of other writers" (PDP, 39), and in his book's second edition he cites with approval Victor Shklovsky's paraphrase of this thesis: "Dostoevsky's plans contain by their very nature an open-endedness which in effect refutes them as plans" (cited PDP, 39) in the usual sense. In Bakhtin's account, Dostoevsky worked by first imagining "voice-ideas"—characters whose identity was fused with an ideology—often based on real Russian thinkers. He then brought these characters into dialogue, argued with them himself, imagined their replies to a multitude of hostile or friendly questions, and then watched carefully how a character originally modeled on Herzen or Turgenev wound up saying things those thinkers never said in reality. He also places them in extreme situations to *test* what they would say.[12] Bakhtin proposes that Dostoevsky learned to create characters able to stand on their own by a long series of such imagined tortures.

Dostoevsky provokes what people *might* have said, and they become different in the process. Then, with these more complex characters, he creates more tests, lets them argue in different combinations, about new things, and in varying specific situations. At each step, his characters depart further from their models and surprise their creator more frequently. Pyotr Stepanovich (in *The Possessed*) was modeled on the terrorist Sergei Nechaev, and Ivan Karamazov on the critic Belinsky, but they differ considerably from their models. It is as if Pyotr Stepanovich was once a mere Nechaev—so he is called in the early notebooks for the novel—but outgrew his model by acquiring layers and layers of new characteristics and new ideologies, which were at best merely potential when he was "Nechaev." In actualizing old potentials, the character acquires new ones, unimaginable at the outset of the process. Only when Dostoevsky sensed a character as sufficiently rich in potential for the unexpected did he actually begin writing the novel.

So that characters might surprise him, Dostoevsky did not determine their fate in advance.[13] For Dostoevsky, a plot is simply the record of what happens to happen. As Bakhtin phrases this point, the author refrains from "ambushing" his characters with knowledge about themselves that the characters could not possess. A critic of Bakhtin's theory might object that Dostoevsky's notebooks do in fact contain plot outlines. But we may reply on Bakhtin's behalf that there are so many contradictory plot outlines and they change so rapidly that they do not seem to be real plans for future events. Rather, they seem to be either mere mechanisms for bringing the characters together for a dialogue or else ways of understanding heroes by seeing what they *might* do and what they are capable of doing. They do not seem to dictate the future but instead project the possible futures that form and disappear moment by moment, in his text as in life.

In Dostoevsky, therefore, plot loses its inevitability as structure disappears and "rhythm" yields to "loopholes." Like real people, characters act *into the open future,* and not in fulfillment of an overall plan laid down at the outset. The polyphonic author's problem is not how to get the character plausibly to do what is needed for the plot to work, as it must be for authors with a specific sequence of events in mind, but how to provoke the character to do things that are both surprising and interesting. The work is always directed forward but without teleology. Thus, the plot of a polyphonic novel is sensed as "one of many possible plots and is consequently in the final analysis merely accidental for a given hero" (PDP, 84).

It follows that what some critics have taken as instances of foreshadowing or structural correspondences planned from the outset are nothing of the sort, any more than we would be justified in real life should we attribute our habit of making the same old mistakes to some sort of advance planning.[14] Repetition may result from mere habit. Or, to use Kierkegaard's language, we find not recollections but repetitions: "Repetition and recollection are the same movement, only in opposite directions; for what is recollected has been, is repeated backwards, whereas repetition properly so called is recollected forwards. Therefore repetition, if it is possible, makes a man happy whereas recollection makes him unhappy."[15] One need only substitute "free" for "happy" to understand Bakhtin's point about Dostoevsky's creative process.

Strange Synchronies

> Rereading is here suggested at the outset . . . rereading draws the text out of its internal chronology ("this happens *before* or *after* that") and recaptures a mythic time (without *before* or *after*) . . .
> —ROLAND BARTHES

Bakhtin observes that a Dostoevsky novel "takes place not in the past, but right now, that is, in the *real present* of the creative process. This is no stenographer's report of a *finished* dialogue, from which the author has already withdrawn and *over* which he is now located as if in some high decision-making position" but a real dialogue recorded in the making, in "the real present" (PDP, 63). The present referred to is the character's present.

This crucial point has far-reaching implications. Dostoevsky's major novels depend on a peculiar kind of *simultaneity* in which the real time of the creative process and the fictive time of the characters—two distinct ontological realms—somehow take place together. The clocks of parallel universes tick in unison. This is a simultaneity not in time but of times: the author makes his decisions as the characters make theirs. And the reader senses this simultaneity, which is why the work seems as open as the real world. No prior decision mandates what characters say or do. No need for ultimate structure or closure dictates a pattern of behavior for characters to fulfill unawares.

In this way, the *an*isomorphism that we have seen in some other novels— the contradiction between their assertion of freedom and the planned whole of the work—is overcome. As the plot of the *Oedipus* matches a structure based on foreshadowing to a vision of fatalism, so Dostoevsky's polyphonic novels develop a shape that corresponds to the characters' freedom.

Bakhtin's model invites further development: one might suggest that all novels presuppose four distinct kinds of time. Within the fiction, we have two temporalities: the time of the fictional characters and the public time in which they live.[16] The two may be joined in an opening statement: "In Petersburg in the year 187-, a certain young man lay dreaming in his garret." " 'Well, Peter, not in sight yet?' was the question asked on May 20, 1859, by a gentleman a little over forty." [17] The public time exists in a sequence we know, which is why in historical novels Napoleon cannot win the battle of Waterloo and, in works set closer to the present, Petersburg cannot flood unless it did.

In the public time of novels, leeway for invention exists only with facts too obscure to be part of general knowledge.[18] Thus, part of the art of the realist novel, whether historical or contemporary, is to develop a smooth continuum between invented characters and those who really existed. Such novels therefore rely on a steady gradation from facts that everyone knows, through those known only to some, to those no one could know either because they are completely obscure or entirely invented. If the realist novel is to work, there must be no sudden jolts along the way.[19]

Most fictional characters belong to the group of people that is obscure to us. Thus, in reading *War and Peace*, we know that there were aristocrats of a certain type in 1805, but we do not know who most of them were: so it violates no external knowledge for there to have been one named Andrei Bolkonsky and another named Natasha Rostova. In a novel set in the present, like *Anna Karenina*, readers do not know who all Russian officers are, so it contradicts nothing for there to be one named Vronsky. Whether historical or contemporary, novels also typically include an intermediate type of character whose real world status we cannot determine. It would take a historian to tell us whether this particular character is made up or not. In *War and Peace*, for instance, all readers are expected to recognize Napoleon as real, but how many know whether Bazdeev, the leader of the Freemasons, or Annette Scherer, "lady-in-waiting and *confidante* to the Empress Marya Fyodorovna," really existed? The presence of these intermediate characters allows the historical and the private to be smoothly blended.[20] Public time and private time shade into each other, and readers are expected to be certain only at the extremes of the continuum.

At the extremes we recognize differences in temporality. Generally speaking, invented characters, as possible but not historically documented people, enjoy greater freedom.[21] Napoleon is destined by the readers' external knowledge to win or lose a given battle, whereas the author may either permit or prevent Princess Marya from marrying whom she chooses. On the other hand, invented characters also face certain limitations. Pierre cannot kill Napoleon, as he hopes, because Napoleon did not die at the hands of a Russian assassin; and although Marya might or might not marry Nikolai Rostov, she cannot marry the Duke of Wellington.[22]

The third time of novels is that of the author, which is usually (as Bakhtin says) *later* in meaning, in the sense that the work *has already been written* and the world of the characters has been constituted by decisions already made. Our experience of reading the work, indeed, usually depends on the assumption of this kind of "lateness." It is our assurance that the author is in control, that textual features are not random, and that our efforts to detect pattern are likely to be rewarded. Even in the case of stories we hear, rather than read, we usually assume the speaker knows the outcome and we are therefore typically disappointed should we discover that the speaker has been making it all up, without a point or goal, while narrating. We feel deceived into misdirecting our attention. That is why a good storyteller who is indeed composing as he or she goes along usually tries to convey the opposite impression, the sense of total control. In this context, we may view acknowledged improvisations as exceptions proving the rule. They are supposed to display the effects of authorial lateness when the author is known to be not later but "in time" with his audience. They are successful *as* improvisations when the improvisor can achieve as he goes along the impression of total control and advance planning even though the audience is constantly aware that could not possibly be the case.

The time of reading constitutes the fourth type of time. When Tristram Shandy asks his readers whether enough reading time has elapsed for a character to have traveled to his destination—as if there need be ten minutes' worth of prose about a character taking a ten-minute walk—he is playing upon the usually tacit fact that these two times do not coincide.[23] That is why we do not worry what the characters might be doing when we are not reading about them.

And yet, authors and critics have noticed that reading time and fictional time cannot be entirely separated either. To take one celebrated example, Poe stressed the importance of brevity so that a story or poem could be read in a single sitting and thereby produce an effect uninterrupted by the ongoing time of daily life.[24] Poe was concerned to achieve a certain loose kind of synchrony. Such an effect of brevity is clearly not available to novelists, who, on the contrary, would be wise to take advantage of what Gillian Beer aptly calls the *intermitted* nature of reading long works: "The intermitted reading of long narrative means that it broods within all our current life-activities. These other activities—and landscapes also—may come to form part of our repertoire of memory when we look back on the text."[25]

When works are especially long—like *War and Peace* and *Remembrance of Things Past*—they offer favorable ground for exploring the nature of memory, as both works do, because their length and the necessary interruption of reading by other activities mean that there is ample time for memory lapses and the distortions introduced by shifts of attention. In general, the skilled author takes reader's time into account. That is indeed one reason that types of plotting in serialized novels typically vary with the length of each excerpt.[26] The brief installments of the "novel-feuilleton" (Eugène Sue's *Mysteries of Paris*, for example) may lead to more frequent crises and create a different pace than would be likely with longer installments (as in Tolstoy's *Anna Karenina*). Thus, authors of serialized novels often revise and smooth chapters or section breaks when the novels are published in book form.[27]

Bakhtin's concept of polyphony represents an attempt to *synchronize two distinct clocks*. In novels before Dostoevsky, Bakhtin may mean to suggest, the time of creating and the time of fictional characters are brought together only for comic or metaliterary effect, as in *Tristram Shandy*.[28] In such cases, wit depends on the jolt produced by the unnatural combination and thereby testifies to its artifice; we must perceive the juxtaposition of times *as* a device for it to have its effect. But in Dostoevsky's case, our attention is not called, as it is in metaliterary works, to the *fact* of synchronization. We may be entirely unaware of it, and presumably readers before Bakhtin were unaware of it. Rather, the novel depends on the *effect* of synchronization. That effect pertains to our experience not of the device but of the characters. We respond to them as free because we sense that they are not preordained to act as they do. They make— are making—the work as they live and choose.

What about the reader's time in a polyphonic novel? In one sense, of course, it cannot be simultaneous with the time of the work's creation because the work is necessarily read after it has been written. But in a different way, some aspects of simultaneity of readers with the author can be retained.

In most novels, the author is later than not only the characters but also the readers because as they read they do not know what is going to happen but he does. And as we have seen, the reader relies on this extra knowledge, this lateness of the author, as a guarantee that the work is sufficiently controlled to be worth reading. With most novels, the reader approaches the author's position only when *re*reading the work. Foreshadowing may be viewed as an attempt to give even a first reading important characteristics of rereading.

By contrast, the reader of a polyphonic novel is closest to the author during a first reading. To be sure, once a novel is written, its events have already been decided—in the case of a polyphonic novel, they have been decided by both characters and author together—but as the reader comes upon an event, he or she does not know its outcome any more than the characters do. In this way, *ignorance* of an outcome is made to correspond with *uncertainty* of outcome, the uncertainty experienced by both characters and polyphonic author. For somewhat different reasons, neither reader nor author nor hero knows what happens until it happens, although all three are presumably trying to guess. Thus a strange (if partial) triple synchronization takes place.

In most novels, the implicit equation of ignorance of outcome with an outcome still undetermined—an equation that might be called "the suspense convention" of novelistic reading—is what allows readers to identify with *characters*. In a polyphonic novel, this sort of identification extends to the author in the process of creation as well. In nonpolyphonic novels, the contemplation of the work from the author's perspective (as a completed structure) weakens suspense. In a polyphonic novel, one can adopt the author's and characters' perspectives together. This extension of Bakhtin's analysis suggests that it is perhaps to such tripling that the amazing intensity of Dostoevskian suspense may be attributed.

These observations also suggest that readers of Dostoevsky may experience *less* of the work's essential quality when rereading, which would not be the case if the work depended on structure rather than on eventness. This difference may be one reason that critics, who are almost by necessity rereaders, have somehow seemed especially remote from the experience of *reading* Dostoevsky. Perhaps special effort should be taken to recapture the thrill of first exposure.

Is it possible to bring the reader even closer to the author? Could the two be not just in a similar kind of time but in the same time—literally simultaneous in the usual sense of the word? That is, could the author actually be composing while the reader is reading? In oral performances, such simultaneity is of course possible, as Pushkin stresses in his well-known story about an improvisatore, "Egyptian Nights." In the improvisatore's rendition, characters are choosing while the improvisatore is composing while the audience is listening, all in the same room at the same moment. And the theme of the improvisatore's poem is itself one selected by members of the audience, which makes them, as the agents of chance, participants in creating the poem. In Pushkin's story, the only time not synchronized with the rest is the public time of the improvisatore's fiction, which he sets in ancient Egypt. Could something approaching this literal kind of triple synchronization take place with a written work?

Dostoevsky in fact attempted something very close to that. His most radical experiment in literary form, *A Writer's Diary: A Monthly Publication*, was not just published *in* a periodical, as Dostoevsky's novels were published, but actually took the form *of* a periodical.[29] Dostoevsky served as editor, publisher, and sole contributor to this enterprise, which combined fiction and plans for fiction, finished sketches and mere outlines, recollections of past events and diverse forms of reportage about incidents still happening. Here readers would find recent real events (described by the author) suggesting outlines for possible stories, which in turn sometimes lead to a finished piece of fiction. As critics have noted, part of this work's appeal derived from readers' sense that they were admitted to the usually secret processes of a writer's laboratory, that they were witnessing the gestation and eventual birth of art as it happened.[30] Readers would see the author stumble, go off on tangents, or make and correct mistakes, a process that would leave its trace on any finished story that would eventually appear. They could, so to speak, read the stories both horizontally and vertically. Because the *Diary* appeared monthly, readers were *almost* simultaneous with the act of creation, and that, too, was part of the appeal.

Some of the *Diary*'s most compelling narratives consisted of Dostoevsky's reports on ongoing trials. After retelling the facts of a case, he typically imagined more details and projected continuations, sometimes several at a time. At one point Dostoevsky became convinced that a convicted defendant, Kornilova, should have been acquitted, and he tried to use his speculations and predictions of her future behavior to obtain a retrial. When she was in fact granted a new hearing, the *Diary* made the case for her acquittal and was again successful. Thus it might be said that Dostoevsky was not only author but also character in this story, whose outcome he could influence though not (like other authors) absolutely control. No more than his readers did he know in advance his narrative's outcome, which was located in the real future. Excitement was generated both by the knowledge that a real person's fate was at stake and by the location of author, characters, and readers all together on the very *edge of the historical present*. Making stories, both fictional and nonfictional, from topical events, the *Diary* cultivated the excitement of time as it flows and events-in-the-making.

Bakhtin's Third Stage: Wisdom of the Chronotope

> The field available for representing the world changes from genre to genre and from era to era as literature develops. It is organized in different ways and limited in space and time by different means. But this field is always specific.
>
> —BAKHTIN

A few years after writing his book on Dostoevsky, Bakhtin returned to its core problem, the representation of a world in which people are free. It appears that in the interim Bakhtin increasingly came to question one aspect of Dostoevskian temporality. In order to render palpable the act of choosing, Dostoevsky focused everything on the moment in which choice is made. Bakhtin had argued that Dostoevsky is at his most Dostoevskian when time becomes nothing but "the cross section of a single moment" (PDP, 29): sequence is overcome, the past fades from view, and only an intensified present is felt. Thus Dostoevsky strives to "concentrate, even at the expense of credibility, as many persons and themes as possible in one place at one time" (PDP, 28). He thereby creates a "whirlwind" motion of events, which expresses "not only the triumph of time, but also the triumph over time, for speed is the single means for overcoming time in time" (PDP, 28). In the third period of his thinking, Bakhtin deeply distrusted this "triumph over time."

When time is only an intensified present essentially disconnected from the past, then a rich sense of biographical and historical continuity must be missing. In his book on Dostoevsky, Bakhtin explained that in Dostoevsky's novels "that which has meaning only as 'earlier' or 'later' . . . is for him nonessential and is not incorporated into his world" (PDP, 29). For this reason, Dostoevsky's characters—unlike those of Tolstoy or George Eliot—"have no biography in the sense of something past and fully experienced" (PDP, 29). Instead, they are all present, and the only things they remember about their pasts are those that still compel present choices—crimes, humiliations, unexpiated sins. What does not torment Raskolnikov now we do not learn. Unencumbered by any other past, Dostoevsky's characters seem maximally free in the present. But such freedom posed ethically troubling questions to Bakhtin, who came to regard it as false to our fundamentally historical nature.

Bakhtin therefore turned to the problem of temporality as experienced by the character. Setting aside the relation of author to hero, he focused on the portrayal of time within the narrative itself. Each narrative genre, he reasoned, has its own way of understanding time, a unique and specific "density and concreteness" distinguishing it from all other genres and (in most cases) from all abstract philosophy. In each genre, Bakhtin wrote, "time, as it were, thickens, takes on flesh, becomes artistically visible; likewise, space becomes charged and responsive to the movement of time, plot and history" (FTC, 84). Taken together, literary genres offer an encyclopedia of temporalities.

Bakhtin's argument begins from a quite simple insight. It is obvious that events plausible in some genres are extremely unlikely, if not impossible, in others. Reading adventure stories, for example, we expect escapes in the nick of time that would be odd in a realistic novel. Common to some narrative forms are sudden changes of fortune, whereas in others change usually happens gradually by imperceptibly small steps. Standards of plausibility are generically given, as are concepts of human agency. In some genres, human initiative measurably affects outcomes that in others must be left to fate. Each of these, and many other qualities, defines *a field of possibilities* characteristic of the given genre. Bakhtin calls such a field a "chronotope." Strictly speaking, the chronotope is not itself present *in* events but rather specifies the possibility *of* events. It is not directly represented in the work but is "the ground essential for the . . . representability of events" (FTC, 250).

In the variety of genres developed over millennia of tradition, time has been conceived in many distinct ways. From this perspective, deterministic or "logarithmic" time turns out to be far from the only alternative. It is, rather, a limiting case, in which the field of time is reduced to a single line. Much as the Russian mathematician Nikolai Lobachevsky, who invented a non-Euclidian geometry, demonstrated that space may be conceived in many different ways, so Bakhtin offered his survey of temporalities to demonstrate that we must *choose* which to adopt. Once we recognize chronotopic multiplicity, we can no longer view time "naively," as if only one kind exists. Which one governs a particular part of natural or social life or best models social life as a whole cannot be presumed in advance.

His next step was to use the treasure house of narrative to identify key differences among genres. He might then propose as the most realistic the one that offered the richest and most accurate sense of biographical and historical time, the one that gave freedom and responsibility their most profound meaning. For Bakhtin, the superior genre turned out to be the nineteenth-century novel. Greater and more profound than any philosophical model of time are the realistic fictions written by Balzac, George Eliot, and Turgenev. The most profound temporal wisdom in *War and Peace* is to be found not in its essays on history but in the richly detailed chronotope from which its plots arise.

"Real Historical Time"

Bakhtin regarded the novel as closer than its rivals to an approximation of "real historical time." Following are just a few of the important features of the novelistic chronotope:

1. Genres evidently differ in their sense of *how change happens.* In the Greek romance, for instance, "fate and the gods hold all initiative in their hands, and they merely inform people of their will" (FTC, 95). What happens in these romances is what has been predestined to happen, and so the life of heroes becomes a long test of endurance, a test whose outcome is also predestined. Thus in Greek romances the gods give the heroes prophetic dreams, which foreshadow what is bound to come—not so that the heroes can struggle with their fate, which is unchangeable, but so that they can bear it more easily. In Greek romances, therefore, time is indeed a single line.[31]

Quite different is the temporality of what Bakhtin calls the ancient "adventure novel of everyday life." A logic of sudden metamorphosis governs this world: nodes of choice punctuate long sequences governed by the iron logic of fate.[32] In Apuleius's *The Golden Ass,* for instance, Lucius's choice of debauchery leads to his transformation into an ass; after a long imprisonment and the harassment of fate, a dream prepares him for another choice. A goddess allows him to exchange his status as an ass to become her human devotee, and Lucius, choosing correctly, is transformed back into a man. In this chronotope, therefore, time "unfolds not so much in a straight line as spasmodically, a line with 'knots' in it" (FTC, 113).

In realist novels, indeterminacy characterizes *all* moments. We always have some measure of freedom, however small, and large changes are as a rule made cumulatively, by the steady exercise of small chances and choices. It follows that every moment of our lives, not just occasional moments of crisis, has ethical value. One suspects that Dostoevsky's use of "crisis time" especially disturbed Bakhtin's ethical sense, for the temporality of crisis makes all other moments ethically neutral.[33] By way of contrast, Bakhtin praised Goethe's sense of constant small accumulations over a lifetime (or even lifetimes).

2. Each model of change implies a specific sense of *human identity and individual development.* At one extreme, the heroes and heroines of Greek romances are ever the same people; for them, time is "reversible" in the sense that nothing in their character would make it impossible for an author or reader to reverse the sequence of their adventures. But one cannot rearrange the incidents in the life of Anna Karenina because as the novel progresses her character gradually changes. Placed in the same situation, she would behave differently.

Identity is also a given in various forms of ancient biography. Change happens, but change itself changes nothing essential. In Plutarch's *Lives,* for instance, a kind of entelechy governs character: as acorns grow into oaks, Demosthenes develops into an orator and Alexander into a conqueror. In such biographies, "the ultimate purpose of development . . . is at the same time its first cause" (FTC, 140). Time may impede or encourage the expression of inborn qualities, and events may lead even to a person's death before those qualities have been fully expressed. But time cannot essentially alter a person. "Character itself does not grow, does not change, it is merely *filled in*" (FTC, 141). In the realist novel, by contrast, people are always in the process of making themselves, and they change throughout life. Character tends to no goal but rather acquires qualities as life goes on. Unpredictable circumstances and their own actions make heroes and heroines different; they do not live in completed selves. It follows that they are ethically responsible not only for what they do but also for how they transform themselves—not only for their actions but also, over time, for a considerable part of their character.[34] Such transformation takes place at every present moment. One reason for Bakhtin's distaste for Freudianism was its sense of the essential completion of the personality at a young age. For Bakhtin, unfinalizability is coterminous with life, and Freudianism therefore appeared to him a philosophy of death. Perhaps one reason that many Freudian interpretations of novels seem reductive is that they *de-novelize* the novelistic chronotope by substituting a more primitive one in which character is finalized.

3. Also important for Bakhtin was a genre's sense of the *historical process*. In some genres, that process is ignored; action is not intrinsically dated or located in the history of a particular people. In Greek romances and various kinds of adventure narratives, there is no one moment or country in which the action would have had to take place. Shipwrecks require a sea and chases an expanse but which sea or expanse does not matter. For this reason, romances and adventure stories can easily be adapted to various times and places. Substitute a French or Russian name for a Greek one, and the romance is easily moved; but it is hard to see what comparable substitutions could relocate *Middlemarch* to Russia or *Anna Karenina* to the Soviet period.[35] In this sense, the action of the Greek romance is both historically "reversible" and socially "replaceable."

By contrast, realist novels depend on a rich sense of anachronism and of "anatopism." Just as one cannot reverse the order of incidents in Anna Karenina's life, so actions in novels are tied with great specificity to certain societies at particular times. "In the year 187-"—the common formula—restricts the action to a decade; Turgenev often situates his action still more precisely in a given season of a specified year (May 1859 in *Fathers and Sons*) and indicates why it would be implausible earlier or later. In the novel, people are temporal to the core.

In Bakhtin's view, the novel presumes that for societies, as for individuals, the past constrains choices in the present.[36] In this sense, the novel is profoundly anti-utopian; from the novelistic perspective, utopian thinkers typically misunderstand these constraints. They tend to forget or explicitly refuse to acknowledge that not all options are open at every moment. In realist novels satirizing utopian thought, therefore, characters must learn the hard lesson that one cannot, without disastrous results, dream up the perfect republic and then simply put it into practice.[37] For the novel, politics can never be a matter of just applying the right timeless principles because the attempted application necessarily takes place at some specific moment shaped in particular ways by its unique historical past.

But if the novelistic past constrains the present, it does not determine it. As biography limits but does not eliminate choice for individuals, so history at every moment contains some options. Indeed, from the novelistic perspective, one effect of historical contingency is to create ever-new possibilities. At every moment new choices become imaginable, while old probabilities come to seem fantastic. History is a sequence not only of unrepeatable events but also of unprecedented options.

4. Particularly important for Bakhtin is the novel's sense of *the relation be-*

tween biographical and historical time. Not only are both individuals and society continually "becoming," they also shape each other. The novel represents the *interaction* of social milieus with particular people; it portrays the incessant and unpredictable concatenations of biographical and historical development. Because these processes impinge upon each other, personalities cannot exactly repeat from age to age or place to place. On the one hand, social milieu is never mere background; on the other, individuals are never mere instantiations of an epoch. These two temporalities engage in a complex and open-ended dialogue.

Time in the Historical Novel

Each of these characteristics of novelistic time derives from the novel's fundamental orientation toward presentness. Constrained by the past and open to multiple futures, novelistic presentness is characterized above all by its incompleteness, the possibility of diverse outcomes that will in turn contain still more diverse options. Each present is "in principle inconclusive; by its very nature it demands continuation, it moves into the future, and the more actively and consciously it moves into the future the more tangible and indispensable its inconclusiveness becomes" (EaN, 30). As a result, the novel subjects all received truths and currently fashionable ideas to a peculiar *"chronic" skepticism:* whatever their claims or however devoted their advocates, these ideas will soon be dated by a future still unimagined.

The novel speculates in categories of ignorance. It is at this point in his argument that Bakhtin arrives at a formulation reminiscent of, but still significantly different from, the Dostoevsky book. With the rise of the novel, he writes, "the temporal model of the world changes radically; it becomes a world where there is no first word (no ideal word), and the final word has not yet been spoken" (EaN, 30). Every object, person, institution, and idea is brought into contact with "the incomplete process of a world-in-the-making" and so becomes "stamped with the seal of inconclusiveness" (EaN, 30). In short, the novel gives us unfinalizability, but without the crisis time and unnaturally intensified present of the Dostoevsky book.

For Bakhtin, a paradoxical conclusion followed from this analysis. Precisely because the novel best understands presentness, it is the genre best able to comprehend the past. That is because it understands each past moment as just another present moment. As modern geology was made possible by uniformitarianism—the principle that the forces governing the physical world have not changed qualitatively—so the novel reflects the discovery that time has always been a sequence of present moments.

For the novel, understanding a moment in the past therefore involves grasping two basic principles. First, every moment in the past had a specific field of possibilities different from our own. To understand a past moment is to reconstruct its field and thereby to discern not only where the moment did lead but also where it might have led. The second principle immediately follows: the outcome that did result, namely, ourselves and our present, was not inevitable. We must always resist the temptation to treat the past as if our own time were already somehow present in it. Bakhtin calls this common error "modernization and distortion."

Historical novels, as Bakhtin describes them, avoid this error:

> The depiction of the past in the novel in no sense presumes the modernization of this past. . . . On the contrary, only in the novel have we the possibility of an authentically objective portrayal of the past as the past. Contemporary reality with its new experience is retained as a way of seeing, it has the depth, sharpness, breadth and vividness of that way of seeing, but should not in any way penetrate into the already portrayed content of the past, as a force modernizing and distorting the uniqueness of that past. After all, every great and serious contemporaneity requires an authentic profile of the past, an authentic other language from another time. (EaN, 29–30)

Bakhtin exaggerates historical novels' resistance to "modernization." They do remind us repeatedly of our own relation to the period described. Thus we have Scott's title, *Waverley, or 'Tis Sixty Years Since*. Even Tolstoy, who was supremely sensitive to the possibility of results other than the one that produced us, recognizes that his novel cannot escape its location in one particular line of development, the one that did result. "He [Prince Vasily] spoke that courtly French in which our grandparents not only spoke but thought," he tells us in the first chapter of *War and Peace* (W&P, 30).

We might therefore modify Bakhtin's point about historical novels in this way: the historical novel as a genre brings into interaction two conflicting temporal perspectives. On the one hand, readers never forget that the events described are not only over but have led (even if they were not destined to lead) to the readers' own world. In this way, foreshadowing penetrates the narrative because it is given in the very perspective that the novelist, himself the product of the events described, offers the readers. That is why the author of *War and Peace* had to take such pains to resist foreshadowing. On the other hand, the past is described *novelistically*, that is, as open and as having had many possible outcomes. The peculiar piquancy of the genre, its special appeal, derives from the interweaving of these perspectives, from the light they shed on each other, and from the ironies they make possible in *both* directions.

Many Realities, and the Surplus of Humanness

For Bakhtin, the single most important feature of novelistic time is the new relation established between the hero and the plot and therefore between an individual and his or her biography. Again, the problem of the Dostoevsky book is now approached in terms set internally by the work rather than in terms of the author's relation to the character.

The epic and tragic hero, in Bakhtin's view, is neither more nor less than what he is. There is nothing else he could be. "Hopelessly ready-made," he completely "coincides with himself"; there is no "gap" between his identity and his life (EaN, 34). Therefore the plot expresses him utterly. "Outside his destiny, the epic and tragic hero is nothing; he is, therefore, a function of the plot fate assigns him; he cannot become the hero of another destiny or another plot" (EaN, 36). By contrast, the life led by a novelistic hero does not exhaust his identity. He could have been different. We sense that, in potential, he has more lives than one: "One of the basic internal themes of the novel is precisely the theme of the hero's inadequacy to his fate or his situation. The individual is either greater than his fate, or less than his condition as a man. He cannot become once and for all a clerk, a landowner, a merchant, a fiancé, a jealous lover, a father and so forth" (EaN, 37). If the hero does become coincident with his condition, then he ceases to be a major character—by definition, perhaps, because in novels noncoincidence is what defines characters as major. If a novel with a coincident hero continues, then interest shifts to some other character, who still "exceeds" the plot. Whoever is the center of attention possesses "unrealized potential" (EaN, 37).

It is in explaining these aspects of the novelistic hero that Bakhtin produces his most remarkable statement about the relation of character to time. He is clearly speaking not only of novelistic heroes but also of real people. Our defining quality as people is what Bakhtin calls "the surplus of humanness":

An individual cannot be completely incarnated into the flesh of existing sociohistorical categories. There is no mere form that would be able to incarnate once and forever all of his human possibilities and needs, no form in which he could exhaust himself down to the last word . . . no form that he could fill to the very brim, and yet not splash over the brim. There always remains an unrealized *surplus of humanness;* there always remains a need for the future, and a place for this future must be found. . . . *Reality as we have it in the novel is only one of many possible realities;* it is not inevitable, not arbitrary, it bears within itself other possibilities. (EaN, 37; italics added)

The essay containing this passage was not published until 1975, more than three decades after it had been written. For it is virtually impossible not to detect in these lines a critique of Soviet Marxism, which asserted that individuals can indeed be exhaustively explained by existing sociohistorical categories and which sought to produce a "new Soviet man" without a surplus. The target of this passage is not only Marxism, but all philosophies, sociologies, and psychologies that close down time.

In polyphony, the plot is only one of many possible plots; in the novel, reality is only one of many possible realities. By different routes, both theories—of polyphony and of the novelistic chronotope—arrive at the concepts of noncoincidence, the loophole, and the existence of genuine alternatives. And yet neither of the two theories entirely succeeds in Bakhtin's terms. Polyphony, as Bakhtin describes it, misunderstands the past by seeing the present as essentially discontinuous and therefore ahistorical. On the other hand, the chronotopic theory of the novel never addresses the problem of a work's *already written* quality and the sense of destiny that such a quality imposes.

Perhaps the value of Bakhtin's theories lies in their deepening of the problems to be solved in any attempt to represent time as open. His very exaggerations, about Dostoevsky and about the novel, serve to foreground central issues. However, Bakhtin omitted what may be the most important method employed by novelists and others to convey a sense of real alternatives: *sideshadowing*. What this term means, and how the method can be used, is the topic of the next chapter.

PART TWO

Sideshadowing and Its Possibilities

CHAPTER FOUR

Sideshadowing

You know, it's a matter of a whole lifetime, an infinite multitude of ramifications hidden from us.
—IPPOLIT TERENTIEV, in *The Idiot*

What is open time? We now come to the core concept of the present study:
sideshadowing, a way of understanding and representing the plurality of possibilities.

The Possibility of Possibility, and the Middle Realm

*Fore*shadowing robs a present moment of its presentness. As we have seen,
foreshadowing lifts the veil on a future that has already been determined and inscribed. Somehow, a specific later event is already given at the time of an earlier
event. Thus the sense of many possible futures, which we experience at every
present moment, is revealed as an illusion. What *will* be *must* be; events are
heading in a single direction; time is entirely linear or, as the underground man
says, "logarithmic," because the future is either known for certain or calculable
(at least in principle) with mathematical certainty.

Wisdom in such a world consists in the appreciation of inevitability. As
readers or viewers of a story with foreshadowing, we recognize a character's
struggle for alternatives as doomed and deluded. If the real world is governed
by the same kind of temporality, then we would do well never to forget the
singularity of the future. Whether or not we hear the voice of Tieresias, the
time in which we live is oracular.

As we have seen, those who have believed time to be genuinely open have
sought to invent ways of telling a story that elude foreshadowing and closure.
They have sought to restore presentness to the present. To do so, Dostoevsky
and Tolstoy made effective use of a device that may be viewed as the antithesis
of foreshadowing: sideshadowing.

Whereas foreshadowing works by revealing apparent alternatives to be mere

117

illusions, sideshadowing conveys the sense that actual events might just as well not have happened. In an open universe, the illusion is inevitability itself. Alternatives always abound, and, more often than not, what exists need not have existed. *Something else* was possible, and sideshadowing is used to create a sense of that "something else." Instead of casting a foreshadow from the future, it casts a shadow "from the side," that is, from the other possibilities. Along with an event, we see its alternatives; with each present, another possible present. Sideshadows conjure the ghostly presence of might-have-beens or might-bes. While we see what did happen, we also see the image of what else could have happened. In this way, the hypothetical shows through the actual and so achieves its own shadowy kind of existence in the text.

In sideshadowing, two or more alternative presents, the actual and the possible, are made simultaneously visible. This is a simultaneity not *in* time but *of* times: we do not see contradictory actualities, but one possibility that was actualized and, at the same moment, another that could have been but was not. In this way, time itself acquires a double and often many doubles. A haze of possibilities surrounds each actuality.

When sideshadowing is used, it seems that distinct temporalities are continually competing for each moment of actuality. Like a king challenged by a pretender with an equal claim to rule, the actual loses some temporal legitimacy. It can no longer be regarded as inevitable, as so firmly ensconced that it does not even make sense to consider alternatives. Or to adapt one of Bakhtin's favorite metaphors, a present moment subjected to sideshadowing ceases to be Ptolemaic, the unchallenged center of things. It moves instead into a Copernican universe: as there are many planets, so there are many potential presents for each one actualized.

The actual is therefore understood as just another possibility that somehow came to pass. It was perhaps not entirely accidental, but it came without guarantees and it was preceded by no annunciation of its coming. Sideshadowing therefore counters our tendency to view current events as the inevitable products of the past. Instead, it invites us to inquire into the other possible presents that might have been and to imagine a quite different course of events. *If only* that chance incident had not happened, if only a different choice had been made, if only a favorable sequence of events had not been interrupted or had been interrupted a moment later—what would have happened then? Sideshadowing constantly prompts questions of this sort. Michael Bernstein identifies the recurrent trope of inevitability as *"little did they know that ... ."*[1] By contrast, sideshadowing leads to the subjunctive and the contrary-to-fact conditional: what if, if only, had it not been, were it not for—what would have taken place then?

In permitting us to catch a glimpse of unrealized but realizable possibilities, sideshadowing demonstrates that our tendency to trace straight lines of causality (usually leading to ourselves at the present moment) oversimplifies events, which always allow for many possible stories. When a sequence of events seems so coherent as to be necessary, we are usually deceived by our own presence at the sequence's culmination. The mirage is not other possibilities but the necessity of the actual one. What happened did not have to happen, and whatever exists, including ourselves, might not have existed. Sideshadowing therefore induces a kind of temporally based humility.

Sideshadowing restores *the possibility of possibility*. Its most fundamental lesson is: to understand a moment is to grasp not only what did happen but also what else might have happened. Hypothetical histories shadow actual ones. Some nonactual events enjoy their own kind of reality: the temporal world consists not just of actualities and impossibilities but also of real though unactualized possibilities. Sideshadowing invites us into this peculiar *middle realm.*

Time as a Field

In its inclusion of contrary-to-fact expressions and tenses, our language displays an appreciation of potentialities in excess of actualities—of the *surplus of temporalities*. In this sense, we may speak of the wisdom of tenses. Time ramifies, and the present we know is one of many possible presents. Every actual moment could have been other, and it could lead to many possible futures, some more likely than others, but none inevitable, as often appears.

Once we are conscious of the lessons of sideshadowing, we may also wish to apply them to the past. It may well be that we are mistaken about past actualities, and that the sequence leading to us differs from the one we imagine. Even if we are right about which events did happen, we may be mistaken in tracing straight lines between them. If we had a more accurate picture of the past, the significance of present configurations might look quite different. The same facts might really possess other vectors; the product of different pasts, they might be directed to a different set of futures. Later in this chapter I will discuss how Dostoevsky made ample use of *past sideshadowing* to unsettle a given sense of the present. Whether he has past, present, or future in mind, Dostoevsky, with his varied use of sideshadowing, dislodges Ptolemaic temporality.

Sideshadowing relies on a concept of time as a *field of possibilities*. Each moment has a set of possible events (though by no means every conceivable event) that could take place in it. From this field a single event emerges—perhaps by chance, perhaps by choice, perhaps by some combination of both with the inertia of the past, and in any case contingently. To later observers, the other possibilities usually appear invisible or distorted. Thus a field is mistakenly reduced to a point, and, over time, a succession of fields is reduced to a line. Sideshadowing restores the field and thereby recreates the *fullness of time* as it was. Sideshadowing suggests that to understand any moment is to grasp its field of possibilities.

As we saw in chapter 3, an escape in the nick of time is not the same thing in an adventure story as in a realistic novel. In one case, it is probable, in the other almost miraculous. But if we know only of the event and not the generic context, this difference might not be visible. We would miss the field of possibilities that gives the event its meaning. The same is true of events in the real world: their significance depends on the nature of other possibilities, on the whole field of alternatives that could have happened.

Sometimes sideshadowing suggests that even unactualized possibilities may somehow leave their mark on history. When an author advances this suggestion, the importance of understanding the field grows: not only does such an understanding allow us to appreciate the significance of actual events in relation to their alternatives, but the alternatives themselves somehow leave strange messages in the shadows of existence. To switch metaphors for a moment: it is as if one possibility out of many became actual but carried another as a sort of recessive gene, invisible to the eye but capable of affecting future generations of events. In this way, a present somehow grows partly out of an unactualized as well as an actualized past. Time exists not just "phenotypically" but also "genotypically."

However and wherever applied, sideshadowing multiplies stories.

The Extraordinary Number of Facts, If Only They Are Facts

Let us consider some examples from a master of sideshadowing, Dostoevsky. Used extensively in his fiction, the device nevertheless dominates some novels more than others. It is essential to the temporality of *The Possessed*, in which it serves as a counterpoint to the utopianism of the revolutionaries. The linear time of their theories is silently opposed by the novel's open time, as their drive toward completion vies with the work's temporality of continuing and open-ended sequence. Operating both in major events and in the most minor scenes, sideshadowing endows the novel with a sense of the unexpected and the mysterious. *Other possibilities* threaten to erupt at any moment and cast their shadow over everything that actually happens.

More often than not, Dostoevsky's chronicler (a resident of the town) tells us what might have happened or what could have happened. Moreover, the "actions" he does describe are frequently checked impulses, which might or might not indicate a possibility contemplated but not actualized. Such actualities are themselves aborted possibilities, and they evoke the middle realm of things that could have happened. Remembered by the character who "performs" them, and perceived by witnesses, these possibilities acquire a substantiality of their own. *The Possessed* is thick with events that might have happened.

At about the midpoint of the novel, several characters, in order to relieve their boredom, take a trip to the mad "prophet" Semyon Yakovlevich. Having completed a lengthy description of the journey and of the visit itself, the chronicler unexpectedly announces that none of these events is important. "At this point, however, there took place, I am told, an extremely enigmatic incident, and I must own, it was chiefly on account of it that I have described this expedition so minutely" (P, 341), he announces. Here, as elsewhere, the chronicler has evidently given us "too many facts," including all sorts of apparently "irrelevant" details about the expedition. We recognize their presence as characteristic of Dostoevskian narration. Too many facts, presented with no clear explanation and an air of mystery, lead us to construct or intimate many possible stories. What is irrelevant to one account, after all, may be central to another, and the reader, like many characters in the novel, seeks to reconstruct many stories from each one.

Stories also multiply if the facts may not be facts at all or if other "facts" lie behind the ostensible ones, with ever-receding layers of possibility and orders of suspicion. Although the chronicler has himself witnessed a great deal, has collected firsthand accounts, and has apparently spoken with almost everyone about almost everything, he seems, for all his research, to be unable to decide on a single version of events. Instead, he typically reports a range of rumors, doubts his own best sources, and obsessively offers alternative possibilities. "Some say," "others affirm," "it is absurd to suppose," "the papers were surely mistaken to say," "now everyone at the club believed with the utmost certainty," "it is maintained in all seriousness"—these and countless similar expressions give each of his accounts an aura of endless alternatives and an air of unresolvable enigma. That is surely true of the "extremely enigmatic" incident—if incident it was—at Semyon Yakovlevich's.

It appears that as everyone was leaving, Stavrogin and Liza Nikolaevna, whose relations everyone regarded as profoundly mysterious, jostled against each other in the doorway. Or, at least, "I am told" they did, says the chronicler:

> I fancied they both stood still for an instant, and looked, as it were, strangely at one another, but I may not have seen rightly in the crowd. It is asserted, on the contrary, and quite seriously, that Liza, glancing at Nikolai Vsevolodovich [Stavrogin], quickly raised her hand to the level of his face, and would certainly have struck him if he had not drawn back in time. Perhaps she was displeased with the expression of his face, or the way he smiled,

particularly just after such an episode with Mavriky Nikolaevich. I must admit I saw nothing myself, but all the others declared they had, though they certainly could not all have seen it in such a crush, though perhaps some may have. But I did not believe it at the time. I remember, however, that Nikolai Vsevolodovich was rather pale all the way home. (P, 341)

Readers will identify this rhetoric as quintessentially Dostoevskian. "Though . . . though . . . however"; "I fancied," "perhaps," "it is asserted quite seriously": with qualification piled on qualification, tentative judgments no sooner made than withdrawn and perhaps ambiguously reasserted, the narrator claims not to be sure what he himself has witnessed. Reports of others are (probably) even more unreliable and apparently contradictory, though not necessarily groundless. Frivolous people with a taste for scandal seriously say things that differ from what the narrator himself has seen, although, of course, he may have missed such a vague event and does not trust his own eyes "in such a crush." He concludes by saying he did not believe in the reported event—does he accept it now?—and then giving evidence that it might just be true anyway. Moreover, the action in question was checked before it happened, and so one has in any case to distinguish between an unrealized possibility and nothing at all.

Something may or may not have happened, and if it did, it may have been one thing or another. Liza and Stavrogin may have simply stared strangely at each other or, "on the contrary," she may have intended to slap him. If that was her purpose, it may have had various motivations, including, presumably, others not mentioned here at all.

What we are given here is not one but *many possible stories*. The real point is that whatever did happen, any of these incidents could have happened. What is important is the field of possibilities, not the one actualized. By depriving any version of undeniable actuality, Dostoevsky reveals the field itself. The sideshadows crowd out the actual event. Indeed, nothing may have happened, in which case the sideshadows themselves are all there is.

We see here one of the reasons that Dostoevsky uses a chronicler to tell the story. Conscientious but often uncertain, the narrator frequently presents various accounts: Dostoevsky means for him to be unsure. In the notebooks for the novel, Dostoevsky makes this function explicit: "N.B. Whenever the meetings of the conspirators are mentioned, the Chronicler adds this note: 'It is possible that they had more meetings—of course they did—I don't know, but presumably the actual course of events was this ... ' " (NP, 122). Dostoevsky's chroniclers are often described as stronger on facts than on insight; but it might be more accurate to say that their importance lies not only in what they know but also in what they do not know. They weigh evidence to determine what did happen; and Dostoevsky uses their various versions for a different purpose, to suggest that reality includes what might have happened.[2]

Rumor as Hero

> In those days Rumor took an evil joy
> At filling countrysides with whispers, whispers,
> Gossip of what was done, and never done.
> —VIRGIL, *The Aeneid*

With facts perpetually uncertain, rumors predominate in *The Possessed*. No matter what happens, rumors circulate countless versions. Indeed, rumors serve as one of the prime movers of action in the novel. Stepan Trofimovich fears the various drawing room accounts of why he is being married to Dasha, and Pyotr Stepanovich seeks to maximize the power of his revolutionary organization by conveying exaggerated impressions of its size and power; or is he, on the contrary, seeking to hide the extent of its power by discrediting accurate versions as mere rumor? It is hard to know, and though we, like the townspeople, may suspect one thing or another, the matter is not resolved, which is just the effect at which Pyotr Stepanovich aims. As he explains to Stavrogin, in a sea of rumor truth itself may serve as a dodge because anything is possible and possibilities carry more weight than actualities.

And so everywhere Pyotr Stepanovich goes he drops hints or refutes what no one has yet imagined. He spreads misinformation and preempts information; concocts lies as he insinuates truth; and sows trust while inspiring disbelief. Using a method that eerily echoes the chronicler who describes him, Pyotr Stepanovich relies on providing too many facts:[3] he patters on, digresses, and recounts "irrelevancies," which, taken together, intimate many more stories than he actually tells. His audience believes these stories the more readily because they take pride in having discerned what they think Pyotr Stepanovich has unwarily revealed. As Pyotr Stepanovich explains,

> By the way, I always say a lot, that is, use a great many words and talk very fast, and I never speak well. And why do I use so many words, and why do I never speak well? Because I don't know how to speak. People who can speak well, speak briefly. So that I am stupid, am I not? But as this gift of stupidity is natural to me, why shouldn't I make skillful use of it? And I do make use of it. . . . So I made up my mind finally that it would be best to talk, but to talk stupidly—that is, to talk and talk and talk—to be in a tremendous hurry to explain things, and in the end to get muddled in my own explanations. . . . Do you suppose anybody will suspect you of mysterious designs after that? (P, 223)

As it happens, this very explanation (which I have shortened a good deal) is itself an example of such patter, inasmuch as in this very confession Pyotr Stepanovich is again using truth as a dodge to deceive Stavrogin even as he admits how he goes about doing so. Although Stavrogin is a good deal smarter than the others, he finds it hard to decide what is really going on. Intrigued by intrigue, the townspeople find themselves sorting through countless versions and feeling clever when they arrive at an appealing one, only to see it soon dislodged; the readers of the novel, though they may smile at the townspeople's simplicity, do the same thing. Nothing is ever as it seems, and the novel ends with many mysteries unresolved and the plurality of possibilities unreduced to singularity. *The Possessed* offers a haze of stories about a haze of stories.

It might almost be said that rumor is the main character of *The Possessed*. Before Pyotr Stepanovich arrives, Liputin serves as chief rumormonger, but as the book progresses it becomes apparent that rumors seem to spread on their own, even in situations in which there was no one to spread them. They do so because they reflect and evoke the field of possibilities surrounding all actions and all nonactions. Throughout the novel, what did happen competes uncertainly with what might have.

The cumulative effect of the chronicler's qualified hesitations, the busy verbosity of Liputin or Pyotr Stepanovich, and the frenetic activity of disembodied rumor is to direct attention away from actualities and toward possibilities. Clouds of story hover over the narrative landscape. We are used to thinking of stories as moving from event A to event B to event C, but *The Possessed* proceeds from one indistinct field of possible events to another, no more definite. It moves not from point to point but "from smudge to smudge."[4]

The Workers Rebel, or Do They?

The hopes of the revolutionaries and the fear of the authorities center on the town's factory workers, the "Shpigulin men." On "a fatal morning," the chronicler tells us, some seventy of those workers came to the governor's house and demanded to see him. Who were they? Why did they come? At whose urging? Were the revolutionaries involved? It is clear that the political significance of the novel's key events depends on an answer to these questions because the handful of revolutionaries by themselves would probably be incapable of shaking the state (although even here both Pyotr Stepanovich and the chronicler sometimes suggest otherwise). The chronicler tries to sort out the actions and mentality of the workers, but he instead gives us his usual assemblage of diverse possibilities.

First of all, he asks, who were the seventy or so workers? Were they chosen representatives? "Some people still deny that there was any election of delegates" and confidently assert that the crowd consisted only of those who had been most unfairly treated at the factory. If so, "the general 'mutiny' of the factory workers, about which there was such an uproar later on, had never existed at all" (P, 442). However, "others fiercely maintained that these seventy men were not simply strikers but revolutionists," who had been influenced by the radicals' manifestos (P, 442). The chronicler does not believe this more sinister story, but the more he refutes it, the more credible it seems.

The chronicler stoutly maintains that the workers do not read manifestos, would not understand them if they did, and would in any case regard any call for an uprising as stupid. He repeatedly describes the workers as utterly loyal and as moved only by a real but entirely local injustice. He admits, however, that "Pyotr Stepanovich, Liputin, and perhaps some others—perhaps even Fedka [the dangerous escaped convict] too—had been flitting about among the workpeople talking to them (and there is fairly good evidence of this)" but insists that the would-be instigators could not have approached more than a very few (P, 443). The chronicler immediately concedes that "Fedka was a different matter. . . . Two workmen are now known for a fact to have assisted Fedka in causing the fire in the town" (P, 443), which does indeed sound as if considerable damage was done by influencing the workers, whether directly or indirectly through Fedka.

The chronicler contends that intellectual revolutionaries cannot do much harm, but he also provides just the argument needed to demonstrate the opposite. In turbulent times, he allows, a handful of "advanced" people may indeed have great success because a lot of riffraff is available to serve as raw material:

> Moreover, this riff-raff almost always falls unconsciously under the control of the little group of "advanced people" who do act with a definite aim, and this little group can direct all this rabble as it pleases, if only it does not itself consist of absolute idiots, which, however, is sometimes the case. It is said among us now that it is all over, that Pyotr Stepanovich was directed by the *Internationale,* and Yulia Mikhailovna [the governor's wife] by Pyotr Stepanovich, while she controlled, under his rule, a rabble of all sorts. (P, 470)

In short, it is possible that there was no workers' revolt and that the revolutionaries had almost no effect. But it is also possible that they successfully produced a violent confrontation, burned down the better part of the town, and were able not only to infiltrate the factory but also to direct the government, through the governor's wife. The revolutionaries may therefore be an essentially harmless, if ruthless, group, but they may equally well represent a genuine threat to the state; and there are countless possibilities between these two extremes. *The*

Possessed never settles on a single set of events or interpretation but invites us to contemplate this range of political possibilities.

At first the head of the police responds to the assembled workers, and then, when he arrives, the governor takes over. In each case, the chronicler again reports not what did happen but the countless things said to have happened. As for the police chief, "it was not true that he galloped to the spot with three horses at full speed, and began hitting out right and left before he alighted from his carriage," although it is true that he had behaved with even less restraint on other occasions (P, 444). "There is a still more absurd story that soldiers were brought up with bayonets, and that a telegram was sent for artillery and Cossacks; those are legends which are not believed now even by those who invented them. It's an absurd story, too" that people were drenched by water from the fire brigade (P, 444). In the chronicler's opinion, this last account, which was repeated in the Moscow and Petersburg papers, evidently derived from the fact that the police chief shouted that "he wouldn't let one of them come dry out of the water" (P, 444). If the chronicler is right, then language itself seems to generate stories, as rumor progresses by an energy of its own. Whatever did happen, any of these events might well have happened.

Still more confusing was the behavior of the governor, who was later declared mad. Once someone is known to be mad, of course, it is possible to believe he did almost anything. "From the facts I have learned and those I have conjectured," the chronicler characteristically begins his account, "it's an absolute fabrication that everyone was flogged; at most two or three were" (P, 452). "It's a nonsensical story, too, that a poor but respectable lady was caught as she passed by and promptly thrashed," even though this story, as well, was reprinted in the Moscow and Petersburg papers and even though the chronicler himself not only believed in the story but also contributed to a subscription for the poor lady, who, it turned out later, did not even exist (P, 452). In short, it is virtually impossible to tell what did or did not happen, and no version makes sense of everything. Whatever possibility was actualized this time, a different one could easily take place on a similar occasion. The chronicler's uncertainty in ascertaining facts becomes the author's way of evoking the field of possibilities present in chaotic or politically charged situations.

Twice *Possessed*

The Possessed interweaves two plots, the story of Pyotr Stepanovich's conspiracy and the story of Stavrogin's search for meaning. Pyotr Stepanovich manufactures secrets, and Stavrogin conceals mysteries behind the "mask" of his face. In each story, an immense number of contradictory possibilities emerge. Sometimes it eventually becomes clear what happened, but only after a long interval of uncertainty in which the reader has become accustomed to contemplating fields rather than points. Other mysteries are never resolved, and contradictory explanations remain possible. For example, we never learn who killed Fedka. Liputin is struck by the fact that shortly after an angry Pyotr Stepanovich predicts Fedka's death, the escaped convict is indeed found murdered, and the reader no doubt shares Liputin's suspicions. And yet it is apparently determined that someone with no connection to Pyotr Stepanovich committed the crime. Or was that determination itself simply the result of deceit? Liputin never learns, and neither do we.[5]

Such multiplicity unreduced to singularity pertains not only to occasional incidents but also to the novel's central events. Several people suggest that Pyotr Stepanovich may in fact be a police agent, either an infiltrator or a provocateur. Of course, such suspicions are bound to arise in any case. Nevertheless, they cannot be easily dismissed. How else did Pyotr Stepanovich manage to return from his exile abroad, move about freely, and even obtain recommendations from influential officials in Petersburg? At the end of the novel, he receives secret information from Petersburg that allows him to avoid arrest, and, un-like his associates, he escapes. The other revolutionaries suspect him, and even Stavrogin puts the question directly:

"And listen, Verkhovensky [Pyotr Stepanovich], you are not one of the higher police, are you?"

"Anyone who has a question like that in his mind doesn't utter it."

"I understand, but we are by ourselves."

"No, so far I am not one of the higher police." (P, 394)

"So far" [pokamest]—this is a denial that almost cancels itself. Does it mean that Pyotr Stepanovich is trying to prove himself so as to join the higher police? He may be working for the authorities even if not for the "higher" police. Is he perhaps lying altogether, as any police agent would? And what if he is both a genuine revolutionary and a police spy at the same time, a sort of double agent, working ultimately—for whom? Possibilities multiply. If Dostoevsky had not meant to suggest them, there would have been no need to insist so frequently and so explicitly that Pyotr Stepanovich may be the opposite of what he seems.[6]

As it is usually read, *The Possessed* depends on Pyotr Stepanovich being, like his real-life model Nechaev, a genuine revolutionary. If he is an agent of the secret police, then the whole significance of the events changes. *The Possessed* then becomes a different novel, a sort of sideshadow of itself.

To be sure, the most likely interpretation is that Pyotr Stepanovich is not a police agent but cultivates the rumor that he is in order to increase his power with the authorities, just as he probably invents his connections with the Internationale to magnify his power with the revolutionaries. And yet Dostoevsky allows these rumors to go unrefuted, draws attention to them, and leaves mysteries easily explained by them to go unresolved. As particular incidents in the novel seem haunted by shadows of contradictory alternatives, so does the novel as a whole.

This doubling of the novel takes place in yet another way. As usually read, *The Possessed* develops an allegory of generations; like *The Raw Youth* and *Karamazov*, it is a reworking of Turgenev's *Fathers and Sons*. The liberal father, Stepan Trofimovich, shirks traditional family responsibilities and so begets the radical son, Pyotr Stepanovich, who horrifies and helps to destroy him. Symbolically, radicalism is the parricide of liberals, who (the novel suggests) perhaps deserve it. It might well be said that the satire of *The Possessed* is directed less at the sons than at the fathers and that its primary target is what the narrator disdainfully calls "the higher liberalism," which is a matter of fashionable beliefs and words. That is presumably why the novel both begins and ends with Stepan Trofimovich.

And yet, despite the novel's reliance on this theme, Dostoevsky cannot resist suggesting that Pyotr Stepanovich might not be Stepan Trofimovich's son at all! Angered by his son's disrespectful treatment of him, Stepan Trofimovich asks, "Tell me, you monster, are you my son or not?" This rhetorical question provokes an unexpected answer:

> "You know that best. To be sure all fathers are disposed to be blind in such cases."
> "Silence! Silence!" cried Stepan Trofimovich, shaking all over.
> "You see you're screaming and swearing at me as you did last Thursday. You tried to lift your stick against me, but you know, I found that document. I was rummaging all the evening in my trunk from curiosity. It's true there's nothing definite, you can take that comfort. It's only a letter of my mother's to that Pole. But to judge from its character ..."
> "Another word and I'll box your ears." (P, 312)

As Michael Bernstein argues, a similar passage in *The Brothers Karamazov* suggests that Smerdyakov, the murderer of Fyodor Pavlovich Karamazov, may not be the old man's illegitimate son after all: some rumors attribute the rape of Smerdyakov's mother to the escaped convict Karp. And yet *Karamazov*, even more than *The Possessed*, is structured around parricide and the conflict of generations. Critics rarely mention the passages from either novel that cast doubt on the paternity of the vicious son. For what sense would the stories make if Karp or the Pole were the fathers? And yet Dostoevsky raises these disconcerting and unrefuted possibilities. In each novel, he has it both ways. He relies on one lineage to construct his plot and introduce major themes, but he also allows, if just barely, for a second lineage, which would radically change the meaning of the novel as a whole. A sideshadow is cast on each work, which thereby becomes, in yet another way, its own double.

As it happens, Dostoevsky apparently used a version of this doubling technique in an earlier book. When he wrote *The House of the Dead*, Dostoevsky, as his readers well knew, had recently completed a sentence in Siberia, part of which was spent in a prison camp. Thus this novel necessarily acquired a ghostly second presence as a factual memoir. And in fact, the work explicitly contains contradictory accounts of its status. It is first offered as an extract from the reminiscences of a fictional character, Goryanchikov, who has been sent to Siberia for murdering his wife. But in the course of the story the narrator is also described as a political prisoner, which was Dostoevsky's, but not Goryanchikov's status.[7] So glaring is this contradiction that it seems inconceivable to attribute it to mere carelessness.[8]

Rather, *The House of the Dead* seems to play deliberately on its double status. Depending on how we take it, the parts fit into different wholes, and whichever interpretation we prefer, some things do not fit. The differences are fundamental. If we interpret the book as Goryanchikov's memoirs, we will focus on the editor's opening account of Goryanchikov's life after prison, a life of tortured isolation and perhaps insanity. The despair of that later life necessarily infects the whole narrative and seems to deprive it of any sense of redemption. But if we read the story as Dostoevsky's memoirs, attention focuses instead on the book's optimistic conclusion, with its symbolic promise of resurrection. Critics have attempted to resolve the difference by explaining one interpretation as contained within the other, but I think there is a real doubling. *The House of the Dead* seems to *resonate* between two narratives subsisting within the same covers. Each sideshadows the other. The reader is given a choice, as we all are, between the suffering that deforms and the suffering that ennobles.

Gaps in the Text

Curiously enough, the textual history of *The Possessed* seems to continue its practice of sideshadowing. As originally published, the novel omits a chapter, "At Tikhon's," which the publisher evidently found too salacious for public consumption. (It tells the story of Stavrogin's visit to a monastery, where he gives the monk Tikhon a printed confession describing his seduction of a young girl.) And yet the original readers did not notice the gap, which would seem to indicate that the book works as a coherent whole either with or without it. Evidently, there are so many unsolved mysteries in the novel that the absence of one revelation was not apparent; and even with the Tikhon chapter included, much remains unexplained. From internal evidence, there is no reason that there could not be yet another omitted revelation.

The missing chapter was not discovered until after the fall of the tsarist regime, and subsequent editions have made different decisions with regard to it. The Modern Library version—for many years the most widely used American edition—includes "At Tikhon's" in an appendix, while indicating where it was originally designed to be placed. This sensible solution in effect doubles the novel, for we may read it either as originally written or as originally published. Or we may read it both ways and speculate about the difference.[9] The thirty-volume Soviet edition of Dostoevsky's complete works chooses a similar solution. *The Possessed* has become two books.[10]

Still more curiously, although Dostoevsky obviously did not know what would happen to his novel, the Tikhon chapter almost seems to anticipate this doubling. For it, too, sideshadows and doubles itself. Stavrogin visits Tikhon because he is haunted by a "derisive and rational" demon, who is apparently the manifestation of the "other self" living within him. Evidently, there are two Stavrogins, which is presumably why, throughout the novel, he seems capable of suddenly altering his behavior in strange ways and has often raised suspicions that he is mad. Stavrogin keeps trying to escape his derisive demon and to become a single, integral person. Thus he has adopted a series of ideologies in a quest for commitment and, "seeking a burden," married the mad cripple Marya Timofeevna: but she above all recognizes that he is an imposter. Trying to be whole, he insistently denies that he is mad, and the townspeople repeatedly alternate between confident assertions of his sanity and of his insanity. When Stavrogin at last hangs himself, he does everything to banish all doubt about his mental state. The cord had evidently "been chosen and prepared beforehand," and he left behind an unused nail—"evidently an extra one in case of need" (P, 688). The novel ends, "Everything proved that there had been premeditation and consciousness up to the last moment. At the inquest our doctors absolutely and emphatically rejected all idea of insanity" (P, 688). But the overemphatic denials, the history of misdiagnoses, and our knowledge of Stavrogin easily leave open the possibility that Stavrogin himself sought to create this verdict. It remains unclear whether he is mad, sane, something in between, or both in turn.

Thus Stavrogin's every action invites a range of inconsistent interpretations and derives from various conceivable histories and motivations. In the Tikhon chapter, the chronicler suspects that the printed confession Stavrogin gives the monk to read could be "the work of the devil who had taken possession of this gentleman" (P, 701). Possession is of course the controlling metaphor for the novel as a whole, and so we see that Stavrogin, too, is a sort of double agent. The link with the novel's plot about the conspirators is also made clear by the confession's appearance: printed abroad, it looks at first glance like a revolutionary pamphlet. Everywhere we encounter disguise and imposture. Marya Timofeevna identifies Stavrogin with one pretender to the throne, and Pyotr Stepanovich plans to turn him into another.

The Tikhon chapter exists in more than one version, and the most interesting one seems to cultivate doubling at every possible point. Other stories lurk at every turn. When Stavrogin arrives at the monastery, he is surprised to find out that he is recognized and assumes it is because he resembles his mother. But Tikhon reminds Stavrogin that he visited the monastery four years before, an incident that—if it really happened—Stavrogin does not remember and knows that he could not have forgotten. The discrepancy between the two histories is never resolved.

In introducing the document, the chronicler, apparently pursuing his suspicion that its author was the other, demonic Stavrogin, raises a number of doubts about it:

> And, who knows, perhaps all that, to wit, those sheets intended for publication, are nothing else but another way of nipping the governor's ear [one of Stavrogin's practical jokes]. Why this occurs to me now, after so much has been explained already, I cannot understand. But I'm not bringing forth any proofs, nor do I assert at all that it is a false document, that it is a completely invented and fabricated thing. Most likely, the truth must be sought somewhere in the middle. (P, 702; PSS 12:108)

The document may be genuine and truthful; but it may also be a tissue of lies, concocted as a grotesque practical joke. Most critics have assumed that the confession is false in the sense that it is not based on a true desire for repentance, as the term *confession* suggests, but that it nonetheless reports actual events. That is indeed the most likely possibility, but, once again, Dostoevsky does not allow the most plausible interpretation to be the only possible one. The truth perhaps lies somewhere in the middle realm.

As if to insist on the alternative reading, Dostoevsky creates (in this version of the chapter) a strange gap. At the crucial point in the story, when the seduction appears imminent, Stavrogin withholds information. When Tikhon asks for page two, Stavrogin instead gives him page three. "But there is a gap here," Tikhon remarks, and Stavrogin answers with an awkward smile: "The second sheet is under censorship for the present" (P, 706; PSS 12:110). "Well, sheet two or three—it's all the same now," Tikhon comments (P, 706; PSS 12:110). But Stavrogin takes offense at the assumption that the seduction necessarily happened.

> "What do you mean—all the same? Why?" Stavrogin made a sudden eager movement toward Tikhon. "Not at all. Ah, in your monkish way you are ready to suspect the worst. A monk would be the best criminal prosecutor!"
> Tikhon watched him narrowly in silence.
> "Calm down. It's not my fault if the little girl was foolish and misunderstood me ... Nothing happened. Nothing."
> "Well, God be praised," Tikhon crossed himself.
> "It would take too long to explain ... it was ... simply a psychological misunderstanding ..." (P, 706; PSS 12:110–11; note the many ellipses in original).

The logic of the novel, when it includes this chapter, seems to depend on the reality of the seduction. Why else would Stavrogin experience the guilt and hallucinations he describes? There would seem to be no reason for Dostoevsky to create this gap and this denial, and in another version of the chapter there is no missing second sheet.[11] And yet, almost compulsively, Dostoevsky inserts an apparently unnecessary second possibility contradicting the first, much as he allows the suspicion that Pyotr Stepanovich is not Stepan Trofimovich's son. We discern a pattern of sideshadowing: even the most crucial and seemingly inevitable events, demanded by the logic of the novel, come accompanied by the possibility that they did not happen.[12]

In general, for every important event in the novel (and for many unimportant ones) Dostoevsky gives us first a probable version, then one or more less probable but still believable alternatives, and at last, in some cases, an additional, extremely remote possibility, often described as "utter nonsense" as soon as it is mentioned. Whenever he can, he moves us from the domain of actuality to the middle realm of real possibilities. As a result, other novels hover in the wings and wait to seize control of the text, much as Pyotr Stepanovich's conspirators proclaim the sowing of doubt as a method for seizing political power. In this way, *The Possessed* is itself conspiratorial. Because the Tikhon chapter both is and is not part of the novel, its history of suppression and rediscovery seems eerily to match the novel's own methods.

The Past as "An Indistinct Abstraction"

> About the Idiot there are only stories.
> —DOSTOEVSKY, notebooks to *The Idiot*

I had thought, much and often, of my Dora's shadowing out to me what might have happened, in those years that were destined not to be. I had considered how the things that never happen, are often as much realities to us, in their effects, as those that are accomplished.
—DAVID COPPERFIELD [13]

Pyotr Stepanovich continually multiplies possibilities for the present. By contrast, Stavrogin, who does very little in the present, serves to pluralize the past. "Pyotr Stepanovich is Busy" (the title of a chapter) but Stavrogin *was* busy. He is the novel's primary vehicle for *past* sideshadowing. Anything might have happened to him, all possible relations with other characters might have taken place somewhere and sometime, and any of those connections might suddenly surface. Each possible past that might have been changes the very nature of the present by giving each current moment a new direction and a new significance. It is as if there were an infinite fund of possible prior events—primarily in Switzerland, where many characters met and about which countless rumors circulate—and so it is as if we saw the past continually shifting before our eyes.

Everyone in the novel tries to find out not only what is happening but also what happened, and suddenly, at the most unexpected moment, an incident will take place that makes sense only if the past contains something no one has suspected. When Shatov gives Stavrogin a blow, one wants to know why he did so and what suddenly prompted the reckless act. And why did Stavrogin restrain himself from killing Shatov on the spot? The narrator describes Stavrogin's possible reactions and his efforts at restraint for two pages—and so Stavrogin's "response" (another checked impulse) becomes one of the most remarkable nonactions in all of Dostoevsky. Surely, we think, something in the past explains what happened and what did not happen, and we are given many possibilities, including Stavrogin's liaison with Shatov's wife and his treatment of Shatov's sister, but these possibilities—even if all are actual events—do not seem sufficient explanation for Shatov's blow and Stavrogin's uncharacteristic restraint. By the time Shatov does explain, the other possibilities have become well fixed in our thoughts.

For that matter, nobody knows why Stavrogin has returned to the town at all, and his arrival is a surprise even though many reasons for it come to mind. In his notebooks, Dostoevsky records both the possible reasons and their inadequacy. Then he comments, "His mother (and several other persons) are anxious to find the principal reason for his return. N.B. There is no principal reason, just *an indistinct abstraction*" (NP, 196; italics in original). We are used to looking for causes and reasons, but there may be none in the usual sense of a chain of actual events: there may instead be nothing more than a thickening haze of possibilities.[14]

The novel contains numerous mysterious scenes evoking questions about Stavrogin's life before the novel. Each hints at strange and unknown pasts modifying the present we thought we knew. In *The Possessed,* past sideshadowing makes time seem to ramify backward as well as forward.

Pseudo-Foreshadowing

To create sideshadowing, Dostoevsky also uses a device that at first glance seems to preclude it. At times he appears to employ a form of foreshadowing, which, one might suppose, allows the future to dictate possibilities to the present and therefore to close down time. On closer inspection, however, these passages exhibit what might be called pseudo-foreshadowing: though using the tropes of foreshadowing, they produce the opposite effect.

Readers of Dostoevsky are aware that his narrators often allude to a future catastrophe, which is, indeed, what has motivated them to tell the story in the first place. *The Possessed* begins, "In undertaking to describe the recent and strange incidents in our town, till lately wrapped in uneventful obscurity, I find myself forced in absence of literary skill to begin my story rather far back, that is to say, with certain biographical details concerning that talented and highly-esteemed gentleman, Stepan Trofimovich Verkhovensky" (P, 3). We have here an allusion to the future, which will contain "strange incidents," but no statement as to what those incidents will be. Something is promised, but we do not know what.

Throughout the novel, the chronicler often begins a sequence of events by saying that they contributed to a later catastrophe, but just what the nature of that catastrophe was—and how it affected the major characters—is left obscure. Although this sort of rhetoric could easily have its place in a novel based on foreshadowing, here it serves a different function.

The first thing to note about pseudo-foreshadowing is that it closes off virtually no options. To be sure, it tells us that there will be some sort of disaster—although a strange event is not necessarily disastrous—but that much is always a given in any Dostoevsky novel. This sort of vague warning has a double effect. First, it alerts the reader to the importance of forthcoming details that have the *potential* for catastrophe. Second, it promises that something otherwise unforeseen and sensational will take place. We focus keenly on possible futures. The result is a sense that *anything may happen*—which is just what Dostoevskian sideshadowing creates. Whereas foreshadowing severely limits options, pseudo-foreshadowing does the reverse. Instead of anticipating some specific outcome or course of events, readers come to expect the radically unexpected.

Dostoevsky's notebooks make clear that he used this device quite consciously even when he had not settled precisely on what would follow and when foreshadowing therefore could not have been his aim. Long before he had settled on a specific plot, for instance, he included the following plan for the opening passage just cited:

> N.B. ... Our recent fires and other strange developments in our, i.e. S—a province notwithstanding, I shall begin my narrative with T. N. Granovsky [the model for Stepan Trofimovich, who at this point of composition had not yet acquired that name]. . . . Timofei Nikolaevich [Granovsky] did not understand nihilism and used to argue about it with Shatov. Yet these are digressions, of which many are needed; also, introduce as many particular events as required . . . then all of a sudden bring in a truly promising plot. Finish it with some major event and a lot of noise. (NP, 177)

"Some major event," "a truly promising plot": apparently, virtually any major event or dramatic plot would accord with the initial vague prediction. And virtually no possibilities for sensational events are precluded.

At the beginning of *The Idiot*, another remarkable example of pseudo-foreshadowing occurs:

> In one of the third-class carriages, two passengers had, from early dawn, been sitting facing one another by the window. Both were young men, not very well dressed, and travelling with little luggage; both were of rather striking appearance, and both showed a desire to enter into conversation. If they had both known what was remarkable in one another at that moment, they would have been surprised at the chance which had so strangely brought them opposite one another in a third-class carriage of the Warsaw train. (I, 3)

Everything about this first meeting of Myshkin and Rogozhin (as the two turn out to be) suggests their future involvement in sensational events. The sequence of "both" clauses intimates a vague parallel between their life stories, and the comment that "if they had . . . known what was remarkable" in each other they "would have been surprised" at the strange chance bringing them together seems to intimate the hand of destiny or, at least, a mysterious causal chain. For critics who know the whole novel and who are rereading this passage, the friends' fatal rivalry over Nastasya Filippovna seems already contained here. Both Rogozhin's attempt on Myshkin's life and the novel's tragic end seem present at the beginning, like a future dictating subsequent events.[15]

On the other hand, this prediction is so vague that it does not specify what or how important the connection between the two may turn out to be. Whatever happened subsequently might look in retrospect as if it had been intimated here. In principle, this passage could be an instance either of foreshadowing or of pseudo-foreshadowing, which is often the case. First readers experience a vague prediction that makes them attentive to potentials, rereaders see future actualities already present. Which interpretation shall we choose?

Despite a reluctance to rely on external evidence unavailable to most readers as a way of solving problems of this sort, I would note that, if we have in mind Dostoevsky's intention when he wrote and when he published this passage, the answer is clear. As Joseph Frank observed a long time ago,

> The first part of *The Idiot* was conceived and written as a self contained unity, which may perhaps best be read as an independent novella. After this point, however, it is clear from Dostoevsky's notebooks and letters that he had no satisfactory idea of how to continue the action. This uncertainty persists all through the middle sections of the book (Parts II and III), where Dostoevsky is obviously writing from scene to scene with only the loosest thread of any central narrative line.[16]

The notebooks to *The Idiot* reveal conclusively that even after Dostoevsky had published the first part, he had little idea of how to continue. To mention just a few important questions of plot, he did not know whether Nastasya Filippovna would marry Rogozhin or Myshkin; whether she would kill herself, be killed, or die naturally; or whether Rogozhin would be damned or saved.[17] In terms of the story, it would be hard to imagine much greater openness. After finishing part I, Dostoevsky was about as uncertain of future events as his readers. In fact, even toward the end of his notes for part III (written between August and October 1868), Dostoevsky was still considering whether to marry Myshkin to Aglaia. The magnificent ending to the novel—surely one of the most memorable in Russian literature—does not appear in his notebooks until October 4. We sense the thrill of discovery when it occurs to him: "2nd half of the 4th Part. N. F. is engaged to the Prince. . . . Goes to Rogozhin in despair. (He murders.) Summons the Prince. Rogozhin and the Prince beside the corpse. Finale. *Not bad.*"

Thus David Bethea correctly comments that to read later events into Myshkin's first meeting with Rogozhin would be "another instance of literally 'getting ahead of ourselves' where the history of the text does not warrant it."[18] Dostoevsky wrote so that many continuations could grow out of this scene and so that we would be alert to possibilities. His description does not close down time, as foreshadowing does, but alerts the reader to its openness while allowing the author to go in many directions.

If nothing significant had grown out of Rogozhin's and Myshkin's first meeting, what significance would rereaders attribute to this scene? Probably none, which means that the assumption of foreshadowing can almost always be confirmed but can rarely be disconfirmed. Instances in which foreshadowing could have been present but is not are usually not noticed. Nevertheless, when such negative examples are pointed out, they may cast doubt on the ascription of foreshadowing (rather than pseudo-foreshadowing) to scenes like the one in the Warsaw train.

As it happens, part I of *The Idiot* contains much stronger signs of a future conflict between Myshkin and Ganya—constant misunderstandings, insults, vague threats, and a blow—all of which seem to lay the groundwork for them to be significant enemies. When Ganya ominously (and eponymously) calls Myshkin an idiot, the full weight of the title seems to promise a dramatic clash.[19] But in fact Ganya turns into a minor, though frequently present, character, and nothing significant or "fatal" takes place between him and Myshkin. In part I, Dostoevsky evidently planted the potentials for many future tragedies without limiting himself to specific ones. In the notebooks written after the publication of part I, he reminds himself to do something more with Ganya but never does. If the vague promises about Rogozhin turn out to be justified, those about Ganya do not. Reflecting on both of Myshkin's early conflicts, we may suspect that neither outcome was inevitable. Both are instances of pseudo-foreshadowing, which works along with sideshadowing to suggest a field but not to fix an outcome.

In the epigraph to *The Possessed* drawn from Pushkin's "Demons"[20] the speaker of the poem is lost in a storm that conjures supernatural terror:

> Strike me dead, the track has vanished,
> Well, what now? We've lost our way,
> Demons have bewitched the horses,
> Led us in the wilds astray.
> . . . . . .
>
> What a number! Whither drift they?
> What's the mournful dirge they sing?
> Do they hail a witch's marriage
> Or a goblin's burying?

Something vague and terrible seems to threaten, but it could be almost anything. Possibilities are multiplied. For Dostoevsky's readers, too, attention is riveted on mysterious processes whose capacity to inspire terror is all the greater because they can lead to many possible outcomes.

Karamazov: "Both Versions Were True"

In *The Possessed*, sideshadowing intimates a world of radical instability. Respectable society's presumptions of order are upset by eruptions of unsuspected other stories. In *Karamazov*, Dostoevsky uses sideshadowing for different purposes. It serves to elucidate the complexity of psychological, ethical, and theological issues haunting Dostoevsky's world.

At the beginning of *Karamazov*, the chronicler reports on what might have happened to Adelaida Ivanovna, the first wife of old Fyodor Pavlovich Karamazov, after she ran away to Petersburg with a divinity student. Fyodor Pavlovich receives news that "she had somehow suddenly died somewhere in a garret, according to some stories—from typhus, but according to others—allegedly from starvation."[21] We note the use of numerous hypothetical expressions and vague qualifiers in this sentence. The two versions of Adelaida Ivanovna's death evidently contradict each other, and, of course, neither may be true. If (sudden?) starvation was the cause of her death, we would be led to construct a whole different narrative—about her relations with the divinity student, for instance. And how could a wealthy woman have allowed herself to starve to death? From self-lacerating pride?[22] To enact a romance, as she imagined she was doing when she married Fyodor Pavlovich? Out of spite or from some principle? If she did not die of starvation, then who spread the rumor she had, and why; and why did it gain currency?

As the passage continues, a different sort of doubling of possibilities is described: "Fyodor Pavlovich was drunk when he heard of his wife's death, and it is said that he ran into the street and began shouting with joy, raising his hands to Heaven: 'Lord, now lettest Thou Thy servant depart in peace,' but according to others he wept without restraint like a little child, so much so that, they say, people were sorry for him in spite of the repulsion he inspired" (BK, 6). We again note the frequent use of phrases indicating dubious report. Fyodor Pavlovich's two alleged reactions, each the subject of rumor, differ considerably and would seem to testify to incompatible states of mind and qualities of character. The reader might be inclined to think that one of them, weeping without restraint, might have been an act and therefore not so different from the buffoonish "shouting with joy," but in one of the novel's most memorable psychological asides, the narrator immediately insists that the weeping might in fact have been sincere: "It is quite possible that both versions were true, that he rejoiced at his release, and at the same time wept for her who released him. As a general rule, people, even the wicked, are far more naive and simple-hearted than we suppose. And we ourselves are, too" (BK, 6). In this case, too, it is not important which story is true or what actually happened. What matters most is that either version or both together could have been true. The chronicler allows that even Fyodor Pavlovich's character admits of radical alternatives, not reducible to a single possibility. And the same applies to ourselves. This observation is central to Dostoevskian psychology.

In *Notes from Underground*, the underground man chooses as an example
of human character a friend who "is a compound personality, and therefore
it is somehow difficult to blame him as an individual" (NFU, 20). In *The
Idiot*, Prince Myshkin outlines his theory of "double thoughts": it is common
for people to be guided simultaneously and independently by a noble and an
ignoble motive. A Freudian, or the many two-bit psychologists who populate
Dostoevsky's novels, would be inclined to regard the noble motive as a mere
mask for the ignoble one, but Myshkin explicitly rejects such an interpretation.
Both motives may be perfectly sincere and irreducible to each other. In the
assumption that the two thoughts must somehow be one, Myshkin discerns a
rush to oversimplify, and in the automatic belief that the "real" thought must
be the base one he finds a kind of *reverse sentimentality.*[23]

In *Karamazov*, Dmitri describes a similar kind of double thinking as he
recognizes, in himself and in others, a longing for Sodom at the same time
that he sincerely worships the Madonna. Such psychological states have no predetermined outcome: it is entirely possible that Dmitri either will or will not
kill his father. And even Fyodor Pavlovich, who explicitly identifies himself as
the incarnation of all evil, has a decent side of which he himself is unaware.
Psychology in Dostoevsky allows us to comprehend human freedom, not to
eliminate it. For every personality and almost every motive has its sideshadow.

Karamazov: Responsibility and the Middle Realm

In one usually overlooked passage, Dostoevsky's chronicler indicates that
the repulsive Smerdyakov, who eventually murders old Karamazov, arranges
for one of his brothers to be accused of the murder, and drives another to go
mad from guilt, might well have done something quite different. Smerdyakov,
the narrator allows, might be a "contemplator," something like the peasant
depicted in Kramskoy's painting *Contemplation:*

> He stands, as it were, lost in thought. Yet he is not thinking; he is "contem-
> plating." If any one touched him he would start and look at one as though
> awakening and bewildered. . . . if he were asked what he had been think-
> ing about, he would remember nothing. Yet probably he has hidden within
> himself, the impression which had dominated him during the period of con-
> templation. Those impressions are dear to him and no doubt he hoards them
> imperceptibly, and even unconsciously. . . . He may suddenly, after hoard-
> ing impressions for many years, abandon everything and go off to Jerusalem
> on a pilgrimage for his soul's salvation, or perhaps he will suddenly set fire
> to his native village, and perhaps do both. There are a good many "contem-

platives" among the peasantry. Well, Smerdyakov was most likely one of them, and he most likely was greedily hoarding up his impressions, hardly knowing why. (BK, 150)[24]

Save his soul, burn his village, or both: this common type is eminently capable of all three, and whichever one he chooses, the others were no less possible. Could Smerdyakov, then, have been capable of saintly sacrifice as well as treacherous murder—of being more like his mother than his father? That would indeed have made a different story. And what is the weight of the repeated qualification "most likely" (*naverno*) in the last sentence? For the contemplative, many things are possible, and it is possible that Smerdyakov either is or is not a contemplative.

Sideshadowing in *Karamazov* serves in part as a weapon against psychological determinism of all sorts, whether the neurological explanations favored by Rakitin (belief is caused by the vibrating of little neural tails in the brain) or the psychological reductions favored by the experts at Dmitri's trial. When the impoverished Captain Snegiryov refuses the two hundred rubles brought by Alyosha, Alyosha recognizes that the humiliated former officer might just as likely have accepted the money. Until the decision was made, Alyosha realizes, either outcome was possible: "I assure you," he tells Lise, "up to the last minute, he did not know that he was going to trample on the notes" (BK, 255). Before the actual decision (and perhaps during the trampling itself), Snegiryov was always of two minds. Whenever he inclined toward one choice, the other was there, too, as a sort of "presentiment" (BK, 256), as a lurking sideshadow of the other choice. For choice in *Karamazov* is real and palpable—that is one of the novel's fundamental lessons—and alternatives always sideshadow every choice and every motive.[25]

Of course, doubling of characters itself serves as a fundamental principle of plot construction in *Karamazov*.[26] Indeed, there is hardly a Dostoevsky novel in which major characters do not possess a series of doubles, ranging from highly delineated main characters to degraded caricatures, each of whom acts out possible lives for a doubled and redoubled hero. In *Crime and Punishment*, Svidrigailov is the Raskolnikov who might have killed himself, Luzhin the Raskolnikov who wants "all his fortune at once," and Lebeziatnikov the paltry theorist who imagines that he is superior to ordinary people. *The Possessed* seems overpopulated with Stavrogin's many doubles, to the point where he seems trapped in a hall of mirrors and bound by a plot that his alternative selves have made—an amazing variation on the myth of Narcissus, perhaps. In *Karamazov*, Rakitin and Kolya double Ivan, who is eventually trapped by the double for whom he has utter contempt, Smerdyakov; and when Ivan goes mad, the devil, whom he recognizes as yet another double, projects endless lives and incidents that all exhibit the same banality, as if, for all the variety in the world, nothing could make anything better out of Ivan. The devil hints that alternatives may exist but do not matter.

The central moral lesson of the novel turns on Ivan's theory that, even if morality does exist and even if all is not permitted, right and wrong still pertain only to actual events and not to merely possible ones. Or as Ivan observes, he controls his actions but "in my wishes I reserve myself full latitude" (BK, 170). Alyosha instinctively recognizes this doctrine as the opposite of Christ's in the sermon on the mount: "You have heard that our forefathers were told, 'Do not commit murder. . . .' But what I tell you is this: Anyone who nurses anger against his brother must be brought to judgment" (New English Bible: Matthew 5:21–22).

Dostoevsky offers a sort of realistic proof of Christ's doctrine by showing that evil derives primarily not from actions but from wishes, for *wishes shape the fields of possibility.* Crime happens because our wishes create those possibilities, one of which is bound to be realized. To focus only on the proximate cause of a crime would be to overlook the fact that it might just as well have come about in a different way, and probably would have, because the field of possibilities is rife with criminality. And that is because we all harbor criminal wishes. We must change the middle realm, the realm of possibilities, if we are to change actuality. Therefore we must try to change everyone's, not just the criminal's, habits of thought if we are truly to prevent evil. As Zosima explains, everyone contributes to evil, and so all bear responsibility.

The idea that criminality results from the field of possibilities allows Dostoevsky an astonishing variation on the detective story plot. In the typical detective story, an array of false clues leads to a labyrinth of possible explanations, and the detective must find the unique correct account. Many stories compete, but only one is destined to win. The moral lesson of *Karamazov,* however, makes the very search for "whodunit" a false lead. Responsibility pertains not only to Smerdyakov, who actually committed the murder, but also to Dmitri, who might easily have done so, and to Ivan, whose wish facilitated the crime; beyond that, it pertains to the many townspeople who, though they profess to be horrified by the parricide, take a voyeuristic interest in it. All create the atmosphere, the field, that makes murder possible. To read *Karamazov* as a detective story or as a tale about how the wrong man was tried for a crime would be entirely to misread it by eliminating its sideshadows. And what is true of this crime is true of crime in general, the novel suggests: moral thinking must attend not just to the linear sequence but also to the evolving concatenation of wishes, desires, and probabilities. One is chosen, but many are called.

Ivan never quite learns this lesson about responsibility and the middle realm. He persists in thinking with only two categories. If Dmitri killed father then

I am innocent, he reasons, but if Smerdyakov killed him then I too am the murderer. Both of these conclusions are wrong. Even if Dmitri were the killer, Ivan would still have helped create a murderous scheme. It is the same scheme regardless of who legally committed the crime. On the other hand, although Ivan surely is to blame, he is not to blame in the same way or to the same degree as Smerdyakov. A person is responsible for evil wishes, but even if those wishes are somehow realized they are still not morally equivalent to actions.[27] That, I take it, is the logic behind Alyosha's puzzling statement to Ivan that it was "Not You, Not You!" (chapter title, BK, 727) who murdered father. "You have accused yourself . . . But you didn't do it: you are mistaken: you are not the murderer. Do you hear? It was not you! God has sent me to tell you so" (BK, 732). Unless one acknowledges the middle realm, this statement makes nonsense of the novel because the whole burden of the plot has been that Ivan is not innocent. What, then, can Alyosha's declaration mean? It means, I think, that Ivan is responsible, but his responsibility pertains not to the realm of actuality, as his binary logic suggests, but to the middle realm of possibility.

Kairova Time and Processual Intentionality

Karamazov reworked a number of journalistic accounts of crime that Dostoevsky had written for his one-man periodical, *A Writer's Diary*. In these articles, Dostoevsky reported on real crimes and trials, which he used in part as a vehicle to upset received notions of intentionality. He was particularly concerned with discrediting what he called "linear" accounts, in which an ironclad chain of events leads (in principle) directly from intention to action. Dostoevsky objected that in such accounts intention is understood simplistically because it is closed off, made immune to the effects of changing circumstances, and, above all, insulated from the *process* of ongoing choice. For Dostoevsky, intention is rarely linear or singular. More often, it changes in interaction with other ongoing experiences and exists among a plurality of shifting sideshadows.

Perhaps the most striking of the *Diary*'s analyses, and one of the most profound pieces of crime reporting ever written, concerned the notorious Kairova case. Kairova, the mistress of a married man, knew that her lover Velikanov was again living with his wife. She purchased a razor, went to the bedroom where the couple was sleeping, and attacked the wife. The two awoke and prevented Kairova from continuing the attack; she was tried and acquitted.

Dostoevsky deplores the pseudo-liberals who applauded the verdict as somehow progressive, but he also indicates that the question put to the jurors was so psychologically simplistic that conviction was impossible. They were asked

whether Kairova, "having premeditated her act," intended to kill Mme Velikanova "but was prevented from the ultimate consummation of her intent"
by the couple (AWD, 5/76, 1.3). Even though Kairova was doubtless guilty
of some crime, Dostoevsky argues, this question cannot be answered either
positively or negatively because its psychological presuppositions are simplistic and false. Acquittal was therefore necessary.[28] But why was the question
unanswerable?

According to Dostoevsky, this case defies linear intentionality. It may well
have happened, he writes, that Kairova's intention was not fixed at the outset
(was therefore not "premeditated") but evolved bit by bit along with her behavior. When she bought the razor, Kairova might still not have known whether
she would attack Velikanova with it, much less whether she would kill her:

> Most likely she hadn't the slightest idea of this even when sitting on the
> steps with the razor in her hand, while just behind her, on her own bed, lay
> her lover and her rival. No one, no one in the world could have the slightest
> idea of this. Moreover, even though it may seem absurd, I can state that
> even when she had begun slashing her rival, she might *still not have known*
> whether she wanted to kill her or not and whether *this was her purpose* in
> slashing her. (AWD, 5/76, 1.3)

The charge to the jury presupposes a complete intention and a series of actions
that may have been designed to realize it. It assumes that either Kairova did
mean to kill Velikanova all along but was prevented by external circumstances
or else that she did not mean to kill her all along and would not have done
so even if she had not been restrained. Either way, the intention was fixed.
Sometimes that is indeed the case, Dostoevsky argues, but often it is not.

Dostoevsky contends that Kairova's intention was never complete in the
way that the court's question suggests. It was vague, unformulated, and processual. At each moment, Kairova's incomplete intention may have allowed for
many possibilities, and to understand her actions one must grasp that multiplicity. Dostoevsky cautions that he does not mean to say that she was insane
or that she acted unconsciously. No, she was aware of what she was doing at
each moment, but she could not tell in advance what she meant to do the next
moment.

Had she not been restrained, Kairova *might* have done several radically different things, and Dostoevsky sketches out the field of possibilities. She might
have passed the razor over her rival's throat "and then cried out, shuddered, and
run off as fast as she could" (AWD, 5/76, 1.3). Or she might have taken fright
and turned the razor on herself. Or, on the contrary, she might have flown
into a frenzy "and not only murdered Velikanova but even begun to abuse the

body, cutting off the head, the nose, the lips; and only later, suddenly, when someone took that head away from her, realized what she had done" (AWD, 5/76, 1.3).

Dostoevsky's point is that the incomplete intention did not predetermine a single outcome, even if no external obstacles had intervened. All these very different possible actions "could have happened and could have been done by this very same woman and spring from the very same soul, in the very same mood and under the very same circumstances" (AWD, 5/76, 1.3). If it were possible for the scene to be repeated several times—if, say, the universe allowed for duplicate worlds, as it does in Dostoevsky's story "The Dream of a Ridiculous Man"—then in each duplicate world the outcome might vary. Identical circumstances leading to different results: there could be no more definitive statement of the openness of time.[29] To understand such temporality one must grasp a field of possibilities and project multiple sideshadows.

Dostoevsky was apparently so struck by the implications of this motif—someone seizing a weapon without having arrived at any specific intention—that he used it again to structure pivotal events in *Karamazov*. It will be recalled that in his frenzied jealousy, Dmitri seizes a pestle in the presence of a witness and runs off with it. When, after Dmitri's father has been found murdered, the investigating lawyer asks Dmitri why he seized the pestle, if not to murder the old man, Dmitri is unable to give a coherent purpose, precisely because he had none. He was angry, murderously angry, and he suddenly seized a weapon that happened to be in view, and that is all. He did not yet have a specific intention; like Kairova's, his intention was to evolve bit by circumstantial bit. It might indeed have led to murder, though in this case it did not; even if it had, the murder would not have been premeditated. The intention was not formulated until the last possible moment when Dmitri was standing over his father's head with the weapon in hand.

The investigator, working from a legalistic, linear idea of intentionality, insists that Dmitri must have had some purpose in mind *when* he seized the pestle, much as the prosecution in the Kairova case made the same assumption about the razor:

"But what object had you in view in arming yourself with such a weapon?"
"What object? No object. I just picked it up and ran off."
"What for, if you had no object?" . . .
"Bother the pestle!" broke from him suddenly.
"But still ..."
"Oh, to keep off the dogs ... Oh, because it was dark ... . In case anything turned up."

"But have you ever on previous occasions taken a weapon with you when you went out, since you're afraid of the dark?" . . .

"Well, upon my word, gentlemen! Yes, I took the pestle ... What does one pick things up for at such moments? I don't know what for. I snatched it up and ran—that's all." (BK, 571)

Dmitri sounds unconvincing, but in fact he is being entirely truthful here. He had no specific objective in picking up the pestle, and he might have done various things or nothing at all with it. He does not know why he snatched it, he just snatched it. The investigator assumes, as we generally do, that actions follow from preformed intentions, but here, as in the Kairova case, Dostoevsky shows how actions may, instead of following from intentions, be part of the process by which intentions themselves evolve over time. Throughout the process, the intention may be vague and, like time itself, open.

Dostoevsky is so often interpreted from a Freudian perspective (and was so interpreted by Freud himself) that it is worth stressing the difference. Dostoevsky's point is not that there is some *sub*conscious intention guiding and preceding Kairova's and Dmitri's actions. They did not have an intention, whether conscious or subconscious; rather, *they were in a certain disposition.* From a processual standpoint, subconscious intentionality is really not that different from conscious intentionality, and both are equally inapplicable to Dmitri and Kairova. Neither can it be said that Dmitri was unaware of a repressed intention: for one thing, he knows very well that he hates and desires the death of his father, and for another, the intention to kill him on this occasion was not repressed, not hidden, but unformulated. In this light, a Freudian reading is almost as simplistic as the investigator's.

For Kairova and Dmitri, time was still open. The doctrine of a prior intention, whether conscious or unconscious, significantly closes down time by reducing a field of possibilities to a line. If their only choice was whether to carry out their plan, then time merely enacts or fails to enact what was there from the outset but does not shape anything. Time so conceived does not possess a developing plurality of possibilities. To use Ilya Prigogine's terms, linearity transforms time from an operator into a mere parameter.[30] By contrast, the prosaic intentionality of "Kairova time" develops with constant sideshadows, as the state of mind responds unpredictably to evolving circumstances. Time and intention exhibit multiple potentials changing from moment to moment.

The Devil's Potentials: The Coordinates of the Other World

In the famous devil chapter of *Karamazov*, Dostoevsky seems to concentrate and almost to parody his own ideas about time. The devil who haunts Ivan is of course his most tormenting double, as Ivan recognizes when he calls the devil the parodic incarnation of all his basest impulses and most banal thoughts. And as Ivan's ideas are extreme versions of the latest intelligentsia theories, the devil offers a double of contemporary ideology as well. He fleshes out each of Ivan's philosophical arguments into the guiding principle of a whole alternative universe.

As the devil describes it, the other world is not fixed but varies in accordance with the latest ideas of intellectuals. It is a cosmic parody of those ideas. It follows that the other world is historical, and this idea of the historicity of a supposedly eternal realm is the source of the chapter's dazzling metaphysical comedy. Eternity had a middle ages and, in fact, "we've everything that you have, I am revealing one of our secrets out of friendship for you; though it's forbidden" (BK, 782). Cosmology changes along with human ideas about it:

> We are all in a muddle over there now and all through your science. Once there used to be atoms, five senses, four elements, and then everything hung together somehow. . . . but since we've learned that you've discovered the chemical molecule and protoplasm and the devil knows what, we had to lower our crest. There's a regular muddle, and above all, superstition, scandal; there's as much scandal among us as among you, you know; a little more in fact, and spying, indeed, for we have our secret police department, where private information is received. (BK, 781–82)

When denizens of the other world are "superstitious," what do they believe? The devil's most famous lines—for example, his claim to be an agnostic—reflect the historicizing of heaven and hell.

The devil gradually reveals that the other world exists as a realm of *possibility*. Just as Russia imitates the West, so the other world copies ideas and institutions existing on earth, but with a few variations that might have or might still come to pass. It is like earth, but "a little more, in fact." Thus Ivan misunderstands when he claims that the devil, as his hallucination, can say nothing new, and is surprised when the devil offers a witticism he has not thought of. The devil explains:

> *C'est du nouveau, n'est-ce pas?* . . . Listen, in dreams and especially in nightmares . . . a man sees sometimes such artistic visions, such complex and real actuality, such events . . . with such unexpected details from the most exalted matters to the last button on a cuff, as I swear Leo Tolstoy has never

invented. . . . A statesman confessed to me, indeed, that all his best ideas came to him when he was asleep. Well, that's how it is now, though I am your hallucination, yet just as in a nightmare, I say original things which had not entered your head before. (BK, 777)

The devil comes from a world analogous to dreams, which do not just repeat life but rework it into new combinations and new possibilities. The other world is not another actual universe, somehow complementing ours, but is an ever-changing set of possible variations.[31]

But for that very reason, the devil continues, it is tedious for those otherworldly beings (if "beings" they are) who long for real life. Neither existent nor nonexistent, the other world feels like nothing but shadows. And so, the devil concludes, I come to visit you, because life on earth is so concrete and defined. One thing or another happens, not all possibilities in a haze: "Here when I stay with you from time to time, my life gains a kind of reality [*moia zhizn' protekaet vrode chego-to kak by i v samom dele*] and that's what I like most of all. You see, like you, I suffer from the fantastic, and so I love the realism of earth. Here, with you, everything is circumscribed, here all is formulated and geometrical, while we have nothing but indeterminate equations!" (BK, 776). Indeterminate equations have innumerable solutions, and so one cannot arrive at a given one unless additional information is provided. Earth somehow provides that information, which is why particular things can actually happen. On earth there are actualities as well as possibilities. Things are "formulated" and have definite shapes (are "geometrical"), whereas the other world is pure potential. Real people suffer, the devil continues, "but then they live a real life, not a fantastic one" (BK, 780), whereas "I am . . . a sort of phantom" (BK, 781). Trapped somewhere between being and nonbeing, the devil (in a terrible but characteristic pun) "suffers from the fantastic" and dreams of "becoming incarnate once and for all and irrevocably in the form of some merchant's wife weighing eighteen stone" (BK, 776).

Ivan keeps trying to apply a binary logic: either the devil exists or he does not. The excluded middle here is the middle realm of real possibilities that are nevertheless not actualities. The devil, on the other hand, plays at breaking down binary formulations. "I want to join an idealist society," he jokes. "I'll lead the opposition in it, I'll say I am a realist, but not a materialist, he-he!" (BK, 774). Of course, this whole scenario not only alludes to the problem of possibilities and to the novel's war on various determinist philosophies. It also evokes the moral danger of trying to live, as Ivan has done, in a permanently uncommitted position, as a mere observer who watches from the shadows but takes no role in action. For life consists not only of possibilities but also of irrevocable actualities.

The Hunger for Possibilities

. . . that imagined "otherwise" which is our practical heaven.
—MIDDLEMARCH

I have focused on Dostoevsky because he was a master of sideshadowing. His philosophical concern with human freedom, his interest in the complexities of psychology, and his restless formal experimentation led him to create diverse versions of this technique. But the impulse to sideshadowing is by no means restricted to novelists. In literature, religion, and popular culture it appears wherever the impulse to the hypothetical is felt.

A few examples may illustrate how widespread the device is. That ever-popular film *It's a Wonderful Life* of course depends on a kind of sideshadowing: the story of what the town would have been without the hero justifies the life that was in fact lived. The tape is replayed, an alternative history unfolds, and the superiority of the actual to an alternative possibility is demonstrated.[32]

Historical crises often evoke magazine articles guessing at the consequences of possibilities narrowly avoided: what would have happened if JFK had lived, if Hitler had won the war, if Napoleon had invaded Russia a few months earlier, or if Trotsky had outmaneuvered Stalin? Britain always has a shadow cabinet, and Russia today seems concerned with its shadow history, the course of events that might have happened if the Bolsheviks had not seized control ("the Russia that did not happen"). Science fiction stories about time travel to the past often appeal to the same kind of curiosity, as do games that allow one to replay famous battles by trying out various strategies. For we understand where we are by understanding where else we might have been.[33]

People long for more stories about people or events that matter to them. Folklore, rumor, or dubious tabloid articles carry an immense appeal even when one knows that the events reported might well be exaggerated or untrue, so long as they are not clearly false. An interesting principle of analogy seems to underwrite such stories: The penumbral region of uncertainty about *what may have been* serves as a stand-in for the hypothetical realm of *what could be*. Insufficiency of documentation, the unreliability of testimony, or the possible existence of unproven conspiracies feeds speculation about alternatives to the present we know.

But hypothetical time seems too unsubstantial. And so unrealized alternatives are projected onto the line of real time. Unactualized possibilities are translated into possible actualities.

Public fascination with certain figures and the lives they lead turns them into subjects of all sorts of stories about what they might do, presented as things they perhaps did. The lives of such figures interest us because of what they allow, because of what we might do in their place, and not only because of what their biography actually is. To satisfy our imaginations, John Kennedy, Elvis Presley, and members of the British royal family would each need to have led many more lives than one.[34] Because a famous person's actual life does not exhaust his or her interest for us, we grow tolerant of the use of dubious, though not absolutely unbelievable, report. To many readers, it is not so important whether Kitty Kelley's juicy stories are true, only that they might be true. They occupy the middle realm of real possibilities.

In this respect, tabloid accounts of famous people may also be seen as a debased but recognizable version of historical fiction. Both appeal to the impulse for other stories, for possible (even if not actual) adventures. To be sure, such writers peddle their wares as genuine, but readers may well understand that they are quasi-fictional. (Laws that make it harder for public figures to prove slander seem to offer unwitting recognition of this intermediate status and to encourage its exploitation.) For that matter, many forms of historical fiction offer themselves as painless introductions to the real past. People who read James Michener this way point to his extensive "research." We lack a single term for forms that play on the possibility that they *may* be true or assert that they are largely but not entirely true—forms that situate themselves indeterminately between fact and fiction—but readers respond to the genre even without the term. These forms might best be called "the literature of the middle realm."[35]

The rough equivalent in sacred writing would seem to be apocrypha. Apocryphal texts were not necessarily regarded as false or heretical, but rather as noncanonical, and so their accounts often occupied an intermediate position favorable to sideshadowing. One wants to know more about Jesus, Mary, or the Creation, and so one is receptive to more stories. In Russia, there were a number of such texts that seemed to migrate between inclusion in orthodox collections and prohibition by an index. At times regarded as heretical, a given text might at other times be used to fight heresies.[36] In Judaism, Midrash fills in the gaps in Torah and explains discontinuities, often by providing more stories. Many of the best-known stories about biblical figures are in fact drawn from Midrashic literature. Although these additional narratives were regarded as sacred, their appeal, like that of folklore, may well have derived in part from the need to explore other possibilities.

Readers often seek such additional "information" about their favorite fictional characters as well, especially those from voluminous and riveting novels. A reader has lived so long, has identified so strongly, with beloved heroes or heroines that worries about them have become a treasured part of real life. That may be especially true of serialized works because so much of the reader's own life has unfolded along with the characters'. When the hero or heroine has faced disaster, a reader may have imagined many outcomes that did not in fact happen. The period between installments provokes speculation, as we also see in soap operas, which have generated their own forms of journalistic speculation. Such journalism thrives on the interim between adventures, and so long as the story lasts there is always an interim. Audiences commiserate and anticipate. The process of doing so, which has given pleasure and served as a catalyst for thoughts or fantasies, seems too precious to give up just because the last page or episode has been reached.

Part of the appeal of picaresque fiction (or drama) is that it is almost infinitely extendable. Each possibility may be presented as another adventure in the sequence, and readers know not to calculate biographical time too closely lest they discover there were not enough years for all the adventures. The same is true of certain forms of popular culture: "M*A*S*H" ran far longer than the Korean War, but the appetite for more stories and the fact that each program was not set too precisely with respect to all the others made it possible to extend the sequence so long as interest lasted. Dick Tracy goes right on solving crimes for decades longer than he could have lived. In each case, possibilities are projected onto a real time line so hypotheticals need not be presented as such.[37]

When a beloved novel is over, some readers turn to the author's notebooks. Events omitted from the final draft may acquire the compelling interest of possibilities. Occupying the middle realm, they achieve a sort of apocryphal status. Neither false nor true, they appeal as sideshadows, as indications of what the character might have done. Sometimes the existence of two authorial endings to the same story may deprive either of a sense of inevitability and endow the whole work with a sideshadow: the alternative conclusions of *Great Expectations* and of Tolstoy's story "The Devil" seem to invite this kind of interest. The whole narrative may be contemplated as one that somehow occupies two contradictory temporal lines: but both could have been possible. In general, any time a work of great appeal exists in two texts, readers will be likely to experience sideshadowing.

When a work has been left unfinished, like *The Mystery of Edwin Drood*, multiple completions by other authors may create a veritable labyrinth of sideshadows, none of which can be taken as actual because none belong to the original author. And yet readers feel that one (or more) of these later authors *may* have discerned what the original author had in mind—if he had already settled on a single ending. The existence of many completions, and the ever-present promise of more to come, spreads an open-ended maze of possibilities.[38]

Paraquels and Parodies

In their hunger for possibilities, recent readers seem to be fascinated by a peculiar genre that has sideshadowing at its core. One writer continues, fills in, or gives the prehistory of a famous story by another writer. Jean Rhys's *Wide Sargasso Sea,* John Gardner's *Grendel,* Lin Haire-Sargeant's *H.,* and Alexandra Ripley's *Scarlett* give us more where more cannot be. The original author is dead, and we know these apocryphal continuations are written by someone else. They cannot be authoritative. Yet they do satisfy the desire for more of a favorite work. They are, in fact, almost entirely dependent on familiarity with the original or at least with some version of it (with a knowledge of the plot or, in the case of *Scarlett,* with the film version).[39] Continuations by other authors thereby acquire the mysterious penumbral status, plausible but not "actual," in which sideshadowing thrives.

These continuations may be set after the events in the original work (sequels); there are also "prequels," taking place before, and "interquels" (like *H.*), which fill in temporal gaps within the original story. The precise timing is largely irrelevant to the interest that sustains the form: what is important is that there be more events, other events, "side" events that could have happened. Because these novels usually do not explicitly raise philosophical questions about time—they presume but rarely discuss hypothetical temporality—a place must be found for them somewhere on the established time line. They are, in the root sense of the word, parodies—"beside songs"—but because that term has taken on the meaning of discrediting an original, the form might best be called *paraquels.*

Parody, in the usual meaning of a text that alludes to and discredits another, may be regarded as *an unwelcome sideshadow.* When parodies become famous and interesting enough, a peculiar doubling of works takes place. Once one has read Fielding's *Shamela, Pamela* will not read the same way again. For modern readers, Richardson's novel comes already sideshadowed, preread, and preparodied. The most successful parodies adhere to the originals in this persistent way. One senses the original trying to shake off or ostentatiously to ignore the unwanted sideshadow. As with Dostoevsky's underground man, who tries to *show* his friends that he is "paying no attention whatsoever to them" (NFU, 70), the very futility of the effort increases the comedy. Whichever work one reads, the original or the parody, one senses both, with the parody having the upper hand.

At times, however, originals do successfully resist even an influential parody, and the two therefore seem to compete on equal terms. For Russian readers, *Notes from Underground* and Chernyshevsky's utopian fiction *What Is to Be Done?* have long survived as parallel texts: which one a person prefers describes his or her sense of the world. Whole genres may compete in this way with parodic antigenres, as each casts a sideshadow on the other. Plato, More, Bellamy, and Wells now come already answered by, and already answering, Swift, Samuel Johnson, Zamyatin, and Orwell.

At times, the parody may utterly replace the original, so that in a sense the sideshadow displaces the event itself. Retrospectively, the pretender seizes the throne. If this sort of displacement has happened in a culture or epoch remote from us, we may even mistake the parody for the original. Signs of exaggeration or other marks of parody evident to first readers may not be recognizable to those with no knowledge of the culture's expectations or conventions. Bakhtin has shrewdly observed that much of our heritage may consist of such unrecognized parodies.[40]

A parody may even be too successful by prolonging the life of an original that might otherwise have been forgotten. How many current readers would know of *Amadis of Gaul* if it had not been parodied by *Don Quixote*? For Western readers, *What Is to Be Done?* and Nekrasov's sentimental verses about a fallen woman survive because they are mocked so savagely by Dostoevsky's underground man. The danger of being too successful a parody is that the original, like the minority opinion in a court case, may survive long enough to be accepted anew when the values informing the parody eventually become objectionable. The romantic revival of medievalism after the Enlightenment may be a case in point.

Whether parodic, reverent, or something in between, paraquels (unlike parodies) are usually written when the original author is dead. But that is by no means always the case. Particularly when copyright laws are nonexistent or lax, it is always possible to cash in on the popularity of a current work by adding to it. In such circumstances, the original author may have the chance to respond with his own "authentic" continuation, thus creating a strange dialogue of sideshadows.

In part II of *Don Quixote*, for instance, the knight of the doleful countenance overhears with indignation two people reading aloud from a continuation of his adventures written by another author. Resolving to expose "the forgery of this new historian," Don Quixote alters his plans so as not to appear where the paraquel placed him.[41] The two readers immediately acknowledge that the knight before them is indeed "the true Don Quixote of La Mancha . . . in spite of him who has attempted to usurp your name and annihilate your exploits, as the author of this book, which I deliver to you, has tried in vain" (DQ, 950). Sancho then suggests that "the Sancho and the Don Quixote of that history must be different people from those who appear in the one written by Cide Hamete Benengeli" (DQ, 952). For if (as Don Quixote reasons) the stories of Amadis are true, or else they could not have been published, perhaps the fake

Quixote is the true story of another knight and squire? Perhaps there are two Don Quixotes and two Sancho Panzas? One of the two readers, Don Juan, proposes that there should be a law specifying that only Cide Hamete (no mention is made of Cervantes) may write about the pair. The true Don Quixote, then, is the one described by the fictive author, Cide Hamete, whereas the real author of the continuation has either perpetrated a fiction or created a quite "different" knight and squire.

Of course, the very possibility of mistaking the false Don Quixote for the true indicates that the continuation by the other author is plausible. In this scene, the second volume of Cervantes's (or Cide Hamete's) *Quixote* becomes the sideshadow of the sideshadow. Moreover, Cervantes seems to be suggesting, all fiction is a sideshadowing of reality in the sense that it reports events that could have happened but did not, a point that Don Quixote, who believes all hypotheticals to be actual, evidently fails to appreciate.

Many of the incidents in the second part of the *Quixote* derive from the same impulse that created the false continuation in the first place, namely, readers' hunger for more stories. Thus readers of volume one appear as characters in volume two, where they have the rare experience of encountering their favorite fictional hero. Deceiving him, they provoke new incidents and invent strange narratives in order to generate more adventures, fresh stories, and other possibilities. "In fact, Cide Hamete says that he considers the hoaxers to be as mad as their victims, for the duke and duchess came within a hair's breadth of looking like fools for taking such immense trouble to play tricks on a pair of fools" (DQ, 1023). As the second volume progresses, it becomes increasingly difficult to say which fiction encloses which and which reality is the real reality. The world becomes an endless layering of hypotheticals, as it may perhaps "really" be.

Resurrections

In the nineteenth century, novelists sometimes created their own continuations. In Balzac, Dumas, and Trollope, for instance, characters are recycled from novel to novel. One of the attractions of novel series, like the six-volume chronicle of the Pallisers, is the pleasure of encountering an old friend from an earlier story. Each novel may be read as a completed structure not requiring knowledge of earlier works, but each will also be somewhat different for those who know the whole series. When we come upon the main heroine of the first Palliser novel, Alice Vavasor, later in the series, readers who know her biography have the pleasure, usually unavailable when a novel is over, of catching a glimpse of a character's *life after closure*. Returning to familiar locales, we may recall what else happened there and discern the continuing thread of an earlier story. Closure in these novels is only temporary; so long as we read, we may chance upon old heroes and heroines the way we sometimes meet old friends in real life. Thus, the extraordinary ending of *The Last Chronicle of Barset* derives its power from the fact that this time the finale is really final. The last lines conclude not just a novel but a series, and not just a story but a world:

> And now, if the reader will allow me to seize him affectionately by the arm, we will together take our last farewell of Barset and the towers of Barchester. I may not venture to say to him that, in this country, he and I have wandered often through the country lanes. . . . I may not boast that any beside myself have so realized the place, and the people, and the facts, as to make such reminiscences possible as those which I should attempt to evoke by an appeal to perfect fellowship. But to me Barset has been a real county, and its city a real city, and the spires and towers have been before my eyes. . . . To them all I now say farewell. That I have been induced to wander among them too long by my love of old friendships, and by the sweetness of old faces, is a fault for which I may perhaps be more readily forgiven, when I repeat, with some solemnity of assurance, the promise made in my title, that this shall be the last chronicle of Barset.[42]

What Trollope describes as the pleasures of the author are also those of the readers. But even this farewell was not quite as final as might seem. Trollope continued to use some of its characters in later novels.[43]

Perhaps the most interesting recycling of characters belongs to Tolstoy, who in the course of his long career continued to write about Dmitri Nekhliudov. Nekhliudov appears in four stories or novellas from the 1850s and then reappears as the hero of *Resurrection* (1899). What is especially interesting is that the various stories cannot be linked to form a biography of the hero. Thus one astute critic, Andrew Wachtel, suggests that instead of a single Nekhliudov there are various distinct "characters named Nekhlyudov" and that Tolstoy "does not seem to expect readers to connect these various Nekhlyudovs to one another."[44] There are many Nekhliudovs, just as a character named Anna Karenina, who is not *the* Anna Karenina, appears in Tolstoy's play *The Living Corpse*. Perhaps the most compelling argument one could advance in support of Wachtel's position is that at the end of "Notes of a Billiard Marker" Nekhliudov kills himself, and so this could hardly be the same character who appears in *Resurrection*. Nevertheless, the hero of *Resurrection* recalls his old friend Irtenev (whom he knew in *Youth*), and his psychology recognizably recalls the Nekhliudov of the Billiard Marker story. How is one to understand the inconsistency?

The explanation, I think, is that this is the same Nekhliudov, but that his various adventures do not belong to a single biography. They each distill one possibility from a field, but they do not lie on a line. Given who Nekhliudov is, he could have found himself in the situation that drives him to suicide in the early story or he could have lived to follow a convict to Siberia, as in the late novel. The stories do not form a sequence but neither are they entirely distinct. They are related as sideshadows of each other. Nekhliudov actually lives, as we all would be capable of living, more lives than one: had we but worlds enough and times.

Tolstoy and Contingency

> Contingency is Tolstoy's cardinal theme in all his great novels.
> —STEPHEN JAY GOULD

Perhaps no writer had a deeper appreciation of contingency than Tolstoy. As Tolstoy knew, contingency is an odd and puzzling concept. It seems to lie somewhere between determinism and sheer chance and may, depending on context, be used as a synonym for either. At times, the assertion of contingency denies freedom by stating a cause: we say that something is entirely contingent on something else. But at other times, contingency is opposed to overarching laws, as when we describe an event as contingent rather than necessary.

The reason for this apparent discrepancy is that a contingent event is one that is dependent on a cause, but the cause itself may or may not arise. It is caused but not mandated. Freedom (or chance) exists at one remove; a contingent event is a possibility, but not a certainty. Thus we speak of taking measures to guard against a given contingency.

A contingent event happens "for some reason"—Tolstoy's favorite phrase in *War and Peace*. By using it, Tolstoy means to indicate that although there are indeed causes or reasons for each historical event, those causes do not add up to any overall structure or pattern. It is not as if more knowledge would reveal that events are guided by a set of laws and that contingency is a mere illusion derived from ignorance of those laws. No, for the author of *War and Peace* life is radically contingent. If we were to accumulate more knowledge about each contingent event and trace the cause of each cause of each cause, we would discover not underlying laws showing the inevitability of things but an infinitely expanding labyrinth. We would never arrive at a reason that the course of events could not have been different.

Unlike so many Russian (and Western thinkers) of his time, Tolstoy utterly rejected the existence of laws of history. He singled out laws of progress, the mania obsessing thinkers "from Hegel to Buckle," but he also had in mind any other laws one might imagine. "To subordinate history to the idea of progress is just as easy as to the idea of regress, or to any other historical fantasy that you like," Tolstoy wrote. "I will say more: I see no necessity whatsoever to seek out general laws of history, not to mention the impossibility of doing so."[45] Nothing guaranteed that history would produce the world we know. At countless moments, in fact at virtually every moment, it might have taken a somewhat different turn. Our world is one possibility out of "a hundred million," just as any alternative possibility would have been.

The wise officers in *War and Peace* know that there can be no science of battle, just as there can be no science of history. The naive Pierre (one of the book's heroes) believes that a skilled commander can "foresee all contingencies"—a phrase that recurs throughout the narrative—which would mean that there are really no contingencies at all. But his wiser friend Prince Andrei learns that most events, especially in battle, happen not according to any conceivable plan but just "for some reason." "What are we facing tomorrow?," he asks Pierre on the eve of the battle of Borodino. "A hundred million diverse chances, which will be decided on the instant by whether we run or they run, whether this man or that man is killed" (W&P, 930). At his last council of war, Andrei asks himself, "What science can there be in a matter in which, as in every practical matter, nothing can be determined and everything depends on innumerable conditions, the significance of which becomes manifest at a particular moment, and no one can tell when that moment will come?" (W&P, 775).

"On the instant," "at a particular moment": Andrei here stresses the importance not only of contingency but also of time. At each moment the field of possibilities subtly changes in ways that in principle cannot be foreseen. Every moment offers an array of opportunities and dangers, each of which would shape future opportunities differently. Time ramifies not only at infrequent historical nodes but constantly, which is why possibilities are incalculably large. History is thus a ravelment of possibilities. Moreover, these instantly changing fields vary with each local situation, which is why Andrei decides to give up his position in the central command and to serve in the ranks.

As if to illustrate the truth of these observations, Tolstoy provides a concrete example of the sort of temporal sensitivity that does make a difference. Watching the French climb a hill toward his soldiers, the line officer Nikolai Rostov contemplates the changing and unpredictable patterns of their movement. As each French soldier chooses one way or another around small obstacles, their overall deployment changes moment by moment. At one point Rostov, guided not by military theory but by his experience as a soldier and a hunter, perceives that the passing present moment offers an unanticipated opportunity. "He felt instinctively that if his hussars were to charge the French dragoons now, the latter would not be able to withstand them, but that it would have to be done at once, instantly, or it would be too late" (W&P, 786). No advance plan of the battle, no matter how detailed, could have predicted this moment. Rostov's successful charge results instead from his ceaseless attention to contingency and from his constant monitoring of the field of possibilities. In Tolstoy's view, it is the sum total of actions like these that decides the outcome of battles. That is why the wise general Kutuzov recommends, as the best preparation for battle, "a good night's sleep." In a domain governed by laws, it is knowledge of those laws and the work of applying them that create success. But in a universe of radical contingency, what matters most is experience and alertness; and alertness requires not late-night planning but sound sleep. As Andrei understands, this logic applies to "practical matters" generally.

Each moment has multiple potentials, but narratives almost by their very nature tend to edit out such multiplicity. The need for coherence, the demands of readability, and the understandable but unjustifiable privilege accorded to what was actually realized—all these subtle influences lead historians to reduce an endless ramification to a line and thereby to transform contingency into necessity. In his polemics with "the historians," Tolstoy constantly stresses how the road taken blots out the very awareness that there were other roads. Histories typically select from the past those elements that, in retrospect, led to the historian's own position. In one of his famous similes, Tolstoy compares such narratives to "stencil work," in which "one or another figure comes out, not because the color was applied from this side or that, but because it was laid on from all sides over the figure cut in the stencil" (W&P, 1432). Stencil history purports to discover a pattern that it has imposed in advance.

Tolstoy and Dostoevsky both objected to linear conceptions of time and turned to sideshadowing as a method for showing that other things could have happened. But they preferred different forms of sideshadowing because their understanding of time's ramification differed. Dostoevsky tended to see occasional critical moments allowing for major turning points. By contrast, Tolstoy envisaged each ordinary moment as having a small measure of freedom. Dostoevsky's crisis time makes choice, when it happens, dramatic and palpable; Tolstoy's prosaic time makes it continuous but elusive. For Tolstoy, life is made by "tiny, tiny alterations," each one of which could have been slightly different. The effects of all together accumulate rapidly to major differences.[46]

What meteorologists have come to refer to as "sensitive dependence on initial conditions" (more popularly, "the butterfly effect") always operates in *War and Peace*. In weather, small and unpredictable changes—the flapping of a butterfly's wings in Peking—do not necessarily cancel each other out but may magnify, bit by tiny bit, to larger changes, such as a storm in New York. Thus long-term forecasting is impossible in principle.[47] Such "butterflies" are always flapping in *War and Peace*, which is one reason the novel is so long: we are initiated into numerous tiny alterations of consciousness and behavior, none of which could have been predicted on the basis of some law but some of which may lead to significant consequences.

For Tolstoy, most time, not just moments leading to crime, resembles Dostoevsky's "Kairova time." Action is typically taken processually: constant adjustments to unforeseen contingency alter purposes, however slightly, moment by moment.

Thus Tolstoy stressed the moral importance of what we do at each prosaic moment. Dostoevsky was often drawn to formulate moral problems in terms of extreme situations, as if the test of an ethical perspective was how it would function in "the house of the dead." Prosaics sides with Tolstoy and resists "in extremis" ethical formulations.[48] Like a judge who viewed extreme cases as making for bad law, Tolstoy viewed ordinary life as the true ethical test. Indeed, he thought that even extreme situations are usually best handled by the wisdom accumulated during ordinary experiences. For all of these reasons, Tolstoy, in contrast to Dostoevsky, preferred what might be called prosaic sideshadowing.

Aesthetic Potentiality

So complex were Tolstoy's methods for representing time's continual openness that I can explore only a few of the most striking ones here. Tolstoy saw and repeatedly stated that conventional narratives destroy the openness of time. The aesthetic ideal of everything fitting into a coherent structure visible at a glance results in a kind of time that gathers to a point. In such narratives, everything tends to the ending and nothing is truly contingent. Structure banishes contingency because each incident must have a purpose, must contribute to the overall plot and pattern, or it would not have been included in the first place.

In a narrative based on structure, "the structural union of the parts . . . [is] such that, if any one of them is displaced or removed, the whole will be disjointed and disturbed," as Aristotle observed. "For a thing whose presence or absence makes no visible difference, is not an organic part of the whole."[49] Of course, not all parts need be equally important, but there must be a rough proportionality between the attention a part attracts and its role in the work.

Now, contingent events are by definition those that need not have happened, which for Tolstoy meant that governing ideas of unity make it virtually impossible to represent time as it really is. That is one reason that Tolstoy repeatedly insisted that at the heart of narrative is a lie. In good narratives, as they have usually been judged, things always or almost always fit, but in life they rarely do.

When Pierre is at his dying father's bedside, something happens that may mean something important or may mean absolutely nothing. The old count, having suffered a series of strokes, cannot speak, and as Pierre approaches him, "the Count looked directly at him, but with a gaze the intent and significance of which no man could have fathomed. Either it meant absolutely nothing more than that having eyes one must look somewhere, or it was charged with meaning. Pierre hesitated . . ." (W&P, 118). In *War and Peace*, the reader also hesitates frequently because the book includes numerous events and characters that may have either great consequence or no consequence at all. In Tolstoy's book, both possibilities are always present, as they are in life.

Readers of novels are trained to seek significance. When at the beginning of *Great Expectations*, Pip gives a pie to a convict, the reader knows that this event will mean something or it would not have been narrated. The fact that the work is known to be an artifact, an aesthetic structure planned in advance, guarantees significance. From Tolstoy's perspective, such advance assurance is precisely why artifacts are artificial and why we sense a radical difference between art and life. In *War and Peace* and *Anna Karenina*, there are numerous incidents that occupy a great deal of space but lead nowhere. Nothing follows from them, and from the point of view of "the plot" they might just as well not have happened. Order and chanciness are both present. Time in Tolstoy's works therefore feels unplanned and contingent, just as life is contingent. This feeling partially explains why so many critics and readers have felt, as Matthew Arnold did, that a novel by Tolstoy must not be taken "as a work of art; we are to take it as a piece of life. A piece of life it is." [50]

Those who read *War and Peace* for the first time almost always feel, as its initial critics felt, that the work is therefore difficult to follow. An immense number of characters appear, are sometimes described at length, and then disappear, never to be seen again; and "incidents are multiplied which we expect are to lead to something important, which do not" (Arnold, 260). Or as Konstantin Leontiev observed, "this is precisely what I call redundancy, a ponderosity of petty details. After all, even feathers weigh a lot when there are a lot of them." [51] Although these critics did not understand the reasons for Tolstoy's use of contingency, they did identify its presence and describe its effects with great precision. [52]

The fact that some incidents in *War and Peace* lead somewhere while others do not makes it impossible to presume in advance that mere presence guarantees significance. Even implicit foreshadowing—the kind that is not flagged as such but derives simply from the sense of a structure planned in advance—is ruled out. Thus, when events do work out "novelistically" (for example, when Prince Andrei arrives home just as his wife is dying in childbirth or finds himself among the wounded prisoners tended by the Rostovs), they carry special power because we know from experience that these events might just as readily not have happened. Readers of these scenes are usually deeply moved, much more so than by equivalent scenes in works by other authors, but are usually at a loss to explain why. The answer, I think, is that Tolstoy's events take place in a universe like the one in which we live, where things happen by contingency.

In life, coincidences are remarkable because they need not have happened; they are improbable or we would not regard them as coincidences in the first place. We all are aware that such events resist our attempts to narrate them so as to convey their original excitement. If an event is interesting just because it happened when it could not have been anticipated, then how do we recreate that sense of surprise when the very fact of our telling warns an audience to anticipate something? "You have to have been there," we say in frustration. In novels, we know that coincidences are really nothing of the sort, so they seem somewhat contrived. But in Tolstoy, the overwhelming mass of contingent events from which the rare novelistic coincidences emerge makes the coincidences seem especially noteworthy. As in life, they are gifts that we might just as well not have received.

Tolstoy's readers sense that narrated events did not happen by what Bakhtin calls "aesthetic necessity." They grow accustomed to witnessing some story lines develop, others cease, and still others continue for a while and then unaccountably disappear. As a result, they experience palpably the opposite of aesthetic necessity: call it *aesthetic potentiality*. They sense that the material Tolstoy assembles could easily have sustained many other plots, many other books.

Reading Tolstoy, we wonder about characters who have disappeared from view, and we imagine what might have happened if a given contingent line of events had not affected the main heroes and heroines. The lives of Tolstoy's heroes and heroines seem (as our own do) but one marvelous actualization out of an immense number of possibilities. The fact that so many critics, including those who have faulted Tolstoy for his so-called lapses in form, have nevertheless felt that no one's works have ever seemed so much like life may be taken as evidence that people sense their lives as fraught with contingency. If we did not feel that we, too, were capable of having lived more lives than one, it would be Tolstoy, rather than Hardy or Dickens, who would seem artificial by comparison.

In a few cases, Tolstoy creates what at first glance looks like foreshadowing. In one scene, the immensely proud Prince Andrei refuses to move aside for another proud man, who looks at him with great animosity. When Andrei's protégé Boris asks, who was that man, Andrei replies portentously and "with a sigh he could not suppress" that it was "one of the most remarkable, but to me most distasteful of men—Prince Adam Czartoryski. . . . It is such men as he who decide the fate of nations" (W&P, 310). Everything about this scene marks it as one destined to lead somewhere: everything promises that Prince

Andrei and Prince Czartoryski will meet again, when something dramatic will happen. But nothing of the sort ever takes place. The reader imagines such a meeting, as Andrei and Boris perhaps do, but it remains an unactualized possibility. Always in *War and Peace*, possibilities are not just in excess, but far in excess, of actualities.

Whereas other generals try to imagine two or three possible outcomes of a military situation, the wise commander-in-chief Kutuzov knows that there is an immensity beyond calculation. Tolstoy creates the sense of such an immensity of lives for his characters as well. Thus, although he uses the sort of sideshadowing that appears in Dostoevsky—the sense of a few other events that might also have happened—he aims at an even stronger sense of contingency. Tolstoy's method is not to project more possible outcomes for each critical event but to give countless ordinary events a small range of freedom. Constant tiny alterations multiply to a myriad of possibilities. The prosaics of sideshadowing overwhelms the sideshadowing of crises.

The reactions of Tolstoy's first critics point to another method he used to create the sense of other possibilities. Instead of giving us the cause of psychological changes, he gives us merely the sign that they have happened. When Andrei comes to view the old oak differently, we recognize that some process that has long been taking place within him has at last become visible to Andrei himself and has led to a change in his conscious outlook on life. But what that process is we do not learn. It is surely neither the oak itself, nor the visit to Natasha, nor his conversation with Pierre, nor any other event close in time to his thoughts about the tree that has caused the process of change, though all of these allow us to be aware of its ongoing activity. Because its causes are hidden, the change does not seem inevitable. As the well-known critic Pavel Annenkov observed, in *War and Peace* causes seem to operate "outside the novel, in the empty and obscure expanse between the scenes."[53] As a result, although the reader does not regard changes in a character as "absolutely impossible," neither does the reader "arrive at the conviction as often as he should that nothing else but what did happen could have happened" (Annenkov, 242).

Although Annenkov intended this observation as a criticism, it accurately describes Tolstoy's technique. Annenkov evidently assumed that novels should create a sense of inevitability, but Tolstoy's purpose was precisely the opposite. Readers of *War and Peace* imagine what *else* might have happened to Prince Andrei. If not for that hidden process of change, might he have grown to resemble his irascible father, who, having forsaken the world of public activity, makes work for himself by tutoring (and torturing) his daughter? Or after having renounced ambition, might Andrei, on the contrary, have eventually discovered his sister's wisdom and learned to live according to prosaic virtues?

Sensing the contingency of what did happen to Andrei, the reader projects these and many other possibilities and feels, when Andrei dies, that an infinity of potential has died along with him.

Nineteenth-century novelists reacted differently to the immense prestige of science, which was then almost always interpreted to mean that iron causal laws create a deterministic universe. For some, novelistic plotting served to illustrate a linear temporality, whereas for others the novel's value lay precisely in its power to show time as open and fraught with possibility. A self-conscious archaist opposed to his age's mania for grand systems, Tolstoy fought a war on narrative forms that presuppose linear time.

Vortex Time

The more a work cultivates devices of openness, the more it seems to preclude closure. In such circumstances, an ending (as opposed to a mere stopping point) is likely at best to seem artificial and at worst to defeat the author's fundamental purposes. For if everything tends toward an end in which all threads are tied and at which action necessarily ceases, then patterning will be retrospectively imposed upon the whole. And yet it would seem that for an artwork to be effective at all, it must create some sense of an ending, some sense that a whole has been concluded.

For Henry James, the novelist's art consists in structuring a plot so that the ending, in spite of its evident violation of life's continuity, seems as natural as possible. "Really, universally, relations stop nowhere," James observes, "and the exquisite problem of the artist is eternally to draw, by a geometry of his own, the circle within which they shall happily *appear* to do so."[54] Some authors resolve the problem with an ending that satisfies the demand for closure while slyly parodying its artifice, as Jane Austen does in *Emma;* others directly allude to closural conventions, as George Eliot does in the "Finale" to *Middlemarch.* These relatively soft allusions to necessary artifice were clearly insufficient for Dostoevsky and Tolstoy, whose drive toward openness was so pronounced as to require special techniques to solve the problem of ending.

Bakhtin argued that the very nature of the polyphonic novel made an effective ending almost impossible. In Bakhtin's view, everything in Dostoevsky's novels was so antagonistic even toward a stopping point (let alone effective closure) that there inevitably arose a pronounced and "unique conflict between the internal open-endedness of the characters and dialogue and the *external . . . completedness* of every individual novel" (PDP, 39). With no good solution available, Dostoevsky usually resorted to "a *conventionally literary, conventionally monologic* ending" (PDP, 39) out of keeping with the whole. Bakhtin's example is the epilogue to *Crime and Punishment,* which many readers have indeed regarded as out of keeping with the rest of the book.

In my view, Bakhtin's conclusion derives more from the inner logic of his argument than from the evidence. In fact, Dostoevsky often found remarkably effective ways to end his works: one need only consider *The Idiot,* in which final catastrophe resolves the plot with impressive power. The ending of *The Idiot* does not just finish off a novel interesting for other reasons but is itself one of the work's most memorable parts.

I believe that Dostoevsky combines temporality tending toward openness with temporality tending toward closure. He relies on the latter or on an interesting combination of the two to ensure an effective ending for his work. Sideshadowing works along with another, radically different chronicity that I prefer to call *vortex time.*

Vortex time and sideshadowing work in opposite ways. If in sideshadowing apparently simple events ramify into multiple futures, in vortex time an apparent diversity of causes all converge on a single catastrophe. A hidden clock seems to synchronize this diversity so that, even though causal lines seem unrelated to one another, they not only lead to the same result but also do so at the same moment (see chapter 2, figure 4 [3]).

Several vortices of varying power are revealed in a Dostoevsky novel. When one appears, an otherwise improbable sequence of escalating disasters occurs, with one shocking event following another with ever-increasing force. Vortices draw events into Dostoevsky's thrilling "scandalous scenes," in which unexpected synchronicities create a cascade of crises. Anyone who knows Dostoevsky's fiction recognizes such scenes as carrying the signature of the author.

To take just one example: in *The Possessed,* several causal lines converge when a series of unexpected guests—the mad cripple Marya Timofeevna, the buffoon Lebyadkin, the conniving Pyotr Stepanovich, and at last the mysterious Stavrogin—appear without warning in Varvara Petrovna's drawing room. Each contributes to yet another shock, and each shock at first seems to end the scene, only to be followed by another, and yet another. Each disaster is revealed as a mere catalyst for a still greater one. Distinct causal lines seem to converge in the same place at the same time, although there is no apparent reason for them to do so. Nothing within each causal line relates it to all the others, and yet they all seem directed at this drawing room at this very moment.

Reflecting on the way everything seems to conspire to produce crisis, the chronicler of *The Possessed* observes that "the utterly unexpected arrival of Nikolai Vsevolodovich [Stavrogin], who was not expected for another month, was not only strange from its unexpectedness but precisely from some sort of fateful coincidence with the present moment [*imenno rokovym kakim-to sovpadeniem s nastoiashcheiu minutoi*]" (P, 179). "Coincidence" unites otherwise distinct causal lines, and their interaction has "fateful" results. Dostoevskian vortices always create "fateful coincidence" at a single "moment." Time seems directed, as if from without, to come to a point.

Any reader of Dostoevsky will think of many similar examples. Some vortices lead to local catastrophes sufficient to end one section of a novel (like the scene concluding part I of *The Idiot*, in which Nastasya Filippovna throws a hundred thousand rubles into the fire). Others shape the very premise of the work, as, after a certain point, the vortex is felt and everything leads to a murder, an attempted murder, a suicide, or a descent into madness. Quite various motives lead Dmitri to stand over his father's head with a pestle in his hand: the money he owes Katerina Ivanovna, the rivalry over Grushenka, resentment over his abandonment as a child, his father's counterclaim over the inheritance, Ivan's recently enunciated theory justifying murder, and the old man's loathsome behavior in the elder's cell. We watch Dmitri in a rapidly intensifying frenzy grab at straws more and more desperately as he searches wildly for the three thousand rubles he needs. The closer he gets to the catastrophe, the more evidently does action, no matter to what end it may be directed, draw him with ever-increasing speed to the murder scene.[55]

In much the same way, a diversity of contradictory ideologies all direct Raskolnikov to the murder scene, and several theories that cannot be reconciled with each other all converge for Kirillov in suicide. The whole point here is that each of these ideological heroes (like others in Dostoevsky) adheres to contradictory theories. It is as if the gravitational pull of the act they justify can redirect any sequence of ideas. The character's obsessive dream of murder or suicide draws everything to it regardless of logic and consistency.

When a vortex is strong enough, it attracts everything, any stray thought or chance event, to its center, even if the character struggles against it. In the vortex, all forces, all theories, no matter what their initial trajectory, are redirected to point toward the catastrophe ahead. In the vicinity of catastrophe, foreshadowing is very definitely possible. In the last chapter of *The Idiot* before the conclusion, there are several examples, as Myshkin is drawn forward by accurate presentiment, and his descent to idiocy can be foreseen with increasing clarity.

Like an astronomical black hole, the catastrophe or obsessive idea seems capable of bending space and time. Its immense gravitational pull makes escape increasingly difficult. In *The Idiot*, the narrator uses the image of a magnet, which creates its own attractive field to bend both time and space. When powerful enough, magnets draw objects toward them regardless of where they are pushed. Contingency yields to providence (usually negative providence). How else to explain why the hero of *Crime and Punishment* finds himself in just the right place to overhear chance information facilitating the murder?

The End of Time

As catastrophe approaches, *time speeds up*. Crises recur more and more rapidly until a moment of apparently *infinite temporal density* is reached. For Madame Stavrogina, the chronicler remarks, "The present moment might really be . . . one of those in which all the essence of life, of all the past and the present, perhaps, too, all the future, is concentrated, as it were, focused" (P, 183).

Of all Dostoevsky's novels, *The Idiot* seems most thoroughly dominated by vortex time. Prince Myshkin himself is fascinated by various versions of it, as we see in his repeated descriptions of the last moments of a person condemned to death. Myshkin dwells upon the speeding up of time experienced by the prisoner as execution nears. On the way to the guillotine, it seems to the prisoner as if he has plenty of time. He imagines that his last half hour has room for an immense number of sensations and thoughts, for his mind now works at an extraordinary rate in order to concentrate the energy of a lifetime into those last moments. As the time remaining diminishes, the mind speeds up still more, so that ten minutes, and then five, and then one, and then a fraction of one, contain the energy of a lifetime. The agony of knowing that the absolute end is near also increases geometrically, and with ever-increasing rapidity it transforms all thoughts and all stray impressions—"one of the executioner's buttons is rusty" (I, 60)—into reminders of the imminent horror.

The vortex strengthens as it approaches. "There is one point that can never be forgotten, and one can't faint, and everything moves and turns about it, about that point" (I, 60). At last the prisoner's head is on the block, and what was once concentrated into a half hour now pulsates to a quarter of a second, and suddenly the prisoner "hears above him the clang of the iron! He must hear that! If I were lying there, I should listen on purpose and hear. It may last only the tenth part of a second, but one would be sure to hear it" (I, 60). As the parts of a second shrink, the mind speeds up virtually to infinity. "And only fancy," Myshkin observes, "it's still disputed whether, when the head is cut off, it knows for a second after that it has been cut off! What an idea!" (I, 60). A second is now an immense amount of time, lifetimes long, for time itself has been deformed, intensified, sped up more and more as it is sucked into the vortex. The lifetime's worth of agony that has been concentrated into a tenth and then into a hundredth part of a second must now be lived through a hundred times if that severed head can remain aware for an entire second. "And what if it knows it for five seconds!" Myshkin concludes (I, 60).

For Myshkin, the reason that execution is worse than murder by brigands is that a man attacked on the high road imagines that he may escape and perhaps maintains this hope even *after* his throat has been cut. Thus there is no vortex, or a much weaker one, than when death is certain. For Myshkin, nothing is more horrible than time without possibilities, when everything is foreshadow and nothing is sideshadow.

Myshkin then wonders, "Perhaps there is some man who has been sentenced to death, been exposed to this torture and has then been told 'you can go, you are pardoned'" (I, 20–21). Of course, as readers of the novel knew, Dostoevsky had himself lived through just this experience—had rediscovered possibility when there appeared to be none. Such unexpected survival beyond the vortex, such an escape from inevitability, suggests that certainty may not be so certain after all. No matter how strong the vortex, no matter how much time may seem to close, there remains the *possibility of possibility*.

Myshkin deeply comprehends the experience of a man condemned because the same temporality governs his epileptic fits. Before a fit strikes, he can begin to feel it coming, and this presentiment grows ever stronger. At last in the final minute before the fit he begins to experience an ecstasy as intense as the condemned man's agony. And the ecstasy follows the same logic of geometric increase. The rapidity of consciousness seems to abolish sequence altogether, and at the final instant, Myshkin explains, "I seem somehow to understand the extraordinary saying that *there shall be no more time*. Probably . . . this is the very second which was not long enough for the water to be spilt out of Mahomet's pitcher, though the epileptic prophet had time to gaze at all the habitations of Allah" (I, 214–15).

"There shall be no more time"—Dostoevsky's favorite phrase from the Book of Revelation—links the temporality of execution and epilepsy to the novel's other governing image of a vortex: the approach of Apocalypse. In his interpretations of the Apocalypse, Lebedyev speculates that we live in the age of the third horse, that is, presumably, just when the first signs of temporal acceleration are beginning to be felt.[56]

On one occasion, as Myshkin senses an approaching fit, he recognizes another causal line that leads to catastrophe at the very same time and place. Rogozhin has been following him in order to kill him. Catastrophe seems overdetermined by the vortex, which synchronizes the two attacks—the epileptic fit and Rogozhin's flashing knife—so they occur together on the staircase. And yet, curiously enough, the result is Myshkin's escape, as Rogozhin becomes paralyzed from the sight of the fit and runs away. As with Dmitri holding the pestle, and a man pardoned from death at the last moment, possibility reappears when least likely. Sideshadows lurk in the deepest foreshadows.

After the Vortex

Dostoevsky's novels typically work by combining the antithetical times of sideshadowing and the vortex. He created worlds in which open and closed time compete. Most frequently, Dostoevsky set a vortex plot within a world governed by open and ordinary time. The latter measures the madness of the former, as Pyotr Ilyich's prudence contrasts with Dmitri Karamazov's insane attitude to blood or money (and as Nastasya's contrasts with Raskolnikov's). The hero struggles with the vortex while prudent, prosaically decent people manage to escape its pull.

When Dostoevsky uses this kind of plotting, the vortex derives from the heroes' ideologies and pathologies; it testifies to obsession and reflects illness of body, mind, and spirit. Vortex time is almost always associated with mental disease or "brain fever." It may also be the work of the devil, as it is in *Karamazov* and in *The Possessed*. If so, it may be exorcised, which is one reason that the epigraph to *The Possessed* is Jesus' driving of the madman's devils into the swine "who ran violently down a steep place into the lake." Cured, the former madman returns to normal, and the people see him "sitting at the feet of Jesus, clothed and in his right mind."[57] Some Dostoevsky heroes are cured and some are not, but all live in a world in which obsession is demonic and exorcism is possible.

In Dostoevsky's novels, vortex time typically possesses main characters (and some minor ones) but does not govern the world. Even in *The Idiot,* in which the vortex operates most powerfully, Myshkin knowingly renounces a possible escape from it.[58] Ordinary but decent characters like Vera Lebedyeva, Adelaida Epanchina, Prince S., and perhaps Yevgeny Pavlovich live unaffected by its terrible pull. In *The Possessed*, Stepan Trofimovich attributes the end of his professional career to "a vortex of combined circumstances," but, the narrator tells us, "it turned out afterwards that there had been no 'vortex' and even no 'circumstances'" (P, 4). For other characters, the vortex surely exists but is of their own making.

Dostoevsky therefore contrasts Raskolnikov's self-induced and self-theorized "disease" with the healthy perspective of Razumikhin, who believes not in sudden challenges to fate but in constant small efforts and undramatic exertions. Razumikhin also maintains that history is open, resists all explanatory schemes, and never fits a pattern dreamed up by some "mathematical head" (C&P, 251). In passages like these, he voices the temporality of the novel. The detective Porfiry Petrovich shares Razumikhin's view, but he also understands profoundly the psychology and temporality of the vortex, which is why he is able to identify the criminal and torture him into confessing. Porfiry recognizes the signs of a man caught in an accelerating chronicity, and he knows that, with the right provocation, Raskolnikov will behave like a moth circling ever closer to the flame. The unequal contest between detective and criminal may be viewed as a duel of temporalities in which Raskolnikov's obsessional disease loses.

Because vortex time does not govern a novel's world, sideshadowing and openness may return after a catastrophe. Thus Dostoevsky's novels often end with a dramatic disaster followed by the resumption of normal time. Possibilities are reborn. Raskolnikov in Siberia at last gives up his fatal theory and returns to a faith in the very process of life. From that moment, the remaining seven years of his sentence, which had seemed like merely empty time, are now revealed as filled with potential: they are *"only* seven years!"* (C&P, 532). Raskolnikov at last escapes the vortex and returns to a temporality that fits no preordained pattern.

At the novel's close Raskolnikov's time begins to open. It is to be filled bit by bit with new, unpredictable events. No mere consequence of what has already happened, Raskolnikov's life would now demand another book: "But that is the beginning of a new story—the story of the gradual renewal of a man, the story of his gradual regeneration, of his gradual passing from one world into another, of his acquaintance with a new, till then completely unknown reality. That might be the subject of a new story, but our present story is ended" (C&P, 532). [59] Dostoevsky stresses that Raskolnikov's time is now "gradual" (or "by degrees"—*postepennoe*) for two reasons: it is free from the dizzying temporality of the vortex, and, immersed in contingency, it can only be known as it is lived moment by uncertain moment.

In *Karamazov*, the idea of openness triumphing over the vortex is conveyed by the note of hope in the final scene and by the narrator's promise of a second novel. He reminds us more than once that everything he narrates—all that we know as *The Brothers Karamazov*—is mere prologue. The novel's catastrophe, however destructive, opens into new life and new uncertainties, as the novel's epigraph suggests: "Except a corn of wheat fall into the ground and die, it abideth alone: but if it die, it bringeth forth much fruit" (John 12:24).

At the conclusion of "The Dilemma of Determinism," which I discussed in chapter 3, William James suggests that open time may share the world with Providence. Perhaps God allows for people to choose and does not know their choices in advance; he creates a world with more possibilities than actualities. And yet, depending on contingent circumstances, he is also ready to offer slight, undetected pushes in the right direction by performing miracles so small that they do not come to light. If so, James concludes, "the creator's plan of the universe would thus be left blank as to many of its actual details," which "would be left absolutely to chance; that is, would only be determined when the moment of realization came" (DD, 182). Without knowing what choices people would make, God would guide the world in beneficial ways. Two temporalities could thus interact to shape the world as we know it.

Dostoevsky's novels also combine openness with closure. To be sure, Dostoevskian providence is usually negative, a drive to catastrophe. A terrible vortex provides sufficient closure to the novel, but sideshadowing returns to project ever more stories of uncertain shape and outcome.[60]

Aperture

In *War and Peace* and to a considerable extent in *Anna Karenina,* Tolstoy chose a different solution to the problem of closure, one that makes no concessions to foreshadowing. The reign of sideshadowing was to be as complete in his books as it is in life: in neither work is there ever a moment when all threads are tied together and when the impression of completeness is offered. Tolstoy chose to create so that closure would be unnecessary. To take its place, he invented a new device, which I call *aperture.*

As it happens, Tolstoy elucidated what he had in mind in an essay he published while *War and Peace* was being serialized, an essay that draws on a number of draft introductions to the book. Most novels, he pointed out, tend to a conclusion that the author has planned from the outset, which means that the ending is silently present in the beginning. But this is not the case with *War and Peace,* in which both beginning and ending are arbitrary and independently chosen. Tolstoy explains that he deliberately picked an arbitrary starting point, the year 1805, because history itself is a continuum with no beginnings and endings. For the same reason, he selected a possible stopping point (1856) that he knew he could never reach, so that however much he might write, he could still write more. There would never be a moment at which all threads would be tied up: "In printing the beginning of my proposed work, I promise neither a continuation nor a conclusion for it. We Russians in general do not know how to write novels in the sense in which this genre is understood in Europe; and this proposed work . . . can least of all be called a novel—with a plot that has constantly growing complexity, and a happy or unhappy denouement, with which interest in the narration ends" (Jub 13:54).

Thus the very design of *War and Peace* required that at the end of each installment of this serially published work there be many loose threads and the potential for development in numerous directions. In the next installment, should there be one, some of these potentials would be activated while others would be left undeveloped. The reader would therefore sense the possibility that a different installment was equally possible. Events in whatever section is most recent always allow for various futures; and the future that is eventually realized will neither account for everything nor convey the impression of inevitability. Thus the significance of events is not predetermined because their meaning may vary depending on what happens next.

Foreshadowing was therefore ruled out in principle. To insure that this device could not contaminate events with anachronistic meaning, Tolstoy determined to write each installment not knowing what was to be in the subsequent one (apart from certain historical facts, like the dates of battles, which were of course fixed). As for his fictional heroes and heroines, Tolstoy declared, "I do not foresee the outcome of these characters' relationships in even a single one of these epochs" (Jub 13:55). It follows that serial publication was not simply the way in which *War and Peace* was published—as it was, say, for *Barchester Towers*—but was essential to its form. Of course, for today's readers, who encounter the work as a book, the original experience of reading periodic installments can only be reconstructed.

Serial publication also deprived the work's original readers of knowing how much more of it remained. It was impossible to guess, as readers usually do, at how many plot complications are possible in a given number of pages to come. And in fact, Tolstoy insisted, he did not know how long the work would continue; he only knew that no stopping point would provide a denouement or an ending in the usual sense. One can imagine the frustration of reviewers who (as many did) guessed at outcomes under the assumption that the work would be as long as Tolstoy's previous novel, *The Cossacks;* then as long as a long Russian novel, like the simultaneously published *Crime and Punishment;* then twice as long as that, and so on. Some critics were particularly struck that Dolokhov, who appeared at first to be one of the main heroes, faded from view in later sections.[61] If Tolstoy had chosen to continue events at the same pace for another decade—say, through the Decembrist revolt of 1825—what would have been the status of Prince Andrei, who dies a few hundred pages before the ending as we now have it, in that much larger work? Like life, *War and Peace* goes on and on. This book was designed not as a very long work but as a work of *indeterminate* length.

Closure was to be replaced by aperture. A work that employs aperture renounces the privilege of an ending. It invites us instead to form a relative closure at several points, each of which could be a sort of ending or, at least, as much of an ending as we are ever going to get. There will be no final ending, only a potentially infinite series of relative closures, each encouraging a provisional assessment made in the knowledge that it will have to be revised. In this respect, *War and Peace* is like life and like history; with aperture, it teaches the wisdom of the provisional and presumes the openness of the future.

Thus, in addition to including essays on how endings falsify events, Tolstoy explicitly warned his readers that *War and Peace* would neither have nor require denouement or closure. It would never be anything but a series of installments: "I am convinced that interest in my story will not cease when [the part about] a given epoch is completed, and I am striving for this effect" (Jub 13:56). The end of the work will simply be the last installment Tolstoy has the energy to write, but he will always be able to add another one.

Most dramatically, Tolstoy surprised the readers of *Anna Karenina* by continuing the work after it had evidently ended with Anna's suicide at the end of part VII. Tolstoy later added part VIII, which involves surviving characters in the excitement over the Eastern War. Vronsky volunteers, while Levin argues with Sergei Ivanovich about the morality of Russian participation. Readers today often overlook what must have been obvious to Tolstoy's contemporaries: the events in part VIII *could not* have been part of Tolstoy's original plan because the Eastern War had not yet begun when the novel began to be published. Those who had read the work as complete when Anna died, who had found a structure tying everything together, who had, in short, discovered closure—were shown to be mistaken. Tolstoy wrote so that continuation was always possible. George Steiner drew the correct lesson from the unexpected part VIII when he asked, why not parts IX and X? The effect of Tolstoyan time, wrote Steiner, is that of "a live continuum in which the individual narrative marked a brief and artificial segment."[62] Aperture encourages us to read with such expectations of open and unending futurity so that we become practiced in assessing events forever free of foreshadowing, closure, and final signification. Professional critics have generally not drawn this conclusion: disdaining the naivete of their predecessors who believed part VII was the end, they have usually affirmed how obvious it is that part VIII was required to provide a satisfying resolution to all themes. In so doing, these critics have behaved like the naive historians satirized in *War and Peace*. They find structure by "stencil" reading. Seeing events that echo earlier events, they have ascribed foreshadowing, as if repetition did not occur often enough in life without advance planning or structure.[63]

"I strove only so that each part of the work would have an independent interest," Tolstoy maintained. And then he wrote and struck out the following remarkable words: "which would consist not in the development of events, but in development [itself]" (Jub 13:55). Development itself—that is what aperture is designed to convey. It requires unpredetermined futurity, which means an escape from *all* ways in which an end or structure can be already given. One may put it this way: Tolstoy's war on foreshadowing, structure, and closure was ultimately an attempt to present a written artifact as an artifact still being written, and so closer to lived experience.

Aperture must be carefully distinguished from an apparently similar but essentially different device, anticlosure. As it has been used from Lucian to

Lem, anticlosure paradoxically creates an effective ending out of an apparent refusal to end. Just as the work is in the process of denying it will have an ending, it ends; and this ending ironically proves the most appropriate one. A poem about fleeting inspiration "breaks off," thus creating a "fragment" that is in fact a complete work. Or, as we saw with *Notes from Underground,* a narrator's refusal to stop becomes the very point at which any continuation would be superfluous. The underground man's notes may have been interrupted but Dostoevsky's *Notes* has been artfully completed.

In short, anticlosure is really just another form of closure. As with any other kind of successful closure, the conclusion of the work creates what one theorist has called "a sense of appropriate cessation. It announces and justifies the absence of further development; it reinforces the feeling of finality, completion, and composure which we value in all works of art . . . by providing a point from which all the preceding elements may be viewed comprehensively and their relations grasped as part of a significant design."[64] With the snap of an epigram, anticlosure makes the very act of denial the most perfect assertion.

That is precisely what Tolstoy did not want to do: he provides no point from which it is possible to "view comprehensively" a completed structure, no point at which all preceding elements can be grasped as part of a completed design, and no point at which continuation would be superfluous. The burden of *War and Peace* is to show how dangerous and false is our demand for such privileged viewpoints. Above all, Tolstoy wanted to change our habit of viewing our lives as if they resembled conventional narratives. Our lives have not been authored in advance, but are lived as we go along. They are process, not product, and every moment could have been different, for contingency always reigns. Time exists not under the foreshadow but accompanied by an ever-changing kaleidoscope of sideshadows.

CHAPTER FIVE

Paralude: Presentness and Its Diseases

The shapes of divinity are many, and
The gods accomplish many things beyond hope;
The expected was not fulfilled
And god found a way for the unexpected.
That is how this affair turned out.
—EURIPIDES

Sports Time

In a running gag on the old television show "Magnum, P.I.," Magnum, who lives in Hawaii, can never watch a live game with his favorite team, the Detroit Tigers. When the Tigers are in the World Series, he sets his VCR to record the game and locks himself away so he can watch it before anyone can tell him the final score. He wants to recreate the sense of being a fan at the ongoing game, where cheering makes sense, where the winner is uncertain, where "it isn't over till it's over." Sports events lose an awful lot—not everything, but an awful lot—when they are recorded because exertion in the present is so important to what sports is all about.

We sense certain moments (and potentially any moment) in a live sports event as truly *momentous.* No matter what the "stats" say, a given play may suddenly alter the whole situation, and no one can tell when or if such a play will come. In a World Series game, the outcome of a whole season of hopes and efforts can depend on a single instant, which therefore acquires even more momentousness. Fans remember games in which an unexpected error, out of character with the fielder, made such a difference. Contingency may intervene at any time; the time of the game is one in which players must handle the unexpected on the spot without preparation, and must be ready for whatever the present presents. The ball takes "a wicked hop," and the fans hold their breath during the interval between the fielder's initial bobbling of the ball and what

173

proves to be either successful recovery or an irreversible error. Holding one's breath, cheering, groans: these are all intrinsic to the experience of watching live sports, which depends on *being there now*.

Spectatorship at a sports event involves us in a special temporality of intense presentness, distinct from the temporality of other daily activities, perhaps including actual participation in sports. In some respects, watching sports events resembles reading adventure stories, in which such crucial events as hairbreadth escapes and last-minute rescues happen "in the nick of time." Sports time is etched all over with nicks. But it is, in a real sense, even more adventurous than adventure time because it exhibits an additional quality that even the most suspenseful story lacks. In sports time, the outcome *really* is uncertain, whereas when we read adventure novels or detective tales we know, first of all, that the genre usually prescribes a specific sort of ending from the outset—in these two genres, a happy ending. Perry Mason gets the true criminal to confess on the stand, and the district attorney, defeated yet again, comes back just as confident next time. It is given that he will not learn from his experience in losing dozens of cases about which he was just as confident. Even criminals who know of Hercule Poirot's or Dick Tracy's reputation do not recognize what readers know, that they are battling not just a detective but a genre.[1] But baseball teams battle only each other.

Still more important, when reading adventure stories we know that the outcome has in a sense already happened because the author has already written it down. Their suspense is ultimately—not immediately but ultimately—illusory. We are aware that it is the product of an author's prior deliberation rather than of real contingency in our own present.

Thus in reading even the most suspenseful story we have options unavailable in the real present. If the suspense becomes unbearable, we can close the book and come back later or not at all. We could flip to the end of an adventure story or we may count how many pages are left and so guess at how many new complications are possible. We could read the foreword by Harold Bloom. There are many ways to circumvent the suspense of a published story.

Herodotus tells us, Count no man happy until he is dead. The most important way in which novels are unlike our lives is that novels are *over*. As we have seen, serialized novels may seem less over, which may partially account for their popularity in the nineteenth century. Serialized dramas, for example, "Hill Street Blues" and "L.A. Law," strive for the same effect, which is one reason they tend to incorporate recent real political or social events from episode to episode. Those events lend an episode the mark of presentness. But they also create a special kind of risk.[2]

As in life, and for reasons Herodotus and the Greek tragedians would have understood, current events incorporated into a serialized drama may create unintended ironies and unwanted meanings. They may have unforeseen continuations in life that shed an unwelcome light on the story. That is why, by the time of showing, a disclaimer at the bottom of the screen—or even cancellation of the episode—may be necessary. These are especially noticeable reminders of the risks inherent in the "present effect."

There is an additional cost: nothing fades so fast as up-to-dateness and the openness of the moment. To the extent that shows depend on the present effect, they date especially rapidly. They lose a lot more in reruns than, say, "The Cosby Show" or other dramas in which each incident is a self-contained unit, in which the episodes take place at a not-too-specific time, and in which they can be watched in any order. "M*A*S*H," which cultivates a fake pastness, somehow even gains in reruns. "Hill Street Blues," in contrast to "The Cosby Show" and "M*A*S*H," strives against its status as already recorded, already over. But sports events, unless they are fixed, do not have to strive in this way because they really are not over.

The joke on "Magnum" is that somehow, in spite of all Magnum's precautions to seal off the outside world, news gets through, he learns the final score, and the game is spoiled. And yet one may conjecture that even if he were able to watch the recording without knowing the outcome, the edge of presentness would be dulled. There would still be suspense, of course, as there is suspense in a novel or detective story. But that's the whole point. A novel's suspense is different; it lacks the special momentousness and eventness of live sports. The suspense of a novel or of a *recorded* sports event comes from *not knowing* the outcome rather than from the outcome being still undetermined, as in an ongoing sports event. Wouldn't Magnum feel a little foolish cheering for an outcome, urging his favorite players on, wishing for a hit in a game that is already over and done with and recorded? You might as well cheer for the Athenians to win the Peloponnesian War.

Sports Time: Synchronizing Public and Private

Novels depend on an implicit convention according to which *what is still unknown will be treated as equivalent to what is still undetermined*. Up to a point, the convention is effective, but we nevertheless are aware that it is a convention. Ignorance is not the same thing as indeterminacy, any more than the suspension of disbelief is the same as belief. Narratives use one as a substitute for the other, but we sense the difference. Thus we have the joke about the person so interested in a friend's story about being in mortal danger that he asks, "And did you live?" Such a mistake, like that of a person running on stage to prevent Judas from betraying Christ, is comic precisely because it mistakes a convention to which we are all accustomed for actuality. But in sports time, as in our ongoing lives, indeterminacy is not represented by a substitute, but is real.

Some sports or sportslike events (like live debates between candidates for public office) can maintain interest when recorded. Their potential for doing so depends on what other sources of interest they may have aside from those dependent on the edge of presentness. There may be purely documentary value, which a historian might use in assessing the effect of a debate on a campaign. A coach may use a recording of an error to help a player perform better in the future. Or recordings may acquire nostalgic or allegorical value. For a fan, seeing how the Philadelphia Phillies at last won a world series may evoke again the joy one feels whenever a string of disappointments is at last vindicated by victory. Given the team's later record of losses, such a reminder may have all the appeal of a photograph from one's happy youth.[3]

Despite the fact that an event's initial appeal may have depended on its presentness, if it came to take the shape of a well-plotted drama, it could be viewed and appreciated as such. In such cases, knowledge of the final score would no more destroy the dramatic value of the recording than knowledge of Oedipus's fate would ruin the play. But with sports, this "dramatability" is quite rare, and not only because the contingency of existence creates too many loose ends. In *Oedipus*, we watch the hero deploy a consistent *strategy* and our interest may shift from the fate of the hero to the nature of the strategy. It is given that Oedipus will be defeated, but the strategy may produce unexpected results along the way and exhibit intelligence or profundity we could not have guessed. But consistent strategy is much less important in sports. If it were, computer-models of games would be much closer to real games. What is important in sports is taking advantage of the unforeseen opportunities of the moment. The game is usually oriented not toward a test of an approach or the trying out of a given plan, but to the edge of the present. Almost always, there is little left over when that interest is exhausted.

In short, for sports to feel like sports, we have to be present. Spectators have to be *simultaneous* with the events they watch. To be present in space as well—to be *at* the game—adds to the experience because it makes simultaneity all the more palpable. In short, two times, the time of acting and of witnessing, have to coincide. I can read a novel by myself at any time, and indeed there is a special pleasure in solitary reading. But there is a way in which sports events cannot be solitary: the players, at least, must be exerting themselves *while* I am watching them. Private and public time, the personal and the historical, must tick in unison. And so in the very act of watching sports we are tacitly acknowledging the existence of real historical time outside ourselves. There are no solipsists in the bleachers.

Is this need for simultaneity reciprocal? If fans require players acting in the present, do players also require fans witnessing the game in the present? Like the tree in the forest: if a game were played and no one saw it, would it still be (or feel like) a real sports event? Would something essential be lost? The question is not an easy one because it is obvious that sometimes people play basketball or baseball with no one watching. Nevertheless, it seems to me that the answer to these questions about the players is yes—the players require a simultaneous audience, though not so emphatically as fans require simultaneous players. If the audience is not actually present, it will be imagined.

A group forms a softball team; two people play tennis. Do they imagine an audience? Or do they perhaps treat the game as practice for such an occasion and mentally add what a "real" game would have—an impartial umpire, a professional playing ground, and fans cheering or booing? When children play a game, either by themselves or with others, they tend to narrate the sportscaster's account of what is going on. The child catches the ball while saying so or preparing to say so. Adults, I imagine, tend to do the same, but silently, lest they seem childish. Somehow the game is not a game unless there is a witness, and the sportscaster incarnates that necessary function.

Bakhtin argues that all artworks require a hero as the center around which a concretization of values takes place. But the hero does not have to be directly represented. In landscape painting, for instance, we are given the "emotional-volitional field" in which a hero *could* live and act. The painting conjures up the feeling of occupying and experiencing such a landscape. "In this sense," Bakhtin writes, "every [aesthetic] visualization includes within itself a tendency toward the hero, the potential of a hero; in each aesthetic perception of the object there slumbers, as it were, a specific human image" (KFP, 155). The "potential hero" is not so much absent *from* the work as absent *in* the work.[4] In much the same way, the potential audience is absent in the unwitnessed sports event.

"Longing for the Present"

A sportscaster describes a game as it happens. In the temporality of his narration, there cannot be foreshadowing. On the contrary, everything in his voice is oriented toward the present and the unknown future: possibilities are explored, inferences are drawn from similar games in the past, guesses are hazarded and disconfirmed. Often two sportscasters disagree about what will happen next, and when plays confirm the predictions of one, he exhibits the sort of pleasure that testifies to having taken a risk. There is no known future to guide the play-by-play and no possibility of dramatic irony arising from how misleading actions at one moment seem in light of what will necessarily follow.

Sometimes pregame shows include a tape of an earlier match—last year's Wimbledon, say. If there is an announcer from this year commenting on last year's tape, his voice is bound to differ from that of his predecessor who was simultaneous with the action, even if the two announcers are the same person. Viewers who watch such a tape often experience an eerie feeling, especially if both commentaries are intermittently audible. The excitement one once felt and that the original sportscaster communicated now seems illusory in light of the known outcome, which the later announcer presumes. We may feel disturbed: it is as if all our hopes, all our present activity, were nothing but the raw material for a future narrative and as if the present we now experience might also be just the over-and-dead past of some near future. Such a perspective drains the blood from our own time; the present is bled white. This conclusion is unwarranted, of course, because the fact that one future did take place does not mean that another was impossible. Past efforts may still have mattered, and therefore present efforts may matter just as much. But the overlapping of times, the importation of foreshadowing into experiences whose presentness was once so intense, creates the uneasy feeling that we were living, and therefore may now be living, a "chronic" delusion. In such cases, memory trumps the presentness of the past.[5]

By contrast, old photographs sometimes allow memory itself to be trumped. For memory tends to regularize past events by eliminating what, in the light of later experiences, turned out to be irrelevant, purely contingent, or unproductive. We forget such details and unwittingly eliminate more and more of them over time and with each recollection. Memory operates by a sort of gestalt effect producing smooth forms. And yet it is often those irrelevancies, preserved in the photograph, that best capture the sense of the moment as it was then experienced. Thus it is often the small items in the background of old photographs that create the strongest impression. The things barely noticed at the time and included only by chance may best preserve the feeling of life as it was lived. The furniture long ago discarded, a spot on the wall, a picture we had long ago ignored but that now suggests the habitual life we lived beneath it—these small items remind us of how it felt to live in a room. The intended subject of a photograph can seem much less important in comparison with its background; which is one reason that professional portraits without a background so often seem to miss the very point of photography.

It would seem that temporal layering, a palimpsest of successive moments, may in various circumstances create quite different feelings and suggest distinct conclusions. This fact perhaps offers the key to one of the most interesting nineteenth-century Russian arguments about representing the presentness of the past. Both Dostoevsky and Tolstoy, as we have seen, deeply understood presentness, believed in the openness of time, and appreciated the distorting effects of foreshadowing. Both undertook radical experiments to convey presentness in all its experiential fullness. But they differed profoundly about the wisdom of trying to recapture the presentness of the past. Although Tolstoy is usually (and accurately) remembered as an extreme skeptic and Dostoevsky as an all-too-ready believer, on this question their roles were reversed. It was the author of *A Writer's Diary*, not the author of *War and Peace*, who denied that the presentness of the historical past could be recaptured and warned of pernicious effects from the very attempt to do so.

Dostoevsky thought of himself as the writer most willing to undertake the difficult task of representing the present as it is happening and reproved his great rival for contenting himself with the much easier project of describing historical times. According to Dostoevsky, what makes the present an especially difficult topic is that key social trends have not set, and so the writer does not know what social forms will emerge. It is very easy to be mistaken about what is important. Or to use the language of Dostoevsky's epoch, it is hard to identify what the "types" of the present might be. By contrast, a writer who focuses on the past, as Tolstoy does in *War and Peace*, has the advantage of temporal distance. In Dostoevsky's view, Tolstoy escaped from the problem of "types in transition" in yet another way: even in *Anna Karenina*, which is set in the present, Tolstoy focused on the aristocracy, whose forms of life had long acquired an immediately recognizable finish. For Dostoevsky, such novels are essentially historical, even if they are set in the present, because they avoid the difficult problem of understanding the changing world.

As it happens, Dostoevsky's own relatively formless work *A Raw Youth*, which perhaps suffered from too much concern with the transitional, was rejected for publication in the *Russian Herald*: the space had already been allotted to *Anna*![6] At the end of *A Raw Youth*, Dostoevsky implicitly replied to Tolstoy, whom he rebukes for his choice of subject matter. When the novel's hero, Arkady, submits his life story (which we have read) to his former tutor Nikolai Semyonovich, the tutor observes that it is almost impossible to create a polished narrative about the seething, transitional, and ill-formed types Arkady depicts. Arkady would do better to choose either heroes from the past or the aristocratic "grandson of those heroes" (RY, 605), evidently a reference to Levin and Vronsky as the mere updating of Pierre and Prince Andrei.[7] To be sure, the tutor concedes, "such a work, if executed with great talent, would belong not so much to Russian literature as to Russian history" (RY, 605). On the other hand, with such a topic "the position of our novelist . . . would be perfectly definite": "Oh! and in the historical form it is possible to depict a multitude of extremely attractive and consolatory details! It is possible so to fascinate the reader indeed that he will take the historical picture for the possible and the actual" (RY, 605). Although Nikolai Semyonovich is entirely sincere here, Dostoevsky's irony is palpable. If Arkady insists on writing about the immediate present, the tutor continues, he should be aware that such a narrative "can have no beauty of form. Moreover these types are in any case transitory, and so a novel about them cannot have artistic finish. One may make serious mistakes, exaggerations, misjudgments. . . . But what is the writer to do who doesn't want to confine himself to the historical form, and is possessed by a longing for the present? To guess ... and make mistakes" (RY, 607). Dostoevsky defined his art, and true realism, in terms of the present and presentness; he detected a range of falsities in those who, like Tolstoy, chose either to give the present the finish of the past (*Anna Karenina*) or the past the openness of the present (*War and Peace*). I should like to focus on the latter point—why, in Dostoevsky's view, the artist should not try to represent the past (by which Dostoevsky meant the relatively distant historical past) as open, even though when it happened it was truly open.

Genre Painting and Memory

Dostoevsky's reasoning may be summarized in a sequence of steps: (1) All moments of time could lead, and could have led, to multiple futures. The past did not have to lead to us. (2) Artists should represent time as it really is experienced. (3) Nevertheless, any attempt to represent the historical past as open will necessarily lead to another kind of falsity and hence will entail grotesque distortions. (4) Therefore, artists concerned (as they should be) with capturing temporal experience should represent only the present (or a recent past still felt as present in the sense that it can still lead to multiple outcomes). In effect, the true realist will, like Dostoevsky, avoid historical fiction and set novels in the world we are still experiencing.

The crucial step in this argument is obviously the third: why does art concerned with representing the presentness of the past lead to distortion? The reason, in brief, is that we know the past through memory, which always imports into the remembered event other events that happened later. It cannot help doing so. Therefore, the artist who, like Tolstoy, tries to "subtract" those memories will, in the very attempt to capture the presentness of the past, distort our experience of the ongoing present, part of which is our memories of the past. In the attempt to be true to a historical past, such an artist falsifies a crucial element of his own time, which is not an isolated moment but a moment in a memory-laden sequence.

Curiously enough, Dostoevsky chose to explain these ideas in an article on genre painting ("Apropos of the Exhibition," AWD, 73.9). After evaluating a number of recent efforts on the part of Russian genre painters to capture the sense of current Russian experience in all its openness, Dostoevsky asserts that this form cannot be retrofitted to depictions of open experiences in the past. The result is bound to be a confusion of two distinct kinds of temporality:

> What is genre [painting], in essence? Genre is the art of portraying con-
> temporary, immediate reality that the artist has himself felt personally and
> has seen with his own eyes, in contrast with historical reality, for instance,
> which cannot be seen with one's own eyes and which is portrayed not in
> its immediate but in its completed aspect. . . . Historical reality in art, for
> instance, is naturally not that of immediate reality (genre) precisely because
> the former is completed and not current. (AWD, 73.9)

As Dostoevsky uses his terms, the present is not "completed" because one does not know what will come of it; that incompleteness is essential to our experience of presentness. Genre painting is the art of capturing the sense of the ongoing present, which means it must exhibit incompleteness. By contrast, we experience the past as completed—we know what came of it—and so quite different techniques must be used to represent it.

It follows for Dostoevsky that attempts to paint the past as genre can only lead to shallow notoriety. Such paintings create a shocking effect at the expense of truthfulness and understanding. For they involve "a confusion of concep-tions of reality." Their falsity derives from their attempt to represent the past as if we, like our ancestors, did not know the past's future:

> Ask any psychologist you like and he will tell you that if you imagine some
> event of the past, especially of the distant past—one that is completed and
> historical (and to live without imagining the past is impossible)—then the
> event will *necessarily* be imagined in its completed aspect, i.e., with the
> addition of all its subsequent developments that had not yet occurred at
> the historical moment in which the artist is trying to depict a person or
> event. And thus the essence of a historical event cannot even be imagined
> by an artist exactly as it probably happened in reality. (AWD, 73.9)

Accurate representation of the historical past is impossible—the artist cannot imagine it as it happened—because each past moment was open: it was actually just another present. It had the potential to lead in directions other than the one realized. But we do not experience the past, we remember it, and memory, as we have seen, alters the past by closing it down. We remember what did hap-pen, not what might have; we remember what led to where we are now. Given in memory, events lose the presentness they once had and acquire pastness, which is quite a different thing.

According to Dostoevsky, a recollected event necessarily includes within the event the future that had not yet happened and might well not have happened. Our intellect may tell us that time was open then just as it is now, but our actual experience of the past, through memory, includes one and only one subsequent course of events. In short, memory necessarily eliminates sideshadows and replaces them with foreshadows, the importing of the future into the past. It must therefore falsify the past, which did not somehow include the future that happened to have resulted from it.[8]

Freedom is an attribute of presentness. In Dostoevsky's view, we cannot visualize people of the past as truly free; we cannot imagine their freedom as we directly experience our own, even if we know they were no less free than we are. Any attempt on the part of the artist to "combine both realities—the historical and the immediate" therefore creates an "unnatural combination" from which "arises the worst kind of untruth." Dostoevsky's example is Ge's genre painting of the Last Supper:

> There sits Christ—but is that Christ? It may be a very good young man, deeply hurt by his quarrel with Judas . . . but this is not the Christ we know. . . . we must ask the question: where are the eighteen centuries of Christianity that followed, and how are they connected with the event? How is it possible that from such an ordinary quarrel of such ordinary people gathered to have supper, such as Mr. Ge depicts, there could arise something so colossal? Nothing at all is explained here; there is no historical truth here; there is not even any truth of genre here; everything is false. . . . everything here is disproportionate and out of scale with the future. (AWD, 73.9)

This example does not really justify Dostoevsky's extreme conclusion. After all, an accurate representation of the past as open would at least have to include the possibility, if not the necessity, of the future that did in fact follow. Even by the criteria of realism with sideshadows, the future that did result must have been *one* of the possible outcomes, and therefore its occurrence should not be made incomprehensible, as (in Dostoevsky's interpretation) it is in Ge's painting.

Prosaics and the Presentness of the Past

As Dostoevsky was well aware, *War and Peace* addresses these very questions at length, and so Dostoevsky's comments on Ge constitute yet another oblique answer to Tolstoy. To repeat: the two writers agreed that memory distorts the past by imposing foreshadowing upon it but they disagreed about the artist's proper response to that distortion. Both appealed to realism but in different ways. For Dostoevsky, the realist must attempt to be faithful to *our own* experience, which means that the past must be represented as we experience it *now*. The artist must preserve the *pastness of the past*, which is an effect of memory operating in the present. Thus the past should not be represented with presentness because we cannot know it that way, even though the people living then directly experienced its presentness. For Tolstoy, the realist must be faithful to the *object* of his description, which means that the author must somehow contrive to restore the presentness of a previous time and recapture the sense of life that people then living experienced. Tolstoy's realist must be true not to his or her own experience, but to the experience of others, however much our current impressions may differ.

In Tolstoy's view, artists of the historical past must expend considerable effort to override their intuitions and counter the effects of their own later position in time. Strictly speaking, according to Tolstoy, it is not the knowledge of later events that must be eliminated but the *false impression of necessity* that somehow accompanies that knowledge. We do not have to forget what did happen, we have to remind ourselves that something else could have.

The crucial point is that historians and historical novelists tacitly assume only two points of reference, which is what allows them to draw a straight line between them; the sense of necessity results from this false privileging of two times. But in fact every moment in between may have been as effective as these two, and so the drawing of a straight line is always misleading. Foreshadowing results from what might be called *the bipolar fallacy*.

Memory as well as the historian tends to draw the same straight line, Tolstoy believed. The longer the line, the stronger the false impression of inevitability becomes. If I made a mistake yesterday, I regret it, and I replay it, and I have to remind myself that yesterday is as unchangeable as the Conquest of Peru. For I still sense the other choices I might have made, and alternatives still possess a palpable sense of possibility. But an event remote in time is weighted with so many subsequent events that it seems impossible to imagine that it, too, had alternatives. "It is this consideration," Tolstoy observes, "that makes the fall of the first man, resulting in the birth of the human race, appear patently less free than a man's entry into wedlock today. It is the reason why the life and activity of men who lived centuries ago and are connected with me in time, cannot seem to me as free as the life of a contemporary, the consequences of which are still unknown to me" (W&P, 1444). It follows that a contemporary event appears to be the work of its participants, whose agency and choice we sense, whereas "in the case of a more remote event we see only its inevitable consequences, which prevent our considering anything else possible" (W&P, 1445).

Memory begins the process of conferring necessity. "Imperceptibly, unconsciously, and inevitably" (W&P, 298), memory leads even the most truthful people into falsehood. In *War and Peace* Tolstoy often describes events in detail and then, a few hundred pages later, describes characters' recollections of those events, which differ considerably from what actually happened. Because the original events have been recorded (as they generally are not in our own lives), we may compare the two accounts and measure the distortions that memory has been introducing in the interim.[9] Tolstoy's most brilliant touch was to have his characters introduce the same mistakes that the readers themselves have unconsciously made. Unless we go back to the original passage, we usually do not notice the characters' errors, which we have repeated. Tolstoy keenly portrays the "gestalt" effects of memory, which reprocesses the messiness of reality by eliminating loose ends and unactualized possibilities. It thereby produces a "good" story (as perception produces a "good" form) with relatively straight lines of causality. Historiography multiplies the errors of memory.

To counteract the distortions of memory, Tolstoy used a number of devices, some of which were evidently just the sort that Dostoevsky criticized in his article on Ge. But criticisms of this sort, which Tolstoy understood, seemed unconvincing to him. To be sure, it is hard to imagine events as they happened; but that is precisely the artist's difficult task and is, indeed, one reason that art is necessary. As Tolstoy argued the point in his essay about *War and Peace*, "The historian is concerned with the results of an event, the artist with the very fact of the event" (Jub 16:10). By the "fact of the event" Tolstoy meant the event as its participants experienced it, that is, without knowledge of what came later and with alternatives to actual subsequent events still palpably possible.

By the time Tolstoy wrote, the Battle of Borodino was one of the most famous incidents in Russian history; the little village after which it was named was as familiar a place as Pearl Harbor is to us. But in *War and Peace* the soldiers at the battle know neither of its subsequent fame nor that it is to be named after that village nor even what exactly the village is called. When Pierre surveys the landscape the day before the battle, he asks some soldiers, "What village is that in front of us?" and one answers, "Burdino or something, isn't it?" (Jub 11:194). It is as if, on December 6, 1941, a newly arrived American sailor referred to Opal Harbor.

Dostoevsky may have felt this scene to be a bit gimmicky, as indeed it is, but Tolstoy did not confine himself to such relatively obvious devices. His own sense of history led him radically to rethink historical causality and the relation of past to present. Basically, Tolstoy argued that, in history and in our own lives, we mistake not only causal lines but also the very sort of incidents that shape the future. We tend to limit the number of effective moments to a few critical incidents and then to draw, if not a straight line, then a smooth curve connecting them. But the essential problem of the bipolar fallacy remains, even if we pick not two, but four or five points.

What if such a procedure is based on a fallacy of perception? What if it is not just the few memorable moments that are effective, but every ordinary moment, including those too ordinary to be preserved in memory? What if we would really need some sort of historical calculus, integrating the infinite "infinitesimals" of daily events? Memory and historical documentation tend to preserve dramatic moments that make a good story, whereas history and our own lives are made by the complex interaction of countless ordinary moments; therefore the very historical sources on which we rely mislead us. Like studio photography, memory preserves the foreground of a picture. But the supposed "irrelevancies" in the background of an unprofessional picture, the details we usually overlook or forget, may be just as important in understanding a past time.

Tolstoy uses the following analogy: to argue that great events are important because they are so noticeable is like concluding from a glimpse of a distant hill where only treetops are visible that the region in question has only trees. If history is made by small prosaic actions, most of which are too unremarkable for anyone to record, then we must expend considerable effort to overcome the "optical illusions" of documentation. In Tolstoy's view, that is the task of the historical artist.

The first step is to be suspicious of anything that appears "historic." The very term suggested to Tolstoy a peculiar kind of false drama in which one of two kinds of spurious temporal doubling takes place. Either the historian, judging from the standpoint of his own time, anachronistically confers a special privilege on actions that may well have led elsewhere or nowhere; or, still more distorting, participants in an event act in anticipation of the historical narratives that may someday be written about them. Thus Tolstoy's Tsar Alexander makes speeches and performs actions not because they arise from present circumstances but in imitation of dramatic moments in classic histories; he and others act as if they were already characters in a narrative. Historians in turn seize on such actions and make them the center of their accounts. The result is a kind of mutual reinforcement of falsehoods. In the process, the sort of actions that may really have been effective are overlooked and the whole nature of the historical process is falsely regularized. It is given a shape that has to do with the needs of storytelling and mythification rather than with the actual course of events in all their contingency.

As a rule, Tolstoy insisted, the sort of actions that do shape history are not performed for that reason. Undertaken from prosaic concerns disregarded in most historical accounts, they do not in the least resemble actions taken in imitation of historical narratives. In Tolstoy's view, those who endeavor to be historic have either no effect or one contrary to their intentions, whereas those who act in response to the concerns of the moment—who are immersed in their own present rather than in an anticipated future—may be genuinely effective. If that is often so, historians need to escape from their genre and view the past differently. In one of the book's best-known passages, Tolstoy sums up this line of reasoning:

> We who were not living in those days, when half of Russia had been con-
> quered . . . tend to imagine that all Russians . . . were engaged solely
> in sacrificing themselves, in saving the fatherland, or in weeping over its
> ruin. . . . But in reality it was not like that. It appears so to us because
> we see only the general historic issues of the period and do not see all the
> personal, human interests of the people of the day. And yet actually those
> personal interests of the moment are always so much more significant than
> the general issues that because of them the latter are never felt—not noticed,
> in fact. . . . Those who endeavored to understand the general course of
> events, and hoped by self-sacrifice and heroism to take part in it, were the
> most useless members of society . . . all they did for the common good
> turned out to be futile and absurd. . . . The law forbidding us to taste of the
> fruit of the tree of knowledge is particularly manifested in historical events.
> Only unconscious action bears fruit, and a man who plays a part in an his-
> torical event never understands its significance. If he tries to understand it
> he becomes ineffectual.
>
> The more closely a man was engaged in the events then taking place in
> Russia the less perceptible was their significance to him. In Petersburg and
> in the provinces remote from Moscow, ladies and gentlemen in militia uni-
> forms lamented the fate of Russia . . . and all that sort of thing; but in the
> army . . . no one swore vengeance on the French: they were all thinking
> about their pay, their next quarters, Matryoshka the canteen woman, and
> the like. (W&P, 1126–27)

Because small but effective events are usually undocumented, Tolstoy makes up examples of what they might be like. They are typically performed not by the tsar, not even by the fictional characters who seem most heroic, like Prince Andrei, but by ordinary line officers or even ordinary civilians. The thoroughly "mediocre" Nikolai Rostov seizes an unforeseeable opportunity to charge French soldiers. In quiet disobedience to the mayor of Moscow, who proposes heroic actions to resist the approaching French army, ladies move their families away. With no one planning it, and in spite of all heroic measures on the part of French and Russian officials, Moscow is destroyed because a city made of wood and deprived of its inhabitants is likely to burn down; and so the French cannot remain there for the winter. The city was destroyed and the French forced to retreat not by those who stayed to fight, but by those who "unheroically" left when they could.

People go about their daily lives and, in the process, take small actions that multiply through an incalculable concatenation of effects. The historical sections of *War and Peace* satirize all bipolar, straight line reasoning, which overlooks the effectiveness of each moment. The fictional sections, which identify each moment of time for each person as possessing a small range of freedom, suggest that foreshadowing distracts attention from the prosaic events leading no place in particular but somehow, in combination, producing a result beyond the reach of narrative neatness.

From a Tolstoyan perspective, Dostoevsky's example of Ge's painting is misleading. For one thing, Christ represents the singular case of direct divine intervention, which, for the believer, means that for once the future could be foreseen. Even for the nonbeliever, Christ is at least a historic figure, constantly described and redescribed, which means that it may indeed be impossible to eliminate the weight of events to come. But ordinary people and unrecorded actions are not so burdened with future significance. It is entirely possible to comprehend a Nikolai Rostov without thinking of the consequences of his actions sixty years later. For those consequences have been so affected at each moment by countless other contingent events and small decisions that we are effectively barred from foreshadowing and intuitively resist the imposition of a future perspective. If the representation of Christ without subsequent history seems grotesque, so would the portrayal of a Rostov with it. Dostoevsky's problem is solved once our focus shifts from the historic to the prosaic.

Present and Sequence. The Happiest Moment and Four Diseases of Presentness

Rostov not only deals effectively with fleeting opportunities, he also exemplifies a healthy attitude toward the present. He is quite able to seize happiness in relatively ordinary events without demanding that they fit into some overall story of his life. If the Greek tragedians insisted that happiness can be known only retrospectively, when a life is over and its story is completed, Rostov intuitively understands that happiness may exceed the reach of narrative. He could not express this understanding, but it may be seen in his direct responsiveness to the potentials of the moment.

Home from the army, the young Rostov goes on a hunting expedition. Lying in wait for the wolf, he prays "with that passionate compunction with which men pray in moments of intense emotion arising from trivial causes. 'Why, what is it to Thee,' he said to God, 'to do this for me? I know that Thou art great and that it is a sin to ask this, but for God's sake, make the wolf come my way and let Karai [Rostov's dog] get his teeth in his throat" (W&P, 604). He knows that if one implores God for anything, it should be for something with consequences; but still, he is so immersed in the moment that he asks anyway. And his wish is granted: "The greatest happiness had come to him—and so simply, unheralded by pomp or fanfare" (W&P, 605). That is the only way great happiness comes in the Tolstoyan world beyond foreshadowing. But the wolf begins to escape; then, by sheer chance, it is caught by the dogs. And in that moment on which nothing depends something supremely important happens: "That instant when Nikolai saw the wolf in the gully struggling with the dogs, saw her gray coat and outstretched hind leg under them, her head with ears laid back in terror and gasping (Karai had her by the throat), was the happiest moment of his life" (W&P, 606).

The happiest moment is one of supreme immersion in the present. It escapes autobiographical narrative. If Rostov were some day to be asked about his happiest moment, he would probably not remember this one, which has nothing to do with his love for Sonya or Marya, with his career, or with any of the events that normally figure in the story of one's life. Outside of such sequences, it would elude memory or seem insignificant. Like the important events of history, the happiest moment of a life will usually remain unrecalled, undocumented, unappreciated as such. The intensely lived present possesses an integrity of its own uncompromised by the shadow of the future.

If Rostov exemplifies a healthy attitude toward the present, is it possible to specify unhealthy attitudes? For the remainder of this chapter, I would like to explore four diseases of presentness, four temporal maladies, each of which admits of many variations. So given are we to misunderstanding our place in time and so complex is our experience that this classification, which is not exhaustive, must be preliminary and always open to revision. Nevertheless, it seems worthwhile to specify the following "chronic" diseases:

1. *The Desiccated Present.* We may lose the sense that the present has special importance. All the weight of time may be displaced elsewhere in the temporal sequence, to the past we can no longer affect or to the future taken as already existing.

2. *The Isolated Present.* By contrast, the present may be treated as if the rest of the sequence did not exist or did not matter—as if there were only a present, as if it were an island cut off from tradition and from consequences.

3. *Hypothetical Time.* The entire sequence may come to seem insubstantial, as if we lived "somewhere" else. It may seem as if our lives were merely hypothetical, practice for some more real time or a sideshow to another and more important sequence. In contrast to determinism, in which every possibility is an actuality, hypothetical time feels as if every actuality were a mere possibility. One falsely seems to possess an alibi for time.

4. *Multiple Time.* This sense of time is quite rare and might be classed as a variant of hypothetical time. In multiple time, the temporal sequence in which we live loses its significance because it is not the only sequence; there are somehow many such sequences existing "simultaneously." In this view, every possibility is actualized, if not in our sequence, then in some other. In the absence of any unactualized possibilities, the significance of present choices evaporates.[10]

Disease #1, The Desiccated Present.
Epic Time and Epilogue Time

Sometimes it seems that the present does not especially matter because the really important moments are already over or still to come. Either the past or the future may predominate over the present, and each of these two possibilities admits of many variations. Let us begin with temporalities in which all the weight is placed on past events.

Bakhtin describes epic time as one in which, from the perspective of the epic singer, all of the really important events are over. Adapting Goethe's and Schiller's idea of the "absolute past," Bakhtin describes the time of epic as remote not just quantitatively—it is not just a long time ago—but also, and more important, qualitatively. It is a different kind of time from the one in which the epic singer and his audience live. One cannot reach it merely by "gradual, purely temporal progressions" into the past; "it is walled off absolutely from all subsequent times" (EaN, 15). At some point, lost beyond recovery, the very nature of time changed. We might say that, in the geological sense of the terms, epic is catastrophist whereas the novel is uniformitarian: in the novel's conception, the nature of time has never changed and every past moment was just another present.[11] In the epic, by contrast, the present in which the singer lives and the past of which he sings are not just temporal categories but *"valorized temporal categories"* (EaN, 15).

For the epic singer, the time of heroes is not just an epoch with different concerns but the time in which values were right and true. It is the time of firsts and bests; indeed, "all the really good things (i.e., the 'first things') occur *only* in this past" (EaN, 15). Only a sacrosanct relation to it is possible. One cannot question that time or adopt an experimental attitude toward it, as the novel does with all epochs. "One cannot glimpse it, grope for it, touch it; one cannot look at it from just any point of view; it is impossible to experience it, analyze it, take it apart, penetrate its core" (EaN, 16). One measures oneself by it, but never the reverse: there can be no real dialogue between the time of the audience and the time of the heroes. Exactly the opposite attitude characterizes the novel, in which the values of every past are open to dialogue and in which a skeptical light may be cast on the past as well as on the present. In the novel, everything must enter what Bakhtin often calls "the zone of familiar contact."

Moreover, the epic world is complete unto itself. Because everything important is already over and because there are no significant truths to come, "there is no place in the epic world for any openendedness, indecision, indeterminacy. There are no loopholes in it . . . it suffices unto itself, neither supposing any continuation nor requiring it" (EaN, 16). But novel time always has such "loopholes" to the future.

The advantage of epic time is that it stabilizes values; the danger is that it devalues present activity and may thereby create the sense that even the most pressing moral decisions are of little ultimate consequence. The world of immediate experience may be drained of importance, and yet that is the time in which we live. And the stabilization of values may threaten rethinking required by the present.

These dangers become all the more evident when we reflect that, as Bakhtin observes, epic time need not be set in the historical past at all. It is possible to see a portion of the present world, for example, the "heroic" leaders of one's country, as living in a temporality qualitatively distinct from that of ordinary experience. Here Bakhtin was doubtless alluding to the Stalinist regime's "epicizing" of public political time, apparent in the daily press, in official pronouncements, and in socialist realism.[12] In this context, Bakhtin's comments on epic and his preference for the open time of novels may be taken as an indirect critique of the Soviet system and of all political thinking that displaces importance away from the real, prosaic lives of individuals.

A softer version of epic time might be called *epilogue time*. When realist novels end with an epilogue, temporality changes. Epilogues are deliberately anticlimactic. In epilogue time, characters no longer live their lives but live out their lives. The important story is over, nothing essential will change, and so it is possible to describe in a few efficient strokes the unsurprising events constituting the *rest* of the heroes' lives. The thick description so characteristic of realist novels is therefore replaced by a mode in which mere assertion is enough.

A work that may have devoted hundreds of pages to a few years, months, or even days may now give us decades in a short chapter. Whereas in the body of a novel the narrator often draws us close to the character and allows us to feel something of the throb of presentness in which choices are made, epilogues are typically narrated at a distance, as if they were being told from the remote future or (perhaps more accurately) from a position looking down on the whole sequence of characters' lives. We palpably sense the shift in temporality when an epilogue begins, and this shift becomes an effective closural marker.

Here it might be instructive to consider why the eighth part of *Anna Karenina*, which takes place after the heroine's death and which is shorter than the other parts, was not written as an epilogue. And why have Tolstoy's critics not discussed part VIII as a sort of epilogue, even though, in some respects, it resembles one? We learn what happens to the characters after Anna's death: Vronsky in his grief goes off to the wars; Levin, forever disturbed by his philosophical questions, finds relative peace and wisdom in family life; Stiva and Dolly continue as they have throughout the book. And yet, there is no shift in temporality; the same time governs these events as governs the rest of the work. Tolstoy chose to present these incidents with the same density of moment-to-moment description as he did the rest of the book.

In contrast to what happens in most successful epilogues, important events that may change the characters' lives do continue to take place in part VIII, just as they do in the first seven parts. It appears even that, for Levin, life continues with still greater intensity than it had before and it is here that he makes his most important discoveries. Throughout part VIII there is no sense that nothing substantially different can happen. To be sure, Vronsky chooses to live as if, after Anna's death, the rest of his life is mere epilogue to a tragedy, but the reader apprehends that this way of living is a falsity and a self-indulgence. It is a pose adopted as if in imitation of Anna's constant self-casting as a tragic heroine.

Through Vronsky, Tolstoy uses the final part of his novel to show the dangers of epilogue time. We see its moral cost not only in the anticipation that Vronsky is going to an early and futile death but also in his abandonment of his daughter to do so. On Anna's way to suicide, when Tolstoy uses a technique approaching stream of consciousness to describe the progression of her thoughts, we note that she never once thinks of her daughter and what will happen to her when left motherless. And now the girl's father also abandons her to be brought up by her legal but not natural father, the near-crazed Karenin. We are likely to conclude that Vronsky should heed the call of the present and that he is morally to blame for embracing the consolations of epilogue.

Perhaps one reason that so many readers have criticized the epilogue to *Crime and Punishment* is that it confuses temporalities.[13] It tries to be both word and afterword. Like epilogues generally, it narrates by assertion rather than by the detailed portrayal used in the rest of the novel. Yet it contrives to save Raskolnikov, to bring him to God and repentance, and not by simply continuing an already familiar trajectory but by beginning and accomplishing a conversion, all in a few pages.[14] Real change takes place, something truly surprising in terms of what has happened before, but it is not given the same novelistic density as previous changes. As a result, we feel that Raskolnikov's conversion is unearned, a sort of salvation ex machina.

At the end of part VI, Raskolnikov gives himself up out of sheer exhaustion, not out of remorse. Thus the epilogue begins by describing his still-unrepentant state of mind. He continues to adhere to the idea that there is no such thing as crime and that, even if there were, certain extraordinary people must be exempt from moral judgment. He regards his act of murder not as immoral but as a mere "blunder." But a few pages later Raskolnikov discovers the Dostoevskian truth in a mythic dream. To be sure, scholars justifying the novel's epilogue have correctly related this passage to the novel's early dreams and have linked its trope of disease to the novel's recurrent language of illness. Both the first six parts and the epilogue use symbolism and myth. Nevertheless, the rest of the novel works primarily by describing psychic states in terms of a dense texture of quotidian experience. Changes are made plausible through a series of minute steps. The epilogue relies on myth alone, and so it seems contrived. An epilogue is no place—and no time—for a final reversal. If such a reversal is contemplated, we expect not an epilogue but a final section, like that of *Anna Karenina*, set in the same temporality as the rest of the book. Epilogue time presumes that all important incidents have already happened and that further changes are mere extensions of what has gone before.

Real people sometimes live as if their lives were set in epilogue time, so that no present actions could make any real difference. Such lives are often suffused with a delicious nostalgia, a poetic sense of constant distance from a beautiful and irrecoverable past, or a painful recognition of changeless regret (as with Vronsky).[15] The master of such states of soul was Chekhov; his drama measures the wasted potential and missed opportunities they entail.

In the opening scene of *The Cherry Orchard*, the play's only active character, Lopakhin, fails to meet the train with the arriving family because he—he, too—has fallen asleep. It is as if even he cannot resist the estate's temporality of missed opportunity as soon as he sets foot on it. We find him sitting in what the first stage direction refers to as "a room that is still called a nursery." He dozes in a place that, like the whole estate, is still consecrated to an outmoded function and is now frozen in a constant provocation to nostalgia or the contemplation of loss:

LOPAKHIN: The train is in, thank God. What time is it?
DUNYASHA: Nearly two. [*Blows out the candle.*] It's already light.
LOPAKHIN: How late is the train, anyway? A couple of hours at least.
[*Yawns and stretches.*] I'm a fine one! What a fool I've made of myself! Came
here on purpose to meet them at the station and then overslept .... Fell
asleep in the chair .... It's annoying .... You might have waked me.
DUNYASHA: I thought you had gone. (ChP, 315)

Anyone who knows Chekhov recognizes scenes like this as his trademark. He
specializes in actions that fail to happen. *The Cherry Orchard* in particular
dramatizes moments when action is needed but is not performed because the
present is deemed vulgar in comparison to the poetic past. One reason that
Chekhov's plays consist largely of nonactions is that so many of his characters
live in epilogue time, when, they feel, nothing they could do would change
anything essential because the essential is long since over.

This play requires no epilogue and probably could not sustain one because
it is pretty much all epilogue. In the last scene, the superannuated and senile
servant Firs, who incarnates the play's temporality, has been left behind because each person thinks that someone else has attended to him and that at some
time he has already been provided for. The family's unwitting but nonetheless
inexcusable cruelty to the old man takes place because they must help him in
the present, but at each moment they all prefer to think that it has all been done
in the past. In their temporality, action is always already over and so is never
taken. As the play ends, we contemplate Firs's approaching death and wonder
at its needless loneliness after a lifetime of faithful service. When we reflect that
the cause of his death may prove to be starvation, our sense of the poetry of
nostalgia is tempered by a realization of its horror.

Disease #1, The Desiccated Present.
Epilogue Time and the Generations

Crime and Punishment abuses its epilogue and *The Cherry Orchard* does not
require one because it is one. Perhaps the most successful epilogue in Russian
fiction is to be found in Turgenev's *Fathers and Sons.* Its power derives primarily
from the fact that the novel's very theme is temporality, especially the difference
between the immediacy of presentness and the remoteness of epilogue time.

Both generations understand the difference. The fathers of Arkady and
Bazarov make every effort to keep up with the latest intellectual trends so as to
share the lives of their sons. But as the sons relentlessly point out, those efforts
are futile because they bespeak a concern for family alien to current nihilistic

values. Old Kirsanóv has gone to Petersburg to learn such strange truths; and old Bazarov boasts that he, too, keeps up with medical discoveries. They try to be up-to-date, but the sons, though they dearly love their fathers, will allow them only epilogue:

> "Yes; I see you have here *The Friend of Health* [a medical journal] for 1855," remarked Bazarov.
>
> "It's sent me by an old comrade out of friendship," Vassily Ivanovich [Bazarov's father] made haste to answer; "but we even have some idea of phrenology, for instance," he added, addressing himself principally, however, to Arkady . . . "we are not unacquainted even with Schoenlein and Rademacher."
>
> "Why, do people still believe in Rademacher in this province?" asked Bazarov.
>
> Vassily Ivanovich cleared his throat. "In this province .... Of course, gentlemen, you know best; how could we keep pace with you? You are here to take our places. In my day, too, there was some sort of a Humoralist school, Hoffmann, and Brown too with his vitalism—they seemed very ridiculous to us, but, of course, they too had been great men at one time or other. Some one new has taken Rademacher's place with you; you bow down to him, but in another twenty years it will be his turn to be laughed at."
>
> "For your consolation I will tell you," observed Bazarov, "that nowadays we laugh at medicine altogether, and don't bow down to any one."
>
> "How's that? Why, you're going to be a doctor, aren't you?"
>
> "Yes, but the one fact doesn't prevent the other."
>
> Vassily Ivanovich poked his third finger into his pipe, where a little smouldering ash was left. (F&S, 93–94)

Since the novel is set in 1859, a journal of 1855 is only four years old, but in those few years a whole mentality has changed. Old Bazarov, cringing lovingly before his son, still manages to hint that the process of generational change is itself a constant. The sons, he suggests, are not really that different from the fathers, are not exactly ahead of them but simply at a different stage of the cycle of youth and age. Where the sons imagine historical progress, with the past left further and further behind, the fathers suggest that what appears to be time's arrow is really its cycle. Sons are simply fathers-to-be, superannuated figures in the making. But the sons have difficulty imagining a future in which the present will be just another past. Their naivete, no less than the fathers' sense of estrangement from the times, lends the novel a profound sense of the tragedy of anachronism.[16]

Bazarov understands his father's idea that as Rademacher succeeded Hoffmann and somebody or other has replaced Rademacher, so someone in the future will anachronize the authority of today. Not so, Bazarov counters, because we nihilists have disposed of authorities altogether. To this, Vassily Ivanovich has no answer, but Turgenev, as elsewhere in the novel, tacitly provides one. For Arkady, Bazarov himself is an authority. So often have we seen Arkady look to Bazarov for approval while telling his father that nihilists deny all authority, that Arkady's mere presence as onlooker in this scene is enough to evoke irony. His adulation suggests that, for all its pretensions, nihilism is just another phrenology or vitalism. Bazarov's claim to have transcended the past by stepping out of the sequence altogether is itself a familiar one and will doubtless be succeeded by another school distinguishing itself from all predecessors, including all those outmoded nihilists.[17]

Arkady's father, Nikolai Petrovich, reacts somewhat differently to displacement by the young. As always, he tries to be fair, or even too fair, and if it is necessary for him to accept an epilogue life, so be it. Talking with his brother Pavel Petrovich, he too evokes the cycle of generations, this time in favor of conceding the present to the young:

> "So that," began Pavel Petrovich, "so that's what our young men of this generation are! They are like that—our successors!"
>
> "Our successors!" repeated Nikolai Petrovich, with a dejected sigh. . . . "Do you know what I was reminded of, brother? I once had a dispute with our late mother; she shouted, and wouldn't listen to me. At last I said to her, 'Of course, you can't understand me; we belong,' I said, 'to two different generations.' She was dreadfully offended, while I thought, 'It can't be helped. It's a bitter pill, but she has to swallow it.' You see, now our turn has come, and our successors say to us, 'You are not of our generation; swallow your pill.'"
>
> "You are really too generous and modest," replied Pavel Petrovich. "I'm convinced, on the contrary, that you and I are far more in the right than these young gentlemen, though we do perhaps express ourselves in old-fashioned language, *vielli*, and have not the same insolent conceit." (F&S, 43)

In a sense, Pavel Petrovich is right. The mere statement that disputants belong to different generations is not an answer, unless one assumes that by some historical law later is necessarily wiser. Dismissing appeals to youth, Pavel Petrovich insists on arguments—to the point of becoming quite argumentative. His logic about the irrelevancy of generations in assessing positions is doubtless correct, and yet he is less wise than his brother, for whom the most important issue is not how to refute but how to live.

Unlike his brother, Nikolai Petrovich is willing to accept life in what his son effectively treats as a mere epilogue and to make of it its own sort of present.

He shifts the field of activity from grand ideas about society to the quotidian. His ideas may be old-fashioned, but he remarries, devotes himself to his son and his new family, and lives a present that is in fact no epilogue. "The prosaics of the quotidian" may appear to the young intelligentsia as poor consolation for an active public life, but it may well be the most vital sphere.[18]

Such wisdom is not for Pavel Petrovich, who insists on fighting the young on their own ground—he literally fights a duel with Bazarov—and rejects the quotidian present, which, no less than his nephew, he sees as somehow not real. Exaggerating his old-fashioned manners, aristocratic demeanor, overscrupulous dress and refined scent, he turns himself into a museum of the old way, a displaced monument to his generation's ideals. One does not bring children into a perfectly ordered museum, and so he remains unmarried, sterile. He can neither cling to the present of the young nor live the present of the middle-aged. Thus he becomes prematurely old and lives almost posthumously. After the duel, Pavel Petrovich advises Nikolai to marry his serf mistress Fenichka, and his brother, who has been reluctant to offend Pavel with a misalliance, thanks him:

> "What is he thanking me like that for?" thought Pavel Petrovich when he was left alone. "As though it did not depend on him! I will go away as soon as he is married, somewhere a long way off—to Dresden or Florence, and will live there till I drop."
>
> Pavel Petrovich moistened his forehead with eau de cologne, and closed his eyes. His handsome, emaciated head, the glaring daylight shining full on it, lay on the white pillow like the head of a dead man .... And indeed he was a dead man. (F&S, 134)

When we encounter Pavel Petrovich in the novel's epilogue, he has in fact gone for good to Dresden to live out his life. The great pathos of this portrait of him, "still handsome, elegantly dressed," derives from our sense that here at last he is in his proper place, in both his life and the novel (F&S, 164). He is at home abroad, far from the flux of his culture, and outside of all those Russian concerns that date so quickly. Contemporary with an epilogue, he lives where presentness no longer threatens and change itself is outmoded.

The epilogue ends with Bazarov's parents at his graveside. Bazarov has contracted typhus while helping at an autopsy with a doctor who did not have equipment for the simplest preventive measures. Evidently assuming that even in this backward province caustic must long since have become available, Bazarov had not brought his own. In short, he fails to understand the present in which he lives. If Pavel Petrovich has *out*lived his time, Bazarov has *pre*lived his.

Throughout this novel, characters fail to synchronize their lives with their epoch. Only those who ignore "the times" and locate their present in private, quotidian life manage to live in a present of meaningful activity. Nikolai Petrovich marries Fenichka, and Arkady, having outgrown the nihilist's future, marries Katya. Their double marriage ceremony, with which the epilogue begins, celebrates the triumph of the private, the prosaic, and the quotidian. Those characters, major and minor, who try to occupy the public present either die before they have lived or live when they are already dead. If they survive at all, they live into an alien future that dispenses with them and in which, their time past, they can accomplish nothing. The uncanny power of this novel's epilogue derives from the fact that it has been immanent all along.

One may ask, however, whether it is ever wise to treat time as epilogue and whether novels that rely on such endings risk achieving closure at the expense of temporal wisdom. The shrewdest of novelists seem to have asked this question. On the one hand, they invite us, in the spirit of epilogue, to contemplate lives as if the pattern we know will continue to govern events. After all, drawing straight lines may teach us something, if not of the future, then of our present situation. To understand one's situation, it is often helpful to imagine the rest of life *as if* it were an epilogue. But it is usually dangerous to forget that such a projection is only one of many possibilities; and that every moment will have options, accidents, and sideshadows. The straight line is the rare exception. The laughable results of past predictions and of superseded futurologies should warn us, more often than they do, that contingency reigns.

Thus a wise novelist, while giving us an epilogue, may also choose to qualify it with a cautionary note. For the alert Russian reader, the epilogue to *War and Peace* gives only a temporary vantage point sure to be superseded by Pierre's dangerous activities in the capital. And in the famous "Finale" to *Middlemarch*, George Eliot, before explaining what happened to her characters, reminds us that projections are as uncertain as they are attractive:

> Every limit is a beginning as well as an ending. Who can quit young lives after being long in company with them, and not desire to know what befell them in their after-years? For the fragment of a life, however typical, is not the sample of an even web: promises may not be kept, and an ardent outset may be followed by declension; latent powers may find their long-waited opportunity; a past error may urge a grand retrieval.[19]

There is no guarantee that after-years will be a mere extension. The web is never even. Eliot suggests that novelistic time, with all its density and contingency, governs even after a narrative achieves a satisfying closure, and so closure itself may mislead. "The expected was not fulfilled / And god found a way for the unexpected," Euripides repeatedly reminds us in his tragedies; in novelistic time, the role of the gods is played by quotidian life and the prosaics of sideshadowing.[20]

The most commonplace events, barely noticeable to those who experience them, may have unpredictable and important consequences, if not within one life then in the next. *Middlemarch* ends with the author's suggestion that the story of Dorothea and of many people too prosaic even for prose may affect us in ways unseen:

> Her finely-touched spirit had still its fine issues, though they were not widely visible. Her full nature, like that river of which Cyrus broke the strength, spent itself in channels which had no great name on the earth. But the effect of her being on those around her was incalculably diffusive: for the growing good of the world is partly dependent on unhistoric acts; and that things are not so ill with you and me as they might have been, is half owing to the number who lived faithfully a hidden life, and rest in unvisited tombs. (Eliot, 795)

Here the novel gestures beyond itself to mention those unhistoric acts too "incalculably diffusive" for story. Novels are often divided into a main part and an epilogue, but life, Eliot reminds us, has no epilogue. Instead, we may recognize a different division. Temporality consists of constant, if small, surprises; on rare occasions, some concatenation of events seems regular enough to narrate. The rest consists of unhistoric moments that are too diffusive for story but that nevertheless possess their own prosaic effectiveness and indistinct sideshadows.

Disease #1, The Desiccated Present. Eschatology and Utopia

> Measure
> Each detail
> By the great
> Purpose
> —MAYAKOVSKY

If epic time and epilogue time devalue the present as a mere extension of the past, then eschatology and utopia typically reduce it to a way station to the future. Whether the end of history is imagined as catastrophic or perfect, the present and immediate future into which we live cease to be truly important. As Bakhtin observes, those who focus on history's finale usually see "the segment of a future separating the present from the end as lacking value; this separating segment of time loses its significance and interest, it is merely an unnecessary continuation of an indefinitely prolonged present" (FTC, 148).

As with epilogue time, a utopian mentality may produce "Chekhovian people" who neglect present opportunities, which they regard as insignificant. Unlike epilogue time, however, utopian temporality often has the sinister consequence of transforming all present circumstances into raw material for revolution. Because the final goal is all, people alive today may become the eggs for the socialist omelette. The Russian intelligentsia was thoroughly devoted to this kind of thinking, and their critics offered insightful warnings about its danger.

Perhaps the most frequently cited warning occurs in Alexander Herzen's *From the Other Shore*, written in the wake of the revolutions of 1848. Herzen has been honored as "the first Russian socialist," but in this book he demonstrates his capacity to interrogate, not just advocate, his ideals. One chapter, structured as a dialogue between an ardent believer in the Future and a skeptic less willing to sacrifice the present, addresses in detail the relative importance of the two times. The believer sees everything tending to a goal guaranteed by the law of progress; the skeptic suggests that there may be no such law and (still more disturbing to the believer) that criteria of progress may look different to each generation. The goal itself may change, and old ideals of perfection may soon be viewed as models of tyranny. How then could it be justified to create present misery in the name of a future goal? "I prefer to think of life, and therefore of history, as an end attained rather than as a [mere] means to something else," the skeptic observes.[21] Each time, each person, has an irreducible integrity, which must not be sacrificed, especially in the name of a goal so distant and so vaguely defined that one cannot be sure what it is, how the sacrifice will lead to it, or whether it would be as desirable as we imagine. "Each age, each generation, each life had and has its own fullness; *en route,* new demands arise, new experiences, new methods" (FTOS, 37).

And what if time has no end, and each generation, sacrificing itself for an infinitely distant utopia, ruins each present? Then the ostensibly noble goal will insure perpetual misery. In the book's best-known lines, the skeptic asks,

> If progress is the end, for whom are we working? Who is this Moloch who, as the toilers approach him, instead of rewarding them, only recedes, and as a consolation to the exhausted, doomed multitudes crying "morituri te salutant", can give back only the mocking answer that after their death all will be beautiful on earth. Do you truly wish to condemn all human beings alive to-day to the sad role . . . of wretched galley slaves, up to their knees in mud, dragging a barge . . . with the humble words "progress in the future" inscribed on its bows? Those who are exhausted fall in their tracks; others, with fresh forces take up the ropes; but there remains . . . as much ahead as there was at the beginning. . . . This alone should serve as a warning to people: an end that is infinitely remote is not an end, but, if you like, a trap; an end must be nearer—it ought to be, at the very least, the labourer's wage, or pleasure in the work done. (FTOS, 36–37)

Herzen's caution seems to have inspired many of the radical intelligentsia's critics over the decades. It is echoed, for instance, in the most sensational attack ever launched on the intelligentsia, a true intellectual scandal if Russia ever had one: the anthology *Signposts: A Collection of Articles on the Russian Intelligentsia* (1909).[22] Taking a predominantly liberal rather than radical or utopian view, the contributors to *Signposts* faulted the radicals for their neglect of current needs in order to achieve "the happiness of the last generations, who will triumph on the bones and blood of their forebears."[23] Several contributors deplored the violence and terrorism that such a mentality justified. They pointed out that "the people," in whose name the violence was perpetrated, were typically viewed merely as a passive object whose only role was to be saved. In the revolutionaries' practice, the people were instructed, not consulted, a habit that did not bode well should the revolutionaries ever attain the power they sought.

For Semyon Frank, the danger of the intelligentsia's mentality was best seen in their contempt for helping real, individual people of today. Like Lenin, who was to become their most successful representative, members of the intelligentsia usually condemned philanthropy as useless or even counterproductive because it was directed at alleviating suffering in the present rather than at advancing utopia. "Once a person has been seized by this optimistic faith," Frank wrote,

> he can no longer be satisfied with direct, altruistic day-to-day service to the people's immediate needs. He is intoxicated with the ideal of the radical, universal achievement of the people's happiness. In comparison with this ideal, simple, individual, person-to-person aid, mere relief from current sorrows and anxieties . . . even seems . . . a betrayal of mankind and its eternal salvation for the sake of a few individuals close at hand. . . . Holding as it does the simple and true key to the universal salvation of mankind, socialist populism cannot help but scorn and condemn prosaic, unending activity of the kind that is guided by direct altruistic sentiment. (Signposts, Frank, 142–43)

To be sure, Frank continues, in theory socialists are also altruists, but the object of their efforts is the future; they are concerned with the utopian, not the "current" and "day-to-day." Like so many critics of the intelligentsia, Frank suggests that one should love one's neighbor more than humanity in the abstract or else one will become inured to ideologically justified cruelty. For the utopian,

> the abstract ideal of absolute happiness in the remote future destroys the concrete moral relationship of one individual to another and the vital sensation of love for one's neighbors, one's contemporaries and their current

needs. . . . Since he is sacrificing himself to this idea [of the future], he does not hesitate to sacrifice others as well. . . . Thus, great love for future humanity engenders great hatred for [living] people. (Signposts, Frank, 143)

Since the fall of Communism, *Signposts,* which was unavailable in Russia from 1917 until its reprinting in 1990, has come to seem prophetic, more accurate than its contributors could have dreamed. Dissidents discovered that they had been repeating its arguments, especially when they stressed how the deplorable conditions of Russian daily life result not only from collectivism and a failed economy but also from the Communist habit of sacrificing the present for the future. For Sinyavsky and Joseph Brodsky, the real symbol of Communism is not so much the Gulag but life without privacy in a sordid communal apartment.[24] "Measure / Each detail / By the great / Purpose," the ever-receding age of true communism. The human truth, however, is that each person lives and always will live in his or her own "now." "People cannot burn with revolutionary fervor forever in the name of bright ideals," Sinyavsky concludes. "Their life depends on the present, not some radiant future; they must live in their own house, not on a universal scale" (SC, 173).

Disease #2, The Isolated Present

> If time is eternally present
> All time is unredeemable.
> —T. S. ELIOT

> Those whose minds have no impressions but of the present moment, are either corroded by malignant passions, or sit stupid in the gloom of perpetual vacancy.
> —IMLAC, in Samuel Johnson's *Rasselas*

The second kind of temporal malady may be understood as the opposite of the first. Instead of fading away, the present may grow so intense that it almost banishes both memory and anticipation. Only now matters, and now is so overwhelmingly powerful and so different from what has gone before or is likely to come that it seems like a temporal island, entirely cut off from life in the past and future. When this malady strikes, it seems that one has lived only for such a present and that the future is well sacrificed for it.

This temporality feels like what in chapter 4 I called vortex time: a moment of infinite temporal density is reached, and one achieves what Prince Myshkin, thinking of the last moment before his epileptic fits, calls "the direct sensation of existence in the most intense degree" (I, 214). For Myshkin (and apparently for Dostoevsky), epilepsy possessed a peculiarly dangerous attractiveness not only because this "mystic" state was bought at the risk of self-destruction but also because it sometimes seemed worth it. Myshkin meditates on the baneful bliss:

That second was, of course, unendurable. Thinking of that moment later, when he was all right again, he often said to himself that all these gleams and flashes of the highest sensation of life and self-consciousness, and therefore also of the highest form of existence, were nothing but a disease, the interruption of the normal condition; and if so, it was not at all the highest form of being, but on the contrary must be reckoned the lowest. And yet he came at last to an extremely paradoxical conclusion. "What if it is a disease? . . . What does it matter that it is an abnormal intensity, if the result . . . remembered and analysed afterwards in health, turns out to be the acme of harmony and beauty, and gives a feeling, unknown and undivined till then, of completeness, of proportion, of reconciliation, and of ecstatic merging in the highest synthesis of life?" . . . Since at that second . . . he had time to say to himself clearly and consciously, "Yes, for this moment one might give one's whole life!" then without doubt that moment was really worth the whole of life. He did not insist on the dialectical part of his argument, however. Stupefaction, spiritual darkness, idiocy stood before him conspicuously as the consequence of these "higher moments"; seriously, of course, he could not have disputed it. . . . What was he to make of that reality? (I, 214)

This disease is so precious that health seems trivial.

Myshkin is well aware that such a temporality is also morally dangerous. The "highest" moment lies beyond good and evil, inasmuch as good and evil depend on consequences. The infinite present renders all other moments inconsequential. The desire to reach a moment of ecstasy—of "standing outside" the temporal flow—fatally attracts other Dostoevsky characters as well. It serves for them as yet another route to the idea that "all is permitted." Previous commitments vanish and anticipated results do not count.

This is a kind of addiction to which Dostoevsky himself was subject. It is expressed as well in Dostoevsky's compulsive gambling, in his desire to risk everything on an intensified moment. And as Jacques Catteau has acutely observed, the ecstasy of risk also partially accounts for Dostoevsky's habit of accepting money in advance for novels he promised to provide in an impossibly short time. The most famous such incident occurred on July 2, 1865, when he signed a contract with the unscrupulous entrepreneur Stellovsky to provide a novel by November 1, 1866. Stellovsky was counting on the forfeit provisions, which allowed him nine years to publish all Dostoevsky's works for free. Dostoevsky went abroad, played roulette, borrowed more money, and worked on *Crime and Punishment* until it became clear he could not finish it in time. At last, with only a month remaining, he hired a stenographer and in twenty-eight days dictated another novel, completed one day before the deadline. Perhaps not just because of its topic, he entitled the work *The Gambler*.[25]

The narrator of *The Gambler*, Aleksey Ivanovich, becomes intoxicated by the thrill of risking everything on the turn of the wheel. Winnings themselves do not matter; when he does win, he gives away or squanders the money. What does matter is the metaphysical jolt he experiences when (as he feels) he overcomes the laws of nature and society with a win against all odds. One moment he is a beggar, and the next a millionaire, with everyone fawning on him. "The point is that—one turn of the wheel, and all will be changed" (G, 118). Gambling is a sort of unwitting parody of incarnation, a way to man-Godhood: and yet, it is not the transformed state but only the moment of transformation itself that attracts him. By the end of the novel, Aleksey Ivanovich lives only in anticipation of such moments. He works as a lackey just long enough to have something to stake; he thinks of nothing but an ecstatic and maximally improbable sequence of turns of the wheel. Because he has given up all personal and public concerns, this is the only sequence he knows.

When his sensible English friend Mr. Astley discovers him in this state, the Englishman reminds him of the cost: "You have not only given up life, all your interests, private and public, the duties of a man and a citizen, your friends (and you really had friends)—you have not only given up your objects, such as they were, all but gambling—you have even given up your memories" (G, 121). Living without memories in a temporality contracted virtually to a moment or to an archipelago of isolated moments, Aleksey Ivanovich has in a real sense lost his humanity. When Mr. Astley informs him that the woman he once loved hopelessly now loves him, and when Mr. Astley offers him money if he will return from gambling to prosaic life, Aleksey can only dream of one more game of roulette when "in one hour I can transform my destiny!" (G, 126).

Disease #2, The Isolated Present. Gambling with History

> The decisive part in the subjugation of the intelligentsia was played not by terror and bribery (though, God knows, there was enough of both) but by the word "Revolution," which none of them could bear to give up. It is a word to which whole nations have succumbed, and its force was such that one wonders why our rulers still needed prisons and capital punishment.
> —NADEZHDA MANDLELSTAM

For Mr. Astley, Aleksey Ivanovich's fascination with sudden transformation rather than gradual change, his willingness to ruin ordinary bourgeois life for a quasi-mystical thrill, is characteristically Russian.[26] "To my mind all Russians are like that, or disposed to be like that," he observes. "If it is not

roulette it is something similar. . . . You are not the first who does not understand the meaning of work (I am not talking of your peasantry). Roulette is
a game pre-eminently for the Russians" (G, 125). He (or Dostoevsky through
him) is speaking above all of the intelligentsia. The psychology of roulette, of
life viewed as occasional moments of infinite density amid a diffuse expanse of
time, haunts Dostoevsky's intelligentsia heroes.

In *Crime and Punishment,* written along with *The Gambler,* Raskolnikov
also disdains work for a few coppers because he wants "all his capital at once"
(C&P, 30). Murder appeals to him as a way to break out of life's prison at a
stroke. His sister Dunya agrees to marry the despicable Luzhin because she,
too, wants her "capital" (Dostoevsky uses the same word) in an instant. In *The
Possessed,* the revolutionaries are guided, in part, by a similar impulse to sudden
transformation. They are attracted by a time when the past is abolished, when
anything can happen in an infinitely intensified present. This "mystical" view
of revolution—this "revolutionism," as it was called—was often remarked on
by the intelligentsia's critics. Distinct from the desire for the utopia to follow
revolution is the desire for the revolutionary moment itself, no matter what
follows.

The contributors to *Signposts* viewed large portions of the intelligentsia as
addicted to gambling with history, which meant, with other people's lives. The
thrill of terrorism derived in part from the belief that, at the risk of one's own
life and the lives of innocent bystanders, the course of history might be changed
in a moment. Sinyavsky linked this ethos to the intelligentsia's fascination with
proclaiming complete breaks with the past and marking those breaks with un-
compromising manifestos or gestures of violence. In such a mentality, violence
takes on the quasi-religious aura of an expiatory sacrifice and a transcendence
of the mundane. It becomes an essential part of "a revolutionary bacchanalia
wherein the participants assume the role of holy assassins or holy sinners. . . .
From here it is only a stone's throw to the deification of the revolutionary
dictator who has seized supreme power and applies violence. The very idea of
violence and power can imbue communism and the revolution with a sacred,
even mystical aura" (SC, 7).

Not all revolutionaries share this ethos, of course. In *Signposts,* Frank points
out that "one can participate in a revolution without having the world-view of
a revolutionary" (Signposts, Frank, 143). One could, for instance, recoil from
revolutionary violence, much as one recoils from war, and yet believe there is
no alternative. One could be fully aware that revolutions often lead to a reign
of terror, which one is prepared to forestall. Frank believes that such reluctant
revolutionaries are rare among the intelligentsia, which is not so much convinced of the necessity of revolution as it is captivated by revolutionism. The

anarchist Michael Bakunin best epitomized this stance: "The will to destroy," wrote Bakunin, "is also a creative will."[27] Frank comments, "The qualifier 'also' has long since disappeared . . . "destruction is no longer seen as *one* of the means of creation, but has been identified with it altogether, or, more accurately, has completely replaced it" (Signposts, Frank, 144).

For both individuals and society, the attraction to sudden moments of change, to a present that swallows up past and future, led to a neglect of daily life, which, the intelligentsia's critics repeated, is the life we all really live. Real time is prosaic time, which members of the intelligentsia regard the way Aleksey Ivanovich regards the intervals between bouts of gambling. As Mr. Astley understands, roulette and revolution, those Russian obsessions, are really the same obsession. Opportunities are missed in a life focused on maximally intense moments.

In *The Possessed,* Kirillov, a former revolutionary who has become a peculiar kind of mystic, seeks to turn all of life into an "infinitely dense present" without end—a perpetual last moment before the epileptic fit. It is hinted that Kirillov may in fact show early signs of epilepsy. He hopes that a completely irrational act of suicide will abolish sequential time, so that the promise of the Apocalypse—*there shall be time no longer*—will be fulfilled. "You've begun to believe in a future eternal life?" Stavrogin asks.

"No, not in a future eternal life, but in eternal life here. There are moments, you reach moments, and time suddenly stands still, and it will become eternal."

"You hope to reach such a moment?"

"Yes."

"That'll scarcely be possible in our time," Nikolay Vsevolodovich [Stavrogin] responded slowly and, as it were, dreamily; the two spoke without the slightest irony. "In the Apocalypse the angel swears that there will be no more time."

"I know. That's very true; distinct and exact. When all mankind attains happiness then there will be no more time, for there'll be no need of it, a very true thought."

"Where will they put it?"

"Nowhere. Time's not an object but an idea. It will be extinguished in the mind."

"The old commonplaces of philosophy, the same from the beginning of time," muttered Stavrogin with a kind of disdainful compassion. (P, 239–40)

Here and elsewhere, Stavrogin cannot help thinking that each attempt to overcome time takes place at a given moment and that there is a long history of futile escapes from history. When we see Kirillov's brains spattered on the floor a moment *after* he has "abolished time," we may reflect on the horror of all such projects. There shall be a lot more time; and whatever the revolutionists say, the new man will resemble the old. We live in freedom by necessity and in temporality forever.

Disease #2, The Isolated Present. The Mutable Past

The subject of this lecture is found in the proposition that reality exists in a present. The present of course implies a past and a future, and to these both we deny existence.
—GEORGE HERBERT MEAD

Our pasts are always mental in the same manner in which the futures that lie in our imagination ahead of us are mental. . . . they are subject to the same test of validity to which our hypothetical futures are subject. And the novelty of every future demands a novel past.
—GEORGE HERBERT MEAD

Day by day and almost minute by minute the past was brought up to date. . . . All history was a palimpsest, scraped clean and reinscribed exactly as often as was necessary.
—GEORGE ORWELL, *1984*

The Russian revolutionaries sought utterly to destroy the inherited world, but they did not cast doubt on the very existence of the past. On the contrary, the reality of the past, with all its horrors, was the starting point of their arguments. Reasoning from quite different philosophical premises and with quite different purposes in mind, some thinkers have overprivileged the present by making it in effect the only reality.

The temptation to treat the present as the only real time sometimes seems irresistible. After all, the future does not exist and never did exist, and the past is over forever. We act and live only in the present. It is characteristic of this line of thought to make the past (no less than the future) dependent on the present, rather than the reverse, as we are usually inclined to believe. It follows that time is symmetrical, insofar as the past and future are equally hypothetical and equally open to revision. Man makes history: in both directions. Our past is not the same as our ancestors', even when we exclude the intervening period.

In chapter 2, I noted that one way to abolish temporal asymmetry was to argue that, in the mind of God or an ideal observer with perfect knowledge, everything is simultaneous: the future is just the portion of time that we less-than-ideal observers do not yet know. The thinkers with whom we are now concerned abolish temporal asymmetry in the reverse way. Rather than make the future just as determined as the past, they make the past just as undetermined as the future.

This approach is not as new as we are sometimes inclined to think. George Herbert Mead (1863–1931) adopted such a position in order to defend the existence of genuine novelty. For Mead, the world continually generates the new and surprising. Time and emergence are real in the sense that the present creates what cannot be wholly accounted for by what came earlier. For example, new scientific discoveries are for Mead not mere predictable extensions from the past. On the other hand, he believed, scientists themselves typically explain past events in terms of deterministic laws, which Mead did not wish to deny. Thus Mead wanted to accept both determinism and novelty beyond determinism's reach.

To resolve this paradox, Mead proposed that *each present generates its own past.* "The past is [simply] the sure extension which the continuities of the present demand."[28] From the standpoint of any given present moment, all earlier moments are exhaustively determined, but the present present moment is novel. But only when it is present: once past, it will be determined from the standpoint of some new present, which will project its own extension, differing from previous ones. The past varies with the present, and so new pasts continually arise behind us.

The past is therefore both revocable and irrevocable, depending on our perspective. From the standpoint of each present, it is irrevocable. But a new present will bring with it a whole new sequence.[29] "There is, that is, the past which is expressed in irrevocability, though there has never been present in experience a past which has not changed with the passing generations" (Mead, 2), and indeed the past must continue to change in this way. "The character of irrevocability is never lost" because we are always in a present with an irrevocable past (Mead, 3). But "the importance of its being irrevocable attaches to the 'what it was,' and the 'what it was' is what is not irrevocable. There is a finality that goes with the passing of every event. To every account of that event this finality is added, but the whole import of this finality belongs to the same world in experience to which this account belongs" (Mead, 3).

Mead of course anticipates the objection that there must be some sense in which the past exists "independent of any present" (Mead, 7). There must be some sort of "in itself" past, we may be inclined to say. It may also be objected that "our research work is that of discovery, and we can only discover what is there whether we discover it or not. I think however that this last statement is in error, if it is supposed to imply that there is or has been a past which is independent of all presents" (Mead, 7–8). Mead replies that the demand for an "in itself" past is "metaphysical" and, from a pragmatic standpoint, unnecessary. The past is our construction of it, and constructions are always changing:

To say that the Declaration of Independence was signed on the 4th of July 1776 means that in the time system which we carry around with us and with the formulation of our political habits, this date comes out in our celebrations. Being what we are in the social and physical world that we inhabit we account for what takes place on this time schedule, but like railway timetables it is always subject to change without notice. Christ was born four years before A.D. (Mead, 27)

For Mead, there can be no past that is just there, independent of our present needs and research problems. He speaks of facts no less than of interpretations. After all, "a reality that transcends the present must exhibit itself in the present" (Mead, 11). We do not and cannot have any direct access to the past. We know it only through documents and memories that exist in the present. It is not as if there is "behind us a scroll of elapsed presents, to which our constructions of the past refer, though without the possibility of ever reaching it" (Mead, 30). We have only information in the present and the need for action directed toward the future. Our constructions of the past do not pertain to anything like the scroll. They refer "not to events having a reality independent of the present which is the seat of reality, but rather to such an interpretation of the present in its conditioning passage as will enable intelligent conduct to proceed" (Mead, 29). Present needs do not just shape what we select from or say about our past but actually determine it.

Mead maintains (much as I have done) that there is a difference between the idea of the past and the idea of earlier presents: "A string of presents conceivably existing as presents would never constitute a past" (Mead, 30). However, he proceeds to argue that history and science have no concern with the concept of earlier presents, which is metaphysical and unattainable, if not self-contradictory. The historian's concern is precisely *the past* that leads to his own time, which is what he needs in order to take action directed toward the future. There is no way to place oneself in another present because the very effort to do so takes place in the present present. From this temporal locale there is no escape. And if one somehow could be transferred to an earlier present, the result would be useless:

When one recalls his boyhood days he cannot get into them as he then was, without their relationship to what he has become; and if he could, that is if he could reproduce the experience as it then took place, he could not use it, for this would involve his not being in the present within which that use must take place. (Mead, 30)

If, *per impossible*, we were to reach that past event as it took place we should have to be in that event, and then compare it with what we now present as its history. This is not only a contradiction in terms, but it also belies the function of the past in experience. This function is a continual reconstruction as a chronicle to serve the purposes of present interpretation. (Mead, 48)

Dostoevsky (as we saw) questioned whether authors could accurately represent the presentness of the past, but Mead goes much further. In his view, it is not just very difficult, but self-contradictory and useless, to try to imagine the presentness of the past. The past must always have pastness and only pastness.

Like similar arguments formulated since Mead, this one relies heavily on an interesting rhetorical shuffle. Mead presents himself as the plain man appealing to evidence immediately at hand and characterizes his opponents, who believe in some sort of unreachable, permanent past, as "metaphysical." In this way, he is able to shift the burden of proof to his opponents, who must demonstrate that such a past is real. They have the theory so they must defend it. The whole rhetorical power of Mead's discussion depends on this move.

And yet, upon reflection, Mead is hardly advancing a commonsense argument. The plain man and working historians presume that the truth about the past is what really happened. Evidence about that truth is necessarily fragmentary and only shakily and probabilistically reliable. That is why new evidence often changes our assessments of what happened. But Mead's argument seems to depend on a tacit verificationism: he implicitly adopts the view that the meaning of a statement is given by its assertability and/or verification conditions. When we talk about distant or inaccessible things—like the past—we are really just using a shorthand for talk about proximate things, the evidence we have in the present. That is why the past is metaphysical and why, when present conditions change, the Meadian past changes along with it.

It seems evident that this position, for all Mead's pragmatist rhetoric, is no less metaphysical or in need of justification than the working historian's view. Mead offers a rather complicated construction as the plain man's view. One is moved to say in reply: Let's just drop all this talk about who is metaphysical. If we are to presume that any position defying common sense is what requires justification, then the burden of proof lies with Mead. But it would perhaps be best to concede that all these views are "metaphysical" and ask Mead to recognize that there is no pragmatist high ground to occupy.

Mead's rhetorical shuffle—let us call it the plain man fallacy—is one of the more pervasive and unfortunate legacies of pragmatism for modern literary theory.

Disease #2, The Isolated Present.
The Dialogue of Times, and a Strange Catastrophism

Mead's argument entails another fallacy that has become rather common, which might be called "the prison house of perspective." The central idea here is that one cannot understand things one does not believe and cannot adopt a perspective other than one's own. Somehow, understanding entails being. This is also hardly a plain man's view because we are all aware of an operational test to judge whether one understands another's view: we can paraphrase what someone who held that view would say in a given situation. This test is used all the time, and we often judge whether we are understood by asking for such paraphrases. Moreover, if each of us were really locked in the prison of perspective, almost everything done by someone different would come as a shock. A Meadian would go around continually flabbergasted by the non-Meadians of the world. And it would also be hard to see how novelists could have created so many characters different from their authors and from other characters. One imagines a Meadian novelist perpetually stymied when trying to figure out what his character would do next.

Let us suppose that a witness to a quarrel recommends that the two disputants try to see the situation from "the other's point of view." Having experienced the value of such advice in the past, the first agrees. He makes an effort to imagine what led the second to see the situation as he does. Reconstructing the circumstances from a previously unsuspected perspective, he at last grasps what concerns his antagonist. Perhaps our first disputant employs the skills of novelists imagining the consciousness of characters alien to themselves; or perhaps he just "places himself in the other's position" as best he can. The situation now looks different to him. He might still maintain the rightness of his original position or he might be moved to change his judgment, but in either case his view is richer and more complex.

The second disputant, however, rejects the mediator's suggestion. The well-meaning witness, he contends, is muddled; for what is recommended is an impossibility, if not a contradiction, inasmuch as any attempt to see the situation from the other's point of view would still be made from his own point of view. And if, *per impossible*, he could achieve the other's perspective, he could not compare it with his own (for he would no longer be in his present position) and so it would be useless. One can see the world only through one's own eyes.

There is of course a sense in which this reply would be true; any reconstruction of the other's perspective is made from one's own perspective. But the objection nevertheless misses the point. There is a significant difference between making the effort to put oneself in another's place and not doing so, even though, whichever one does, one still sees the world through one's own eyes. The first disputant knows from experience that the effort is often rewarded with insight into another's perspective and that sometimes such insight can be confirmed by questions or direct interaction. He recognizes that morality almost always demands this effort of imagination and that exercising these perspectival skills can enrich one's moral sense. The second disputant, however, believes that the recommended exercise is spurious and so does not make it. From a practical standpoint, his cleverness impedes his development of skills that (as he reasons) cannot in fact be acquired and that are justified by muddled reasoning. Ethically speaking, his world becomes a poorer and less complex place.

If the second disputant should be a literary theorist, he might want to deny the meaningfulness of understanding a classic text from the perspective of its author, culture, or period. For all one can know about the work is what our own culture and period predispose us to see. Any view of the author's culture would necessarily be our view: there is no escape from the prison-house of our own times. And the misguided effort to do the impossible distracts us from using the text so as to solve present problems and allow intelligent conduct to proceed.

Should he turn his attention to history, our second disputant would be unlikely to develop the habit of imagining the world with the information available at the earlier time. He would tend to see the past more anachronistically than need be. The issues of the past would acquire a wholly present coloration instead of something closer to their original tinge. Insofar as historical insight involves seeing other times more closely to the way they saw themselves, the second disputant might prove less effective in solving current practical problems, his own criterion for knowledge.

Moreover, he would probably be inclined to see the past as leading inevitably to the present. He would be inclined to what, in chapter 6, I shall call backshadowing. Mead, it will be recalled, is a determinist with respect to the past, and if determinism is combined with the hypothesis that the past is the creation of the present, it would seem difficult to avoid neglecting all those potentials that are invisible from a present perspective and that might have led elsewhere. Our first disputant might catch a glimpse of a few sideshadows, but it would be hard to imagine the second doing so.

The second disputant could not be further from Bakhtin's position about the value of entering into dialogue with other times and other cultures. Such dialogue requires the imagination of an alien perspective without losing one's own. The resulting interaction may yield what Bakhtin calls creative understanding, that is, a new view contained in neither perspective but resulting from the conversation between them. For Mead, such a dialogue would be impossible because we cannot put ourselves in the earlier position at all; and if we could, we would be unable to use that position for present purposes. Mead at best imagines one perspective or the other but rules out the possibility of dialogic exchange.

Bakhtin argued that to understand the present one must resist the temptation to view it as unlike all other times. By contrast, Mead's view entails a perpetual temporal catastrophism. At each present moment, the present is qualitatively different from the past inasmuch as the past is wholly determined but the present exhibits truly novel features. But it is hard to imagine why the present present moment should be so different from every earlier moment, and still harder to grasp why what is now true of this moment will soon turn out to have been (or to be) untrue of it. What causes this alteration?

If one believes that the future will show present novelty to have been determined, then it is difficult to see how one could believe quite so strongly in that novelty. We are aware (we cannot help being aware) that the present is the past of the future. If the future (the present to come) is sure to change the basic character of the present present, then it would seem some shadow of pastness is bound to fall on the present even *while* it is present, at least for those who believe Mead's account. The novelty of the present present would seem to depend on the enduring novelty of past presents, that is, on the sense that earlier moments not only *have* pastness but also *had* presentness. In suggesting that we believe in the novelty *only* of the present, it is Mead who would seem to be recommending an impossibility.

Disease #2, The Isolated Present. Commemoration

> I dedicate this to all those who did not live to tell it. And may they please forgive me for not having seen it all nor remembered it all, for not having divined all of it.
>   —ALEXANDER SOLZHENITSYN, *The Gulag Archipelago*

Finally, and most important, Mead's view seems to create important moral and political problems. Our sentiment of remorse depends on our belief in irrevocability—an irrevocability entailed not just by the present present but also by all future presents. That sentiment would seem to be decisively compromised by the Meadian knowledge that the past we rue will soon be replaced by another, perhaps quite different one.

The history of the twentieth century, the century of totalitarianism, may illustrate the unfortunate political implications of Mead's position. Jews studying the Holocaust and Russians investigating the Soviet period are often moved

to *establish the facts*, to prove what really happened to the millions who perished. They often do so from a belief in memorializing and thereby honoring
the dead. These activities seem to depend on the past being what Mead calls
metaphysically real. To such investigators and memorializers, assertions that
there is nothing like a scroll and that the dead we can number today may not
have died tomorrow might seem grotesque. When they say that so many Jews
died during Nazi rule and that so many Soviet citizens were executed in 1937
they mean something more, let us say, than that "in the time system which we
carry around with us and with the formulations of our political habits, these
dates come out in our celebrations" or commemorations. If they recalculate
the number, they do not mean that the number has changed but that it has
been more accurately ascertained by the standard of what "metaphysically"
happened.

Russians in particular insist on the reality and absolute irrevocability of the
past because the rewriting of history, the denial of facts according to the current needs of the Party, was so commonplace under the Soviet regime. (Perhaps
Holocaust revisionism will have a similar effect on Jews.) These Russians often
understand that interpretations may change, but they still maintain that the
facts themselves do not. In light of actual experience, the idea that facts may
alter like railway timetables is likely to appear not just a philosophical theory
but a sinister practice. Mead's approach to time may appear less a daring philosophical paradox than an unwitting justification of a horror through which they
have lived.

Mead assumes that as presents "slide" into each other, the memories and
documents that figured in the previous past will be preserved, thus assuring that
there will be reasonable continuity between presents. But what if that is not
the case? In *1984*, Orwell dramatizes the implications of a world in which each
present not only generates its own past but is able to control the documentation
and probably even the memories inherited from earlier times. Thus we have the
"memory hole" and the doctrine of "the mutability of the past," according to
the Party's slogan: "Who controls the past controls the future: who controls
the present controls the past." [30] In explaining this theory, O'Brien insists that
no falsification is going on because there is no "real past" outside our records,
or, more accurately, no real past outside the "mind of the Party," which controls the records. When Winston Smith appeals to the idea that there must
be some real past, O'Brien, whose philosophy is a sinister version of extreme
pragmatism, dismisses such a concern as metaphysical.

Of course, the Soviet Union was unable to go quite so far. Documents
could be destroyed or altered, events once acknowledged could become nonevents, and people could be eliminated from photographs, but memories, at

least, proved more difficult to eradicate. It is perhaps for this reason that Russians today are so concerned to discover, publish, and establish the facts of human suffering during the Communist period. They were taught the Leninist doctrine that the standard of truthfulness and morality is utility to the Party. Having seen such a doctrine in practice, they assert, with a moral fervor that is hard to gainsay, that the millions of deaths they commemorate quite simply *really happened*, and *will always have happened*, irrespective of the vicissitudes of future presents.

Disease #3, Hypothetical Time. Edited Life

Epilogue time drains the present of significance in the name of the past and utopian time drains it in the name of the future. In hypothetical time, the entire sequence of past, present, and future comes for one reason or another to seem insubstantial. It is as if real time were in some other dimension, to which we have no access; as if our lives were a dream and real life were something we can only dream of. In hypothetical time, we dwell, as it were, in the middle realm of mere possibilities, and we sense each moment as if it were only the shadow of some other actuality, existing elsewhere or nowhere. When life feels this way, decisions lose significance and the soul of ethics dies. No matter what happens, it does not count. "It's all the same," as Chebutykin keeps repeating in Chekhov's *The Three Sisters*.

Hypothetical time comes in various forms. It easily borrows the rhetoric of other temporalities that drain the present of meaning (the various forms of disease #1); in its grip, people indiscriminately invoke the languages of fatalism, epilogue time, utopianism, or anything else that renders the present unimportant. These borrowed discourses function only negatively, not to stress the meaningfulness of some other time but only to deny the meaningfulness of this one. Those who see the world hypothetically may appeal to the future, but they do not really believe in it and do not strive for it. If they speak nostalgically of the past, it too seems to be insubstantial, unclear, and fading even from memory. Hypothetical time is purely subjective, governed by the contrary-to-fact conditional. Past and future, when referred to, become mere counters for that which does not exist and probably could not exist.

Of course, Chekhov was the master at describing this psychology and its baneful effects. His characters typically live in a dreamy world of wishes, indeed of mere velleities, which do not lead to action. People are always speculating about the wonderful future too far away (if realizable at all) to be more than a dream and too unclear for any specific effort to bring it about. They wish life, all of it, were somehow different in its essence. The most important Chekhov play devoted to hypothetical time is *The Three Sisters*, which would reward examination in some detail.

In this play, the wish for an essentially different temporality is expressed as the heroines' desire to "go to Moscow," which is less a specific place than a different temporal dimension. In Moscow, in the meaningful temporality beyond reach, perfect lovers are to be found, all vulgarity will disappear, and life will be inexpressibly beautiful.

From the opening scene of the play, time dominates its discourse.[31] If one were to catalogue all the scenes in which time is discussed, one would have pretty much reproduced the entire play. When the curtain rises on the Prozorovs' house, conversation focuses on a double anniversary:

> OLGA: Father died just a year ago today, on the fifth of May—your name day, Irina. . . . I felt as though I should never live through it, and you lay in a dead faint. But now, a year has gone by, and we think of it calmly; you're already wearing white. . . . [*The clock strikes.*] The clock was striking then, too. [*Pause*] I remember there was music when Father was carried out, and they fired a salute at the cemetery. He was a general, in command of a brigade, yet there were very few people walking behind his coffin. But then, it was raining. Heavy rain and snow.
>
> IRINA: Why recall it? (ChP, 235)

Since the clock strikes every hour, it is hardly surprising that it struck then, too. Clocks, in fact, figure almost as another kind of character in the play. When Kulygin enters, he comments that the clock is seven minutes fast; in act 3, Chebutykin breaks an expensive clock, and in act 4 he describes his clever watch and makes it strike. People are always asking the time, counting months, enumerating years, and mentioning their ages, all while continually waiting for something that does not happen. Act 2 begins with the sisters' anticipation of the mummers' visit, which never takes place, just as within each act they imagine going to Moscow within months although the time between acts is measured in years. Thus the stage directions at the beginning of each act comment ironically on action not taken. Time passes, years slip by, and almost nothing happens except anniversaries and comments on passing time.

Even the past fades, as Olga's opening speech intimates.[32] Memories gradually but relentlessly disappear, and there is no true memorial, just as few people attended Father's funeral. Experience fails to accumulate because life is a continual forgetting. Typically, we catch the characters just at the point where a memory is barely strong enough to come to mind but rapidly fading out.

> OLGA: Now I remember you. I remember.
>
> VERSHININ: I knew your mother.

CHEBUTYKIN: She was a lovely woman ... God rest her soul.

IRINA: Momma is buried in Moscow.

OLGA: In the Novo-Devichy ....

MASHA: Imagine, I'm already beginning to forget her face. And we won't be remembered either. We'll be forgotten.

VERSHININ: Yes, we'll be forgotten. Such is our fate, we can do nothing about it. What to us seems serious, significant, highly important—a time will come when it will be forgotten, or seem unimportant. (ChP, 245)

The present is simply the forgotten past of the future, and the characters sense the forgetting to come. Thus the present, with no staying power in memory, has no weight even as it happens. In elegy, at least, the poem itself acts as memorial, but these characters live beyond the possibility even of elegy.

Vershinin, who is always moving out of one temporary lodging into another and who longs to have flowers but believes that "nothing can be done about it now" (ChP, 250), compensates for the empty present and rapidly disappearing past by "philosophizing" about the glorious future. "In two or three hundred years life on this earth will be unimaginably beautiful, wonderful," and we must live by dreaming about it, he intones (ChP, 249). With a sigh, Irina replies that "really, all that ought to have been written down ..." (ChP, 249). For that matter, everything of importance—if we could only tell what it is, which Vershinin says is impossible—ought to be recorded before it is forgotten; perhaps that is why Fedotik and Roday repeatedly wander about photographing everything in sight.

Kulygin evidently could stand to record his gifts because he gives people the same one more than once. The present moment in which he gave it before has passed from memory, which is all the more ironic because the gift is a history book. He lives in a state not of déjà vu but of *jamais vu:* things that have happened are as if they have never been.[33] Nothing stays. Love itself is powerless against time. "Did you love my mother?" Masha asks Chebutykin. "Very much," he replies. "And did she love you?" Masha continues. After a pause, he answers, "That I no longer remember" (ChP, 299).

Throughout the play, we sense that the failure to take present action leads to terrible waste. If it is to be taken at all, action must at some point be taken *now;* if it is always postponed or regretted, wished for or deemed no longer possible, it will never take place, even though at any moment it could. At any moment Vershinin could plant or buy flowers, but he prefers to speculate on the pattern of his life that has somehow not included them. Chebutykin has never gotten married, as he has wished to, in part because somehow he never got around to it. And of course the three sisters plan to go to Moscow but never go because one can go to Moscow only in the present, and their actions are always to be performed at some other time. Thus at the beginning of the play Moscow lies in the future, and by the end Irina decides that fate has prevented her from ever going, although even at that moment she could: "I am alone, I'm bored, I have nothing to do, and the very room in which I live is hateful to me.... So I have made up my mind: if I am not destined to be in Moscow, then so be it. It is fate. There is nothing to be done.... It's all God's will, that is the truth" (ChP, 299).

Irina's string of fatalistic synonyms recalls that the sisters believe, or speak as if they believe, in omens. Masha, who admits to being superstitious, finds it ominous that "just before Father died, there was a wailing in the chimney, just like that" (ChP, 262), and in act 1 Irina has played solitaire to ascertain her fate:

> IRINA: The game is coming out, I see. We shall go to Moscow.
>
> FEDOTIK: No, it's not. You see, the eight falls on the two of spades. [*Laughs.*] That means you won't go to Moscow. (ChP, 268)

To be sure, this is a rather pale fatalism. If they happen to play cards, they look and see what their fate might be, but there is no energy, no real conviction, even then. That is perhaps because what actually happens does not much matter.

We see as well that this attitude leads to the triumph of evil when it could be resisted. Natasha, the sisters' sister-in-law, gradually takes over the house, displaces the sisters from their rooms, openly takes a lover, bans the mummers without telling the sisters, and is cruel to the servants. The sisters find all rudeness and conflict unendurable, and so, paradoxically, they allow it. For to prevent it they would have to engage in conflict and take present action. So Natasha has her will without opposition. Andrei, her husband and the sisters' brother, knows, of course, that he should not mortgage the house to give Natasha the money, especially because the house also belongs to the sisters. But he, who also cannot bear conflict, commits the fraud, and they do not stop him, thus becoming, in a peculiarly Chekhovian way, passive accomplices to it. The progress of evil is unremitting as the sisters escape from present responsibilities to some other kind of time.

Theirs is the time of their favorite tense, the contrary-to-fact conditional, and of their favorite phrases, "If only ..." and "We should have": "OLGA: . . . it seems to me that if I had married and stayed home all day, it would have been better. [*Pause.*] I should have loved my husband" (ChP, 237). She and Irina will marry only in the subjunctive and never in the indicative. "IRINA: I kept thinking that we'd move to Moscow, and there I'd meet my true love, I dreamed of him, I loved him" (ChP, 290). "I dream" is the other repeated form of hypothetical existence, and the sisters are always dreaming, dreaming only, of Moscow, Moscow!

> OLGA: . . . Being in school every day, then giving lessons till evening, my head aches continually, and I'm beginning to think like an old woman. . . . day by day I feel my youth and strength draining out of me. Only one dream keeps growing stronger and stronger ...
> IRINA: To go to Moscow. To sell the house, make an end of everything here, and go to Moscow ...
> OLGA: Yes! To go to Moscow as soon as possible.
> [*Chebutykin and Tuzenbach laugh.*]
> IRINA: Brother will probably become a professor [in Moscow]; in any case, he won't go on living here. (ChP, 236)

Andrei's dream of escape is no less hypothetical (or laughable). To Ferapont, the old and deaf servant, he confesses his disappointment:

> ANDREI: My God, I'm the Secretary of a District Board . . . and the very most I can hope for—is to become a member of that Board! I, a member of a District Board, I, who dream every night that I am a professor at the University of Moscow, an illustrious scholar of whom all Russia is proud!
> FERAPONT: I wouldn't know ... I don't hear well ...
> ANDREI: If you could hear well, I probably wouldn't be talking to you. (ChP, 259)

Most Chekhov characters do not listen and Ferapont cannot listen, yet his deafness does not hinder purely hypothetical conversation. Senile as well as deaf, Ferapont barely senses the present, and Andrei's very dreams are spoken in a dialogue without a listener. This is a substitute for conversation, and its topic is Andrei's substitute for meaningful activity.

The essential temporality of the play is voiced first and most explicitly by Vershinin:

> VERSHININ [*walking about the stage*]: I often think, what if one were to begin life over again, but consciously? If one life, which has already been lived, were only a rough draft, so to say, and the other the final copy! Then each of us, I think, would try above everything else not to repeat himself, at least he would create a different setting for his life, he would arrange an apartment like this for himself, with flowers and plenty of light.... (ChP, 250)

The life we live is a sort of rough draft, and the real life, if there were such a real life, would be edited. Life is a sort of rehearsal, and nothing in it really matters as it would in a real performance. Of course, there is no real performance, but somehow the life we live is nevertheless mere practice, only preliminary, nothing more than a rough draft. We dwell in a stream of hypothetical time with no real time to come.

It is Chebutykin who spells out the implications of this view. "It's all the same," "nothing matters," *vse ravno*, he repeats: most cruelly, he does not prevent the duel in which Tuzenbach is senselessly killed. "One baron more or less—what does it matter?" he asks (ChP, 301). Perhaps the duel did not happen, perhaps it only seems to us that things happen, perhaps it was a rough draft, perhaps we only apparently exist:

> CHEBUTYKIN: Maybe I'm not even a man, and am just pretending I have arms, and legs, and a head; maybe I don't even exist, and only imagine I'm walking about, eating, sleeping. [*Weeps.*] Oh, if only I didn't exist! (ChP, 283)

> CHEBUTYKIN [*drops the clock, which smashes*]: Smashed to smithereens!
> [*Pause; everyone is upset and embarrassed.*]
> KULYGIN [*picking up the pieces*]: To break such an expensive thing—oh, Ivan Romanych, Ivan Romanych! You get minus zero for conduct.
> IRINA: That was Mama's clock.
> CHEBUTYKIN: Maybe ... Mama's, so it was Mama's. Maybe I didn't break it, and it only appears to have been broken. Maybe it only appears that we exist, but, in fact, we are not here. I don't know anything. Nobody knows anything. (ChP, 285)

Chebutykin is too ignorant to know the philosophical dicta to which his paradoxes allude—he barely knows who the famous critic Dobroliubov was—but Chekhov understands the parody of Descartes and perhaps Kant as well. For those who live in hypothetical time, existence—real existence—is very definitely a predicate which they imagine does not apply to them.

Nobody prevents the duel in which Tuzenbach is killed, and Irina herself, who is grieved at his death, contributes to it. It is, in fact, something of a suicide in response to her inability to love—not just him, we know, but anybody existing outside a dream and living in the actual world. Just before going off to the duel, he holds a last conversation with her. He pleads for "something" like love, but her soul is "locked" forever. He goes off to escape from this time into some other:

> IRINA: . . . I'll be your wife, faithful and obedient, but it's not love, I can't help it! [*Weeps.*] I have never in my life been in love. Oh, how I have

dreamed of love, dreamed of it for a long time now, day and night, but my soul is like a fine piano that is locked, and the key lost. [*Pause.*] You look troubled.

TUZENBACH: I haven't slept all night. There is nothing in my life so terrible as to frighten me, only that lost key racks my soul and will not let me sleep .... Tell me something .... [*Pause*] Tell me something ....

IRINA: What? What shall I say? What?

TUZENBACH: Something.

IRINA: Don't! Don't! [*Pause*]

TUZENBACH: What trifles, what silly little things in life will suddenly, for no reason at all, take on meaning. You laugh at them, just as you've always done, consider them trivial, and yet you go on, and you feel that you haven't the power to stop. . . . I feel elated, I see these fir trees, these maples and birches, as if for the first time, and they all gaze at me with curiosity and expectation. What beautiful trees, and, in fact, how beautiful life ought to be with them! [*A shout of: "Aa-oo! Yoo-hoo!"*] I must go, it's time .... There's a tree that's dead, but it goes swaying in the wind with the others. So it seems to me that if I die, I'll still have a part in life, one way or another. Good-bye, darling .... [*Kisses her hands.*] The papers you gave me are on my table, under the calendar. (ChP, 303–04)

The "trifles" Tuzenbach has in mind are the petty insults that have led to the duel with Solyony. They have immense power now, as they so often do in Chekhov, in part because the presence of mind and will it would take to stop the duel does not seem worth the effort. He does not will to will. The final reference to the calendar is so explicit, so otherwise unnecessary, that it verges on a false step on Chekhov's part. Finding a real love and life to be beyond his reach and accepting death more by inertia than by choice, Tuzenbach imagines a future life that is neither life nor death, "life, one way or another." It is like a swaying in the wind and, ironically, like the half-life of unactualized possibilities that he and the other characters have always led. He does not know it, but Natasha plans to cut down these very trees.

What would life have to be like for the sisters to regard it as meaningful? What sort of temporality do they demand before they would leave the middle realm of possibility for present actuality? In act 2, Vershinin, Masha, and Tuzenbach hold a long conversation about time, in which Masha, evidently voicing the beliefs of her three siblings, makes their position clear (ChP, 264–67). The conversation begins, characteristically, because there is nothing else to do, not even (for some reason) tea to drink, and so Vershinin proposes that they all "philosophize a little."

"Let us dream," Vershinin says, "of the life that will come after us in two or three hundred years." He imagines that this life will be beautiful and glorious in every possible way, if not in two or three hundred years, then "let's say a thousand years—the time doesn't matter." It never does. For Vershinin, our miserable life today has meaning only as a moment leading to that future, but the future is so remote, so dreamlike and hypothetical, that we are completely in the dark about what actions in the present contribute to the happy life supposedly to come. He alludes to his earlier comment that Columbus and Copernicus may turn out to have been insignificant, whereas some crank we ignore may really be paving the way.

In reply, Tuzenbach insists that technology will make unimaginable advances, but the miserable essence of life will remain just the same, an inscrutable mixture of fears and hopes. Even in a million years, he says, life will follow its own laws, which have nothing to do with us and have no meaning at all, at least in human terms. Even if birds should learn to "philosophize," they would encounter the same difficulty in explaining the world and their actions, which, like ours, are guided by something other than present volition. This assertion of meaninglessness even in the remote future and even among the absurdly imagined avian Vershinins to come, prompts Masha's demand to know what it is all for:

> TUZENBACH: . . . Birds . . . will still go on flying, not knowing where or why. They fly and will go on flying no matter what philosophers spring up among them; and let them philosophize as much as they like, so long as they go on flying....
>
> MASHA: But there is a meaning?
>
> TUZENBACH: A meaning ... Look, it's snowing. What meaning has that? [Pause]
>
> MASHA: It seems to me a man must have some faith, or must seek a faith, otherwise his life is empty, empty.... To live and not know why the cranes fly, why children are born, why there are stars in the sky ... Either one knows what one lives for, or it's all futile, worthless. [Pause]
>
> VERSHININ: In any case, it's a pity youth is over....
>
> MASHA: Gogol says: It's boring in this world, gentlemen!
>
> TUZENBACH: And I say: It's difficult arguing with you, gentlemen! Well, let it go ...
>
> CHEBUTYKIN [reading the newspaper]: Balzac was married in Berdichev. (ChP, 266–67)

Masha, like her sisters, demands an unattainable kind of meaning, one that would reveal the significance of actions to us as we take them, that would reach beyond our time to show the pattern of actions past, passing, and to come. One must work, she says, but one must also know why one works and what its effect will be. One must know whether Columbus will turn out to have been a crank and whether a knowledge of Italian contributes to culture or is a sort of mental "sixth finger." Otherwise, everything actual is nothing but pointless factoids (if it is even that), like the place of Balzac's marriage.

Perhaps in Moscow they have such knowledge! But unless it is available, the time we live in is meaningless, at best a "rough draft" for some future life in which we would truly *know*. This knowledge would be apocalyptic, the sort available only at the Last Judgment, when history and time are over. In the play's closing scene, Chebutykin is once again reading pointless facts from a newspaper and once again saying that everything is "all the same," while the sisters once again long to escape from temporality as we know it. They still dream of a time in which everything is perfected and all meanings are given:

> MASHA: Oh, listen to that music! They [the regiment] are leaving us . . . we are left alone to begin our life over again. We must live.... We must live....
>
> IRINA [*lays her head on Olga's breast*]: A time will come when everyone will know what all this is for, why there is all this suffering, and there will be no mysteries; but meanwhile, we must live. . . .
>
> OLGA [*embracing both her sisters*]: The music plays so gaily, so valiantly, one wants to live! Oh, my God! Time will pass, and we shall be gone forever, we'll be forgotten, our faces will be forgotten, our voices, and how many there were of us, but our sufferings will turn into joy for those who live after us, happiness and peace will come to this earth, and then they will remember kindly and bless those who are living now. . . . The music is so gay, so joyous, it seems as if just a little more and we shall know why we live, why we suffer ... If only we knew, if only we knew! . . .
>
> CHEBUTYKIN [*softly sings*]: "Ta-ra-ra boom-de-ay, sit on the curb I may." ... It doesn't matter! It doesn't matter!
>
> OLGA: If we only knew, if we only knew! (ChP, 312)

The demand for perfect knowledge and the use of the contrary-to-fact conditional: the repeated final phrase, prepared for by each lament, captures with all the power of a fading epitaph the sisters' lugubrious hypothetical temporality. The present lacks all substance; and actuality is drained of all value in the face of a dream time beyond human reach.

Disease #3, Hypothetical Time. The Impurity of Freedom

We may better understand human freedom if we recognize that it must be limited to be genuine. Absolute freedom would not be freedom at all.

If it is dangerous to deny the existence of unrealized alternatives, it is no less so to admit *only* possibilities. There are unactualized possibilities, but they do not have the same moral weight as actualized ones. As surely as meaningful ethical choice depends on an awareness that something else may have taken place, it also depends on the knowledge that something truly did. We might have chosen otherwise, but we did choose this way. To attempt to keep options forever open so as not to limit them is to dilute the very meaning of choice and is itself a choice.

That is precisely what Dostoevsky's underground man tries to do. In rebellion against absolute determinism, he demands pure freedom and attempts to live a life of pure potential. He senses that any concrete action will serve to define and therefore to limit him. Thus his refusal to do anything but dream and his attempt to live solely in the unreal world of books and fantasies reflect a fear of the actual. In one of his most daring paradoxes, he denies that he *does nothing;* rather, he insists, he *does not do anything.* As he explains, to do nothing—to be "a sluggard"—would be to define oneself positively; it would mean one possesses an actual characteristic:

> Oh, if I had done nothing simply out of laziness! Heavens, how I would have respected myself then. I would have respected myself because I would at least have been capable of being lazy; there would at least have been in me one positive quality, as it were, in which I could have believed myself. Question: Who is he? Answer: A sluggard. . . . After all . . . it would mean that I was positively defined, it would mean that there was something to be said about me. "Sluggard"—why, after all, it is a calling and an appointment, it is a career, gentlemen. . . . every passer-by would have said, looking at me: "Here is an asset! Here is something really positive!" And, after all, say what you like, it is very pleasant to hear such remarks about oneself in this negative age, gentlemen. (NFU, 17–18)

The underground man has chosen rather to remain radically undefined, even more "negative" than the age. The problem, however, is that such a choice is also a commitment and defines him as a particular type, which this novel precisely identifies: the type of the underground man. His choice not to choose entails a life of waste and cruelty. What the underground man does not recognize, but Dostoevsky does, is that freedom cannot be pure. To be real, it must commit itself and close off some possibilities by embracing others. Freedom always operates under constraints, in a particular situation and at a particular moment. Its options are more than one, but less than infinite. Freedom is the sort of thing that can only be impure.[34]

Disease #3, Hypothetical Time. Crime and Chronicity

It was his [Raskolnikov's] conviction that this eclipse of reason and failure of will power attacked a man like a disease, developed gradually and reached its highest point just before the perpetration of the crime, continued with equal violence at the moment of the crime and for longer or shorter time after, according to the individual case, and then passed off like any other disease. The question whether the disease gives rise to the crime, or whether the crime from its own peculiar nature is always accompanied by something of the nature of a disease, he did not yet feel able to decide.
—DOSTOEVSKY, *Crime and Punishment*

Raskolnikov did not live his true life when he murdered the old woman or her sister. When murdering the old woman herself, and still more when murdering her sister, he did not live his true life, but acted like a machine, doing what he could not help doing—discharging the cartridge with which he had long been loaded. One old woman was killed, another stood before him, the axe was in his hand.
—TOLSTOY, "Why Do Men Stupefy Themselves?"

Dostoevsky understood that hypothetical living can result not only in a wastefully passive life but also, strange as it may seem, in active and violent crime. When *Crime and Punishment* begins, we see Raskolnikov suffering from a "disease," whose most obvious symptom is abstraction from the present. He is "so completely absorbed in himself" that he does not notice his poverty (C&P, 3). Nothing related to his immediate situation interests him: "He had given up attending to matters of practical importance; he had lost all desire to do so" (C&P, 3). The narrator reports that it would scarcely have been possible to live in greater slovenliness, but Raskolnikov has long since ceased to notice his surroundings and, despite his hunger and weakness, would not even remember to eat if the maid, at her own expense and out of the goodness of her heart, did not bring him food. Raskolnikov is hungry not so much from lack of money as from lack of attention.

Although he dreams of the perfect crime, which demands perfect presence of mind, Raskolnikov walks about the street talking to himself, ironically enough, about rationality and planning. He does not plan but dreams of planning; he does not make meticulous preparations but argues abstractly that they could be made. Remote from the here and now, he never seems to know what time it is and, at the end of part I, is even late keeping his engagement to murder.

The novel's first action is the visit to the old lady, which Raskolnikov thinks of as his "rehearsal" or "trying out" [*proba*] of his plan. He arranges to visit the pawnbroker's apartment to look around once more and to anticipate what the murder would be like if he should actually decide to do it. And yet even as a rehearsal this incident is not quite "the real thing," only a shadow of what he tells himself it is (C&P, 72). "Even his late trial run," he recalls shortly before the murder, "was simply a try at a trial run" ["*Dazhe nedavno probu svoiu . . . on tol'ko proboval bylo delat'*"]. It was hypothetical action at two removes from actuality (C&P, 71–72).

Nevertheless, it is closer than his daydreams, which are at best mental rehearsals for such a second-order rehearsal. Thus, despite its remoteness from actual murder, the trial run has a terrible concreteness for him. For one thing, it brings him outside himself: he must really see the victim of his mental murder and experience her actual behavior, which inspires him with hatred. The time of this episode is tantalizingly close to a real criminal action, close enough to make him giddy and inspire him with the thrill of possible danger, though nothing is yet at risk. For he still does not believe that he could ever do anything more than dream, plan, and rehearse, over and over again.

Raskolnikov has long been obsessed not so much with crime as with the *possibility* of crime. It is precisely as a possibility that it attracts him, which is why he never concretely works out the details; he has never even considered how he is to obtain the axe when necessary. A man dreaming of the perfect crime winds up relying on chance to get the murder weapon! That's all "trifles," he tells himself, and postpones considering them while concentrating, when he can concentrate at all, on the theory of crime and the thrill of danger. Planning for an actual crime entails knowing precisely what one will do, but Raskolnikov plans only for a possible crime.

Rehearsal and hypothetical planning overcome all desire to do anything else. For that matter, even after the murder, Raskolnikov finds himself drawn in the same way back to the scene of the crime, not out of guilt, but to *re*-enact it as he has *pre*-enacted it. Without knowing how he got there, he finds himself at the old woman's former apartment, rings the door bell, then rings it again and again, each time experiencing "the hideous and agonisingly fearful sensation he had felt then. . . . He shuddered at every ring and it gave him more and more satisfaction" (C&P, 170). He cannot cease "experimenting." He has tantalized himself with terror, and he cannot relinquish its fearful pleasure. He seems to be repeating not only the crime but also the rehearsals for it, the time when it figured as a persistent possibility that need never become actual.

Indeed, even the murder itself is undertaken as if it were just another rehearsal. The fact is, Raskolnikov never decides to commit the murder, which is one reason he later has so much trouble in ascertaining *why* he decided to do so. Instead of actually resolving, he remains in what feels like hypothetical time; and yet, the steps entailed by hypothetical living translate into actual and terrible action. Dostoevsky is at the height of his powers here. He shows us a murder, a dramatic and active event if there ever was one, consciously and freely committed by someone who never truly decides to do so and lives passively at several removes from reality. What makes such a strange action possible?

Throughout part I, Raskolnikov remains in the territory between resolving on murder and renouncing it. His supposed resolutions are more like resolutions to resolve, and even these are unacted upon. After he has gotten up late and is rushing frantically to get to the murder scene on time, the narrator makes this state of mind explicit:

> We may note in passing one peculiarity in regard to all the final resolutions taken by him in the matter; they had one strange characteristic; the more final they were, the more hideous and absurd they at once became in his eyes. In spite of all his agonising inward struggle, he never for a single instant all that time could believe in the carrying out of his plans.
>
> And, indeed, if it had ever happened that everything to the least point could have been considered and finally settled, and no uncertainty of any kind had remained, he would, it seems, have renounced it all as something absurd, monstrous and impossible. But a whole mass of unsettled points and uncertainties remained. (C&P, 71)

He does not settle details *in order to* remain in uncertainty, *in order to* stay in the territory between deciding to act and deciding not to act. But that territory gradually shrinks to a point. He at last arrives at a moment when not renouncing the action necessitates doing it, though without a decision to do so.

The sequence of events leading to the crime begins with Raskolnikov's dream of the beating of the mare, after which he prays, "Lord, show me my path—I renounce ... that accursed dream of mine" (C&P, 61). But he has not renounced it, only considered renouncing it. Almost immediately a test confronts him. By sheer chance—though Raskolnikov wonders if it is fate—he learns that the old lady will be alone at a particular hour. He could never again hope to obtain such a valuable piece of information without risk of detection. If he does not continue to act as if he might still decide to act, he will indeed have renounced his dream forever. And so, clinging to the shrinking space between resolution and renunciation, he continues to do the sheer minimum necessary to keep the dream alive. But with a specific time set, that minimum is enough to bring him to the murder scene, axe in hand.

In almost sleeping too long, he leaves just enough time to keep the possibility alive. Throughout the killing, he does the very least he can do at each moment to make the next (but only the very next) moment one in which the dream will still exist. As a result, he behaves "almost wholly mechanically: as if someone had taken him by the hand and pulled him along irresistibly, blindly, with unnatural force, without objections. As if a piece of his clothing had been caught in the cogs of a machine and he were dragged into it."[35] At the murder scene, he is "almost unconscious of his body" (C&P, 76). In fact, he had anticipated as much, which is why he long ago chose an axe, a weapon requiring no accuracy or presence of mind to use, rather than a knife (C&P, 71). Even in his dreams, apparently, he imagined doing it dreamily.

He kills the old woman when "he had not a minute to lose. He pulled the axe quite out, swung it with both arms, scarcely conscious of himself, and almost without effort, almost mechanically, he brought the blunt side down on her head. He seemed not to use his own strength in this" (C&P, 78). He uses the blunt side because it does not require aiming. When the old woman's meek sister, Lizaveta, enters through the still-open door, Raskolnikov must, by sheer inertia, kill her, too. Dostoevsky's description removes the agency from the murderer to the action itself, as if the sheer momentum of mechanical activity were sufficient, without any decision, to make the possibility an actuality: "The blow landed directly on the skull, with the sharp edge, and immediately split the whole upper part of the forehead, almost to the crown. She collapsed."[36]

To live as if there were no actuality, as if possibilities were all, is to renounce responsibility altogether. If one acts as if there were only sideshadows, the most horrible actuality may come about. Indeed, it may well be that most murders happen in just this Dostoevskian way, committed by people operating in hypothetical time who have never quite decided to do what they have done. In such a case, responsibility rests on one for falling into this state of mind in the first place. There is no alibi for attentiveness to the real present and near future.

Disease #4, Multiple Time.
The Garden of Forking Paths

> The parallel worlds idea, in fact, is not widely accepted because it appears to posit such a strange universe.
> —FRED ALAN WOLF, *Parallel Universes*

If determinism threatens choice by reducing the possibilities of each moment to one (the actuality), another, much less familiar way of thinking threatens choice by expanding actualities to encompass *all* possibilities. The sequence of time in which we live loses substantiality by losing singularity; the universe (or universe of universes) abides in *multiple time.*

I refer to a number of thinkers who have posited multiple (or "parallel") universes. According to this strange model, whatever possibility is not realized in one universe is realized in another.[37] There are no unactualized possibilities, and so no middle realm of real but unactualized possibilities. For Bakhtin, the present is only one of many possible presents, but in this view the present is one of many actual presents.

Various considerations have led thinkers to adopt this model, which comes in several versions. Fred Alan Wolf's *Parallel Universes* proposes multiple universes as a way of resolving paradoxes raised by quantum physics and relativity theory; David Lewis's *On the Plurality of Worlds* multiplies universes (or worlds, in his terminology) in order to solve, as neatly and simply as possible, philosophical enigmas raised by counterfactuals.[38] The essential questions pertaining to multiple time are most clearly seen in Jorge Luis Borges's well-known story "The Garden of Forking Paths."

Borges's story evidently belongs to the genre of the philosophical parable. Going back to antiquity, this genre includes tales of the wisdom of Solomon, many Talmudic narratives, Voltaire's "Story of the Good Brahmin," and Stanislaw Lem's *Cyberiad.* Among Russian classics, it is closest to Pushkin's "The Queen of Spades," Dostoevsky's "The Dream of a Ridiculous Man," Chekhov's "The Bet," and, perhaps, the absurdist parables of Daniil Kharms. In all of these works, a philosophical question is rendered through a brief narrative in which plot and question interweave in complex ways. Often this form enriches our sense of the issues without providing a definitive answer. True to the genre, Borges does not defend but explores the idea of infinite universes. In this crucial respect, he is unlike Wolf and Lewis. The sort of objections, moral and other, that might be advanced against Borges's idea are themselves an implicit or explicit part of the story. Borges's parable therefore avoids the moral naivete typical (in my view) of those who actually defend the existence of other worlds "quasi-simultaneous" with our own.

"The Garden of Forking Paths" is double; it consists of an outer story cast in the mode of a detective/spy narrative and an inner story in which a scholar reveals the amazing solution to a problem in Sinology. Both have a linear plot. The inner story recounts the history of the scholarly question and provides the new solution explaining all earlier mysteries. In the outer story, the motive for a strange and apparently incomprehensible murder is revealed in the last paragraph, so that Borges's narrative achieves, in terms of form, the sort of strong closure characteristic of detective fiction. In terms of content, however, the matter is rather different: for both stories within the story raise philosophical questions about the nature of time that, far from being resolved, seem to ramify (like time itself?) endlessly. Such a combination of strong formal closure and philosophical openness is in fact rather common for philosophical parables.

The outer story treats a set of issues with which we are already familiar: presentness, freedom, and fatalism; and the psychological consequences of a doctrine's philosophical tenets. Its plot is relatively simple. During World

War I, Dr. Yu Tsun, a Chinese working in England as a German spy, discovers that a British agent, Richard Madden, has just captured or killed another German spy. Yu Tsun knows that he will be next. His problem is how to communicate to the Germans the name of a town in France they should bomb. To do so, he must solve three subsidiary problems. First, he must communicate the message so that the Germans will pay attention to it amid the din of war and the overflow of reports. Second, the message must be so coded that the Germans will understand it but the British will not. Finally, he must do so, having no secure means of communication at his disposal, before Madden arrests or kills him.

Yu Tsun hits on a plan, which is clarified only at the conclusion of the story. He looks up a name in the telephone book, takes a train to Ashgrove, and inquires the way to the house of Stephen Albert. After walking through the labyrinthine garden to Albert's house, he finds its owner. Yu Tsun enters into conversation with Albert (during which the inner story is told) and then kills him. At that moment, Madden arrives and arrests the murderer. Madden soon deduces the reason for the crime: the name of the town the Germans were to bomb was Albert, and the news reports of the strange murder communicated this information to the Germans. Unfortunately, as we know from the beginning of the story, the result made no difference beyond briefly postponing a British attack.

All of this information is provided in a statement by Yu Tsun, who also records the repeated speculations about time in which he engaged during these events. On the one hand, he recalls, the necessity for rapid decisions and the palpability of the present crisis repeatedly provoked the thought that people always live in the present and that every moment has always been characterized by presentness: "Then I reflected that everything happens to a man precisely, precisely *now*. Centuries of centuries and only in the present do things happen."[39] On the other hand, Yu Tsun kept sensing the present moment as insubstantial—either as a mere repetition of the past or as already dictated from the future. If dictated from the future, the beleaguered Yu Tsun reasoned, it should display prophetic signs. When he learned that Madden was pursuing him, he records, "It seemed incredible to me that that day without premonitions or symbols should be the one of my inexorable death" (Borges, 20). Even now, when recording the episode, Yu Tsun does not seem to notice the significance of the fact that he did not, in fact, die on that day of his "inexorable death," as the record itself tacitly testifies. But on the day in question he soon found the "premonitions" he had at first missed.

Despite the unmistakable palpability of presentness, Yu Tsun continued to find instances of foreshadowing indicating that his and other presents are all already written from the future. If such signs are true, he reasoned, then the present moment has no more openness than it does when it is already over and recorded in a completed narrative—as it is, of course, for Borges's reader. Or is it the impression of foreshadowing that is the mirage? Yu Tsun recalls that when he saw Madden just miss the train to Ashgrove, he told himself that "this slightest of victories foreshadowed a total victory. I argued (no less fallaciously) that my cowardly falsity proved that I was a man capable of carrying out the adventure successfully" (Borges, 22).

Yu Tsun never decides whether foreshadowing exists in the real world, but he does arrive at a paradoxical piece of advice: *"The author of an atrocious undertaking ought to imagine that he has already accomplished it, ought to impose upon himself a future as irrevocable as the past"* (Borges, 22; italics in original). To act resolutely in the present, one must, strangely enough, adopt a species of fatalism. The exercise of will is enabled by the belief (or imagination) that the desired future is in any case already irrevocably decided, indeed, already accomplished. Although philosophically speaking, choice requires *a*symmetrical time in which the past but not the future is fixed, psychologically, choice apparently demands (at least for "atrocious undertakings") the belief that time is symmetrical, that actions are unalterable, and that choice itself is unreal. And yet in saying that one *ought* to *impose* such a fatalistic perspective, Yu Tsun seems to be acknowledging that, regardless of what psychology requires, the future is not irrevocable and that choice is real. And what is the psychology involved in imposing a psychology? Is one involved in a strange form of double-think (or double-feel)? The opposition of a doctrine's psychological to its philosophical implications constitutes the central paradox, and probably the central point, of the outer narrative.

Whether time is closed or open, symmetrical or asymmetrical, fated or free, Yu Tsun assumes throughout the outer narrative that it is singular: that there is one and only one actuality at each moment. The inner narrative questions this assumption. As it happens, the Sinologist Stephen Albert has solved the mystery of Yu Tsun's great-grandfather, Ts'ui Pen, a powerful politician who abandoned the world to live in the Pavilion of Limpid Solitude, where (according to the sources) he worked on two projects, a novel and an infinite labyrinth. When he died, no traces of the labyrinth were found, and the novel appeared to be nothing but rough drafts. Apparently, even the plot had not been worked out: in one chapter a character dies yet in the next he is alive. But Albert has discovered an additional piece of evidence that explains the mystery of Ts'ui Pen.

That evidence is the fragment of a letter, in which Ts'ui Pen wrote, *"I leave to the various futures (not to all) my garden of forking paths"* (Borges, 25). Albert immediately realized that the novel and the labyrinth are one; that the manuscript is not unfinished but a finished fragment from an infinite book; and that the book represents time as Ts'ui Pen understood it. Time *is* a garden of forking paths. In Ts'ui Pen's labyrinth, the forks are not in space but in time. In the story's best-known passage, Albert explains,

> In all fictional works, each time a man is confronted with several alternatives, he chooses one and eliminates the others; in the fiction of Ts'ui Pen, he chooses—simultaneously—all of them. *He creates*, in this way, diverse futures, diverse times, which themselves also proliferate and fork. . . . In the work of Ts'ui Pen, all possible outcomes occur; each one is the point of departure for other forkings. Sometimes the paths of this labyrinth converge; for example, you arrive at this house, but in one of the possible pasts you are my enemy, in another, my friend. (Borges, 26)

Whenever there are two or more possibilities, each occurs in a different universe, a different temporal sequence. Time bifurcates and all choices are always made. "In contrast to Newton and Schopenhauer, your ancestor did not believe in a uniform, absolute time. He believed in an infinite number of times. . . . This network of times which approached one another, forked, broke off, or were unaware of one another for centuries, embraces *all* possibilities of time" (Borges, 28). But if all choices are made, the reader may ask, in what sense is there choice at all?

Moreover, in Ts'ui Pen's model the temporalities of each universe are synchronized (or hypersynchronized, since these are synchronies not in time but of times). Thus, as in a spatial labyrinth, their paths not only diverge but also converge, which means that a given moment may be the outcome of two quite different sequences.[40] It follows that a moment may not be identical to itself because the same situation may have resulted—almost certainly did result—from different pasts. Ghostly other universes have made us, and Yu Tsun begins to sense that the humid garden may be "infinitely saturated with invisible persons. Those persons were Albert and I, secret, busy, and multiform in other dimensions of time" (Borges, 28).

The outer story presents contradictory versions of singular time, the inner story an image of multiple time—of an infinite plurality of times. Of course, we are reading not two stories but one parable containing both, and the relation of the two taken together suggests a third possibility about time. It is an odd coincidence, we may reflect, that the man chosen simply because his name is Albert should turn out to be mysteriously connected to Yu Tsun's ancestor and that, in choosing this method of communicating to his superiors, the spy should have wound up killing the one person whose work is of supreme value to him.

"In every one [of the possible times]," I pronounced, not without a tremble to my voice, "I am grateful to you and revere you for your re-creation of the garden of Ts'ui Pen."

"Not in all," he murmured with a smile. "Time forks perpetually toward innumerable futures. In one of them I am your enemy" (Borges, 28).

Time creates possibilities—and if Ts'ui Pen is right, each possibility is an actuality—with truly "atrocious" and unanticipated meanings. In the last sentence of the story, Yu Tsun reports that his German chief may have deciphered his message, but "he does not know (no one can know) my innumerable contrition and weariness" (Borges, 29). Whether time is open or closed, singular or plural, it is certainly two other things: an unfathomable mystery and infinitely (or innumerably) ironic.[41]

Disease #4, Multiple Time. Multiple-Universe Determinism

The multiple-universe models I have encountered are exhaustive: every contingent event is enacted in some universe, there are no unactualized possibilities, and all choices are made.[42] These models encounter several troubling problems. For one thing, the multiplication of times threatens personal identity. If my self splits, then which am I? How am "I" responsible for my actions? Who am I if I have been capable of yielding to every temptation that has come my way? Insofar as identity depends on what we choose and what we forego, what happens to it if nothing is foregone? We took the road not taken. For another thing, because all choices are made somewhere, the totality of good and evil in existence becomes a zero-sum game. All we affect (if anything) is where evil occurs. Finally, and most strangely, the fact that possibilities do not exceed actualities reintroduces determinism by a new and unexpected route. Everything that happens had to happen, and nothing that could have taken place fails to take place.

In exhaustive multiple universe models, for every present moment there are other corresponding presents. Each of us has duplicates or counterparts in other universes. Neither the self nor the universe in which we live has the singularity we usually assume. No universe and no self has any privilege; none is in any sense primary or more real than its counterparts. That is why identity becomes a vexed problem. Contingency no longer means something that might or might not happen, but something that happens in some but not in all universes. Everything possible happens somewhere, and there are no gaps in logical space (Lewis, 86).

It is therefore evident why such models are, *ex hypothesi*, deterministic in a peculiar way. In a deterministic singular universe, everything that could be is, and so with the plurality of universes. The difference is that multiple-universe determinism applies not to any one universe but to the universe of universes (to the meta-universe). Because there can be no unactualized possibilities, there are no sideshadows; for whatever in a singular and open universe would be a sideshadow is here an actuality somewhere else in the meta-universe. Somewhere Fyodor Pavlovich is the father of Smerdyakov, and somewhere Karp is. If this Raskolnikov kills the old woman, another does not. In some universes, the events in *Karamazov* are fictional but in others factual. Dostoevsky has written the true story of a crime somewhere else.

In the meta-universe the totality of good and evil is fixed because no choice could possibly alter the balance. Choice loses much of its significance insofar as the significance of a choice depends on its singularity and on what possibilities were left unactualized. The present fades to a mere shadow of its former self if the present is exhaustively multiplied. This is a "Copernican revolution" with a vengeance. What difference does it make what I do, if I also do the opposite? Both personal identity and morality would seem to be seriously threatened. This implication is, I think, suggested by Borges's story. For Wolf, too,

> this thought bothers me. It gnaws at me. If this is true, do we really have any choice at all? If every time I choose, all of my parallel *mes* are also choosing, then is there really any choice? If any choice means all of them, then perhaps choice is just another illusion. There really is no free choice, because all of the results of any choice always manifest. We may be machines after all, but just existing in more dimensions that we are aware of in any single universe. I ask the reader to consider the possibility. (Wolf, 98)

If selves split with each choice, as they do for Ts'ui Pen and Wolf, then decision would seem to lose all meaning. There is no room for remorse, only regret that one is in the wrong universe. Ethics would seem to require a singular universe as surely as it requires multiple possibilities. There must be sideshadows.[43]

CHAPTER SIX

Backshadowing

The handwriting on the wall may be a forgery.
—RALPH HODGSON

Backshadowing Defined and Characterized

Backshadowing may be defined as foreshadowing after the fact. The past is viewed as having contained signs pointing to what happened later, to events known to the backshadowing observer. Visible now, those signs could have been seen then. In effect, the present, as the future of the past, was already immanent in the past. A more or less straight line is drawn between the past period under examination and the observer's present (bipolarity).

Alternatively, backshadowing may be based on three significant times: the period under examination; the outcome of that period; and the present, in which the backshadowing observer passes judgment on the earliest period. There is a bipolar story, with an observer located after its completion. The first period contained signs pointing to the second and read in the third. The signs are clearest in light of what happened later, but they were legible from the first. When backshadowing is used, a past period is treated as if its participants could in principle have seen the future that loomed and was in fact to happen.

Those who failed to foresee are therefore typically regarded as blind or self-blinded. Like Oedipus, they could have known what would happen next. But in many cases, they are more to blame than Oedipus because unlike that fated king they might have taken action to alter or attenuate the forces threatening them. A particular tone of superiority therefore characterizes the backshadowing observer, who passes judgment on those who failed to take responsible action.[1]

One key problem with backshadowing lies in its assumption that the past contained legible signs of the future. Were such signs in fact present and visible? And if the possibility of what in fact happened later could have been foreseen, were there not also countless other possibilities? Not knowing, as later observers do, what was to happen, could people in the past have foreseen which of all possibilities was to be realized? And might not later observers be mistaken when they assume that what did happen later was the most likely possibility?

Not all judgments of past actions involve backshadowing, of course. If the likelihood of what did happen later could have been foreseen without the added knowledge that only a future perspective could provide—if nothing resembling foreshadowing is ascribed to past times—then such judgments would not involve backshadowing. If the people of the past are seen as having no more access to their future than we have to ours, backshadowing is not involved in evaluating their actions. Those who support dictators committed to a totalitarian ideology and then are surprised when freedom of speech is suppressed might justly be convicted of naivete because the experience already available to them offered sufficient reason to fear such an outcome. A person who squanders money and keeps no records might be expected to foresee the danger of financial difficulties. In passing moral judgments, it is important to distinguish between standards that involve backshadowing and those that do not.

The historical researcher who wishes to avoid backshadowing needs to ascertain what the past looked like to its participants. What the researcher must avoid is conferring an unjust privilege on later events and on the researcher's own present, as if later events were necessarily visible before they happened. It is wise to keep in mind that, from the perspective of an earlier time, other outcomes—sideshadows to us—may have been just as (or even more) likely. Because sideshadows are not as palpable as actualities, it is of course difficult to do so. A kind of temporal egotism leads us to endow our own actual present with special privilege.

"He Should Have Known": Premises of Backshadowing

Like foreshadowing, backshadowing tends to eliminate sideshadows. It involves a series of questionable assumptions about time. The backshadowing observer may never articulate or even be aware of those assumptions, and he might well reject them if a critic should point them out. To be sure, backshadowing sometimes results from the application of an explicit theory justifying the practice, but it also derives from a natural tendency to privilege one's own time.

Just as there is such a thing as ethnocentrism, so, too, there is *chronocentrism*. Taking our own moment as somehow special and the prejudices of our own time as wisdom requires no persuasion and demands no prior theory. We do not have to be argued into it; it is much more likely that we need arguing out of it. In much the same way that it requires effort, practice, and skill to see the world from alien cultural perspectives, it requires the same qualities to imagine the past without the surplus knowledge that our own situation provides.

Backshadowing in effect turns the past into a well-plotted story. Everything conspires to produce the outcome we know; loose ends, which intimate other possibilities, are drastically reduced or entirely eliminated in backshadowing narrative. Such narratives consequently feature various tropes of irony, which presuppose the greater wisdom of the narrator and readers. "And yet they did not see"; "Little did he know that"; "Meanwhile, as these people were absorbed in their petty affairs, a storm was gathering"—these and many similar narrative devices are the characteristic language of backshadowing. We see; they should have seen.

In Ilf and Petrov's celebrated Soviet satire *The Golden Calf*, a group of office workers frightened by an approaching inspection learn that one of them has checked himself into an insane asylum:

> "He is feigning madness. At this very moment I'm sure he is roaring with laughter. There's a smart fellow for you! I even envy him."
>
> "What's the matter? Is there something wrong with his parents? Were they merchants or some other alien element?"
>
> "Of course, not only is there something wrong with his parents, but, between you and me, at one time he had a drugstore. Who could have known that some day there would be a revolution? People made their way in the world as best they could; some managed to get a drugstore, and there were people who even had a factory. Personally, I don't see anything wrong with it. Who could have known?"
>
> "He should have known," Koreiko said coldly.[2]

He should have known: this is the essential trope of backshadowing. And indeed, if one is a Marxist-Leninist, the laws of history were indeed known and the revolution was an inevitability. Those who did not see it coming were at best naive and at worst engaged in a desperate attempt to profit from injustice as long as possible.

In short, backshadowing typically involves the following (often concealed) premises:

1. History (or some portion of it) fits a relatively neat pattern.

2. That pattern is now clear to us, and we see it correctly. The story, with beginning, middle, and end, is now over, and we are in a position to contemplate it in its entirety. We can assess its meaning as we would assess the meaning of a novel.

3. History (or a particular portion of it) is teleological. It was directed to a particular outcome known to us.

4. Signs of that outcome, of the direction of history, were visible all along.

5. Therefore the pattern should have been visible to those in the past as clearly, or almost as clearly, as it is now visible to us.

6. It is consequently possible to measure the wisdom or folly, guilt or innocence, of our predecessors according to the facts now known.

7. The standards of judgment we use are the proper ones for judging people in the past. The values that lead us to assess actions as progressive or reactionary, good or evil, apply to the earlier time because the same story seamlessly links past and present.

8. Either sideshadows of the past were entirely absent—history had to lead to us—or were, at most, limited to the alternative path or paths we identify now. What happened later was either inevitable or highly probable. Characteristically, the option of inevitability is chosen by those who believe the outcome of history to be correct, whereas the option of a single missed path (or a few missed paths) is chosen by those who view it as incorrect or evil. What is lacking in either case is a serious attempt to see the sideshadows that might have been possible or visible at the earlier time, especially those that later events have obscured and those not relevant to our present problems. It is the end of the story that prescribes what options, if any, were available at the beginning or middle.

9. A bipolar model of temporality is favored. It is as if time had but two significant moments, then and now; or (in the three-part variant of the model) time had three significant moments, the beginning of the story, the end, and ourselves, who observe the whole accomplished narrative. By contrast, sideshadowing invites us to attribute causal effectiveness to countless intervening moments, which might have continually altered options, possibilities, and appropriate standards of judgment.

The tendency to backshadowing may be stronger or weaker and more or less extensive. In some cases, it embraces the whole of history and the present dispensation is thought to offer a key to understanding all prior events. In others, backshadowing is applied only to a particular sequence that is of special interest to the observers, and it is only a single truth or moral lesson that is held to be certain. Sideshadows may be completely eliminated or it may still be possible to glimpse a few vague beginnings of other possibilities. Even if no serious effort is made to reconstruct them, sideshadows may appear, if only vaguely and indistinctly, as improbable alternatives. In such cases, the skeptical reader may read through a backshadowing narrative to glimpse other shapes and recognize, if not specific other possibilities, then at least the reward of looking for them.

As a rule, the more explicit and more conscious the philosophy of history on which backshadowing depends, the more thoroughly are sideshadows eliminated. By the same token, such explicit backshadowing rarely falls into the temporal incoherence characteristic of its more intuitive and unwitting practitioners. It is those to whom backshadowing comes naturally and without reflection who are most often surprised and discomfited when the method's concealed assumptions are pointed out.

Retrospection and Reciprocity

> Treason doth never prosper: what's the reason?
> For if it prosper, none dare call it treason.
> —SIR JOHN HARRINGTON

Tolstoy regarded what I have called backshadowing as a fundamental falsity affecting most narratives about the past. He distrusted it for the same reasons that he rejected foreshadowing, and he saw the same mental tendencies contributing to these twin errors. Both derive in part from the requirements of good storytelling: to be tellable and effective, narratives impose neatness on events. Structure, the elimination of loose ends, the creation of a beginning, middle, and end—all these and a host of related narrative techniques that we take to be natural and perform almost automatically lead to an unjustified privileging of the moment of narration when an entire pattern is purportedly visible. As a result, the past looks as if it were predestined to lead to the present and as if the signs of our own time were already there for those willing to see them.

In his comments on the design of *War and Peace*, Tolstoy recounted how he arrived at his narratological suspicion. He describes how, as a soldier at Sevastopol, he often had the opportunity to interview soldiers immediately after an engagement and then read the narrative accounts that were later written about it. Whoever performs such an exercise honestly will be conscious of the enormous gap between the two. When the battle is still fresh, soldiers will offer

> a sublime, complex, infinitely varied and grim, indistinct impression; and from no one—least of all from the commander in chief—will you learn what the whole affair was like. But in two or three days the reports begin to be handed in. Talkers begin to narrate how things they did not see took place; finally a general report is compiled and the general opinion of the army is formed according to this report. Everyone is relieved to exchange his own doubts and questions for this false, but clear and always flattering

presentation. A month or two later, question a person who took part in the battle, and already you will not sense the raw, vital material that used to be there, but he will narrate according to the official reports. (Jub 16:11)

What Tolstoy describes here is the transformation of presentness into pastness, which typically involves the construction of a neat whole from parts that in fact did not cohere or lead in a single direction. Backshadowing almost always results from this transformation.

Perhaps the cleverest (though not the wisest) character in *War and Peace,* the Russian diplomat Bilibin, is so keenly aware of this process that he describes it in advance. Before a historical event happens he provides the descriptions that will later be written about it; understanding the structure of such narratives and the kinds of judgment they will serve, he can predict the stories to come. He realizes very well that he has no capacity to predict events, but that does not prevent him from foreseeing stories about events. Facts are infinitely various, but the kinds of narrative distortion are relatively few, and all must allow for backshadowing judgments with clear lines of causality.

Before the Battle of Austerlitz, for instance, Bilibin tells his friends that, whatever happens, "the glory of Russian arms is assured" because even if the Russians lose, there is sure to be a story—and he knows which story—justifying Russian prowess and assigning blame to a single and non-Russian cause. No matter what chain of events might lead to defeat, backshadowing narrative will select (or fabricate) the incidents leading to such a flattering story. It will proceed by "stencil work," in which what appears is what the narrator needs. When the Russians do lose the battle, Bilibin is proven right: just such stories are told. Bilibin's narrative prescience testifies to the falsity of histories and of the patterns we see.

Tolstoy's own version of Bilibin's insight is his famous simile about a group of men preparing to haul a log. "Each of them gives his opinion as to how and when to haul it. They haul the log away and it turns out that it has been done in accordance with what one of them said. [Therefore we conclude retrospectively that] he ordered it" (W&P, 1434–35). Whatever happens in a sequence of historical events, it is always possible to find someone who predicted it, if only because so many people are advancing so many possibilities that something resembling one of them is bound to come true. Retrospective narrative then attributes to the one who offered the confirmed prediction special insight or power.

After the fact, people ask, Why did others not foresee what that man foresaw and what to us is so plain? *They should have known.* But however natural it may be, such a conclusion is almost always unjustified. The grounds on which the prediction was made may well have been entirely spurious and no better than rival predictions, given the evidence available and possibilities existing at the time. Had another prediction come true, retrospective narratives would have seized on it with equally good (or bad) justification.

"Retrospection" is one of several closely related fallacies Tolstoy identifies as contributing to backshadowing. He in fact describes too many to recount here. But one more is worth discussing, the fallacy of "reciprocity":

> besides the law of retrospection, which represents all the past as a preparation for future events, the law of reciprocity comes in, confusing the whole matter. A good chess player who has lost a game is genuinely convinced that his failure is due to a mistake on his part, and looks for that mistake in the opening, forgetting that at each stage of the game there were similar blunders, that none of his moves was perfect. The mistake on which he concentrates his attention has been noticed simply because his opponent took advantage of it. How much more complex is the game of war, which takes place within certain limits of time, and where it is not a question of one will manipulating inanimate objects, but of everything ensuing from countless collisions of diverse wills! (W&P, 854)

Like retrospection, this fallacy also derives from bipolar thinking. One draws a straight line from one event in the past to the present situation. The earlier event is seen as determining all intervening events. But in fact causality is a constant ravelment of possibilities. There may be no single turning point, and the identification of one derives not from the way events happen but from the manner in which solutions are sought. If that is true of chess, it is all the truer of actual historical events, for example, battles, in which the number of agents is much greater and the power of intervening choices and chances is much larger.

Indeed, even battles are too simple an example and conceal yet another problem with backshadowing. Like games of chess, military engagements end, which means that accounts of them are written by those who no longer participate in them. But history proceeds continually and any demarcation of ends, any periodization, is necessarily arbitrary. The observer has a natural tendency to place himself at the conclusion of a story, but a later historian will be sure to see his predecessor as being in the middle of it. Assessments of the Russian Revolution made so confidently in 1930 are now easily describable as among its results. The later historian may look down on the shortsightedness of his predecessors, who did not see forces about to disconfirm their evaluations, but, governed by the same natural tendency, the later historian is likely not to give proper consideration to his own middle position in some future narrative. One is always wise to suspect backshadowing and its accompanying fallacies whenever the standards of the present are offered as if they were somehow final or based on considerations intrinsically superior to those available at earlier times.

Whiggism

What elegant historian would neglect a striking opportunity for pointing out that his heroes did not foresee the history of the world, or even their own actions?—For example, that Henry of Navarre, when a Protestant baby, little thought of being a Catholic monarch; or that Alfred the Great, when he measured his laborious nights with burning candles, had no idea of future gentlemen measuring their idle days with watches.
  —*MIDDLEMARCH*

Though it does not refer to Tolstoy, Herbert Butterfield's study *The Whig Interpretation of History* catalogues many of the fallacies described in *War and Peace* and adds a few more. Once quite familiar, this book seems to have passed from controversy, especially among literary scholars, who perhaps need it most.

The target of Butterfield's polemic is a recurrent view of history exemplified by (but not limited to) the Whig historians of his time. As he describes them, these historians tended to see the past as a preparation for the present, traced history as the triumph of Whiggish liberty, evaluated movements on the basis of their contributions to this cause, and assumed the role of final judges delivering the verdict of History. They produced a neat story in which progressives advanced and reactionaries tried to forestall the British constitution, saw Protestantism as favoring liberty and Catholicism relentlessly opposing it, and, in general, offered a comforting picture of history as the gradual triumph of forward-looking over backward-looking forces.

Butterfield means us to understand that this method of thinking is by no means confined to Whigs but is an ever-present temptation to those who narrate the past. In this broader sense, *Whiggism* also "describes the attitude by which the men of the Renaissance seem to have approached the Middle Ages. It describes the attitude of the 18th century to many a period of the past"; and there are countless other examples because the underlying logic of Whiggism is not tied to any particular political perspective:[3]

> The whig interpretation of history is not merely the property of whigs and it is much more subtle than mental bias; it lies in a trick of organisation, an unexamined habit of mind that any historian may fall into. . . . It is the result of the practice of abstracting things from their historical context and judging them apart from their context—estimating them and organising the historical story by a system of direct reference to the present. (WIH, 30–31)

The defining Whiggish practice is to assume the essential correctness of present political and social values and then to narrate history as the story of their long and arduous triumph. History so conducted can only "ratify whatever conceptions we originally had in regard to our own times" (WIH, 62). The historian assumes the special role, denied to ordinary people and to earlier historians, of vindicating past sufferers and condemning evildoers from a perspective that nothing can ever gainsay.

So flattering is this role and so congenial this activity that it is no wonder it remains, through countless ideological changes, a powerful temptation. "By the very finality and absoluteness with which he has endowed the present he [the historian] has heightened his own position. For him the voice of posterity is the voice of God and the historian is the voice of posterity" (WIH, 107). Such a historian becomes a judge when his trade fits him, at best, to be only a detective: "His concern with the sphere of morality forms in fact, the extreme point in his desire to make judgments of value, and to count them as the verdict of history" (WIH, 107).

Anachronism necessarily results from such a practice. Characteristically, a timeless Progress and an unchanging Reaction fight a Manichean battle across the centuries. It is therefore easy to describe Luther's Protestantism as if it were essentially the same as the Protestantism of today and to see past conflicts as mere translations of recent issues into other terms. Whiggism tends to see the likenesses between past and present, but we must rather learn "the elucidation of the unlikenesses" (WIH, 10). The truly historical impulse, Butterfield contends, is to appreciate why questions that now seem empty once seemed as compelling as our own: "Real historical understanding is not achieved by the subordination of the past to the present, but rather by our making the past our present and attempting to see life with the eyes of another century than our own. It is not reached by assuming that our own age is the absolute to which Luther and Calvin and their generation are only relative" (WIH, 16).

Whiggish history involves what Butterfield calls a "magnet." Countless small events tending in all directions are made to line up (like iron filings in a magnetic field) in a single direction, which points to us. This magnet "can draw out of history the very things that we go to look for" and allows us readily, but fallaciously, to "see in Luther a foreshadowing of the present" (WIH, 27). But real historical work disposes of the magnet and foreshadowing.

One of Butterfield's most interesting arguments concerns the opposition of particular to general histories, the latter usually made by abridging the former. General histories tend to strengthen the magnet because in most cases what is abridged out are all the contingencies and messiness of history: these abridgments rely on what I have called a bipolar model. In Butterfield's view, a good abridgment would preserve proportionately as much ramification, disorder, and sense of contingency as the various fine-grained descriptions of the particular or specialist histories; but what almost always happens is that abridgments, like plot summaries of novels, leave out the complexities and create a mendaciously neat, smooth story. The result is a spurious sense of a direction to history, as if the seeds of later events were present in earlier ones. A straight line is drawn, say, from the Reformation to nineteenth-century England, whereas in fact countless contingent events intervened, each of which was as causally effective as the ones with which the narrative began: "Any action which any man has ever taken is part of that whole set of circumstances which at a given moment conditions the whole mass of things that are to happen next. . . . it is not easy to work out its consequences, for they are merged in the results of everything else that was conspiring to produce change" (WIH, 20).

For Butterfield, real contingency is essential to history. That is why good historical work involves not the elaboration of overarching theories or stories but ever-finer details, which serve constantly to make the picture more complex. It may be said that anyone who writes as if there were "an unfolding logic in history" and as if there are people who cooperate with Progress itself, "does not believe there is an historical process at all" (WIH, 42). That is because time, the time of contingency, does not "unfold" but acts unpredictably. "It is not by a line but by a labyrinthine piece of network" that things change and emerge; the history of religious liberty and of so many other complex facts "is born of strange conjunctures, it represents purposes marred perhaps more than purposes achieved, and it owes more than we can tell to many agencies that had little to do with either religion or liberty" (WIH, 45).

To evaporate the contingent is to dispense with history. One cannot get at the essence of history by eliminating vicissitudes and accidents or by factoring out local circumstances and personal factors because such "incidentals" *comprise* the historical: "The thing which is unhistorical is to imagine that we can get the essence apart from the accidents" (WIH, 69). And if that is so, then history did not have to lead to us but could have led in countless other directions.

Backshadowing is most readily discernible when historical figures, movements, or works are placed on one side or the other of an eternal contest of progressive with reactionary. Typically overlooked is the possibility that later situations resulted from the interaction of two sides rather than from the triumph of one and that they represented a result desired by neither. Ascribed to a simple clash of wills is "something that probably no man ever willed" (WIH, 46). The Whiggish historian assumes that everyone was always concerned with the questions of his own day, as if those were always there and were not as ephemeral as those of the past.

Time Line: The Progressive

Many who would abjure the set of assumptions Butterfield describes never-theless follow them often enough in practice. Teleology infects the most anti-teleological of thinkers, as in the curious recent display of historical and episte-mological relativists outlining the story by which their truth at last came to be accepted. Or consider the common practice of refuting some ideas by calling them backward-looking and recommending others as forward-looking. This practice could be valid only if history had a direction that somehow guaranteed that later was better. If it does not, then the old idea might just as well be better than the new. We can all think of instances—the fascism or Bolshevism of the young in the early part of this century—in which that was so and when the "backward-looking" was preferable. But it is common enough for people who recoil at the notion of an inevitable law of progress nevertheless to make an essentially temporal characterization a recommendation or criticism.

After the Bolshevik coup, it was quite common for Russian intellectuals who on other grounds recognized the danger of a Marxist dictatorship to sup-port it because it was "the wave of the future." To oppose it seemed like going against history itself. To some, anything less than enthusiastic support resembled adherence to paganism at the time the Roman Empire had become Christian.[4]

What is especially poignant is that in post-Bolshevik Russia the thinkers who did remain in opposition are now honored as forward-looking heroes who warned against taking a disastrous road. Still more curious is that in the past de-cade it has become common to refer to Communists and socialists as conserva-tives or right-wingers and to free-marketeers and proponents of Western-style democracy as liberals or left-wingers. Has History suddenly reversed direc-tion? Why not continue to refer to Communists as left-wingers but say that one opposes the left? The answer, one suspects, is that, almost by definition, for these Russians what is left is good and therefore if capitalism has suddenly become good, it has become left. And that is because left and right are mentally arranged on a time line, with left facing the future and right facing the past.

What this sort of thinking disables is evaluation of positions in terms of evi-dence and logic. An appeal to "the future" substitutes for all other evaluative criteria. What is leftist or radical must be forward looking and therefore must be good; there is no need to suspend judgment long enough to weigh evidence. People become paralyzed by an implicit teleology, even when, upon reflec-tion, they would not accept it. For those called progressive, this model (though weakening thought) offers the rhetorical advantage of a presumption of their own correctness. But why conservatives do not object more often and more vigorously to the language of this time-line characterization, which so evidently works against them, is harder to understand. Perhaps it is because, often enough, they too accept that History is against them—a form of victimization that has its own Dostoevskian consolations.

Arthropodic Whiggism: Wonderful Life

In the sciences, the most powerful critic of what we have called backshadowing has been Stephen Jay Gould. His argument has figured as part of a larger critique concerning the nature of time in scientific reasoning. Gould wants us to appreciate that different sciences work with different concepts of time—with different chronotopes, as Bakhtin would say—and that fallacies are bound to arise when one temporality, developed in a particular science, is assumed to govern the domain of all others. Gould believes in what Bakhtin would call a Galilean chronotope consciousness. Specifically, physics, because of its enormous prestige, has acquired a special privilege, which has worked to distort reasoning in other sciences, such as Gould's own speciality, evolutionary biology.

In physics, time is reversible, in the sense that physical laws usually incorporate symmetrical time. Laws of motion allow us to retrodict and to predict with equal certainty. Applying the law, one knows where a given body in motion was at an earlier time as easily as one knows where it will be at a future time. If one could go back to an earlier time and recreate the conditions in which that body was, and then "replay the tape," it would repeat the same path. That is because the laws governing its motion uniquely determine a specific sequence. But that is not true of evolution, Gould maintains. If one could replay the tape of life's development, it is extremely likely that a quite different sequence would emerge because laws of evolution, unlike laws of motion, do not determine all details. Rather, they exist as general regulating principles operating in the background, while in the foreground contingency plays an important role: *"laws in the background* and *contingency in the details"* is the Darwinian formula.[5] There is considerable loose play in this system; in William James's sense of the term, there is indeterminacy. Sounding very much like James, Gould observes that "the universe is not so tightly interconnected that the fall of a petal disrupts a distant star, whatever our poets sing" (WL, 309).

Replay the tape and contingent events—countless chances—would almost certainly have been different, thus leading to different outcomes. Predictability and retrodictability are both impossible. For Gould, evolution is truly a historical science in the sense that contingency, unrepeatable facts, and unpredictable details play an important part (much as they do in battle as described by Tolstoy).

Nevertheless, many scientists and laymen have been led into thinking away contingency. Typically, they have imagined Darwinian laws as predetermining a specific outcome, namely, us. Their "Darwinism" holds that from the very beginning conscious beings like ourselves, who would some day learn the laws of evolution that produced them, were already implicit, already foreshadowed. This view is comforting but false, Gould insists. Replay the tape of life and there might well have been no human beings or other species with which we are familiar. The world might well have been radically different.

In problems that touch us less personally than our own existence, some specialists in evolution have also been misled by an underestimation of contingency. In such cases, they have reasoned backward—backshadowed—from a known outcome in order to understand earlier periods in life's history. This scientific Whiggism (as one might call it) presupposes an inevitable path leading to what did result. It blinds one to other possibilities equally likely to have developed; more concretely, it has led some scientists to misperceive and misclassify life forms from remote times. Gould's most extended example of such an error is the discovery and interpretation of the Burgess shale fossils.

The story may be told briefly. In 1909 Charles Doolittle Walcott, the premier paleontologist of his time, discovered in the Burgess shale a rich trove of fossils dating from the early Paleozoic. He interpreted these remarkable organisms as early, "primitive," "ancestral," "precursor" forms of later-known organisms and placed them into categories derived from the classification of those later organisms. Decades later, Harry Whittington, Derek Briggs, and Simon Conway Morris reexamined the fossils. Step by step, and against their own traditionalist presuppositions, they were led to a quite different picture. They concluded that most Burgess shale organisms did not belong to the classes of arthropods or crustaceans in which Walcott had placed them; they belonged to radically different groups that have no modern (or even later) representatives. Among the Burgess shale arthropods, for instance, there are numerous body plans (classes) radically different from the four into which modern arthropods fall. Indeed, there are even whole new phyla, and some of the supposed arthropods were not arthropods, or members of any other previously known phylum, at all. Evidently, Walcott had "shoehorned" the amazingly disparate organisms he had discovered into a classification system too narrow for them. Why?

As Gould tells the story, Walcott's errors derived from what I have called backshadowing. He assumed a progressivist view of evolution based on a "ladder of life" and a "cone of increasing diversity." Taken together, these metaphors suggested that life tends over time to greater diversity, increased complexity, and generally superior forms, the supreme example of which is ourselves.[6] Evolution resembles a branching tree, and it "unfolds as though the tree were growing up a funnel, always filling the continually expanding cone of possibilities" (WL, 39). Moreover, because the tree is also a ladder of progress, higher on the tree is not just later but better: "In a literal reading, up and down should record only younger and older in geological time: organisms at the neck of the funnel are ancient; those at the lip, recent. But we also read upward movement as simple to complex, or primitive to advanced. *Placement in time is conflated with judgment of worth*" (WL, 39). It follows from this perspective that earlier forms must be simpler and more primitive versions of later ones. The law of evolution ensures that the path is ever upward; natural selection is taken as dictating that later forms are better than earlier ones. Thus it was possible for Walcott to conclude that "in *Marella* [a Burgess shale organism] the trilobite is foreshadowed" (cited WL, 108). In general, according to this way of thinking, "we must somehow grasp all that came before as a grand preparation, a foreshadowing of our eventual design" (WL, 45).

In fact, however, many Burgess shale organisms were not earlier (let alone more primitive) forms of later organisms we know but members of different branches that have no modern twigs. Instead of a funnel expanding in diversity, life seems to have proceeded by first creating a wide disparity, which was then decimated; increasing diversity then followed *within* surviving types. Indeed, this pattern seems to have been repeated several times in evolutionary history. Any attempt to classify by backshadowing is bound to lead the classifier to miss or underestimate just those features of the organism that suggest their radical difference. Backshadowing blinds one to the lines of development that might have led elsewhere; that is, it obscures the sideshadows.

This argument would seem to refute the "cone of increasing diversity," but what about the ladder of progress? Could one not argue that the phyla and classes that died out were somehow more primitive, less adapted to survival, and less amenable to producing complex organisms like ourselves, and that therefore, operating over time, evolution was bound to produce humans or something very much like them? For Gould, this assumption, too, derives from illegitimate retrospective reasoning. Evolution is not progress, although the terms are too often taken as synonymous. For one thing, evolution does not work by a pattern of overall progress but by adaptation to specific and changing environments. For another, contingency enters the picture: an unforeseeable catastrophe (and there have been several) may radically change the environment. As a result,

> groups may prevail or die for reasons that bear no relationship to the Darwinian basis of success in normal times. Even if fishes hone their adaptations to peaks of aquatic perfection, they will all die if the ponds dry up. But grubby old Buster the Lungfish, former laughing-stock of the piscene priesthood, may pull through—and not because a bunion on his great-

grandfather's fin warned his ancestors about an impending comet. Buster and his kin may prevail because a feature evolved long ago for a different use fortuitously permitted survival during a sudden and unpredictable change in rules. And if we are Buster's legacy, and the result of a thousand other happy accidents, then how can we possibly view our mentality as inevitable, or even probable? (WL, 48)

Through catastrophes (the impact of extraterrestrial objects, for instance) and other contingencies, organisms are selected that enjoyed no inherent advantage, in the sense that there would be no way to predict from an examination of them which would survive. If the tape were replayed and the contingencies were different, different body plans might be selected. If one examines the Burgess shale body plans, the ones that survived do not seem to have had any intrinsic superiority over those that perished. To be sure, it is always possible to insist that the arthropods that did survive *must* have been superior to those that didn't; but that is clearly circular reasoning. Had other arthropods or phyla survived, just as good reasons could have been invented for their survival (assuming there would have been some intelligent being to invent them).

"Buster the Lungfish" may survive because of a feature that evolved for a quite different reason and that only by chance also proved useful in a radically changed environment, for which the feature was not originally selected. This is one interesting kind of contingency. Another is the advantage that may eventually be conferred by a mere *by-product* that has not been selected for at all. A given structure that confers an advantage may bring with it a second feature that "hitched a ride" on the first and offers no advantage at all and perhaps even entails a minor disadvantage. But that by-product may itself ensure the organism's survival (or secure its doom) in changed circumstances. If so, natural contingency has again played a role. And what if human intelligence, or some other feature in an earlier organism necessary for the existence of human intelligence, arose as a by-product?[7] It would then be easy to imagine a world without anyone like us.

Gould understands that the mere fact of our existence carries immense persuasive force. It is illogical but natural to assume that somehow if we are here, we had to be here and were destined to be here, if not by God then by laws of nature. Gould therefore tries to give some weight to alternatives by sketching in a few of them. He offers sideshadows, which he calls "possible worlds" (WL, 309).[8] A crucial event in the evolution of life was the development of more complex eukaryotic cells—the complex textbook kind—from simpler prokaryotic cells, a change that required two billion of the three-and-a-half-billion-year history of life on earth. If whatever events led to this development had taken a few billion years longer, the sun might have reached its explosion point long before complex organisms arose at all. "Run the tape again, and the first step from prokaryotic to eukaryotic cell might take twelve billion years instead of two billion years—and stromatolites, never awarded the time needed to move on, might be the highest mute witnesses to Armageddon" (WL, 311). Moreover, at different stages of the evolutionary path as we know it quite other paths were equally possible: it might well have been large birds, rather than small mammals, who filled the ecological niche left by the decimation of large reptiles, as indeed happened for a time in what is now South America. Gould offers these sideshadows in order to provoke us to imagine worlds radically different but no less likely than our own. We might then prove less ready to impute direction and inevitability to a process innocent of either.

Two Fallacies: Hyperselectionism and Inferring History from Current Utility

Like Tolstoy and Butterfield, Gould enumerates several fallacies of perception that derive from an unjustified privileging of the present situation. Contingent results are taken as if they had been inscribed in the universe from the outset. The result of such thinking is the elimination of history—of the possibility of alternative paths and the effectiveness of contingency. Gould has a good eye for detecting varieties of Panglossism: the world is seen as if it had to be the way it is because no better way could be imagined. Vanity and unjustified optimism converge; we result from the very nature of things in their innermost essence.

Gould focuses repeatedly on two closely related fallacies, hyperselectionism and the equation of current utility with historical origin. *Hyperselectionism* names a misconstrual of Darwinism that proceeds from the assumption that natural selection insures optimal design. It leads researchers to believe that any feature of an organism must have arisen from natural selection and must contribute to survival. The organism as a whole must be optimally designed or else it would not have survived in competition with a rival. Hyperselectionists like Alfred Russel Wallace therefore "viewed each bit of morphology, each function of an organism, each behavior as an adaptation, a product of selection leading to a 'better' organism" (TPT, 50). Thus Wallace could conclude that any apparent nonutility in an organism was in fact a sign of our faulty knowledge: a proposition that evidently created its own form of nonfalsifiability. For hyperselectionists, every organism exhibits an "exquisite fit" with its environment (TPT, 50).

The result of such a view may well be to attribute functions where there are none and to postulate histories that did not happen. Gould points out that this view is uncannily like the creationist one it was supposed to replace because both assumed perfect harmony. In one case a perfect plan was realized suddenly by the will of a divine creator, in the other a perfect plan simply took time to unfold. But the chronotope of "unfolding" and perfection, as we have seen, is essentially nonhistorical; true historicity involves surprise, adaptation, tinkering, and therefore less-than-perfect results. Though Gould does not use Bakhtin's terminology, his point is essentially that evolution properly understood involves what Bakhtin calls a chronotope of "becoming," which is closer to the novel than to the unfolding identities of Plutarch's *Lives*.

According to Gould, Darwin accepted neither the inevitability of perfect design nor natural selection as the *only* force shaping evolution. Darwin "was a consistent pluralist gazing upon a messier universe" than Wallace's (TPT, 50). To be sure, natural selection designs structures that work remarkably well, but organisms also exhibit features that do not contribute to survival or may even impede it. Change may be nonadaptive: "Darwin emphasized two principles leading to nonadaptive change: (1) organisms are integrated systems and adaptive change in one part can lead to nonadaptive modifications of other features ('correlations of growth' in Darwin's phrase); (2) an organ built under the influence of selection for a specific role may be able, as a consequence, to perform many other, unselected functions as well" (TPT, 50). Moreover, some features of organisms are evidently not particularly well designed. Gould's trademark example is the panda's "thumb," which is anatomically not a thumb at all but an enlarged wrist bone jury-rigged to serve the function of an opposable thumb. The need for this "digit" arose after the true thumb was already unavailable for such a solution: "An engineer's best solution is debarred by history. The panda's true thumb is committed to another role, too specialized for a different function to become an opposable, manipulating digit. So the panda must use parts on hand [*sic*] and settle for an enlarged wrist bone and a somewhat clumsy, but quite workable, solution. The sesamoid thumb wins no prize in an engineer's derby" (TPT, 24).

Gould's point is that such *im*perfect design is the true mark of history. Neither an omniscient God planning perfection from the outset nor teleological laws would produce such a compromise solution: "Ideal design is a lousy argument for evolution, for it mimics the postulated action of an omnipotent creator. Odd arrangements and funny solutions are the proof of evolution— paths that a sensible God would never tread but that a natural process, constrained by history, follows perforce" (TPT, 20–21).

Evolution proceeds by a broken line, by tinkering with resources at hand; constrained by history, it moves in no fixed direction. The existence of such imperfect solutions testifies to the lack of an advance plan. By contrast, optimal design tends to cover its tracks.

The logic behind Gould's second fallacy of perception should now be apparent. Because optimal design covers its tracks, one cannot infer historical origin from current utility. A feature that serves a current function may or may not have arisen to do so. It may be the by-product of some other feature or it may have arisen to serve one function but then proved amenable to another. Although the long neck of giraffes allows them to eat leaves from the tops of trees, it may not have arisen for any reason related to feeding. Gould's essays offer a catalogue of examples in which backshadowing from current function to a hypothetical history could easily mislead the researcher.[9]

Gould holds that this fallacy is much more widespread and therefore much more debilitating than one might at first suppose because it is often a concealed assumption in a chain of reasoning. It may therefore easily pass unnoticed by the reasoner even if it is contrary to his or her other views. Gould stresses,

> This assumption—the easy slide from current function to reason for origin—is, to my mind, the most serious and widespread fallacy of my profession, for this false inference supports hundreds of conventional tales about pathways of evolution. I like to identify this error of reasoning with a phrase that ought to become a motto: *Current utility may not be equated with historical origin*, or, when you demonstrate that something works well, you have not solved the problem of how, when, or why it arose.
>
> I propose a simple reason for labeling an automatic inference from current utility to historical origin as fallacious: Good function has an alternative interpretation. A structure now useful may have been built by natural selection for its current purpose . . . but the structure may also have developed for another reason (or for no particular functional reason at all) and then been co-opted for its present use.[10]

Three Principles: Anthropic, Misanthropic, and Brassicic

Interestingly enough, it is this second fallacy that Gould discovers in the much-debated anthropic principle in physics. The anthropic principle reflects a sense of wonder that the universe allowed for the evolution of conscious beings like ourselves. For if any of myriad laws and facts of nature had been ever so slightly different, human life would have been impossible. The odds against our existence appear incalculable, and so it seems (as Freeman Dyson observed) that "the universe must in some sense have known that we were coming."[11] If so, might we not do well to assume our centrality in the universe and use this insight as a tool in research? So understood, man becomes "the focal point in nature": the anthropic principle, in this way, reverses the Copernican revolution and, in a quasi-Hegelian way, attributes to the universe a direction leading to the creation of conscious observers (ourselves) capable of knowing it.[12] We are an essential part of "a self-cognizant universe" (AP, 8). As Reinhard Breuer observes,

> If the role of the human race is drawn into scientific observations of the basic physical elements of nature, we shall be returning in some degree to a long-abandoned position, the cosmology of the Greek philosopher Ptolemy. . . . As far as possible, it [the anthropic principle] finally gives credit to the special role in the cosmos played by Man—through the point in time at which we exist; through the place of our existence in a particular planetary, solar, and galactic neighborhood; and beyond this, through our evident close relationship with natural events, whose varied and subtle interaction was necessary before our existence could come about—Man as the linchpin of nature. (AP, 11–12)

Or as Breuer also puts the point, "The closer the relationship between the human race and its cosmic environment, the more inevitably the properties of the natural world and the cosmos must derive from our study of ourselves" (AP, 8).

Such a statement can mean many things, and the anthropic principle comes in several versions. For our purposes, it is sufficient to distinguish two, the strong and the weak. The strong anthropic principle holds that "the structure of the universe and the particulars of its construction are essentially fixed by the condition that at some point it inevitably produces an observer" (AP, 8), someone like ourselves. Thus "the universe is as it is because otherwise it would not produce observers" (AP, 17). Everything tended and was somehow designed to produce us, the discoverers of the anthropic principle.[13] The weak version holds that "because there are observers in our universe, the universe must possess properties which permit the existence of these observers" (AP, 8). There is no mention of inevitability, but the universe must be consistent with our existence.

The strong principle is apparently the more vulnerable and more challenging. It evidently expresses a view of existence that is the direct opposite of Gould's. The dialogue between these two views is immensely interesting, a reconstruction in modern scientific terms of an almost timeless debate (between the "Ptolemaic" and "Copernican" or "Galilean" views of humanity's place).[14]

Gould raises two important objections to the strong anthropic principle. First, its supporters reason from current fit with our environment to a design that made us fit, which is evidently a version of Gould's second fallacy: "This error of sliding too easily between current use and historical origin is by no means a problem for Darwinian biologists alone. . . . This procedure of false inference pervades all fields that try to infer history from our present world"

(BFB, 115). The anthropic principle is Gould's central example from another science. As in evolution, so in cosmology, "the current fit of human life to physical laws permits no conclusion about the reason and mechanism of our origin" (BFB, 115). If another set of laws had produced another set of beings, they, too, would doubtless see themselves as the goal of creation. The fallacy would not be committed only if there were no one to commit it.

Gould's second objection focuses on the probability argument: the odds were so much against our existence that we must infer some design overcoming the odds. For Gould, this argument for the anthropic principle is perilously close to common arguments for divine origin; in fact, the two are virtually the same argument. William James offers the decisive refutation. Confronted with creationist arguments of this sort, James replied that with only a single sample of a universe we cannot compute odds at all. As Gould paraphrases James's point, "Any result in a sample of one would appear equally miraculous when you consider the vast range of alternative possibilities. But something had to happen" (BFB, 319). Or we might offer the following analogy: if a million and one people each buy a lottery ticket, the odds against any person winning are a million to one. Nevertheless, the odds that a million-to-one result will happen are 100 percent, a certainty. Whoever won might mistakenly imagine that he or she was somehow destined to win. The same logic applies to the origin of human life. As James observed,

> Your argument that it is millions to one that it didn't do so by chance doesn't apply. It would apply if the witness had preexisted in an independent form and framed his scheme, and then the world had realized it. Such a coincidence would prove the world to have a kindred mind to his. But there has been no such coincidence. This world has come but once, the witness is after the fact and simply approves. . . . Where only one fact is in question, there is no relation of "probability" at all.[15]

Here we may observe that Gould's and James's argument—which seems convincing—apparently has a surprising consequence. For Gould's argument in *Wonderful Life* also appeals to odds, to the unlikeliness that we should have evolved (so many other paths could have been followed that our existence must be regarded as highly contingent). But if there is no question of probability at all, then Gould is committing the very fallacy he identifies, although for the opposite purpose. Instead of an anthropic principle, he formulates a sort of misanthropic principle: we cannot be the center of things and we must be a mere afterthought because the odds were so much against our existence.

By James's argument it is impossible to calculate odds at all. Let us suppose that evolution and cosmology suggested the opposite state of affairs: that even if the laws of nature and the facts of evolution were radically different, conscious observers like ourselves most likely would have existed. One camp might then have argued that this likelihood is evidence for a design including us, and the other, with equally good reason, that there is nothing miraculous or special about our appearance. It is apparent that both likelihood and un-likelihood can lead to both conclusions; and that, therefore, it is wrong to infer either conclusion from either set of presumed facts. In the debate between Gould and the defenders of the strong anthropic principle, we seem to witness an encounter of two radically different *temperaments,* one with a tendency to see purpose and the other accident; one thinking in terms of laws and the other of contingencies; one placing humanity at the center of things and the other at the margins. Each temperament is predisposed to read the facts in a particular way, and each is correlated with a distinct sense of temporality, which leads to the initially favored reading.

At first glance, the weak anthropic principle seems to avoid the difficulties of the strong. As usually stated, it simply points out that because observers exist, the universe must be consistent with the fact that there are observers; and this is obviously, if not tautologically, true. The universe must be consistent with *any* known fact. The difficulties with the weak anthropic principle come not from what it states but from what it singles out; not from what it affirms but from what it inclines one to do. The question to be raised is, why single out *this particular fact*? Why mention us? The very act of doing so implies that this fact is more significant than all others with which the universe must be consistent; and yet that presumed significance is neither explicitly stated nor exposed to demands for justification.

When human observers are singled out, a tendency to teleology arises. One slides toward many assumptions of the strong principle. In *The Devil's Dictionary,* Ambrose Bierce defines *zenith* as "A point in the heavens directly overhead to a standing man or a growing cabbage."[16] Why select the man rather than the cabbage? The universe must be no less consistent with the existence of cabbages; so why not formulate the "weak brassicic [cabbage] principle"?

Breuer, in fact, seems to draw implications from the weak anthropic principle entailed not by his formulation of it but by his selection of humans as the significant fact. Immediately after stating his definition, he paraphrases it: "In other words, the universe must be consistent with the fact that it contains observers (whose position will necessarily be privileged)" (AP, 8). How does the necessary privilege of observers follow from the fact that the universe must be consistent with their (and every other fact's) existence?

Although the weak anthropic principle at first appears less vulnerable than the strong, upon reflection the opposite is the case. Those who adopt the weak principle presumably do so because they are already uncomfortable with the explicit teleology of the strong; they might therefore be convinced that it implicitly contains the same difficulties in a concealed form. But it is hard to see what arguments might dislodge an advocate of the strong anthropic principle who is aware of and ready to embrace its most anthropocentric claims. We are dealing here with a perspective prior to evidence, a sense of the universe consistent with any evidence. I recognize that the same may be said of the opposite view, to which I myself incline.

Looking Backward

> Once history has attained an ideal state of communism, communism ceases to evolve qualitatively and does not envisage . . . this social system being replaced by another. Just as one doesn't ask what comes after eternity, the question of after communism never comes up; after communism, the ideal state, there will only be more communism, still bigger and better in its "communistness."
>
> —ANDREI SINYAVSKY, *Soviet Civilization*

The more the present moment is regarded as a historical culmination, the stronger the impulse to backshadow is likely to be. It will therefore be strongest when the present is conceived as, at last, "posthistorical" (or as, for the first time, "truly historical"). Backshadowing appeals most powerfully to those who imagine that the vicissitudes of merely historical time have yielded, or are just about to yield, to the perfection of a utopian world. For then the story of humanity is over, and one can evaluate the significance of past actions with the same certainty as one can evaluate the significance of actions in a finished novel.

If history is completed, there are no more changes to come that could falsify present judgments. Utopia outdates outdating. Earlier judgments were made by those within history and were therefore necessarily partial and bound to be qualified by future events. Once history is over, however, the observer stands outside the historical process and judges from a moment when the pattern is revealed.

Posthistorical time is, in effect, apocalyptic time. Each judgment is a Last (and sure) Judgment. It is therefore a commonplace of utopian fiction that the future society has achieved not only perfect happiness but also perfect assessments. Utopians enjoy not only undreamed-of social harmony but also unprecedented epistemic privilege, and the certainty this privilege guarantees is itself one of the greatest pleasures of utopian living. The idea of the supreme perspective from which to contemplate the past is most readily apparent in the title of Edward Bellamy's enormously influential utopia, *Looking Backward, 2000–1887.*

In utopia, matters of opinion have been transformed into matters of fact. Questions that once evoked different opinions, all of which were partial and subject to revision, now have certain answers on which everyone agrees. They would be insane not to. In most utopias, for instance, aesthetic judgments are no longer subject to debate. One can easily rank the great artists and writers, and utopias typically correct the perverted taste of the author's own time, as William Morris does in *News from Nowhere* when we learn that those abominable buildings the Houses of Parliament have at last been consigned to the storage of manure. Of course, Morris here offers a political as well as an aesthetic judgment. It must be one of the great pleasures of authors of utopias that they can frame their own aesthetic prejudices as time's final verdict.

Most utopias therefore propose a radical change in art, a new aesthetics of harmony for a harmonious world. In Bellamy's utopia, the great poet of the future, "Berrian," manages to write engaging stories with no vicissitudes, "sordid anxieties," or conflict of wills at all.[17] (We are not told how.) Morris goes further than most in banning narrative art utterly from the future society: because novels require conflict, which perfection by definition excludes, there is "no place" for them in utopia. There may be news from nowhere, but no news in nowhere. Morris's characters explain that the world no longer needs art because it has become art: "The production of what used to be called art . . . has no name amongst us now, because it has become a necessary part of the labour of every man who produces."[18] Moreover, people have no need to imagine alternative worlds when the real one is perfect. "As for your books," Clara remarks, "they were well enough for times when intelligent people had but little else in which they could take pleasure, and when they must needs supplement the sordid miseries of their own lives with the imaginations of the lives of other people" (Morris, 169).

Alternatives to perfection are necessarily inferior; utopia banishes sideshadows. Anti-utopian writers have focused on this hostility to imagination and alternatives as one feature of the proposed heaven that would make it more like hell. Thus a key scene in many twentieth-century anti-utopian works, from Zamyatin's *We* to Ray Bradbury's *Fahrenheit 451*, is the rediscovery of the literary classics of the past, whose power of imagination is in itself counterrevolutionary. In the anthropology of anti-utopias, a world without sideshadows is contrary to the fundamental needs of real people, whose very identity partakes of and requires open time.

Utopias set in the future almost always engage in what might be called *anticipatory backshadowing:* the author invites readers to imagine how their world will look when viewed by their counterparts in the utopia to come. He passes certain judgments on his own time by projecting them forward onto people who will "look backward." Looking backward from utopia to history is not like looking backward from one historical period to another because it involves perception across a change in temporality itself. Typically, a visitor from our own time arrives in the future and is given a tour of the new world, during which he and his hosts repeatedly contrast it with the world of the past (in which author and readers live). Of course, the comparisons never favor the past.

In *Looking Backward*, the visitor from 1887 has the specially piquant experience of reading Dickens in a world where all social problems have been overcome: Dickens did not see the solution to the miseries he described, but the visitor (and everyone else in 2000) does. Final judgments are passed on previous movements. It turns out, for instance, that the anarchists of 1887 were actually in the pay of the capitalists because their violence delayed the establishment of socialism; utopias, with their belief in simple and symmetrical patterns, have a marked tendency to conspiracy logic.

Utopian tour guides offer praise for those who (like the author and whatever readers may be converted) foresaw and hastened the arrival of the time to come. For signs of the future were everywhere available to those who were not too compromised to find and read them. Thus a common motif is the return of the traveler to utopia back to the world in which he was born. Having seen the truth, he detects the signs of the future he once missed and tries to explain them to the citizens of our own world—to people like us—and is mocked, a motif adapted from Plato's Allegory of the Cave. The plain signs of the future are not noticed by those whose skepticism is itself the sign of a blinding moral corruption.[19] These skeptics imagine many different paths, deny the necessity for things to improve, or may even suppose that there are legitimately different ideas about what improvement would be. They live in a world of mere opinion, not one of Truth, and they often reject not only the possibility but even the desirability of final solutions to human problems. Above all, they cultivate the sense of alternatives and of other possible times. But in the light of the future already realized, these putative other times are revealed as illusions generated by sick souls. There have never been any sideshadows.

The Single Truth and Society as Artwork

Soviet Marxism understood itself to be the realized utopia. Communism, if not yet achieved, was on the horizon, and the path to it was short and clearly marked. It is therefore not surprising that the classics of utopian literature were made available to Russian readers in a series entitled "Forerunners of Scientific Socialism," whose editors seem to have been unconscious of the potential irony in its title. After all, each utopia, when it was written, was offered as a final judgment, superior to all previous ones. For each utopian author, all predecessors were at best forerunners to himself, but his work soon became a predecessor to the next "final" vision. And so time after time each ultimate answer became a penultimate one and then a pen-penultimate one. Why did the editors of the Soviet series not anticipate a similar fate for "scientific" social-ism, and why were they so sure that the sequence of final visions had at last come to an end? Some readers of these works must have been struck by the disagreements among unchallengeable truths and by the irony of a *series* of final words. Now that the Soviet regime has collapsed, the tacit if unintended irony of a series of utopias has become manifest. The putative end of history is now just another historical period.

In recent assessments of the Soviet experience, two features of official cul-ture often predominate, one pertaining to knowledge and the other to what might be called aesthetic politics. So far as knowledge is concerned, the regime claimed that there is a single, final knowable truth and that this truth was in its possession. As a result, all cultural and social questions were already answered, or at least soon would be, with only a little more technical work. Thus, it was common to write the history of philosophy as the story of how Marxism-Leninism was at last discovered: deliberate and explicit backshadowing was common. Each philosopher's views could be precisely assessed in terms of their approach to the known Truth, and the conflict of philosophical schools was given final adjudication. Westerners who encounter this approach are usually struck by its explicit starting point—the absence of all important unresolved questions and the consequent impossibility of learning anything significant from the philosophy of previous centuries. Such Soviet philosophers offered verdicts on their predecessors; they did not enter into dialogue with them.

Applied to the heritage of previous art, the idea of discovered truth admitted of the two principal solutions advanced in the utopian tradition. One might choose to do away with the art of the past—to throw Pushkin and Raphael "from the steamship of modernity," as many in the avant-garde proposed—and begin all over again. Or one could try to preserve a part of tradition by engaging in systematic backshadowing. Because possession of the Truth made reliable assessments possible, one could retell the history of art as an eternal conflict between progressive and reactionary forces. Those on the right side of history would be preserved, and the rest would be consigned to oblivion. The Soviet regime by and large adopted this second solution.

Thus in each period the superstructure of culture had contained forward- and backward-looking forces, and it was now clear which were which. As Boris Groys has aptly observed, the result of this approach was a kind of timeless eclecticism and homogenization.[20] The progressive artists of each period re-semble the progressive artists of all other periods; they all loved the people, struggled against reactionary forces, and anticipated the glorious future. Each progressive artist offered contributions of use to the Soviet people, which could borrow from them as needed. For those who adopt this sense of artistic tradition, time is overcome and everything is "forever simultaneous" because all history tells the same story, leading to ourselves at the end. Soviet Marxism and socialist realism are Whiggism squared. In this view, Groys observes,

> all "progressive" world culture acquires a superhistorical significance and eternal relevance that make it the contemporary of any new "progressive" aspiration, and "antipopular," "reactionary," "decadent" culture assumes a no less superhistorical, universal significance that reveals its inner sameness at any given moment of history. . . . Stalinist culture looks upon itself as postapocalyptic culture—the final verdict on all human culture has already been passed, and all that was once temporally distinct has become forever simultaneous in the blinding light of the final judgment and the ultimate truth revealed in Stalin's *Short Course* of party history. (Groys, 47–48)

The second feature of Soviet culture that has attracted recent commentary, aesthetic politics, is also deeply indebted to the utopian tradition. Society itself was to become a perfectly executed artwork. We have already seen Morris's version of this idea, and it may generally be said that utopian literature describes the ideal society as resembling an aesthetic masterpiece. Anyone who reads the utopian classics will, I think, be struck by their devotion to aesthetics as well as to justice; indeed, the two are typically seen as the same. Perfection, like utopian city planning, is to be symmetrical. Groys begins his study of Soviet art on this note:

> The world promised by the leaders of the October Revolution was not merely supposed to be a more just one . . . it was also and in perhaps even greater measure meant to be beautiful. The unordered, chaotic life of past ages was to be replaced by a life that was harmonious and organized according to a unitary artistic plan. When the entire economic, social, and everyday life of the nation was totally subordinated to a single planning authority commissioned to regulate, harmonize, and create a single whole out of even the most minute details, this authority—the Communist party leadership—was transformed into a kind of artist whose material was the entire world and whose goal was to "overcome the resistance" of this material and make it pliant, malleable, capable of assuming any desired form. (Groys, 3)

As in an artwork, there were to be no inharmonious details: thus totalitarianism derives in part from an aesthetic impulse. So does the ideal of transforming human nature—the creation of the "new Soviet man"—so that there will be no inharmonious behavior.

The state therefore becomes, among other things, the one great artist of society. It follows that independent artistic visions have no place. An artwork must have unity and therefore a single design. Thus the socialist realist artist becomes (like the industrial engineer, with whom he was often compared) not a creator of his own individual designs but an executor of the design prepared above. He helps to transform psychology, becomes "an engineer of human souls." In *The Possessed*, Dostoevsky foresaw that any such regime would soon find it had "to remove a hundred million heads" (P, 413) in order to overcome what Groys calls "the resistance of the material"; he recognized as well that there would be no room for individual artistic (or scientific) visions. In the future society, Pyotr Stepanovich confides to Stavrogin, "Cicero will have his tongue cut out, Copernicus will have his eyes put out, Shakespeare will be stoned." [21]

Of course, it is possible to press this insight about the "aesthetic" nature of the Soviet utopian regime too far. Sinyavsky goes one step further than Groys by attributing considerable artistic gifts (to be sure, of a special sort) to Stalin himself. "A born artist" who loved to use people as artistic raw material and who saw public life as a stage performance, Stalin, as Sinyavsky describes him, was especially talented in creating not only an art of harmony but also a surrealistic art of the grotesque. He alternated disharmony with harmony in brilliant counterpoint. In Sinyavsky's view, socialist realism was only the "diurnal" aspect of Soviet life: "But the principal business is done at night: arrests, executions, political intrigues, and governmental sessions associated with binges of black humor and sinister buffoonery. . . . Glancing back over the Stalin era, I can't find one artist who would have been worthy of Stalin, who could have matched his formidable irrationality, his 'nocturnal' spirit" (SC, 104–05). Having begun with utopian harmony, the regime, so to speak, switched genres. In such passages, Sinyavsky is carried away by his own taste for the surreal and by his own overdeveloped inclination to read history in aesthetic terms. But he is probably right when he observes that many people experienced Soviet life as if they were unwitting actors in a grotesque drama and when he interprets the masterpiece of twentieth-century Russian fiction, Bulgakov's *The Master and Margarita*, as a response to the surreal aesthetic feel of Soviet society.

Time and Opinion

The presumed possession of absolute truth and the socio-aesthetic ideal of perfect harmony both close down time by eliminating the unexpected. The Soviet regime prided itself on unanimity: thus the ritual of elections in which a single candidate received virtually 100 percent of the vote or decades of unanimous votes in the Soviet parliament. Westerners often wondered why it was necessary to hold such elections when the outcome was certain; the answer, in part, is that they were pageantry and ritual more than legality. They expressed the politico-aesthetic ideal of perfect harmony.[22]

From the earliest days of Soviet rule, its opponents often focused precisely on the elimination of surprise as an essentially dehumanizing feature of the regime. They frequently cited Dostoevsky's underground man, with his demand for the unexpected; almost as often, they invoked Dostoevsky's Grand Inquisitor, who attributed the appeal of what would be called totalitarianism not so much to a longing for justice as to a craving for certainty. As mentioned in chapter 1, these two works exercised a key influence on the development of a new twentieth-century genre, the dystopia—a term used for that form of anti-utopia set in the putatively perfect future. The creator of this form, which was to include Huxley's *Brave New World* and Orwell's *1984*, was Zamyatin, whose dystopia *We* could not be published in the Soviet Union.

We pioneered the classic plot of the dystopia—an escape from posthistory back to history, either for the hero or for all of society. As the novel's title indicates, utopian harmony is based on complete collectivity and the elimination of individual will. Life in "the United State" is mathematically symmetrical, and surprise is as impossible as an unexpected answer to a simple mathematical operation: "The ideal (it's clear) is to be found where nothing *happens.*"[23] Thus in *We* unanimous elections have a metaphysical import: they express the beneficent closure of time and the aesthetically pleasing elimination of contingency.

This in no way resembles the disorderly, unorganized election days of the ancients, on which (it seems so funny!) they did not even know in advance the result of the election. To build a state on some non-discountable contingencies, to build blindly—what could be more nonsensical? Yet centuries had to pass before this was understood!

Needless to say, in this respect as in all others we have no place for contingencies; nothing unexpected can happen. The elections themselves have rather a symbolic meaning. (*We*, 129)

Thus one sign of rebellion against perfection is precisely a nonunanimous vote. The novel's heroine, I-330, makes clear that her movement's prime goal is not so much political as metaphysical and not so much social as temporal: the goal is to restore uncertainty, which means that even though the rebellion fails, it has succeeded by virtue of having taken place at all: "'And tomorrow!' She breathed the words through sparkling white clenched teeth. 'Tomorrow, nobody knows what ... do you understand? Neither I nor anyone else knows; it is unknown! Do you realize what a joy it is? Do you realize that all that was certain has come to an end? Now ... things will be new, improbable, unforeseen!'" (*We*, 136–37).

With the rebirth of contingency comes a rebirth of *opinion.* In a world where

Truth is singular, unitary, and known, opinion loses its meaning: there is only truth and error. Opinion in a strong sense presupposes the absence of a final answer and therefore of the legitimacy of conflicting opinions, which unforeseen contingencies may unexpectedly validate. Where there is opinion, there must be opinions. *Opinion requires the middle realm* of real possibilities that may or may not be actualized; it requires the unexpected. Freedom of speech and democracy (with open elections) in turn demand a meaningful sense of opinion; for if there is only truth and falsity, then there is no reason not to establish the truth once and for all and to forbid error. That, of course, is what the Soviet regime did and what utopians of the right as well as the left aspire to do. Perhaps the greatest threat to democracy is well-intentioned people who will not credit that others with opposing views may be guided by honest motives, may be responding thoughtfully to a different set of experiences, and may, just possibly, turn out to be right in our highly uncertain world. (Chapter 7 of this book explores what it may mean to take seriously the value of opinion in open time.)

Vagrant Philosophy and the Script of Time

In *The Master and Margarita,* humor derives primarily from the encounter of Soviet officials' professions of certainty with radically inexplicable events. Their very confidence that they possess the truth invites the devil (who visits Stalinist Russia) to perplex them with events radically beyond the possibility of explanation. He plays games with causality and, above all, with time.

In the opening chapter, the overconfident Berlioz is busy explaining to the poet Bezdomny that Jesus, like all supposedly supernatural beings, never existed at all, when a series of strange events begins. "Berlioz' life was so arranged that he was not accustomed to seeing unusual phenomena."[24] The first unusual phenomenon is the appearance of the disguised devil himself. As if to mock Soviet pretensions to knowledge of the future the "foreign visitor" (as Berlioz takes him to be) claims to be a historian of a rather strange sort: he knows the future in the same detail as the past. "Yes, I am a historian," the visitor calmly remarks, "[and] this evening a historic event is going to take place here at Patriarch's Ponds" (M&M, 20).

Unlike the Soviets, who proclaim a perfectly ordered world, the devil describes one that is fundamentally chaotic and kept in reasonable order only by (literally) supernatural effort. He makes fun of Berlioz's Marxist-inspired dicta that laws govern history and that people who know these laws rule themselves:

> "But this is the question that disturbs me—if there is no God, then who, one wonders, rules the life of man and keeps the world in order?"

"Man rules himself," said Bezdomny angrily in answer to such an obviously absurd question.

"I beg your pardon," retorted the stranger quietly, "but to rule, one must have a precise plan worked out for some reasonable period in the future. Allow me to inquire how man can control his own affairs when he is not only incapable of compiling a plan for some laughably short term, such as, say, a thousand years, but cannot even predict what will happen to him tomorrow?" (M&M, 15)

No wonder five-year plans fail. To be sure, the Soviet regime did not claim to be able to predict every contingent event (which would then not be contingent at all) but only to know the general laws guiding history to its end. But what if a sort of "butterfly effect" reigns: what if contingent events do not "factor out" but combine to produce radically unpredictable results? In fact, as the devil speaks, just such an unforeseeable concatenation of events leading to Berlioz's death has already begun.

Bulgakov's world plays with a reversal of the ancient model: in this novel it is the sublunary world that is (or rather presumes to be) certain while the heavens manifest openness and surprise. In one of the book's most memorable scenes, Pontius Pilate finds himself dreaming—or is it one of the novel's intuitions of the nature of things?—of a walk along a moonbeam with Jesus: "He was walking with [his dog] Banga and the vagrant philosopher [Jesus] beside him. They were arguing about a weighty and complex problem over which neither could gain the upper hand. They disagreed entirely, which made their argument the more absorbing and interminable" (M&M, 310). In *The Master and Margarita*, the ultimate questions are unresolvable even to God. Heaven, but not earth, is a realm that permits opinion.

Of course, the Soviet government was aware that, in spite of its supposed mastery of historical laws, it, too, was subject to contingency, at least in the short run. Many Russian intellectuals have seen the regime's constant rewriting of the past as tacit acknowledgment of the need to revise previous assessments without admitting to doing so and, therefore, as implicit admission of the future's unknowability. That, I take it, is the point of the much-quoted East European witticism: Communism is a system in which the future is known but the past always changes.

In Vasily Grossman's posthumous novel *Forever Flowing*, Nikolai Andreyevich comes to learn another way in which contingency can be eliminated. History may literally be scripted beforehand. He recognizes this feature of Soviet life when he is told in advance of the "spontaneous" popular actions and "wise" government responses that will accompany the anti-Semitic "doctors' plot" campaign:

In the greatest secrecy Nikolai Andreyevich was told by a certain person that the way things would go was this: The doctors would be publicly executed on Red Square; a wave of pogroms against the Jews would roll through the whole country; this would be the signal for the exile of all the Jews to the taiga and to the Kara-Kum Desert to build the Turkmenian Canal. This exile would be undertaken in order to protect the Jews from the just but merciless wrath of the people. And it would be an expression of the eternally vital spirit of Soviet internationalism, which, while it appreciated and understood the people's wrath . . . would nonetheless not permit mass kangaroo courts and repressions.

Like everything else that took place in the Soviet Union, this spontaneous wrath at the bloody crimes of the Jews was thought out ahead of time and planned in full detail.[25]

Nikolai Andreyevich understands that he has encountered the fundamental way in which the Soviet regime deals with contingency:

In exactly the same way, the elections to the Supreme Soviet were planned ahead of time in full detail by Stalin. Secret meetings were held in advance and candidates were picked—and from that point on the spontaneous nomination of candidates took place on a planned and scheduled basis. . . . It was exactly how the workers came to demand . . . that they be permitted to work on their days off. . . . It was how speakers spoke in "open, free discussions": the texts of their speeches had been prepared and approved ahead of time—for if, for some reason, "open, free discussions" were required, they had to be planned in advance. (FF, 27–28)

But even such planning, it turns out, is subject to contingency. Stalin suddenly died, thus disrupting the script of the doctors' plot. "Stalin died without previous planning, without instructions from the administrative apparatus. Stalin died without the personal instructions of Comrade Stalin. In this freedom and spontaneity, the capriciousness of death, there was something explosive, something contradictory to the innermost essence of the Soviet state" (FF, 29).

It seems that even in totalitarian regimes, the asymmetry of time may be preserved, though it is often reversed. To the extent that the future is deemed known, the past vacillates; and the mutability of the past often corresponds to hubristic and unwarranted claims about the predetermination of the future. The more they are denied, the more do contingency and sideshadows create the surprise of unwanted alternatives. Backshadowing narrators find themselves in the middle of a larger and unanticipated story. Possibilities reemerge. The world of diverse opinions and open time, the topic of the next chapter, reasserts itself.

Conclusion

Opinion and the World of Possibilities

Crooked Timber

"Every hour, answered the princess, confirms my prejudice in favour of the position so often uttered by the mouth of Imlac, 'That nature sets her gifts on the right hand and on the left.' Those conditions, which flatter hope and attract desire, are so constituted, that, as we approach one, we recede from another."
—SAMUEL JOHNSON, *Rasselas*

Utopias have their value—nothing so wonderfully expands the imaginative horizons of human potentialities—but as guides to conduct they can prove literally fatal.
—SIR ISAIAH BERLIN

Out of timber so crooked as that from which man is made nothing entirely straight can be built.
—IMMANUEL KANT

The world of opinion is the world of possibilities. It thrives where there are sideshadows and when people recognize that the future may easily differ from their most earnest expectations. We appreciate it most when we acknowledge that the present, and therefore we ourselves, could have been different. Sideshadowing suggests humility and an awareness that our opinions are just that. It teaches us the contingency of each particular opinion and a "Galilean consciousness" with respect to our own beliefs.

If the American Revolution had not happened, would we exist? Would I be writing, and you be reading, a book on time—*this* book, with its present argument? The suggestion that we—the observers of history—might not have been here at all is quite unsettling. And the possibility that we would be here but would see things quite differently is doubtless less unsettling psychologically but much more so epistemologically.

A rich sense of opinion grows from an appreciation that our knowledge is (in both senses) partial and that another set of experiences might well have led us, on equally good grounds, to hold different beliefs. We believe what we do in large part because of contingencies. So realist novels teach. Some other genres (utopias, saints' lives) presuppose a single truth obligatory for all, but the novel resides in the kingdom of opinion. As Bakhtin remarks, it does not know, but asks why we think we know; it speculates in categories of ignorance. This very aspect of novels was eliminated in socialist realist fiction.

Realist novels instruct that ideas are rooted in the particularities and partialities of biography, and we are therefore asked to refer characters' claims of Truth to the special circumstances that have engendered those claims. Philosophical novels therefore typically work by subjecting all ideas to a distinct kind of novelistic scrutiny, which I like to call *the irony of origins*. The character believes, but the novel reveals why he believes. Ideology is referred to biography. No matter how firmly they are held, beliefs are shown to embody the limitations of necessarily contingent experience. Exaggerated claims for them or too strong a faith in their certainty usually leads novelistic heroes to disturbing consequences, and so the irony of origins is complemented by *an irony of outcomes*. A character who believes that love is purely physiological winds up falling desperately in romantic love, as in *Fathers and Sons;* a hero who believes that all is permitted comes to feel guilty for a crime in which he is, at most, an unwitting accomplice, as in *The Brothers Karamazov*. Whatever experience has led to a given theory, other, surprising experiences reveal its shortcomings. In this way purported Truth becomes fallible opinion; there are no final truths. The opinions of others, even if they seem wrong, reactionary, or passé, may represent an honest and considered response to a set of experiences different from our own.[1]

In *Anna Karenina*, Levin comes to recognize the value of learning from, not just arguing against, opinions different from his own, so long as they are arrived at honestly. For all his tendency to dogmatism, he increasingly appreciates the value of opinion itself, which can serve as a key to other experiences. Levin learns to probe, not just to refute, others' beliefs, to try to see them from within and imagine why an intelligent and decent person might hold them. Thus he listens with special attention to a "reactionary landowner," whose views Levin does not share, because "the landowner unmistakably spoke his own individual thought—a thing that rarely happens—and a thought to which he had been brought not by a desire of finding some exercise for an idle brain, but a thought which had grown up out of the conditions of his life, which he had brooded over in the solitude of his village, and considered in its every aspect" (AK, 350). In reconstructing the circumstances and processes of thought that have shaped the landowner's opinions, Levin gains access to considerations he has overlooked, and his own views become all the richer. Whereas others see ideas divided into true and false, progressive or reactionary, Levin cultivates an awareness of the middle realm of opinion and of the complexities that may invalidate the most self-evident of social tenets.

In the process, he comes to question, as Tolstoy did, the simple equation of education with enlightenment and enlightenment with knowledge of the Truth. It no longer seems to Levin that there is a single social Truth, valid for all peoples at all times, any more than there is a single method for organizing agriculture (the topic of the book Levin is writing) valid for all countries in all periods. The need for compromise and constant adjustment, he comes to understand, is not just a tactical way of diffusing conflict but a reflection of the unavailability of final answers.

Levin even comes to suspect that his earlier dream of Truth is not only un-realizable but also incoherent. Such insight does not lead him (or his creator) to any form of vulgar relativism, but rather to a pluralism: he recognizes the advantage of many competing sets of values and perspectives, the necessity of choosing less-than-perfect solutions, and the eternal need for reevaluation. In a world in which time is open and knowledge inevitably partial, he accepts the practical (rather than theoretical) wisdom of adjustments to a middle realm of possibilities and opinions.

Perhaps the most remarkable living thinker to develop this perspective, Sir Isaiah Berlin, has provided an autobiographical account of how, beginning with his study of the Russian classics, he arrived at his pluralistic perspective. Berlin situates this essay very much in our own time, at the end of a century domi-nated by "the great ideological storms that have altered the lives of virtually all mankind: the Russian Revolution and its aftermath—totalitarian tyrannies of both right and left . . . which, interestingly enough, not one of the most per-ceptive social thinkers of the nineteenth century had ever predicted."[2] In one way or another, "prophets with armies at their backs" (CTH, 1) have pursued the millennium at the cost of tens, if not hundreds, of millions of lives. Berlin situates himself among the anti-utopian thinkers of our times.

As he describes his intellectual odyssey, Berlin began with an assumption shared by so many eighteenth- and nineteenth-century social thinkers: progress in the sciences can be matched by social progress, based on a true science of society. Discoveries could be made that would lead, at least in principle, to the perfectly just society. In Berlin's account, this assumption rests on three key ideas: first, that "all genuine questions must have one true answer and one only, all the rest being necessarily errors; in the second place, that there must be a dependable path towards the discovery of these truths; in the third place, that the true answers, when found, must necessarily be compatible with one another and form a single whole, for one truth cannot be incompatible with another—that we knew *a priori*" (CTH, 5–6). The problem of society seemed like a kind of "cosmic jigsaw puzzle" whose pieces might be fit together in the single right way (CTH, 6). This complex of beliefs (which Bakhtin called the "monologic" conception of truth) had to be correct, for if it were not, what meaning would the idea of progress have?

It was the third idea—the compatibility of "truths"—that unraveled first. Reading Machiavelli, Vico, Herder, and some Russians (especially Herzen), Berlin encountered the possibility, "which came as something of a shock, that not all the supreme values pursued by mankind now and in the past were necessarily compatible with one another." It might be false that "there could be no conflict between true ends" (CTH, 8). Perhaps different cultures and periods each have their own values and purposes, which add up to no single whole; perhaps humanity is capable of pursuing diverse goals, none of them solving everything and none revealing all human potentialities; and perhaps there is no single unambiguous standard of progress and "no ladder of ascent from the ancients to the moderns" (CTH, 9). Voltaire's idea that enlightenment is the same whenever and wherever it is attained—that Sophocles, Confucius, and Seneca would have felt at ease with each other—might well be mistaken.

If true values may be incompatible, then the concept of utopia may be not only an unattainable ideal but also "conceptually incoherent" (CTH, 13). There may be no single state of society that would be perfect and no social structure that would realize all human potentials because human potentials and values may be at odds with each other. Utopia conflicts with the essentially dynamic, creative, and processual nature of human beings. It assumes that people

> have a certain fixed, unaltering nature, certain universal, common, immutable goals. Once these goals are realized, human nature is wholly fulfilled. The very idea of universal fulfillment presupposes that human beings as such seek the same essential goals, identical for all, at all times, everywhere. For unless this is so, Utopia cannot be Utopia, for then the perfect society will not perfectly satisfy everyone.[3]

It seems to follow that opinions are not mere approximations that will someday be replaced by a known truth; that there is no unambiguous standard of progress; and that history tends to no single goal. These are apparently fatal objections to all forms of utopianism and, one might add, to all forms of backshadowing. An appreciation of human history and potential requires sideshadows, the other values that were alternatives to our own.

Dialogue and Final Solutions

Berlin's favorite thinkers are those who recognize the need for a plurality of "truths" (or social views) and who deny that all true values are "ultimately" reconcilable. The title of Berlin's best-known essay, *The Hedgehog and the Fox*, interprets Archilochus's dark line—"The fox knows many things, but the hedgehog knows one big thing"—so as to mark a fundamental divide between two kinds of minds:

> For there exists a great chasm between those, on one side, who relate every-thing to a single central vision, one system . . . in terms of which they understand, think and feel—a single, organizing principle in terms of which alone all that they are and say has significance—and, on the other side, those who pursue many ends, often unrelated and even contradictory, con-nected, if at all, only in some *de facto* way . . . these last lead lives, perform acts, and entertain ideas that are centrifugal rather than centripetal, their thought is scattered or diffused, moving on many levels, seizing upon the essence of a vast variety of experiences and objects . . . without, consciously or unconsciously, seeking to fit them into, or exclude them from, any one unchanging, all-embracing . . . unitary inner vision. The first kind of intel-lectual and artistic personality belongs to the hedgehogs, the second to the foxes; and without insisting on a rigid classification, we may . . . say . . . [that] Dante belongs to the first category, Shakespeare to the second.[4]

Berlin classes Plato and Hegel as hedgehogs and Aristotle, Montaigne, and Pushkin as foxes; Tolstoy had both impulses. Berlin clearly prefers Tolstoy as fox: "Any comforting theory which attempted to collect, relate, 'synthesize', reveal hidden substrata and concealed inner connexions, which, though not ap-parent to the naked eye, nevertheless guaranteed the unity of all things—the fact that they were 'ultimately' parts one of another with no loose ends—the ideal of the seamless whole—all such doctrines he exploded contemptuously and without difficulty. His genius lay in the perception of specific properties, the almost inexpressible individual quality in virtue of which the given object is uniquely different from all others" (H&F, 36).

Though he concentrates on the essays in *War and Peace*, Berlin may also have in mind such passages as Pierre's discovery that perfect agreement is im-possible. When Pierre gives his speech to the Masons, he is distressed not so much by those who disagree with him as by those who agree:

> At this meeting Pierre for the first time was struck by the endless variety of men's minds, which prevents a truth from ever appearing the same to any

two persons. Even those members who seemed to be on his side understood him in their own way, with stipulations and modifications he could not agree to, since what he chiefly desired was to convey his thought to others exactly as he himself understood it. (W&P, 528)

Pierre is a utopian; and after this speech he sinks into depression because he immediately recognizes that utopia presupposes perfect agreement, which is not to be had between any two minds, much less among all of them.

In principle, there is no final solution. "Some among the Great Goods cannot live together," Berlin maintains. "We are doomed to choose, and every choice may entail an irreparable loss" (CTH, 13). In practice, too, utopianism falls short because it underestimates contingency, by-products, and emerging new possibilities. Berlin sounds very much like Gould (or Tolstoy) when he observes that even successful solutions cannot be final because "every solution creates a new situation which breeds its own new needs and problems, new demands" (CTH, 14). Utopians typically draw a straight line to the end of history, to the solving of all problems, but even if they could achieve their goals, history would not be over. There would be new problems requiring something other than merely drawing the straight line to utopia a little further. In a contingent, messy universe, advance planning has decided limits:"We cannot legislate for the unknown consequences of consequences of consequences. Marxists tell us that once the fight is won and true history has begun, the new problems that may arise will generate their own solutions, which can be peacefully realised by the united powers of harmonious, classless society. This seems to me a piece of metaphysical optimism for which there is no evidence in historical experience" (CTH, 14–15).

The putatively utopian societies of the twentieth century reveal the danger of abolishing opinion and sideshadows. Those who presume that history's goal is revealed and that standards exist to measure the adequacy of all opinions in effect abolish opinion altogether. Bakhtin had much the same point in mind when he observed that a monologic view of truth "recognizes only one principle of cognitive individualization: *error*. True judgments are not attached to a personality, but correspond to some unified, systemically monologic context. [When truth is monologic,] only error individualizes" (PDP, 81). And what reason is there to tolerate what is known to be error?

As Lenin pointed out, there is also no reason to refrain from sacrificing the lives of those who disagree. To put into practice such valuable and reliable knowledge no cost is too great: "To make such an omelette, there is surely no limit to the number of eggs that should be broken—that was the faith of Lenin, of Trotsky, of Mao, for all I know of Pol Pot. Since I know the only true path to the ultimate solution of the problems of society . . . and since you are ignorant of what I know, you cannot be allowed to have liberty of choice even within the narrowest limits" (CTH, 15).

Also like Bakhtin, Berlin maintains that a recognition of a multiplicity of conflicting goods, perspectives, and desirable possibilities does not necessarily lead to extreme relativism. Pluralism is not relativism. With effort, people of different values can understand each other; otherness is not absolute; a common humanity insures that we can grasp and appreciate what it would be like to cherish what others have cherished. It is possible to overstate, as well as to underestimate, differences: "Forms of life differ. Ends, moral principles, are many. But not infinitely many; they must be within the human horizon" (CTH, 11). And we can expand our own perspective by imagining how it appears from another perspective. That is what Bakhtin meant by dialogue, and Bakhtin, too, insisted that dialogue does not lead to absolute relativism. On the contrary, dialogue presupposes, as total relativism could not, the value of learning from other perspectives. "It should be noted that both relativism and dogmatism equally exclude all argumentation, all authentic dialogue, by making it either unnecessary (relativism) or impossible (dogmatism)" (PDP, 69).

If there are no final solutions, then—Berlin asks that constantly repeated Russian question—"what is to be done?" Nothing final, absolute, or perfect, for that will only lead to terrible suffering. Rather, do not fear compromise, however dull or unheroic it appears in contrast to utopian visions. Be prepared to balance competing values, to establish temporary priorities, and to adjust them in the face of contingency. Because solutions can be only partial and temporary, cultivate the imagination of alternatives. Or, in the language I have been using, value opinions and project sideshadows.

The Church of Philadelphia

If criticism, the authority of which you cite, knows what you and I don't, why has it kept mum until now? Why doesn't it disclose to us the truth and immutable laws? If it had known, believe me, it would long ago have shown us the way and we would know what to do. . . . But criticism keeps pompously quiet or gets off cheap with idle, worthless chatter.
—ANTON CHEKHOV

Like the basic knowledge of a clinical physician, the basic knowledge we rely on in the humanities springs, not from reflecting on the theoretical ramifications of abstract ideas, but from concrete experience of actual cases or circumstances.
—STEPHEN TOULMIN

Chronocentrism and backshadowing come most readily to groups that imagine they possess wisdom inaccessible to their contemporaries and superior to that of their own predecessors. People sometimes believe or act as if they believe that they have special insight by virtue of belonging to a group favored by history and by virtue of living in the present moment.

In the thirteenth and fourteenth centuries, a number of "spiritual" thinkers, at first mostly clergymen and eventually including many laymen, arrived at a doctrine that ensured their special Scriptural insight, which was held to be greater than that possessed by all predecessors in the history of the Church. Following doctrines advanced by Robert of Liege, Joachim of Fiore, Arnold of Villanova, and later by a number of Franciscans, they argued that "spiritual intelligence" progresses over time. Later stages of history allow for deeper and deeper understanding; the possibility of wisdom grows. Thus Joachim and Arnold identified John's vision of "the seven churches which are in Asia" (Revelation 1:4) with seven stages of history, each marked by increasing understanding of Scripture and insight into the nature of things. They understood their own time as that of the sixth church, the church of Philadelphia; that is, they lived in the latest possible era before the seventh church (Laodicians), when spiritual men would receive understanding in such measure that "they would be able to transform human society into the most advanced state of spirituality possible on earth" or (as others believed) "they would be able to taste and touch divine truths as well as see them."[5]

What is crucial about these beliefs is that they guaranteed the growth of spiritual intelligence over time. Wisdom became a coefficient of history. This "progressivist conception of spiritual intelligence" (Lerner, 52) mandated that people of the present were necessarily the wisest. It followed that any spiritual of the thirteenth century had far greater insight than anyone from the remote past. Augustine was hobbled by his century; for all his individual powers of mind, he could not see as deeply as an ordinary thirteenth-century spiritual could. (Neither, of course, could other thirteenth-century people, who were not spirituals but belonged to the "carnal Church.") Moreover, there was little danger that the future could significantly outdate the wisdom of the present as the present had outdated the wisdom of the past because there was only one more "church" left, and it would be a culmination of present insights.

Such a theology offered a justification for what intelligentsias since have often claimed: greater wisdom than other members of society and their own predecessors. That was assuredly true of the Russian intelligentsia. As it happens, we get the word *intelligentsia* from Russia, where it was coined around 1860. In its Russian context, the term suggested a group that was (1) different from the rest of society and (2) characterized by special insight (intelligence, in a deep sense). Almost immediately, the group identified its special powers to understand the world with a unique ability to redeem it politically; as with the medieval spirituals, epistemology was wedded to soteriology. And the Russian intelligentsia also typically imagined that the end of history was at hand; they pursued an imminent secular millennium.

With the salvation of the world at stake, members of the intelligentsia were expected to subscribe without question to a code of philosophical and social beliefs reflecting the latest wisdom. For this reason, the terms *intelligent* (member of the intelligentsia) and *intellectual* are anything but synonymous. If by an intellectual we mean someone who thinks for himself or herself, who questions orthodoxies, and who freely explores ideas wherever they might lead, it becomes evident why, almost by definition, an intellectual could not be an *intelligent*. For an *intelligent* was identified as such by his unquestioning acceptance of the group's received truths. Thus many of Russia's best-known writers were not considered, and did not consider themselves, members of the intelligentsia. Chekhov, for example, indignantly rejected calls to join an intelligentsia circle and savagely criticized the conformist mentality the group demanded. For their part, the intelligentsia typically responded by labeling skeptical intellectuals enemies of the people's salvation. The conflict between *Signposts* and the intelligentsia, which was described in chapter 5, expressed the ongoing dispute between the intelligentsia and its intellectual enemies.

Central to intelligentsia ideology was a progressivist conception of social insight. The continuing Russian story of "fathers and sons"—and later of "grandsons"—was one in which later was assumed to be better. Each generation claimed to possess an ideology superior to those of its predecessors and to be that much closer to the final revelation (and revolution). Diverse systems of this sort succeeded each other, but at all times two unshakeable assumptions were clear: (1) the special role of the intelligentsia and its superiority to the rest of society, and (2) the necessarily greater insight of each successive generation of *intelligents*. The parallel of the *intelligents* with the possessors of spiritual intelligence is obvious.[6]

The intelligentsia's opponents persistently subjected these two tenets to unwelcome examination; without much exaggeration, the Russian novel may be described as the record of such scrutiny. *Crime and Punishment*, for example, focuses on the claim of intelligentsia superiority, which is transformed into Raskolnikov's division of humanity into "extraordinary people" to whom "all is permitted" and ordinary people, who serve as mere breeders. Although Tolstoy also rejected such claims, his most interesting comments pertain to the second intelligentsia tenet, the progressivist conception of social insight.

As we have seen, Tolstoy (whom no one would have considered an *intelli-*

gent) flatly denied that history is governed by a law of progress. There is no good reason to assume that later generations are wiser, he insisted, much as there is no good reason to assume that *intelligents* are wiser than other people. In the epilogue to *War and Peace*, Tolstoy describes with withering irony how historians and critics of his own day judge thinkers and political leaders of the past "progressive" or "reactionary" according to the historians' and critics' own values. They write as if their opinions were not just opinions but had some objective validity established by history itself, whereas their most cherished beliefs are, of course, nothing but the prejudices of a small group of people at a particular time. When they comment on the Napoleonic period and its aftermath, for instance, "all the famous people of that period, from Aleksandr and Napoleon to Madame de Staël, Photius, Schelling, Fichte, Chateaubriand, and the rest, pass before their stern tribunal and are acquitted or condemned according to whether they promoted *progress* or *reaction*" (W&P, 1351–52).

These members of the intelligentsia write as if, by virtue of existing in their own time, they possessed a kind of insight unavailable to predecessors but easily acquired today. Thus we detect the tone of certain judgment, which reflects the assumption that something more than the prejudice of current values— something radically different from the mistaken convictions of the past—is at work:

> There is no one in present-day Russian literature, from schoolboy essayist to learned historian, who does not cast his little stone at Aleksandr for the things he did wrong at this ["reactionary"] period of his reign.
>
> "He ought to have acted in such and such a way. In this instance he did well, in that instance badly. He behaved admirably at the beginning of his reign and during 1812, but acted badly in granting a constitution to Poland, . . . in fostering Golitsyn and mysticism . . . and disbanding the Semyonovsky regiment," and so on.
>
> It would take a dozen pages to enumerate all the reproaches leveled at him by historians, based on their knowledge of what is good for humanity. (W&P, 1352)

But why should we assume the historians and critics have the right standards? Even if we accept that such historians were not just expressing their own prejudices and that the study of history gives one special insight, why should we believe the historians of today rather than those of yesterday or, presumably, tomorrow? Each intelligentsia generation condemns the values of its predecessors as shortsighted or vicious and yet does not seem to foresee that the next generation will say the same thing about it. The spectacle of confident judgments repeatedly revealed as inadequate or worse does not seem to lead either to less certainty or to a more humble tone.

To be sure, later historians judging Alexander have one advantage over him: they know what happened during the next fifty years, as Alexander did not. But they do not know what *else* might have happened and which possibilities were as likely as the one realized. They are likely to overlook or underestimate the alternatives he tried to forestall. In this respect, they may have considerably less insight than Alexander and his contemporaries. The habit of backshadowing, of judging from the security of the present, conceals the sideshadows.

Moreover, current historians do not know and generally underestimate the changes that will occur in the next fifty years after their judgments are made. Standards will shift, though we do not know how; the future we project will almost certainly not be realized, and the projections made today will most likely come to look incredibly naive in light of whatever does happen. In this sense, "it is impossible to say of the activity of Aleksandr or of Napoleon that it was either beneficial or harmful, since we cannot say for what it was beneficial or harmful. If that activity fails to please someone, it is only because it does not coincide with his limited understanding" (W&P, 1353).

What, then, do the historians' reproaches mean? asks Tolstoy. They mean nothing more than that Alexander "did not have the same conception of the welfare of humanity fifty years ago as a present-day professor who from his youth has been occupied with learning, that is, with reading books, listening to lectures, and making notes" (W&P, 1353).

Tolstoy's satirical reminder (or defamiliarization) of what professors actually do continues an argument he advanced frequently.[7] *Intelligents* pass judgments with such confidence because they seem to believe in the superior wisdom conferred by their way of living, which is implicitly or explicitly credited with great epistemological power. The views of others are presumably distorted by class interests, atypical experiences, or other forms of socially conditioned false consciousness from which the intelligentsia is somehow exempt. But from Tolstoy's perspective, the conditions of intelligentsia life distort its views no less than alternative conditions shape the views of others. Tolstoy remarks: if we do not have theories of history that attribute to shoemakers or shopkeepers a decisive role in saving the people, as we have theories of history attributing such a role to the intelligentsia, that is only because it is intellectuals rather than shoemakers who theorize. "History is written by learned men and so it is natural and agreeable for them to think that the activity of their class is the basis for the movement of all humanity" (W&P, 1419–20), just as it is natural and agreeable for people to think that their own time enjoys special privilege.

Epilogue . . .

Everything that belongs only to the present dies along with the present.
—BAKHTIN

So "natural and agreeable" is it to assume the superiority of one's own group, profession, and time that we should be especially suspicious of all theories that seem to presume such superiority. When we readily acquit ourselves of the limitations of vision distorting the views of people in the past and of others today, it might be suspected that the jury has been fixed.

In some cases, of course, convincing justification is to hand. In physics, astronomy, mathematics, and various other sciences, it does seem to be the case that real progress has been made, and that one really is more knowledgeable by virtue of having lived later. What the spirituals claimed of Scripture may really be true of physics: any competent physicist today, even if endowed with no special genius, may know more about physics than Aristotle or Newton. But in matters of culture, politics, and ethics, in areas that purport to explain and evaluate human experience, there is no similarly clear line of progress, irrespective of our prejudices, that can be traced.

The burden of proof, therefore, must lie with those who lay claim to the superior knowledge of a later age. Claims based on intellectual discoveries of recent vintage should only increase our skepticism; recent revelation has not been measured against the human experience it purports to explain. If a cultural, social, or philosophical school has in the past decade or so "overcome" errors previously characterizing the whole Western tradition, it would be wise to remember that earlier schools made similar claims and to suspect that the present school will soon be but another chapter in the tradition it imagines it has transcended. Intellectual revolutions are ill-judged by their contemporaries.

Suspicion should also increase when the capacity of the future to invalidate the present is underestimated, when, implicitly, the school in question writes as if it were close to the end of history. We might, in such cases, remember the doctrine of the "church of Philadelphia" and remind these "Philadelphians" how much history and how many changes of values have passed since earlier claims of near-certainty or near-finality were made.

Failure to acknowledge the problem of chronocentrism in the study of human behavior may in itself be a sign that the work suffers from this limitation. Why is our conviction of superiority, however deeply held, different from those of our predecessors? The question seems especially pertinent when schools adopt (as many recently have) versions of extreme epistemic and cultural relativism. To assert the superiority of schools of our own time because they have at last adopted extreme epistemic relativism is to offer an especially curious claim. But in their solidarity and guild mentality, intelligentsias today can be expected to remain as satisfied with their extreme epistemic relativism as their predecessors were satisfied with absolutist doctrines, so long as the guild's own privileged insight can be maintained.

Moralistic or politically inspired schools that habitually judge the cultural heritage of the past according to the standards of their own groups today are especially prone to chronocentrism. Only a teleological or Whiggish view of history can offer automatic guarantees of superior wisdom to successive generations of ordinary intellectuals. Without that guarantee, there is something vaguely humorous in academics, and their students, condemning or acquitting Shakespeare and Milton according to the latest orthodoxies of the academy: did they support or undermine hegemony, foster progress (in our terms) or abet reaction?

As in Tolstoy's day, so in ours: Wordsworth and Goethe, Dostoevsky and Melville are summoned before the stern tribunal of associate professors. Perhaps it may be pointed out that such a stance borders on the apocalyptic. Such critics, like the historians Tolstoy describes, implicitly seem to presume the sort of knowledge that could be available only at the end of history, when all earlier views are revealed as partial and when no future experience could outdate present values. And so we hear the tone of certainty that only a final Revelation could warrant. Shakespeare and Dostoevsky saw through a glass darkly, but we see face to face.

Or perhaps we might better say that such criticism presumes epilogue time. All the really important changes have taken place, and now the pattern is visible, as in the epilogue to a novel. After all, it is not that such critics deny there will be a future. Rather, one suspects that they do not imagine how naive or shortsighted their own views may soon look. For present experience "is not the sample of an even web" (Eliot, 789). Temporal wisdom would suggest that critics adopt a more *tentative* tone, recall that they themselves might once have thought differently, or make an effort to learn from "reactionary" positions they reject. Like Levin, they might try to imagine why a decent and intelligent person might sincerely disagree with them.

Sometimes these critics convey a strong sense that all values shared before a decade ago were morally offensive. As if situated in epilogue time, they seem to speak as if the process of change had essentially stopped with them—as if the future would undergo change but only by realizing or extending the insights of the present. Epilogue time allows the future to be viewed in terms of a form of anticipatory backshadowing that might be called *pre*shadowing: the future is to be like the present, only much more so.

. . . and Beyond

In rhetoric there is the unconditionally innocent and unconditionally guilty; there is complete victory and destruction of the opponent. In dialogue the destruction of the opponent also destroys that very dialogic sphere where the word lives.
—BAKHTIN

There can be neither a first nor a last meaning; it always exists among other meanings as a link in the chain of meaning, which in its totality is the only thing that can be real. In historical life, this chain continues infinitely, and therefore each individual link in it is renewed again and again, as though it were being reborn.
—BAKHTIN

Stated positively, how can we avoid chronocentrism and backshadowing when studying the past? Sideshadowing invites a special kind of dialogue that can enrich our perspective through an open-ended engagement with alternatives. Such a dialogue would require the following steps:

1. *Imagining, with the help of sideshadows, how the other time, culture, or group saw itself.* What factors seemed important to them in justifying (or questioning) their values and practices? Were there benefits, dangers, or circumstances, now invisible to us, that made such values and practices compelling or desirable? Did opponents of prevailing values raise objections different from ours? If our values had occurred to people living then, what drawbacks would they have seen in applying them to their own world? Would our present practices have been impossible or, if possible, counterproductive in ways we now find hard to see?

Examining the context in which people lived from their perspective would entail asking what they saw as the main threats to their survival and just how threatening anticipated dangers appeared. What were their expectations in the various realms of life? What opportunities did they perceive? Chronocentrists who examine the past are often surprised to find that those who were, in our terms, oppressed, did not view themselves that way. Instead of resorting to concepts like blindness or false consciousness to explain their failure to recognize themselves as victims—instead of depriving them of voice by speaking for their "true" interests—allow them to speak as equals from whom we have something to learn. When, after considering what they might say, we invoke our present values, we may do so as part of a dialogue with no presumed winner.

2. *Reversing the process of judging earlier ages in our own terms by imagining how people of the past would have judged us in theirs.* What benefits and virtues have our own most cherished values and practices led us to overlook, forego,

or underestimate? Although it is natural and agreeable to assume the role of prosecutor, it is also helpful to become a defendant attacked by a talented attorney with the values of another time and culture. This exchange, too, can enrich our sense of both our time and theirs.

3. *Recognizing that the present was not the only possible outcome of earlier times and imagining alternatives to ourselves.* If the projections of twenty, thirty, and fifty years ago had come to pass, and our world looked today more or less as some had anticipated it would, what would such a sideshadow of ourselves teach us? If different policies had been pursued, what might the implications have been for our own time and for all the intervening times? How did the results that were projected from inventions, discoveries, and choices differ from those we now perceive to have resulted? If some contingent historical event had turned out differently, if some invention we take for granted had not yet been made, what might the world look like now? In that alternative world, how would our sense of ourselves differ? What values might now prevail? Reality as we know it is only one of many possible realities, and we may engage in dialogue with our sideshadows.

Each of these dialogues creates a sense that we cannot presume our values but must defend, examine, and reevaluate them. We live in a Galilean universe of opinions and possibilities. By surrendering the sense that later is better and that our own group is somehow favored by history or profession, we may attend to counterarguments otherwise overlooked. We may still wind up adhering to a version of our own ethical preferences, but we will do so less "naively" and without the spurious advantage conferred by chronocentrism and analogous perspectival errors. Ours will form part of an open-ended dialogue of values and, in the process, become more complex. The conviction that informs our beliefs need be no less strong for being aware of viable alternatives; and our defense of them, or some newly altered version of them, need be no weaker in consequence of such dialogues.

We may also learn to sense more profoundly the difficulty of anticipating the consequences that attend our choices and of attempting to bend history to our will. There is no libretto to history. Time and people are not infinitely malleable. Nor are we capable of comprehending the full range of interstices in our network of social relationships. All choices will lead to some unlooked-for results and unforeseen complications. They will ramify and concatenate in surprising ways. Straight lines of development are harder to perpetrate than to attribute after the fact.

At the same time, we should keep in mind that a future we cannot imagine will also be judging us. Supposing they view us chronocentrically, how might we answer their condemnations? Could analogous answers be made by past cultures that we judge? If, on the other hand, our successors should forego chronocentrism and engage in open-ended dialogue with us, what might we learn about ourselves from the experience? People tend not to see many potentials of their own time, some of which—the ones later realized—seem obvious to future observers.

In short, sideshadowing and the openness of time have implications for us as both historical actors and interpreters. We are all captives of our moment, and we live on a small temporal island. Complex moral thinking, informed by a rich sense of temporality, may liberate us from the tyranny of the present instant. The imagination of sideshadows and the process of dialogue with alternatives may expand our temporal horizons and make us more attentive to historical opportunity. Time is open and will always be open. "Nothing conclusive has yet taken place in the world, the ultimate word of the world and about the world has not yet been spoken, the world is open and free, everything is still in the future and will always be in the future" (PDP, 166).

Notes

Introduction

1 See, for instance, the classic study by Stephen Toulmin and June Goodfield, *The Discovery of Time* (New York: Harper and Row, 1965).

2 To take just one example: The idea that we may be a jury-rigged or jerry-built set of compromises that could have been quite different led H. G. Wells to qualify his confidence that the human mind can solve social or other problems. Wells reflected that "in the great scheme of space and time" man is "finite and not final. . . . When you have realised to the marrow, that all the physical organs of man and all his physical structures are what they are through a series of adaptations and compromises . . . and that this is true also of his brain, and of his instincts and of many of his mental predispositions, you are not going to take his thinking as being in any way mysteriously different or better." H. G. Wells, "Appendix: Scepticism of the Instrument," *A Modern Utopia* (Lincoln: University of Nebraska Press, 1967), 376–78.

3 William James, "The Dilemma of Determinism," *"The Will to Believe" and "Human Immortality"* (New York: Dover, 1956), 159. Further references are to DD.

4 A few years ago, when my thinking was in a relatively early stage, Bernstein asked me what I was working on. Expecting he would need an explanation, I replied, "Something I call sideshadowing," but to my surprise he immediately guessed what my neologism must mean. He had arrived at a similar set of ideas from considering different material, especially Jewish narratives about the Holocaust, both fictional and historical. We decided to write a joint book in two parts, but it eventually became clear that it would be wiser to publish two separate, but intellectually linked, books. They are linked as well by the fact that we exchanged ideas and refined concepts together over a long period. Thus, in referring readers to Bernstein's book, *Foregone Conclusions: Against Apocalyptic History* (Berkeley: University of California Press, 1994), I am doing more than just mentioning a related work.

5 The seventy-four years of Soviet culture, based on a set of beliefs radically different from those prevalent in our own society, offer a treasure house of surprising and instructive examples about temporal conceptions. It seems to me that, either because the Soviets were for so long the familiar other or because their time has now passed, their instructive differences have not received the attention they warrant.

6 My thanks to Robert Belknap, who pointed out to me that my thesis here can be viewed as an extension or adaptation of Lessing's core argument in *Laocoön*.

See especially chapters 16 and 17 of Gotthold Ephraim Lessing, *Laocoön: An Essay on the Limits of Poetry and Painting*, trans. Edward Allen McCormick (Baltimore: Johns Hopkins University Press, 1984), 78–90.

7   In a footnote, James cites these words from another thinker, Christoph Sigwart (DD, 148 n1).

8   Robin Feuer Miller suggested to me that the metaphor of sideshadowing seems to presuppose a source of light and asked me to be more specific about it. The question is an intriguing one, but at this point I am not prepared to push the metaphor so far.

9   Some readers of the typescript of this book were disturbed that it mixes analyses of great literature with considerations of popular culture. I do so not because I wish to dignify popular pastimes but because they are so much a part of everyday experience. They can serve as reminders of experiences we have all had or understand.

10   The complex *moral* ramifications of backshadowing are the main focus of Bernstein's *Foregone Conclusions*.

11   Alexander Herzen, *"From the Other Shore" and "The Russian People and Socialism,"* trans. Moura Budberg and Richard Wollheim (Oxford: Oxford University Press, 1979), 39. Further references are to FTOS.

Chapter One. Prelude: Process and Product

1   William James points out that we directly experience a few seconds of time, rather than the imperceptibly small instant, because we experience not the present but the "specious present." If someone waves a light in a dark room, one will see its path— its recent past locales along with its present one—because our experienced present is "speciously" a few seconds long. On this sense of the present and its relation to memory, see the chapter "The Perception of Time" in William James, *The Principles of Psychology* (New York: Dover, 1950; a reproduction of the 1890 edition), 1:605–42.

2   Anton Chekhov, *The Major Plays*, trans. Ann Dunnigan (New York: Signet, 1964), 230–31. Further references are to ChP.

3   The relation of meaning to narrative shape has been a recurrent theoretical concern since Aristotle's *Poetics*. Over the years my thinking has been influenced by Erich Auerbach, *Mimesis: The Representation of Reality in Western Literature*, trans. Willard R. Trask (Princeton: Princeton University Press, 1953); Frank Kermode, *The Sense of an Ending: Studies in the Theory of Fiction* (London: Oxford University Press, 1967); Hayden White, *Metahistory: The Historical Imagination in Nineteenth-Century Europe* (Baltimore: Johns Hopkins University Press, 1973); and Bakhtin's various writings on the problem, especially FTC and BSHR.

4   That is true even of most experimental or metaliterary works that create anticlosure, which (for reasons I shall examine in chapter 6) is really just another form of closure. On anticlosure, see Barbara Herrnstein Smith, *Poetic Closure: A Study of How Poems End* (Chicago: University of Chicago Press, 1968), and Kermode, *The Sense of an Ending*.

5   On "transcription" and related concepts, see the introduction to Morson and Emerson, *Rethinking Bakhtin: Extensions and Challenges* (Evanston: Northwestern University Press, 1989).

6   It might at first seem that the Russian structuralist Yuri Lotman approaches Bakhtin's position, but I believe that they are in fact making quite different points. See Jurij Lotman, *The Structure of the Artistic Text,* trans. Ronald Vroon (Ann Arbor: Michigan Slavic Contributions, 1977), 231–39. In this discussion of plot, Lotman defines events as (1) relative to a scheme assessing significance (incidents that are events from one perspective are nonevents from another), and (2) something that happened but did not have to happen, in the sense that the event "involves the violation of some prohibition" (236). The first criterion makes clear that Lotman's topic differs from Bakhtin's: Lotman's nonevents might still be eventful in Bakhtin's terms. Lotman is concerned not with what events in life are (Bakhtin's topic) but with how narratives designate certain incidents as significant enough to be told. This context indicates that in speaking of events that might or might not have happened, Lotman is not endorsing open time or denying determinism. Rather, he seems to mean that what a storyteller calls a (significant) event is one that violates some set of social norms or expectations (and is therefore newsworthy). But that could easily happen in a universe of closed time.

7   I say "disembodied" because in A&A and KFP, Bakhtin stresses that our location at particular places at particular moments is fundamental to issues of action and choice; this idea led him to interesting meditations on the body. An interest in our "embodiment" was closely linked to Bakhtin's distrust of theoretism.

8   On processual intentions, see Morson, *Hidden in Plain View: Narrative and Creative Potentials in "War and Peace"* (Stanford: Stanford University Press, 1987), 218–23, 236–37.

9   At the minimum, creativity would seem to require both these concepts. First, the act must be valuable (to someone), which is what distinguishes creativity from mere error, although errors, when reflected on and deliberately repeated, are an important source of valuable novelty. Second, the act must be surprising. If we are speaking of human creativity, agency is also involved.

10 Osip M. Brik, "T. n. 'Formal'nyi metod' " (The so-called "formal method"), LEF 1 (1923): 213. Of course, this argument, despite its antiromantic rhetoric, borders on a romanticization of the machine.

11 Edgar Allan Poe, "The Philosophy of Composition," in *Great Short Works of Edgar Allan Poe,* ed. G. R. Thompson (New York, 1970), 529–30.

12 Percy Bysshe Shelley, "A Defense of Poetry," in *The Selected Poetry and Prose of Shelley,* ed. Harold Bloom (New York, 1978), 443.

13 Apparently independently and probably unaware of each other, Bakhtin and Vygotsky both proceeded from a model in which thought was identified with inner speech.

14 L. S. Vygotsky, *Thought and Language,* ed. and trans. Eugenia Hanfmann and Gertrude Vakar (Cambridge: MIT Press, 1962), 45.

15 Of course, people often take offense at abstractions like prejudice or at social facts like pornography, but that is because prejudice and pornography result from human choice and behavior. It is paradoxical to take offense at laws of nature, but not at laws passed by Congress.

16 The underground man's argument here and elsewhere is implicitly directed against the "compatibilist" position that determinism does not contradict freedom because there is a difference between causation and compulsion. In most determinist views, people freely choose but it is still possible in principle to predict what they will

choose because the exercise of choice is itself subject to determinations. The underground man paraphrases the Russian radicals' version of this argument and offers his reply:

> You will shout at me (that is, if you will still favor me with your shout), that, after all, no one is depriving me of my will, that all they are concerned with is that my will should somehow of itself, of its own free will, coincide with my own normal interests, with the laws of nature and arithmetic.
>
> Bah, gentlemen, what sort of free will is left when we come to tables and arithmetic, when it will all be a case of two times two makes four? Two times two makes four even without my will. As if free will meant that! (NFU, 28)

The underground man concedes that causation and compulsion are not the same, but he adds that

1. neither one allows for freedom because freedom requires alternatives, that is, an open temporality;

2. if anything, determinism restricts freedom more than compulsion because it is easy to imagine resisting compulsion; but how does one resist determinism? After all, any attempted resistance must itself have been determined. The underground man's language and behavior represent his own attempt to find some way to violate determinism just as one might resist compulsion;

3. determinism is characteristically used (even by some compatibilists) to *justify* compulsion. For example, utopians often argue that there is no need for "bourgeois" freedom because people are determined anyway;

4. determinism is usually accompanied by a certain sort of smugness on the part of those who "know the laws" or at least recognize the full implications of the existence of laws, whether or not they are known. The gentlemen in their crystal palace are notably characterized by such smugness.

17 The obvious comparison here is with Freud's concept of the death instinct. And yet, the underground man's reasoning seems to be the precise opposite of Freud's because it involves not a "compulsion to repeat" but a *compulsion to surprise*. See Sigmund Freud, *Civilization and Its Discontents,* ed. and trans. James Strachey (Norton: New York, 1961), 73.

18 Perhaps what we need is a sense of purposiveness without a purpose that ever becomes clear or definite?

19 For an intriguing reading of this passage in terms set by general systems theory, see Aron Katsenelinboigen, "Systems Unity: The System's View of the Devil in Dostoevsky's 'The Brothers Karamazov,'" *Selected Topics in Indeterministic Systems* (Salinas, Cal.: Intersystems Publications, 1989), 331–36.

20 This passage and some others like it in Dostoevsky suggest a reading of the Garden of Eden story: the hunger for eventness produced the Fall, and the devil, far from initiating sinfulness, was the convenient means at hand. Sinfulness precedes the Fall. This Dostoevskian reading was adopted (or adapted) in Zamyatin's *We,* in which utopia is a recreation of Eden, and the desire for events produces a new Fall. Prelapsarian "sinfulness" (viewed positively) is, in fact, a topos of anti-utopian literature long before the twentieth century. In *Rasselas,* the "wants of him who wants nothing"—the desire for unexpected events—provokes Rasselas's escape from the Happy Valley.

21 Richard McKeon, ed., *The Basic Works of Aristotle* (New York: Random House, 1941), 48.

22 In my discussion of Aristotle, I have benefited from Paul Horwich, *Asymmetries in Time: Problems in the Philosophy of Science* (Cambridge: MIT Press, 1987), 28–33.

23 Robert Louis Jackson, "Aristotelian Movement and Design in Part Two of *Notes from the Underground*," *The Art of Dostoevsky: Deliriums and Nocturnes* (Princeton: Princeton University Press, 1981), 186.

Chapter Two. Foreshadowing

1 The term *determinism* has many senses. For a recent and intriguing analysis of four uses of the term, see chapter 3 of Stephen H. Kellert, *In the Wake of Chaos: Unpredictable Order in Dynamical Systems* (Chicago: University of Chicago Press, 1993), 49–76. This book examines the implications of chaos theory for determinism. The four listed uses of *determinism* are (1) Differential Dynamics (the future depends on the present in a mathematically specifiable way); (2) Unique Evolution (or Laplacian determinism: if two worlds agree on everything at one moment of time they must agree at all other moments, and so there can be no forks in history); (3) Value Determinateness (physical qualities have exact values, for if they were indistinct the system would be insufficiently set); and (4) Total Predictability (by a superior intelligence). Each step presupposes the earlier ones, and so as we proceed from 1 to 4, the concept becomes stronger. Kellert contends that chaos theory raises problems for total predictability; he goes on to argue that when combined with quantum mechanics, chaos theory raises problems for unique evolution as well.

2 On time as anisotropic and on the asymmetry in knowledge, I follow Horwich, *Asymmetries in Time*.

3 These quotations from Bruno and Leibniz are taken from the article "Time" in *The Dictionary of the History of Ideas: Studies of Selected Pivotal Ideas,* ed. Philip P. Weiner (New York: Scribner's, 1973), 4:393, 394.

4 But of course this fear of teleology is often exaggerated. There are many kinds of teleological explanation; some are unavoidable or even superior. For a survey of its kinds, see chapter 3 of John D. Barrow and Frank J. Tippler, *The Anthropic Cosmological Principle* (Oxford: Oxford University Press, 1988), 123–218.

5 Another device that evidently testifies to the author's essential surplus is multiple plotting, of the type found in *Middlemarch*. Readers become aware of patterns that escape the characters. In such a novel, as Martin Price has observed, "any one story is embedded in a structure of relationships with other stories that have as much prominence for us but may be at the margin of a given character's awareness or totally beyond his ken. We may be Lydgates or Dorotheas, but we do not live our lives in constant juxtaposition with those other selves, as they do in the novel of multiple plot. At its most pointed, this will be dramatic irony; but in more tenuous form it is present everywhere and affects our sense of any character and event." Martin Price, *Forms of Life: Character and Moral Imagination in the Novel* (New Haven: Yale University Press, 1983), 11. It may be added that if someone in real life did choose to live "in constant juxtaposition," he would be novelizing experience in a dangerous way. Nevertheless, this example is somewhat less dramatic evidence of the essential surplus than foreshadowing is because, after all, novelistic characters are sometimes aware of the relation of their lives to those of characters in the

work's parallel stories, as Alice Vavasor is in Trollope's *Can You Forgive Her?* Of course, Alice does not compare her life with Lady Glencora's because she knows they both belong to the same novel but because they are friends who have faced similar problems.

6 Cited in "Time," *The Dictionary of the History of Ideas*, 4:390.

7 *The Hellenistic Philosophers*, vol. 1, *Translations of the Principal Sources with Philosophical Commentary*, ed. and trans. A. A. Long and D. N. Sedley (Cambridge: Cambridge University Press, 1987), 309. Some Stoics made the softer claim that small "accidentals" may differ (a man may not have the same mole on his face).

8 It is much like going around the earth and repeating the same journey endlessly. It is curious to reflect that there must have been people who believed in a flat earth but in a circular time.

9 It might at first seem that at least those living in the first cycle are free, for their future has not been enacted in some earlier past. One might imagine that subsequent cycles will make choice pointless, but not the first, where choice is taking place. But a moment's reflection shows that this conclusion is false. The theory states that each cycle *independently* repeats the same sequence of events. With no influence from the first cycle, the second cycle is identical. Now, choice depends on the notion of alternatives: that if conditions could somehow be repeated another choice might have been made. But in eternal recurrence, the same circumstances are indeed repeated and the same choice is always made, ad infinitum. Such endless repetition demonstrates that even in the first cycle alternatives are absolutely illusory.

10 See chapter 1 ("Substantive and Analytical Philosophies of History") of Arthur C. Danto, *Analytical Philosophy of History* (Cambridge: Cambridge University Press, 1968), 1–16.

11 Could this be one reason for the appeal of Marxism to literary critics?

12 Ibid., 9. Danto borrows this distinction between prediction and prophecy from Karl Popper.

13 I recognize that my purpose in this book differs from Danto's. He emphasizes the retrospective character of narrative sentences typically used by historians. "Narrative sentences refer to at least two time-separated events, and describe the earlier event" (Danto, 159) because a given occurrence "acquires historical *significance* in virtue of its relations to some other . . . [and later] occurrence in which we happen to have some special interest" (Danto, 167). Thus we have "narrative sentences" that an eyewitness to the event described (the earlier event) could not have made: "The Thirty Years War began in 1618," "Aristarchus's theory anticipated Copernicus's," or "Petrarch opened the Renaissance." I largely agree with these observations, but I also wish to emphasize that such narrative sentences often obscure the presentness of past moments and occlude the perception of alternative courses of development, thus leading to what in chapter 6 I shall call backshadowing and chronocentrism.

14 Auerbach, *Mimesis*, 157–58. Auerbach provides my second example of figural interpretation, ibid., 48–49.

15 As cited in Rufus W. Mathewson, Jr., *The Positive Hero in Russian Literature*, 2d ed. (Stanford: Stanford University Press, 1975), 49.

16 As cited in Abram Tertz [Andrei Sinyavsky], "On Socialist Realism," trans. George Dennis, *"The Trial Begins" and "On Socialist Realism"* (Berkeley: University of California Press, 1982), 148. Further references are to OSR.

17 On the fascinating questions connected with rereading, see Matei Calinescu, *Rereading* (New Haven: Yale University Press, 1993).

18 Sophocles, *Oedipus the King*, trans. Bernard W. Knox, in *Man and His Fictions: An Introduction to Fiction-Making, Its Forms and Uses*, ed. Alvin B. Kernan, Peter Brooks, and J. Michael Holquist (New York: Harcourt Brace, 1973), 364.

19 Of course, Tieresias has this knowledge *within* the represented world, because he is a prophet; he has it because the gods of his world have revealed it to him. By contrast, we know the whole story because we exist *outside* the represented world and have heard the story before. The two positions are not identical but are nevertheless crucially similar in one respect: we resemble Tieresias and differ from Oedipus because we are able to assess events as they happen in terms of their inevitable outcome.

20 Jonathan Culler has argued that Oedipus too rapidly accepts that he is the murderer of Laius; Culler proceeds to deconstruct key concepts of causality and narratology. I find both the specific and general arguments to be implausible, though thought-provoking. See Jonathan Culler, "Story and Discourse in the Analysis of Narrative," *The Pursuit of Signs: Semiotics, Literature, Deconstruction* (Ithaca: Cornell University Press, 1981), 169–87.

21 M. Lermontov, *A Hero of Our Time*, trans. Martin Parker (Moscow: Foreign Languages, n.d.), 167.

22 Virgil, *The Aeneid*, book VII. I have combined two translations: by Rolfe Humphries (New York: Scribner's, 1951), 188, and by Robert Fitzgerald (New York: Random House, 1983), 206–07.

23 Sergei Bulgakov, "Heroism and Asceticism (Reflections on the Religious Nature of the Russian Intelligentsia)," in Mikhail Gershenzon, ed., *Signposts: A Collection of Articles on the Russian Intelligentsia*, ed. and trans. Marshall S. Shatz and Judith E. Zimmerman (Irvine: Schlacks, 1986), 36; italics mine.

24 *The Confessions of St. Augustine*, trans. John K. Ryan (Garden City, N.Y.: Image, 1960), 291 (book 11, chapter 18).

25 The concept of hypertime also underlies some nonsense literature. At the Mad Tea-Party, the Hatter tells Alice that if she would only keep on good terms with Time,

> "he'd do almost anything you liked with the clock. For instance, suppose it were nine o'clock in the morning, just time to begin lessons: you'd only have to whisper a hint to Time, and round goes the clock in a twinkling! Half-past one, time for dinner! . . ."
>
> "That would be grand, certainly," said Alice thoughtfully; "but then—I shouldn't be hungry for it, you know."
>
> "Not at first, perhaps," said the Hatter: "but you could keep it to half-past one as long as you liked."
>
> "Is that the way *you* manage?" Alice asked.
>
> The Hatter shook his head mournfully. "Not I!" he replied. "We quarreled last March. . . . And ever since that . . . he won't do a thing I ask! It's always six o'clock now. . . . it's always tea-time, and we've no time to wash the things between whiles" (*The Complete Works of Lewis Carroll* [New York: Modern Library, n.d.], 78–80).

Once there is hypertime, we can speak of the speed of time and inquire how much time it takes for a given amount of time to pass. For the Hatter, time is measured normally within each process but it *does not add up*. And so, willingly or not, one can stay at a given time for a long time.

In the chapter "An Outlandish Watch" in Carroll's *Sylvie and Bruno* (chapter 23), time can be set backward by setting the hands of a certain watch backward. After a cyclist is involved in an accident and lies bleeding in a nearby shop, the possessor of the watch sets it back, returns to the time just before the accident, and removes the obstacle that caused it; and no accident takes place. But as soon as the time when the watch was set back is reached, the cyclist is again lying bleeding in the shop. Apparently, the past has been changed, but the effects of the canceled past on a later moment remain, which provides the extremely odd image of events that have not been caused and, presumably, shared memories of incidents that have not happened. Or have they? For an interval, there were two simultaneous times— except that one happened "first" and the other was superimposed upon it "later."

Also, by setting the "reversal-peg" on the watch, time can be made to go backward in a given locale, and so the possessor of the watch witnesses a conversation in which the utterances occur in reverse order. And yet, curiously enough, each utterance is spoken forward—it does not sound like a tape played backward—with just the sequence of utterances backward. Thus we have two times going in opposite directions, local in one way and "global" in the other.

26 In this section I have benefited from Northwestern University senior theses written by Julie Williams (on the novel and the Garbo film) and by Shannon McLeod (on Kitty).

27 Denis de Rougement, *Love in the Western World*, trans. Montgomery Belgion (New York: Harper and Row, 1974), 15.

28 So Tolstoy argues in his reading of Chekhov's story "The Darling." See Tolstoy, "An Afterword, by Tolstoy, to Chekhov's Story, *Darling* (1905)" *"What Is Art?" and Essays on Art*, trans. Aylmer Maude (Oxford: Oxford University Press, 1969), 323–27.

29 As Helena Goscilo pointed out to me, the saying "to understand is to forgive" could be interpreted less categorically, merely as a general exhortation to remember charity. But it does seem that the unqualified phrasing encourages a categorical reading.

Chapter Three. Interlude: Bakhtin's Indeterminism

1 This is the thesis of "unique evolution." See Kellert, *In the Wake of Chaos*, 59.

2 In fact, the Russian word *izbytok* may be rendered either way.

3 In a footnote, James cites these words from Christoph Sigwart (DD, 148 n1). Chaos theorists have pursued an analogous argument: scientists' focus on linearity did not prove the world was wholly linear (it is linear and nonlinear "in motley alternatives") but distracted them from nonlinear phenomena. See Kellert, *In the Wake of Chaos*, and James Gleick, *Chaos: Making a New Science* (New York: Viking, 1987).

4 James's outline of the various consequences of determinism is lived out by characters in Dostoevsky. Myshkin often inclines toward a kind of panglossism; Ippolit Terentiev and Ivan Karamazov embrace pessimism; Svidrigailov and perhaps Stavrogin try out "gnosticism."

5 So Caryl Emerson and I have argued in *Mikhail Bakhtin: Creation of a Prosaics* and in our introduction to *Rethinking Bakhtin: Extensions and Challenges*, which includes

a summary of Bakhtin's important early essay on ethics, "Toward a Philosophy of the Act" (KFP).

6 For Bakhtin's many examples, see DiN, BSHR, and FTC. On his various definitions of the novel, see Morson and Emerson, *Mikhail Bakhtin*, 300–05.

7 Sigmund Freud, "Creative Writers and Daydreaming" in *Critical Theory since Plato*, ed. Hazard Adams (New York: Harcourt Brace, 1971), 749–53.

8 It is quite common to equate polyphony with "heteroglossia," which, I think, is something like equating polygamy with heterodoxy. The two concepts designate different phenomena, and a novel may easily exhibit one without the other. According-ing to Bakhtin, many novels before Dostoevsky display heteroglossia but none are polyphonic.

9 For a modern example of such thinking, see Katsenelinboigen, *Selected Topics in Indeterministic Systems*, especially the section on "Indetermining the Future" (19–24) and chapter 11, "On One Possible Interpretation of the Authors of the Torah of the Plans and Actions of the Creator" (259–330). Other examples may be found in process theology. See, for example, John B. Cobb, Jr., and David Ray Griffin, *Process Theology: An Introductory Exposition* (Philadelphia: Westminster Press, 1976). Paraphrasing Hartshorne, Cobb and Griffin explain that in process theology "to say that God is omniscient means that in every moment of the divine life God knows everything which is knowable at that time. . . . In each moment of God's life there are new, unforeseen happenings in the world which only then become knowable" (47).

10 Interestingly enough, Shatov (in *The Possessed*), who largely shares Dostoevsky's ideology, achieves real understanding when he gives up the ideological perspective altogether.

11 Martin Price goes some distance toward a Bakhtinian formulation when he writes, "We are all aware of the mixed pleasure and horror an author can feel at finding his characters demanding lives of their own. . . . And there are many authors who count on characters' taking over the direction of the work, as it were, once they come into fictional life" (Price, *Forms of Life*, 43). Polyphony would also require that this "counting on" be the basic principle of the work and that its effects be experienced by the reader.

12 Michael André Bernstein examines the ethical problems involved in such provocation of characters and in the view that one best understands people or tests ideas by placing them in extremis. See Bernstein, *Bitter Carnival: "Ressentiment" and the Abject Hero* (Princeton: Princeton University Press, 1992), and Bernstein, *Foregone Conclusions*.

13 Bakhtin does not note exceptions to this generalization. In *The Idiot*, Nastasya Filippovna's personality (and *some* sort of tragic destiny) were apparently envisaged from the outset, even though the other characters (especially Myshkin) underwent radical transformations.

14 The classic structuralist study of Dostoevsky is Robert L. Belknap, *The Structure of "The Brothers Karamazov"* (1967; repr. Evanston: Northwestern University Press, 1989).

15 Søren Kierkegaard, *Repetition: An Essay in Experimental Psychology*, trans. Walter Lourie (Princeton: Harper and Row, 1964), 33.

16 By novels here I mean realist novels, as discussed above. The relation of times internal to the fiction differs from genre to genre.

17 The first example in the text is made up; the second is part of the first sentence of Turgenev's *Fathers and Sons*. Consider the author's first comment (after an initial statement by a character) in *War and Peace:* "With these words the renowned Anna Pavlovna Scherer, lady-in-waiting and *confidante* to the Empress Marya Fyodo-rovna, greeted Prince Vasily, a man of high rank and office, who was the first to arrive at her soiree on a July evening in the year 1805" (W&P, 29). This first section of the work was originally published under the title *The Year 1805*. For Turgenev's novel, see Ivan Turgenev, *Fathers and Sons*, the Garnett translation revised by Ralph Matlaw (New York: Norton, 1966). Further references are to F&S.

18 Indeed, it might be possible to use novels to estimate the extent of general knowledge.

19 Or the result will be something like the scene in *Fantasia* in which the animated Mickey Mouse shakes hands with the filmed Leopold Stokowski. The frame would be broken and the realist enterprise derailed.

20 One of the remarkable things about Trollope's Palliser novels, especially *The Prime Minister*, is the way they manage to violate these prescriptions. Here we really do seem to have a parallel universe in which a person we never heard of in real life becomes prime minister of England. From a theoretical perspective, it would be well worth examining this important feature of Trollope's art.

21 Tolstoy adroitly exploits this fact in *War and Peace*, in which it serves as a concrete illustration of his theory that the less prominent a person is, the more freedom he or she enjoys; a peasant has more freedom of action than Napoleon. See Andrew Wachtel, *An Obsession with History: Russian Writers Confront the Past* (Stanford: Stanford University Press, 1994).

22 On this constraint in historical drama, see Herbert Lindenberger, *Historical Drama: The Relation of Literature and Reality* (Chicago: University of Chicago Press, 1975), 2.

23 Of course, it might be objected that Tristram is a character in the fiction talking to purely fictive readers. To this objection we may reply, (1) the situation of fictive readers is meant to mirror that of real readers; (2) Tristram here serves simultaneously as himself and Sterne; that is, we recognize Sterne's trick in Tristram's actions; and (3) even from Tristram's perspective, from which the events narrated are as real as he is, there is no reason why an event that took ten minutes to happen should have to occupy ten minutes of reading time. If the reader skims, must the character run? For a translation of a classic essay on time in *Tristram Shandy*, see Victor Shklovsky, "Sterne's *Tristram Shandy:* Stylistic Commentary," in *Russian Formalist Criticism: Four Essays*, trans. and ed. Lee T. Lemon and Marion J. Reis (Lincoln: University of Nebraska Press, 1965), 25–57.

24 Poe contrasts "the short prose narrative, requiring from a half-hour to one or two hours in its perusal" with "the ordinary novel," which "is objectionable, from its length. . . . As it cannot be read at one sitting, it deprives itself, of course, of the immense force derivable from *totality*. Worldly interests intervening during the pauses of perusal, modify, annul or counteract . . . the impressions of the book." Edgar Allan Poe, "Review of *Twice-Told Tales*," *Great Short Works of Edgar Allan Poe*, 522. In "The Poetic Principle," Poe declares that "a long poem does not exist. I maintain that the phrase *a long poem*, is simply a flat contradiction in terms" because it is inevitably experienced as a series of short poems (Poe, "The Poetic Principle," in Adams, ed., *Critical Theory since Plato*, 564).

25 Gillian Beer, *Arguing with the Past: Essays in Narrative from Woolf to Sidney* (New York: Routledge, 1989), 2.

26 As W. J. Harvey observes, serialization allows both writers and readers to experience "a peculiar reality and intimacy in this prolonged concurrence of fictional characters with their own lives." The same may also hold for very long novels; we do not merely read about Tolstoy's and Proust's characters, "we also live with them and the work in some way draws substance from our own lives." W. J. Harvey, *Character and the Novel* (Ithaca: Cornell University Press, 1965), 111.

27 My thanks to William Mills Todd III for pointing out the significance of such revisions.

28 Bakhtin does not discuss a number of works that seem to go some distance toward a Dostoevskian technique. In the Preface to *Clarissa*, for instance, Richardson explains that his epistolary technique was designed to keep the characters' description of action (and presumably the reader's experience of it) as close as possible to the action itself:

> All the Letters are written while the hearts of the writers must be supposed to be wholly engaged in their subjects (The events at the time generally dubious): So that they abound not only with critical Situations, but with what might be called *instantaneous* Descriptions and Reflections. . . .
>
> "*Much more* lively and affecting, says one of the principal characters, must be the Style of those who write in the height of a *present* distress; the mind tortured by the pangs of uncertainty (the Events then hidden in the womb of Fate); than the dry, narrative, unanimated Style of a person relating difficulties and dangers surmounted, can be; the relater perfectly at ease; and if himself unmoved by his own Story, not likely greatly to affect the Reader."

See Samuel Richardson, "Author's Preface," *Clarissa, or the History of a Young Lady*, ed. George Sherburn (Boston: Houghton Mifflin, 1962), xx. Of course, the author (as opposed to the letter writers) may still be "later" than the action. See Ian Watt's discussion of the importance of this technique for the rise of the realistic novel in his *The Rise of the Novel: Studies in Defoe, Richardson, and Fielding* (Berkeley: University of California Press, 1957), 191–96. For Northrop Frye, techniques to keep the action at a "continuous present" and to create "literature as process" rather than as product are definitive of the age of sensibility. See Frye, "Towards Defining an Age of Sensibility," in *Eighteenth-Century English Literature: Modern Essays in Criticism*, ed. James L. Clifford (New York: Oxford University Press, 1959), 311–18.

29 I have offered three quite different interpretations of the *Diary:* (1) "Dostoevsky's *Diary of a Writer:* Threshold Art" (Ph.D. diss., Yale University, 1974); (2) *The Boundaries of Genre: Dostoevsky's "Diary of a Writer" and the Traditions of Literary Utopia* (1981; repr. Evanston: Northwestern University Press, 1988); and, closest to the present comments, (3) "Dostoevsky's Great Experiment," an "introductory study" to AWD.

30 See, for instance, Konstantin Mochulsky, *Dostoevsky: His Life and Work*, trans. Michael A. Minihan (Princeton: Princeton University Press, 1967), 535.

31 Not quite a single line, of course, if the internal reactions to fixed external events can differ.

32 It is a time of "punctuated equilibrium" (in Stephen Jay Gould's and Niles Eldredge's phrase).

33 This is part of Bakhtin's prosaic ethics.
34 Thus the excuse "I could not behave otherwise, given who I am" may easily sound like a rationalization to readers who have watched how a character gradually shaped himself or herself. And that is often true of such excuses in life.
35 Of course, there are stories that seem to rely on such substitutions: Leskov's "Lady Macbeth of Mtsensk" and other works that relocate a hero from an earlier genre. Far from showing that substitutions are possible, they foreground the inevitable difference between the two works as a source of interest.
36 In *Foregone Conclusions,* Bernstein illuminates the ethical problems that arise when historians narrate history without a sense of the constraints and opportunities available at a past moment.
37 In B. F. Skinner's *Walden Two,* Rogers asks in all utopian seriousness, "Why don't we just start all over again the right way?"—a line that could be only a sign of naivete and the object of irony in a realist novel. B. F. Skinner, *Walden Two* (New York: Macmillan, 1948), 9.

Chapter Four. Sideshadowing

1 In *Foregone Conclusions.*
2 Even when Dostoevsky does not use a chronicler, he creates some of the same effects. The omniscient narrator of *Crime and Punishment* frequently pauses to recount that, years later, when Raskolnikov recalled a given incident, he wondered at his state of mind: why did he do what he did or go where he went, when some other equally plausible alternative might have led to a different outcome? Like the chronicler's rumors, these "future recollections" endow the text with sideshadows. The reader learns not only what Raskolnikov did but also what he might have done. Dostoevsky may have adapted this technique from *Eugene Onegin,* which also seems to cultivate sideshadows and to rely on its narrator to do so. On the conditional in *Eugene Onegin,* see Helena Goscilo, "Multiple Texts in *Eugene Onegin:* A Preliminary Analysis," *Russian Literature Triquarterly,* no. 23 (1990): 271–85.
3 In Bakhtin's terms, we might say that Pyotr Stepanovich unwittingly draws the chronicler into his speech zone. He is in this way a sort of co-chronicler, which raises the suspicion that the novel itself may be a kind of decoy.
4 I owe this phrase to Caryl Emerson (conversation). On the temporality of chroniclers and on rumor as historical agent, see Emerson, *Boris Godunov: Transpositions of a Russian Theme.*
5 As Susanne Fusso suggested to me, the intimations that Darya is pregnant are neither confirmed nor dispelled.
6 At the end of "A Meeting," the lame man observes that even though Pyotr Stepanovich has asked whether others would inform, he "hasn't answered the question either; he has only asked it. The remark produced a striking effect" (P, 419).
7 In his later sketch "The Peasant Marey," which is also offered as both story and memoir, Dostoevsky observes that many people who have read *The House of the Dead* "supposed and are even now firmly convinced that I was sent to hard labor for the murder of my wife" (AWD, 2/76, 1.2).
8 Joseph Frank details the inconsistencies and argues that they represent a strategy for dealing with censorship. See Frank, *Dostoevsky: The Stir of Liberation, 1860–65*

(Princeton: Princeton University Press, 1986), 219. Robert Louis Jackson finds this explanation plausible but insufficient and points out that Dostoevsky retained the contradiction when he published *The House of the Dead* (originally serialized) in book form. See Jackson, "The Narrator in *House of the Dead*," *The Art of Dostoevsky: Deliriums and Nocturnes*, 33–69.

9   Dostoevsky first published his story "The Meek One" in *A Writer's Diary* and then republished it separately; the separate version omits an outer frame to the story included in the *Diary*. For an analysis of the difference this omission makes, see Charles Isenberg, *Telling Silence: Russian Frame Narratives of Renunciation* (Evanston: Northwestern University Press, 1993).

10 Michael Katz's fine new version of the novel—*Devils* (Oxford: Oxford University Press, 1992)—places the chapter "where the author originally intended it, rather than in an Appendix" ("Note on the Text," xiv). Some hint of doubling still remains because Katz does not renumber the chapters, and so "At Tikhon's" appears as an unnumbered chapter between chapters 8 and 9. But priorities are reversed: whereas the Modern Library edition encourages us to read the novel first as it was originally published and then read the missing chapter (along with several variants of it), Katz's version leads us to read the novel first with the Tikhon chapter and then mentally to subtract it.

After the Tikhon chapter was rejected, Dostoevsky evidently made changes in the later parts of this serialized novel to include some crucial information and motifs provided in the missing chapter (e.g., a key quotation from Revelation), and so no version can give us the work as Dostoevsky originally intended. There is something to be said for each editorial choice. On the whole, I prefer the Modern Library solution.

11 The Oxford press edition translates a version without this gap. Reading across several variants, one may have the strange experience of an absent absence.

12 *The House of the Dead* also creates gaps. The "editor" has selected only a few of Goryanchikov's chapters and omitted incidents apparently recorded in a state verging on insanity.

13 From chapter 58 ("Absence"). In *Character and the Novel*, W. J. Harvey cites these lines and comments (in my view, correctly), "We sense that our actual life, the line that we do in fact follow, is surrounded by a network of possible lives that we might have led. . . . A novel . . . can allow for . . . this sensed penumbra of unrealized possibilities, of all the what-might-have-beens of our lives. . . . Such speculation frequently becomes, as it does in real life, part of the substantial reality of the identity of any character. . . . he is what he is but he might have been otherwise" (146–47).

14 The same motif is used even more extensively in *Karamazov* to "explain" (that is, mystify) Ivan's return to the town: "Why Ivan Fyodorovich had come amongst us I remember asking myself at the time with a certain uneasiness. . . . It seemed strange on the face of it that a young man so learned, so proud, and apparently so cautious, should suddenly visit such an infamous house and a father who had ignored him all his life, hardly knew him, and would not under any circumstances have given him money. . . . It was only later that we learned that Ivan had come partly at the request of, and in the interests of, his elder brother Dmitri . . . Yet even when I did know of this special circumstance I still felt Ivan Fyodorovich to be an enigmatic figure, and thought his visit rather mysterious" (BK, 14–15). As with Stavrogin,

many reasons are provided for Ivan's return, but neither individually nor together are they sufficient. There perhaps is no reason, only possible reasons forming "an indistinct abstraction."

15 David M. Bethea points out that the idiom for "facing each other" (*drug protiv druga*), used twice in this passage, literally means "friend against friend." See Bethea, *The Shape of Apocalypse in Modern Russian Fiction* (Princeton: Princeton University Press, 1989), 80.

16 Joseph Frank, "A Reading of *The Idiot*," *Southern Review* 5 (1969): 313–14; as cited in Robert Hollander, "The Apocalyptic Framework of Dostoevsky's *The Idiot*," *Mosaic* 7 (1974): 123–39.

17 See especially Edward Wasiolek's "Notes on Part II of the Novel" in NI, 159–65 and his introduction to NI, 1–20. For an excellent study of these notebooks, see chapter 2 of Robin Feuer Miller, *Dostoevsky and "The Idiot": Author, Narrator, and Reader* (Cambridge: Harvard University Press, 1981).

18 Bethea, *The Shape of Apocalypse*, 81. Bethea cites Hollander, "The Apocalyptic Framework."

19 In part I, Ganya calls Myshkin an idiot twice, and on a third occasion he maintains that Myshkin is not an idiot.

20 *The Demons* (or simply *Demons*: Russian has no articles) is the literal title of the novel that Constance Garnett rather freely rendered as *The Possessed*.

21 BK, 6. I have retranslated this and other lines from *Karamazov* because Garnett tends to soften Dostoevsky's hypotheticals.

22 The same motif occurs with the fool-in-Christ Stinking Lizaveta, Smerdyakov's mother. Many people said she refused charity not out of holiness "but only from pride, but that is hardly credible. She could hardly speak, and only from time to time uttered an inarticulate grunt. How could she have been proud?" (BK, 116). But the very raising of this possibility suggests that pride might have played a role, and self-laceration from pride is, of course, a key motif of the novel. If not true of Lizaveta, then perhaps this surmise describes the "recessive gene," the hidden possibility, that afflicts her proud and resentful son.

23 The famous discussion of "double thoughts" occurs on 293–94. The theme reappears explicitly on 344 and implicitly on 401–02 and 498.

24 My thanks to Robert Fisher, who discussed this passage in his Northwestern University senior thesis. On Dostoevsky's acquaintance with this painting, see James L. Rice, *Dostoevsky and the Healing Art: An Essay in Literary and Medical History* (Ann Arbor: Ardis, 1985), 252–59.

25 Katerina Ivanovna also does not make up her mind whether to use her document against Dmitri until the very minute when she does so, and both possibilities have been present to her mind all along—as with Snegiryov. Note as well that the murder itself is sideshadowed for the reader by the gap in the text at the crucial moment: what happens there? Many things could have, and the reader long entertains multiple possibilities.

26 This device is in fact not uncommon in novels. As W. J. Harvey observes, sometimes one function of subordinate characters is "to embody unrealized potentialities in the protagonist, to create the penumbra of alternative histories" (*Character and the Novel*, 148). Dostoevsky uses the device with special obsessiveness and power.

27 The fallacy of assuming a wish is already an act, so that if one has an evil wish

one might as well act on it, underlies Smerdyakov's "jesuitical" reasoning in "The Controversy."

28 One might agree with Dostoevsky's analysis but still think that Kairova, if she was doubtless guilty of some crime, should not have been acquitted. And one might plausibly suggest that no legal system could operate if it required Dostoevskian psychological subtlety to arrive at judgment.

29 "Unique evolution" is rejected. See Kellert, *In the Wake of Chaos*.

30 In using these terms, I allude to Ilya Prigogine, *From Being to Becoming: Time and Complexity in the Physical Sciences* (San Francisco: W. H. Freeman, 1980), and Prigogine and Isabelle Stengers, *Order Out of Chaos: Man's New Dialogue with Nature* (Toronto: Bantam, 1984).

31 The motif of a *mundane other world* (as it might be called) belongs to Menippean satire, where it appears from Lucian and Julian the Apostate to the third book of *Gulliver's Travels*. For a commentary on its use in Rabelais, see Erich Auerbach, "The World in Pantagruel's Mouth," *Mimesis*, 262–84. On the devil's reasoning, see Katsenelinboigen, *Selected Topics in Indeterministic Systems*, 331–36.

32 Or consider *A Christmas Carol*, that other ever-popular story, versions of which are broadcast at Christmas time almost as often as *It's a Wonderful Life*. The Jimmy Stewart film shows what would have happened if the hero had not lived; in the Dickens story, Scrooge learns what will happen if he does not live differently. In both cases, there are two possible plots juxtaposed to and sideshadowing each other.

33 Paul Ricoeur calls attention to the argument that the very concept of historical causality entails the imagination of alternatives that might otherwise have taken place: "This kind of logic consists essentially of the constructing by our imagination of a different course of events, then of weighing the probable consequences of this unreal course of events, and, finally, in comparing these consequences with the real course of events." He cites Max Weber ("In order to penetrate the real causal interrelationships, *we construct unreal ones*") and Raymond Aron ("Every historian, to explain what did happen, asks himself what might have happened"). See Paul Ricoeur, *Time and Narrative*, trans. Kathleen McLaughlin and David Pellauer (Chicago: University of Chicago Press, 1984), 1:183. Aron also paraphrases Weber's point that it is necessary "to restore to events of the past the dimension of uncertainty or probability which characterizes events as we live them or as any man of action conceives them" and therefore one must "re-create imaginary evolutions." See Raymond Aron, *Main Currents in Sociological Thought*, trans. Richard Howard and Helen Weaver (New York: Basic, 1967), 2:199. In the terms of the present study, these thinkers advocate sideshadowing as a way of recapturing the presentness and openness of a past moment.

34 Thus whenever a charismatic figure of good or evil dies, one can be sure that rumors he lives "in hiding" will circulate. In the Middle Ages, the savior king who died would be rumored to be either in hiding or otherwise destined to return; and our tabloids are filled with stories about Hitler, JFK, and Elvis still alive. Their lives are so fascinating that there must be more of them.

35 In *The Boundaries of Genre*, I approached works of this sort from a different perspective and called many of them a type of "threshold art." "Faction" and TV docudramas may also be located in this middle realm. In a matter of weeks, docudramas often satisfy the hunger for more possibilities.

36 With respect to Old Russian literature, Victor Terras notes that "in some instances the dividing line [between apocryphal and canonical] was vague, and Russian churchmen would at times use the authority of apocryphal work in a theological debate. Furthermore the status of some works . . . changed over the centuries." Victor Terras, *A History of Russian Literature* (New Haven: Yale University Press, 1991), 21. Ivan Karamazov cites one such text, "The Journey of the Mother of God among the Torments," in introducing his Grand Inquisitor legend, which is itself offered as another story about Jesus.

37 Or consider the season of *Dallas* at the end of which a whole year of adventures turned out to be a dream, so that the next season could offer an alternative version of the same year.

38 Several completions may eventually be combined into one. In *The D. Case, or the Truth about the Mystery of Edwin Drood*, which includes the text of the novel and lists Dickens as a coauthor, several fictional detectives, from Sherlock Holmes to Dostoevsky's Porfiry Petrovich, survey earlier continuations and offer a panoply of solutions. These solutions pertain not only to the Drood story but also to the "mystery" of the "untimely" death that prevented Dickens from finishing the work. See *The D. Case: The Truth about the Mystery of Edwin Drood* by Charles Dickens, Carlo Fruterro, and Franco Lucentini, trans. Gregory Dowling (New York: Harcourt Brace, 1992).

39 For that matter, film versions of novels that alter the original plot may provide sideshadows—especially if the two versions are almost equally well known, are both classics of their medium, or are for other reasons both "authoritative." The same may be true of operas based on literary works. For the various transformations of the Boris Godunov story, see Caryl Emerson, *Boris Godunov*.

40 "In world literature," he concludes, "there probably are many works whose parodic nature has not even been suspected. . . . And yet we look at world literature from a tiny island limited in time and space" (DiN, 374).

41 Miguel de Cervantes Saavedra, *Don Quixote*, trans. Walter Starkie (New York: Macmillan, 1957), 953. Further references are to DQ.

42 Anthony Trollope, *The Last Chronicle of Barset*, ed. Peter Fairclough (Harmondsworth: Penguin, 1967), 861–62. Thus the title, too, takes on added power because it names not only a novel but also the end of a series. The mention of this (double) title in the work's last phrase achieves especially strong and effective closure.

43 Much later, Trollope responded to requests for another Barchester narrative by writing the rather slight story "The Two Heroines of Plumplington," which, though alluding to some familiar places, is only loosely connected with the original series.

44 Andrew Wachtel, "Resurrection à la Russe: Tolstoy's *The Living Corpse* as Cultural Paradigm," *PMLA* 107, no. 2 (March 1991): 272 n. 20. See also Donna Orwin, "The Riddle of Prince Nexljudov," *SEEJ*, 30, no. 4 (Winter 1986): 473–86. Orwin sees all the Nekhliudovs as one.

45 "Progress i opredelenie obrazovaniia. (Otvet G-nu Markovu. *Russkii vestnik 1862 g.*, No. 5)," Jub. 8:333.

46 The theme of "tiny, tiny alterations" is developed in Tolstoy, "Why Do Men Stupefy Themselves?" *Recollections and Essays*, trans. Aylmer Maude (1937; repr. London: Oxford University Press, 1961). I discuss the essay in Morson, "Prosaics: An Approach to the Humanities," *The American Scholar* (Autumn 1988): 515–28.

47 For a readable summary of this reasoning, see the first chapter of Gleick, *Chaos,* 9–31.

48 See Bernstein, *Bitter Carnival* and *Foregone Conclusions.* In part VIII of *Anna Karenina,* Levin rejects this kind of thinking, which his intellectual half-brother and the novel's eponymous heroine favor.

49 Aristotle, *Poetics,* trans. S. H. Butcher, as reprinted in Adams, ed., *Critical Theory since Plato,* 53.

50 Matthew Arnold, "Count Leo Tolstoy," in Arnold, *Essays in Criticism: Second Series* (London, 1888), 260.

51 Konstantin Leontiev, "The Novels of Count Leo Tolstoy: Analysis, Style, and Atmosphere—A Critical Study" (1890), in *Essays in Russian Literature, The Conservative View: Leontiev, Rozanov, Shestov,* ed. and trans. Spencer E. Roberts (Athens: Ohio University Press, 1968), 295–96.

52 Interpretations by early critics have a special value that is often overlooked. The knowledge that a work is a classic significantly alters the judgment of later critics: even a first reading comes to resemble a rereading. Especially valuable are reviews of serialized works that have not yet been completed. Then it is possible to see the effect that a part makes and to recover one's experience when the ending was still unknown.

53 P. V. Annenkov, "Istoricheskie i esteticheskie voprosy v romane gr. L. N. Tolstogo 'Voina i mir,'" in *L. N. Tolstoi v russkoi kritike: Sbornik statei,* 3d ed., ed. S. P. Bychkov (Moscow: Khudozh. lit., 1960), 246.

54 Henry James, Preface to *Roderick Hudson* in *The Art of the Novel,* ed. R. P. Blackmur (New York, 1934), 5. Francis Dunn discusses a number of similar comments in his study of how Euripides struggled to represent open time within the closural constraints of tragedy. See Dunn, *Tragedy's End: Gestures of Closure in Euripidean Drama* (Oxford: Oxford University Press, in press).

55 But not to the murder, in this case: teasing the reader with "vortical expectations," Dostoevsky suddenly sideshadows, and Dmitri refrains from murder. But we do not learn this until much later.

56 See Hollander, "The Apocalyptic Framework," and Bethea, *The Shape of Apocalypse* who have argued that the Apocalypse structures the novel as a whole.

57 This, the second epigraph to *The Possessed,* is drawn from Luke 8:32–37. The first epigraph, from Pushkin's "Demons," is discussed above.

58 "A terrible longing came upon him to leave everything here and go back to the place from which he had come. . . . He had a foreboding that if he remained here even a few days longer he would be drawn into this world irrevocably and that his life would be bound up with it for ever" (I, 291).

59 I have severely modified the Garnett version. The word *postepennyi* (gradual, step-by-step) appears three times in the original. Perhaps *postepennoe* is meant to echo the title word *prestuplenie* (crime), which results from the refusal to accept *gradual* change.

60 Elsewhere I argue that in *A Writer's Diary* Dostoevsky failed to reconcile the two temporalities. See Morson, "Dostoevsky's Great Experiment," the introductory study to *AWD.*

61 I cite some examples in Morson, *Hidden in Plain View,* 58–59.

62 George Steiner, *Tolstoy or Dostoevsky: An Essay in the Old Criticism* (New York: Knopf, 1959), 105.

63 As chapter 2 explains, foreshadowing requires not just two related events; all cau-
    sality, and pure accident, gives us that much. It requires backward causation, in
    which the earlier event is the consequence and so the preordained sign of the
    later event.
64 Smith, *Poetic Closure*, 36.

Chapter Five. Paralude: Presentness and Its Diseases

1 Occasionally, when the formula has been used so many times that it has grown impossibly stale, authors may create the shock value of having a detective lose a case,
   be defeated by Moriarity, or die (like Superman). But this twist is essentially para-
   sitic on the generically given expectation of success and cannot be repeated often or
   the whole nature of the encounters must change. We might expect a resurrection of
   the hero or a continuation in which the criminal is defeated (though not necessarily
   permanently), thus making the plot cover two stories, rather than one, as it initially
   seemed.
2 Analogously, forgers stamp their work with signs of pastness. Both are spurious
   and both are risky, though not for the same reason.
3 One Chicago Cubs fan I know can watch recordings only of games the Cubs won because otherwise the nostalgia effect would be missing. My thanks to Benjamin Brent.
4 Compare Bakhtin's argument with Paul Ricoeur's contention that even "eventless"
   histories, for example, those produced by the Annales school, necessarily involve
   a "virtual plot" (or "quasi-plot") with "quasi-events" and "quasi-characters." See
   Ricoeur, *Time and Narrative*, 1:206–25.
5 That would seem to be the effect of Pinter's play *Betrayal*. My thanks to Deborah
   Tannen for this example.
6 Hearing such a story, one has to marvel at the good fortune of publishers when
   it was possible to reject a Dostoevsky novel—correctly—because something better
   had come along. Actually, the situation was much more complex and less narrat-
   able than this well-known anecdote suggests. The story may have been significantly
   altered by hindsight, as William Mills Todd (who was kind enough to share his
   research with me) pointed out when reading the present study.
7 See Robert Louis Jackson, "The Problem of Type," *Dostoevsky's Quest for Form: A
   Study of His Philosophy of Art* (New Haven: Yale University Press, 1966), 92–123.
8 It involves what George Kline has called "the fallacy of the actual future." See
   George L. Kline, " 'Present', 'Past', and 'Future' as Categoreal Terms, and the
   'Fallacy of the Actual Future,' " *Review of Metaphysics* 40 (December 1986): 215–35.
9 On memory in Tolstoy, see Natasha Sankovitch, "Creating and Recovering Experience: Repetition in Tolstoy" (Ph.D. diss., Stanford University, 1992).
10 For an interesting new novel exploring diverse temporalities and some of their implications for how life is lived, see Alan Lightman, *Einstein's Dreams* (New York:
   Pantheon, 1993).
11 I paraphrase Bakhtin, but the geological comparison is my own.
12 On such features of Soviet culture, see Katerina Clark, *The Soviet Novel: History as
   Ritual*, 2d ed. (Chicago: University of Chicago Press, 1985); Boris Groys, *The Total
   Art of Stalinism: Avant-Garde, Aesthetic Dictatorship, and Beyond*, trans. Charles
   Rougle (Princeton: Princeton University Press, 1992); and Andrei Sinyavsky, *Soviet*

Civilization: A Cultural History, trans. Joanne Turnbull with Nikolai Formozov (New York: Arcade, 1990). Further references to *Soviet Civilization* are to SC.

13   Scholars, of course, have repeatedly tried to justify the epilogue, but their very need to keep doing so suggests that most readers agree with Philip Rahv, who calls the epilogue "implausible and out of key with the work as a whole." See Rahv, "Dostoevsky in *Crime and Punishment,*" in the Norton Critical edition of *Crime and Punishment,* ed. George Gibian (New York: Norton, 1964), 614.

14   Or perhaps, as John Kieselhorst suggested to me, we do not quite get the conversion, just the turning point that we are told will lead to it.

15   Commenting on this chapter of the present study, Robert Alter wrote, "I hesitantly propose for consideration still another variety of the 'dessicated present,' in which the present is radically subverted because it is inhabited by, imprisoned in, the past. Psychoanalytically, this is repetition compulsion. Literary examples that come to mind are Miss Havisham in *Great Expectations* and, above all, Faulkner."

16   On tragic anachronism, see Thomas M. Greene, "History and Anachronism," in *Literature and History: Theoretical Problems and Russian Case Studies,* ed. Gary Saul Morson (Stanford: Stanford University Press, 1986), 205–20. I have benefited from recent studies of Turgenev: Elizabeth Cheresh Allen, *Beyond Realism: Turgenev's Poetics of Secular Salvation* (Stanford: Stanford University Press, 1992); Jane Costlow, *Worlds within Worlds: The Novels of Ivan Turgenev* (Princeton: Princeton University Press, 1990); and David Lowe, *Turgenev's "Fathers and Sons"* (Ann Arbor: Ardis, 1983).

17   Bazarov's argumentative strategy has been repeated in artistic movements that claim to reject all Western art or philosophical schools rejecting all Western philosophy. This form of one-upsmanship, which offers itself as not just another move but the denial of the game itself, is nonetheless a move in the game. Its effectiveness usually depends on how familiar the intended audience is with this tactic. Turgenev evidently knew it well; and perhaps, in his honor, we might call it "the nihilist's move."

18   As Bernstein stresses in *Foregone Conclusions.*

19   George Eliot, *Middlemarch* (New York: Modern Library, 1984), 789.

20   Five Euripides plays end with these lines (or a slight variation on them): *Helen, Andromache, Bacchae, Alcestis,* and *Medea.* See Dunn, *Tragedy's End.*

21   FTOS, 36. See also the introductory essay by Isaiah Berlin; and Aileen Kelly, "Ideology and Utopia in Herzen and Dostoevsky: *From the Other Shore* and *Diary of a Writer,*" *The Russian Review* 50 (October 1991): 397–416; Kelly, "Herzen and Proudhon: Two Radical Ironists," *Common Knowledge* 1, no. 2 (Fall 1992): 36–62; and Kelly, "Revealing Bakhtin," *The New York Review of Books,* 9/24/92, 44–48.

22   *Signposts* (also known in English as *Landmarks*) was the most widely debated— and vilified—publication of its time. It went through five editions in about a year, and the fifth included an appendix listing over two hundred books and articles written in response. Of the many commentaries on the volume, see especially Leonard Schapiro "The *Vekhi* Group and the Mystique of Revolution," in *Russian Studies,* ed. Ellen Dahrendorf (New York: Viking, 1987), 68–92; Christopher Read, *Religion, Revolution, and the Russian Intelligentsia, 1900–1912: The "Vekhi" Debate and Its Intellectual Background* (London: Macmillan, 1979); and Morson, "Prosaic Bakhtin: *Landmarks,* Anti-Intelligentsialism, and the Russian Counter-Tradition," *Common Knowledge* 2, no. 1 (Spring 1993): 35–74.

302
Notes to Pages 200–28

23 Sergei Bulgakov, in *Signposts*, 37. Further references are to Signposts, contributor, page.

24 See SC and Joseph Brodsky, *Less than One: Selected Essays* (New York: Farrar Straus, 1986).

25 See Jacques Catteau, *Dostoevsky and the Process of Literary Creation*, trans. Audrey Littlewood (Cambridge: Cambridge University Press, 1989). See especially the section entitled "Solvency: the wager of the novel," 136–40.

26 Perhaps there are American examples. On a roughly comparable "presentist" mentality in colonial Virginia, see T. H. Breen, "Of Time and Nature: A Study of Persistent Values in Colonial Virginia," *Puritans and Adventurers: Change and Persistence in Early America* (New York, 1980), 164–96.

27 This line, Bakunin's most famous, occurs in "The Reaction in Germany," in *Bakunin on Anarchy: Selected Works by the Activist-Founder of World Anarchism*, ed. Sam Dolgoff (New York: Vintage, 1971), 55–57.

28 As cited in David L. Miller, *George Herbert Mead: Self, Language, and the World* (Chicago: University of Chicago Press, 1973), 179.

29 See George Herbert Mead, *The Philosophy of the Present*, ed. Arthur E. Murphy (La Salle, Illinois: Open Court, 1959). The volume was first published posthumously in 1932. In my paraphrase I rely also on the editor's introduction, especially pages xvi–xxi. See also the "Prefatory Remarks" by John Dewey, xxxvi–xl; and David L. Miller, *George Herbert Mead*, 172–87. In my discussion of what I call the plain man fallacy, I am indebted to a conversation with Michael Williams and to his book *Unnatural Doubts: Epistemological Realism and the Basis of Scepticism* (Cambridge, Mass.: Blackwell, 1991).

30 George Orwell, *1984* (New York: Signet, 1961), 32.

31 For an interesting analysis of time in *The Three Sisters*, see C. J. G. Turner, "Time in Chekhov's *Tri Sestry*," *Canadian Slavonic Papers* 28, no. 1: 64–79.

32 Note also that what would otherwise be the clumsy device of one character telling another what she must already know—that father was a general—here serves as an early signal of their concern that everything will be forgotten; and so even important and "unforgettable" facts must be repeated. But even lives of repetition fade.

33 *Jamais vu* is actually a rather common phenomenon, as can be attested by any scholar who has laboriously worked out an idea, felt the thrill of discovery, and then come upon old notes showing that he or she made the same discovery and experienced the same thrill once before.

34 This is one reason that arguments against freedom misfire when they do no more than demonstrate the existence of (social, physical, psychological, or other) constraints. Of course there are constraints, and freedom in fact demands them. Only if constraints leave *no* options is freedom impossible.

35 This passage is omitted in the Garnett translation, and so I take it from Richard Pevear and Larissa Volokhonsky, *Crime and Punishment* by Fyodor Dostoevsky (New York: Knopf, 1992), 70.

36 Here again I prefer the Pevear and Volokhonsky rendition, 79. Garnett gives agency to the axe, rather than to the blow (*udar*).

37 Though their formulations might bring Leibniz to mind, these thinkers differ from him. For Leibniz, God in principle might have chosen a different universe, but he did choose only this one.

38 Fred Alan Wolf, *Parallel Universes: The Search for Other Worlds* (New York: Simon

and Schuster, 1988); David Lewis, *On the Plurality of Worlds* (Oxford: Basil Black-well, 1986). See also Lightman, *Einstein's Dreams*, 18–22.

39 Jorge Luis Borges, *Labyrinths: Selected Stories and Other Writings*, ed. Donald A. Yates and James E. Irby (New York: New Directions, 1964), 20.

40 This concept both resembles and significantly differs from *past sideshadowing*, described in chapter 4. In past sideshadowing, there have been many possible routes to the present, but only one actual one. In Ts'ui Pen's model, there may have been many actual paths.

41 In *Parallel Universes*, Wolf explicitly cites and endorses Ts'ui Pen's model. He imagines time as a "wave of possibilities": "When the wave encounters a situation that is logically impossible in a single world . . . the wave does something analogous to the way an ocean wave behaves when it encounters two or more spaces between piers jutting out in the ocean space. The wave splits apart. One part goes running after one possibility and the other part follows other possibilities. Each part is a reality in a different world" (Wolf, 40). In this way, all possibilities are enacted, each in a different world, and the universe as a whole is "a universe of all possible universes" (Wolf, 60). As in Ts'ui Pen's model, times may converge as well as diverge. Wolf also imagines communication among different universes.

In Lewis's model, all possibilities are enacted in different universes, but these universes are completely sealed off from one another: "There are no spatiotemporal relations at all between things that belong to different worlds" (Lewis, 2). In Wolf's and Ts'ui Pen's models, time bifurcates whenever a choice is made, but in Lewis's there are two universes that are absolutely identical up to the moment of choice, after which the universes differ. We do not split, we have counterparts.

For Wolf, the idea of multiple universes solves problems in physics and promises communication among universes. Lewis offers his model (which he insists is both believable and a true description of the way things are) as a way of solving problems in modal logic. (Contrary-to-fact statements are to be understood as factual statements about existing other worlds; Lewis therefore calls his model "modal realism.") Remarkably enough, Lewis appeals to the simplicity and economy of his explanation as a reason for accepting it. As a nonphilosopher, I can only wonder about the weight that certain problems of the discipline have for its members. Occam's razor has here turned into Occam's vacuum cleaner. Instead of cutting away hypothetical entities, it sucks them up; one adds whole universes to save a favorite theory.

42 It would be possible to propose multiple universes that do not exhaust all possibilities, as in the time-loop plots discussed in chapter 2. Both exhaustiveness and multiplicity raise problems for exhaustive multiple-universe models.

43 Lewis claims to avoid any threat to ethics because in his model selves do not branch; rather, I do one thing and my counterpart in another world does the other. To be sure, "it will not matter to reality as a whole how you decide—there will in any case be many just like you who decide one way and many who decide the other—but it still matters to you" (Lewis, 125). For Lewis, morality pertains to what one can be *blamed* for, and one can be blamed only for the evils one causes, in this world. Otherworldly evil "is just as much an evil as this-worldly evil" (Lewis, 126) but nevertheless "they aren't your evils." Lewisian morality therefore becomes essentially tribal; one cares only for what happens to one's own people. Indeed, Lewis extends this point to this world: "Should I lie awake at night bemoaning the evils

of other worlds, and should I celebrate their joys? I see no reason why I should bemoan the evils and celebrate the joys even of remote parts of this world, which I believe in along with everyone else" (Lewis, 126–27).

Lewis's sense of morality seems extremely thin in its understanding of what actual moral choice involves, still thinner in its sense of how an ethical sensibility is formed (moral education), and positively diaphanous in its sense of a moral imagination. For one thing, it is hard to imagine someone developing much ethical sensitivity who limits his or her concern to what he or she can be personally blamed for. Ethical sensitivity is in large part a matter of educated perception, developed by extending concern for other people where there is no question of our being the cause of their suffering. Lewis's use of the word "bemoaning" for such concern is telling. I care for those who die under totalitarian regimes even though I cannot be blamed for their deaths, and I would wonder at someone who did not care. Care extends beyond culpability, and it is part of the process by which we learn to ascertain culpability. The main story of most realistic novels deals with characters' developing moral concern for others beyond the compass of blame; and readers, who identify with people not only remote but fictional, also develop ethical sensitivity in this way.

Much evil is the result of complex causes and less-than-obvious psychological reactions. Dostoevsky never tired of showing that we can correctly understand what we *can* be personally blamed for, and what we contribute to indirectly, only if we first practice moral concern for situations remote from ourselves and our actions.

For another thing, our sense of responsibility is developed in part by our identifying with those in positions similar to our own and asking what one would do in their position; and who is more like oneself than one's exact Lewisian counterpart in another world? If the actions of a person identical to oneself until ten minutes ago do not excite one's approval or regret, whose actions do? "There but for the grace of God go I"—a sentence that in this context acquires new meaning—would seem to be an important basis of sympathy, which is in turn an important basis of moral sensibility.

Finally, Lewis underestimates the effect of knowledge that evil is a zero-sum game on moral behavior, one source of which is the sense that one is lessening the *totality* of evil, not just evil happening right here. It will be recalled that for William James morality depends on a sense of the world being "vulnerable" to injury—a worse place in its entirety—if we should behave badly. Would someone contribute to alleviating hunger in America if he knew that success here would necessarily mean more hungry people in China? Would not the morality of such a contribution, if made, change or diminish? If everyone believed that nothing he or she did would make the totality of evil greater or less, would not human behavior likely be changed for the worse? Not just the desire to avoid blame but also some desire to lessen the totality of evil, wherever and to whomever it happens, would seem to be important to the cast of mind of a virtuous person. And for that, the universe or metauniverse must contain more possibilities than actualities.

Chapter Six. Backshadowing

1 Focusing on Jewish narratives about the Holocaust, Bernstein's *Foregone Conclusions* explores the complex moral as well as historiographical problems raised by backshadowing.

2 Ilya Ilf and Eugene Petrov, *The Little Golden Calf: A Satiric Novel*, trans. Charles Malamuth (New York: Ungar, 1966), 49–50.

3 Herbert Butterfield, *The Whig Interpretation of History* (1931; repr. New York: Norton, 1965), 32. Further references are to WIH.

4 In Russia, Julian the Apostate sometimes symbolized this stance, as he does in Herzen's *From the Other Shore*.

5 Stephen Jay Gould, *Wonderful Life: The Burgess Shale and the Nature of History* (New York: Norton, 1989), 290. Further references are to WL.

6 Gould cites this remarkable passage from Walcott: "In early times the Cephalopoda ruled, later on Crustacea came to the fore, then probably fishes took the lead, but were speedily outpowered by the Saurians. These Land and Sea Reptiles then prevailed until Mammalia appeared upon the scene, since when it doubtless became a struggle for supremacy until Man was created. Then came the age of Invention; at first of flint and bone implements, of bows and arrows and fish-hooks, then of spears and shields, swords and guns, lucifer matches, railways, electric telegraphs" (cited WL, 259). Gould observes that "the entire progressionist credo is rolled up into these few words" and notes (1) how biological and technological "progress" become part of the same process, and (2) inaccuracy: reptiles never replaced fishes, who still dominate the sea (WL, 259–60).

7 For the fascinating issues surrounding this idea, see Stephen Jay Gould, *The Panda's Thumb: More Reflections in Natural History* (New York: Norton, 1982), 47–58. Further references are to TPT.

8 Not in Leibniz's sense: for Leibniz, although other worlds were possible in the sense that they would have involved no contradiction, the nature of God ensured that he would choose to create the best possible world (ours).

9 The point would also be relevant to anthropology and human history insofar as they infer history from function.

10 Stephen Jay Gould, *Bully for Brontosaurus: Further Reflections in Natural History* (New York: Norton, 1991), 114. Further references are to BFB.

11 As cited in Reinhard Breuer, *The Anthropic Principle: Man as the Focal Point of Nature*, trans. Harry Newman and Mark Lowery (Boston: Birkhauser, 1991), 7. Further references are to AP.

12 Two important defenders of the anthropic principle explicitly cite the German idealists, including Hegel, as predecessors: see chapter 2 of John D. Barrow and Frank J. Tipler, *The Anthropic Cosmological Principle* (Oxford: Oxford University Press, 1988), 27–122.

13 There are still stronger versions, such as the "Final Anthropic Principle": *"Final Anthropic Principle (FAP): Intelligent information-processing must come into existence in the universe, and, once it comes into existence, it will never die out"* (Barrow and Tipler, 23). The idea is that otherwise it would make no sense for the universe to have produced intelligence in the first place. Thus there seems to be a sort of metaphysical guarantee of human survival—closely resembling our assurance that certain events

in novels could not happen because then the work would make no sense. Would someone who accepted such guarantees take the threat of nuclear catastrophe or similar threats to human survival less seriously than he might otherwise?

14 Barrow and Tipler trace the history of this debate in fascinating detail, 27–218.

15 Cited from a letter of James, BFB, 319–20. Tolstoy would go on to argue that even framing the argument in advance would not necessarily prove anything: that is the logic of his log-hauling example.

16 Ambrose Bierce, *The Devil's Dictionary* (Garden City, N.Y.: Doubleday, n.d.), 234.

17 Edward Bellamy, *Looking Backward, 2000–1887* (New York: Signet, 1960), 122.

18 William Morris, *News from Nowhere, or An Epoch of Rest, Being Some Chapters from a Utopian Romance* (New York: Longmans, 1910), 149. Further references are to Morris. Note that Morris can offer his work as a sort of fragment—"some chapters from a utopian romance"—because the harmonious world is complete in all its parts.

19 On the Allegory of the Cave as the masterplot of utopias, see chapter 3 of Morson, *The Boundaries of Genre*, 88–92.

20 Groys, *The Total Art of Stalinism*, 46–49. Sinyavsky makes a similar point in OSR.

21 P, 424. Of course, this line looks forward with uncanny accuracy to the Chinese Cultural Revolution, which perhaps went even further than its Soviet counterpart.

22 In effect, unanimous votes were an updating of the old religious argument for God "by the universal consent of mankind."

23 Eugene Zamyatin, *We*, trans. Gregory Zilboorg (New York: Dutton, 1952), 24.

24 Mikhail Bulgakov, *The Master and Margarita*, trans. Michael Glenny (New York: Signet, 1967), 10. Further references are to M&M.

25 Vasily Grossman, *Forever Flowing*, trans. Thomas P. Whitney (New York: Harper and Row, 1986), 27. Further references are to FF.

Chapter 7. Opinion and the World of Possibilities

1 I have discussed the irony of origins and the irony of outcomes in more detail elsewhere. See Morson, *Boundaries*, 77, 88, 118–20, 180; id., *Hidden in Plain View*, 17, 23–24, 115–19, 249, 276; and id., "Genre and Hero/*Fathers and Sons:* Inter-generic Dialogues, Generic Refugees, and the Hidden Prosaic," in *Literature, Culture, and Society in the Modern Age*, ed. Edward J. Brown, Lazar Fleishman, Gregory Freidin, and Richard Schupbach, *Stanford Slavic Studies* 4:1 (Stanford, 1991), 336–81.

2 Sir Isaiah Berlin, "The Pursuit of the Ideal," *The Crooked Timber of Humanity: Chapters in the History of Ideas*, ed. Henry Hardy (New York: Knopf, 1991), 1. Further references are to CTH. In stating that no nineteenth-century thinker foresaw totalitarian tyranny, has Berlin forgotten the author of *The Possessed*?

3 Isaiah Berlin, "The Decline of Utopian Ideas in the West," *Crooked Timber*, 20–21.

4 Isaiah Berlin, *The Hedgehog and the Fox: An Essay on Tolstoy's View of History* (New York: Simon and Schuster, 1970), 1–2. Further references are to H&F.

5 Robert Lerner, "Ecstatic Dissent," in *Speculum: A Journal of Medieval Studies* 67, no. 1 (January 1992): 51, 53. My description of these thinkers paraphrases Lerner.

6 One might say that a group constitutes an intelligentsia in the Russian sense to the extent that (1) its members identify first and foremost as members of that group, (2) it expects its members to subscribe to a code of beliefs, and (3) it adheres to a

belief in its own special role and in the temporal progressivism of insight. Of course, such criteria may be satisfied by right-wing as well as left-wing intelligentsias.

7 To be sure, not all professors were (or are) members of the intelligentsia and, of course, not all members of the intelligentsia were (or are) professors. But there is often a considerable overlap of the two.

Index

In this index, an "f" after a page number indicates a separate reference on the next page; an "ff" indicates separate references on the next two pages. A continuous discussion is indicated by two page numbers separated by a hyphen. *Passim* indicates a cluster of references in close but not consecutive sequence.

This index uses the abbreviations on pages xiii–xiv. In addition, the following abbreviations are used: B = Bakhtin, D = Dostoevsky, T = Tolstoy, sh = shadowing (foresh = foreshadowing), and t = time.

Absent absence, 295
Absolute freedom, 222
Absolute past, 189
Accident, 71, 118, 243, 254, 300. *See also* Chance
Accidentals, 288
Accomplished future, 50–52, 57–61
Action and agency, 22–26 *passim*, 142–45, 147, 156–58, 186, 214–21, 224–27; and chronotope, 106; and contingency, 156–58; and creative process, 23, 25f, 285; and determinism or fatalism, 86, 230; and eventness, 21–22; "historic" and unhistoric, 185–86, 198; as instantiation, 21, 49; mechanical, 224–27 *passim*; and mutable past, 208; and nonaction, 193, 214–21; pre- (or re-) enacted, 225; and processual intentionality, 142–45; as rehearsal, 224–27; scripted, 263–64; and vortex t, 164; and wishes, 142, 296–97
Actuality, 10, 83–84, 96, 189, 223; privilege of, 157; vs. real, 83. *See also* Possibilities
Adventure, 34, 150; stories, 19, 109, 120; t vs. sports t, 174
Adventure novel of everyday life, 107–8
Aeneid (Virgil), 3, 64–65, 66, 123
Aesthetic: judgment in utopia, 256; necessity, 90, 160; politics, 258–60; potentiality, 158–62
Ahistoricity, 87–88, 113
Alertness, 157
Alibi: for attentiveness, 227; for t, 189
Alice in Wonderland (Carroll), 289–90
"All happy families are alike," 72
"All is permitted," 141, 275

Allegory of generations, 128, 193–97, 275
Allegory of the Cave, 257, 306
Allen, Elizabeth Cheresh, 301
Alpha and omega, 18, 54
Already written artifact, 79, 174; and aperture, 171; and Borges, 229–30; and "lateness" of author, 102; life feeling like, 69; narrative as, 36–38, 43–45, 49f; and omens or fate, 61, 63; and polyphony, 113; and presumed significance, 159–60; and reader's t, 103; and suspense, 45
Alter, Robert, 301
Amadis of Gaul, 152
"Ambushing" a character, 99
Anachronism, 1, 6, 109, 170, 185, 211, 242; tragedy of, 194–95
Anatopism, 109
Anisotropy. *See* Isotropic/anisotropic
Anna Karenina (T), 55–56, 71–81, 88, 108f, 299; Anna's, 72f; Annie in, 73, 75; aperture in, 169, 171; and contingency, 6, 78, 160; critics and (re)readers of, 77, 80–81, 171, 179, 191; and epilogue t, 191f; and essential surplus, 77–78; and foresh, 71–81; image of book in, 79; and loose ends, 77–79; and *Oedipus*, 76; omens and prophetic dreams in, 10, 75–77; opening sentence of, 72; and passion, 71–73; peasant in, 75, 77f; prefigural reading in, 55–56; and prosaics, 73f; public and private t in, 101; and RY, 179–80; reactionary landowner in, 268–69, 279; serialization of, 103; structure and identification in, 10, 76, 80

Anna Karenina (Garbo film), 71–72, 73
Anna Karenina (other), 154
Annales school, 300
Annenkov, Pavel, 161
Anniversary, 215
Annunciation, 54, 118
Anthill, 29
Anthropic Cosmological Principle, The (Barrow and Tipler), 287, 305–6
Anthropic principle, 251–55; final, 305–6
Anthropic Principle, The (Breuer), 252, 254
Anthropology, 305
Anti-utopia(nism), 14, 256; D's, 30–33; and dystopia, 33, 261; and novels, 109; and opinion, 267–73. *See also* Utopia(n)
Anticipatory backshadowing, 256, 279
Anticlosure, 12, 171–72, 284
Antigenres, 152
Aperture, 12, 169–72
Apocalypse, 56, 198, 299; and apocalyptic t, 255; and certainty, 222; and external vantage point, 18, 51; and vortex t, 166
Apocrypha, 149, 298
Apocryphal: adventures, 150; continuations, 151
"Apropos of the Exhibition" (D), 181–82, 183–87 *passim*
Apuleius, Lucius, 107–8
Archilochus, 271
Archimedean thinking, 40
Aristotle, 271, 278, 287; and endings, 37–38; on t, 35–36, 70; *On Interpretation*, 35–36; *Physics*, 35; *Poetics*, 158, 284
Arnold of Villanova, 274
Arnold, Matthew, 9, 159
Aron, Raymond, 297
Arrow of t, 18, 194
Art and/vs. life, 8, 44–47, 50f, 69, 82, 174–75; in AK, 77–79; and (an)isomorphism, 20, 38–39; and aperture, 169–72; in B, 82, 88–90; and closure or structure, 8, 20, 38, 78; and coincidences, 160; and contingency, 158–60; and external vantage point, 18–19, 20; and foresh, 45–47, 50, 63; and irrelevancies, 19–20; and omens, 61, 63; and polyphony, 91–92; and presumed significance, 159–60; and society as artwork, 256, 259–60
Art of the Novel, The (James), 299
Arthritic knee, 62

Arthropods, 245f, 248
Artifice, 7f, 82; and essential surplus, 78; of eternity, 40; and foresh, 45, 50, 58, 61; and presumed significance, 159–60; and structure or closure, 38, 162
Astronomy, 3, 278
Asymmetries in Time (Horwich), 46–47, 287
Asymmetry. *See* Symmetry/asymmetry
Attention, 77, 79, 157, 224, 227
Auerbach, Erich, 58, 284, 288, 297
Augury, 61, 69
Augustine, 274; *Confessions*, 45, 47, 50, 70
Austen, Jane, 42; *Emma*, 162
Autobiography, 188
Avant-garde, 81
Avian philosophers, 221
Avoidance of fate, 70

Back to the Future (films), 70
Backshadowing, 13–14, 211, 234–64, 270, 277, 305–6; anticipatory, 256, 279; avoiding, 280–82; Bernstein on, 305; and bipolarity, 234, 237, 240; and contingency, 242–43; defined, 234–35; and ethics, 284, 305; and evolution, 245–55; fallacies and problems of, 13, 234–35, 238–40; and foresh, 234f, 238, 242; and history, 14, 235, 236–37, 240, 241–43, 277; and *Looking Backward*, 255–57; and other judgments of past, 235; premises of, 235–38; and the progressive, 244–45; and sidesh, 211, 235, 237, 270, 277; and Soviet Union, 257–64; tropes of, 236, 239; unwitting, 238, 244; and utopia, 14, 255–64; and Whiggism, 241–43
Backward causation, 7, 10, 47–50, 61–63, 300
Backward-looking, 241, 244
Bakhtin, Mikhail: work as response to Russian novel, 5; Soviet context of, 82, 96, 112–13, 190
—three solutions to representing t and freedom, 10–11, 82, 88; stage 1, 88–90; stage 2, 91–101; stage 3, 105–13
—problems with and extensions of: exaggerates, 93, 111, 113, 291; mistaken, 163; overlooks *Clarissa*, 293; overlooks sidesh, 11, 113; ideas modified or extended, 93, 100–105, 111
—topics: creative process, 11, 21–27, 294; death, 38; dialogue with other times, 211–12; dreams and fantasies,

89; ethics or responsibility, 11, 21–22, 86, 294; Galilean chronotope consciousness, 245; God and theology, 10–11, 82, 86, 95–97; historical novel, 110–11; indeterminism, 10–11, 82, 86–113; Job, 96; pluralism, 268, 270, 272–73; presentism, 278; prosaics, 11, 294; utopian t, 198
—and other thinkers: Einstein, 95; Freud and Freudianism, 89, 108–9; William James, 10f, 82, 84, 86–87, 97; Lotman, 285; Ricoeur, 300; Vygotsky, 27, 285
—terms and concepts: ambushing, 99; characterological traits, 94; chronotope, 3–4, 105–13, 245, 250; creative understanding, 3, 211; dialogue, 93–100 passim, 273, 280; embodiment, 89, 285; emotional-volitional, 177; enter into, 89; essential surplus, 43–45, 47, 50, 77–81, 88f, 97, 287; eventness, 11, 21–24, 27, 31, 34–35, 90; external or internal open-endedness, 162; finalization, 38, 89; forges the new, 97; given vs. created, 23–24; hopelessness, 90; indefinitely prolonged present, 198; information-bearing surplus, 97–98; inner speech, 27, 285; intensified present, 11, 105–6; knots in t, 108; lateness of author, 88–90, 102f, 293; located in, 89; loophole, 90, 99, 113, 190; material, 23; mean directly, 94; modernization and distortion, 111; monologism, 87, 270, 272; naivete, 107, 281; noncoincidence, 92–93, 112–13; nothing conclusive, 93, 282; on the same plane, 97; one of many possible plots or realities, 112–13; outsideness, 38, 89, 94; polyphony, 11, 41, 91–101, 113, 291; potential hero, 177; ready-made, 23–24, 112; real historical t, 107–10; real present of creative process, 100; requiem, 90; rhythm, 90, 99; scaffolding, 24; at second hand, 93; singular singularity, 22; soul vs. spirit, 90f; speech zone, 294; story-line weight, 90; surprisingness, 22; surplus of humanness, 112–13; surroundings vs. field of vision, 89; theoretism, 21, 285; transcription, 21–22, 87, 284; triumph over time, 106; ultimate semantic authority, 94f; unfinalized, 89; unfinalizability, 90, 92f, 97, 108, 110; unnecessary continuation, 198; unrecognized parody, 152;

unrepeatability, 22f; valorized temporal category, 189; voice-ideas, 98; whirlwind motion, 106; world-in-the-making, 110; yet-to-come world, 89; zone of familiar contact, 190
—works: A&A (and AiG), 38, 285; BSHR, 87–88, 284; DiN, 298; EaN, 110–12, 189–90; FTC, 4–5, 105–10, 198, 284; KFP, 21–22, 177, 285, 291; PDP, 91–101, 110, 112–13; 162–63, 272–73, 282; PDP, editions of, 96, 98; PT, 23–24; TRDB, 38, 91, 96–97
Bakunin, Michael, 88, 205, 302
Balzac, Honoré de, 57, 107, 153, 221f; *Eugénie Grandet*, 88
Barchester series (Trollope), 12, 154, 298
Barchester Towers (Trollope), 170
Barometers, 62–63, 71
Barrow, John and Frank Tipler, 287, 305–6
Barthes, Roland, 100
Battle games, 148
Beer, Gillian, 102
Behaviorism, 21
Belinsky, Vissarion, 99
Belknap, Robert, 283, 291
Bellamy, Edward, 152, 255–57
Berlin, Isaiah, 14; *Crooked Timber*, 267, 269–70, 272–73, 306; *Hedgehog and Fox*, 271; introduction to Herzen, 301
Bernstein, Michael André, xi–xii; coins backsh, 13; and sidesh, 6, 283; *Bitter Carnival*, 291, 299; *Foregone Conclusions*, 118, 283f, 291, 294, 299, 301, 305
"Berrian," 256
Betting, 96
Bias of the artifact (and narrative predispositions), 8, 33, 40–41, 60–61
Bible: Hebrew, 55, 96; progressive insight into, 274, 278; corrected by T, 55. *See also specific books of Bible*
Bierce, Ambrose, 254
"Bildungsroman and Its Significance" (B), 87–88, 284
Biography, 106, 110; discontinuous, 154–55; and happiness, 188; t of, 2
Bipolarity 183, 185, 187; and backsh, 234, 237, 240; T on, 240
Birds, 59ff
Blame, 2, 74–75, 303–4
Body plans, 246, 248
Boileau-Despréaux, Nicolas, 25
Book, image of, 79
Borges, Jorge Luis, 13, 228–32, 233, 303

Boris Godunov (Emerson), 284, 290–91, 294, 298
Bradbury, Ray, 256
Brain fever, 167
Brassicic principle, 254
Brave New World (Huxley), 33, 261
Breen, T. H., 302
Brent, Benjamin, 300
Briggs, Derek, 246
Brik, Osip, 25, 285
Brodsky, Joseph, 201
Brothers Karamazov, The (D), 93, 99, 128, 138f, 286, 290f, 298; doubles in, 140–41, 146; epigraph to, 168; and irony of origins, 268; metaliterature in, 52; mysterious return in, 295–96; paternity question in, 128–29; pestle scene, 144–45; responsibility in, 139–42; returning the ticket, 85; sidesh in, 137–42, 144–47, 296, 299; and vortex t, 164, 167f, 299; wishes in, 141–42, 296–97
—chapters of: devil, 31–32, 52, 140–41, 146–47, 297; Grand Inquisitor, 91, 261, 298; "Not You!" 142
Bruno, Giordano, 49, 287
Buckle, Henry, 40, 155
Bulgakov, Mikhail, 14, 260, 262–63
Bulgakov, Sergei, 66
Burden of proof, 209, 278
Burdino, 184
Burgess shale, 245–48
Buster the Lungfish, 247–48
Butterfield, Herbert, 249; *Whig Interpretation*, 241–43, 244
Butterfly effect, 157, 263
By-products, 2, 248, 251, 272

Cabbage principle, 254
Calinescu, Matei, 289
Calvinism, 3, 63–64
Can You Forgive Her? (Trollope), 288
Canaries in mines, 62
Capitalism as left-wing, 244
Care, 304
Carnal Church, 274
Carroll, Lewis: *Alice*, 289–90; *Sylvie and Bruno*, 290
Cartography of space and t, 17–18
Cascade of crises, 163
Catastrophe, 12, 134, 198; in evolution, 247–48; and vortex t, 12, 163f, 168
Catastrophism, 189, 212
Catteau, Jacques, 202, 302
Cause and causality, 21–22, 66, 285–87,

289; backward, 7, 10, 47–50, 61–63, 300; and barometer, 62–63, 71; of cause of cause, 155; and constraints, 69–71; and contingency, 155; and fate or destiny, 64, 68, 74; and foresh, 47–50, 300; and hypertime, 290; insufficient for determinism, 84; in *Master and Margarita*, 262–63; of omens, 61–63, 75–77; and past sidesh, 133; vs. signs, 51, 60, 161; straight lines of, 119, 183, 185; T on, 161, 185, 239–40; unnoticed, 62f; and V-diagram, 46–47; and vortex t, 163, 166. *See also* Bipolarity; Compatibilism; Determinism and indeterminism; Fate and fatalism; Sideshadowing
Certainty, 165; craving for, 261; and external vantage point, 39; in *Forever Flowing*, 263–64; Grand Inquisitor on, 261; and hypothetical t, 221–22; and later = better, 278–79; and *Master and Margarita*, 262–63; in Soviet Union, 257–64; and utopia, 1, 31f, 39–40, 255–57
Cervantes Saavedra, Miguel de, 12, 20, 152–53
Chance, 108, 160; and art vs. life, 78; and contingency, 155; and determinism or indeterminism, 64, 85; and evolution, 245; and field of possibilities, 119; and God, 95; "hundred million," 156; and law, 84, 155; and perfect crime, 225f; perhaps fated, 226; and providence, 168
Change, 255, 299; in different genres, 107–10; in epilogue t, 279; in fields of possibility, 156; and irrevocability, 207, 212–14; nonadaptive, 250; of the past, 206–14; sudden, 2f, 203–6; in temporality in utopia, 256–57
Chaos, 84, 290, 299; theory, 290, 297
Character, personality, and self, 2, 5; historicity of, 11, 19; and multiple t, 232; noncoincidence of, 112–13; and other possible lives, 295; and pure potential t, 223; responsibility for, 294; and surplus of humanness, 112–13; in various genres, 107–10
"Characterological traits" (B), 94
Characters: and foreshadowing, 63; in socialist realism, 58; and structure, 59–61; vs. real people, 51
—and author, 10–11, 50, 90–98 *passim*, 106, 112; and ambushing, 99; and creative process, 80, 100–105, 291; and

dreams or fantasies, 89; and essential surplus, 43–45, 287; and foresh, 47–48, 50; and identification or sympathy, 76, 80; and lateness of author, 88–90, 102f, 293; in life beyond text, 92; and man and God, 82, 88, 95–97; and multiple plotting, 287–88; in *Oedipus*, 59–61, 76; and polyphony, 91–101, 291; simultaneity of, 100–105 —and reader, 90, 292f; argue, 91–92, 94; and epic, 190; and foresh, 63, 117; and freedom, 89–90; of *Oedipus*, 59–61, 289; and outsideness, 89; and polyphony, 91–92; and serialization, 292–93; times of, 100–105

Checked impulse, 120–22, 133

Chekhov, Anton, 39, 57, 273, 275, 302; and hypothetical t, 214–22; "The Bet," 228; *The Cherry Orchard*, 192–93; *The Three Sisters*, 13, 214–22, 302; *Uncle Vanya*, 18–19

Chekhovian people, 198

Chernyshevsky, Nikolai, 56–57; *What Is to Be Done?*, 40, 56, 151–52

Cherry Orchard, The (Chekhov), 192–93

Chinese cultural revolution, 306

Choice, 10, 18, 34, 64, 69, 145; in AK, 71, 75f; and compatibilism, 285–86; critical vs. prosaic, 22, 157–58; and (in)determinism, 85, 87; and epilogue t, 181; and eternal recurrence, 51–52, 288; and eventness, 21–22; and fatalism, 68, 71, 75f; and field of possibilities, 119, 145; and isomorphism, 60; and known future, 51f; as momentous, 22; and multiple t, 189, 227–33 *passim*, 303–4; and novels, 42; and *Oedipus*, 59f; and opinion, 281; and plot, 106–7; and presentness, 191; and process, 9, 28; and providence, 168; and sidesh, 140, 281; while uttering, 27; in various chronotopes, 107–9. *See also* Determinism and indeterminism; Fate and fatalism

Christmas Carol, A (Dickens), 297

Christmas stories, 297

"Chronic": delusion, 178; diseases (*see* Diseases of presentness); skepticism, 110

Chronicler: of BK, 138; and C&P, 294; of P, 120–24, 130–31, 134, 294; of P, and co-chronicler, 294; of P, and rumor, 123–26, 294; of Tikhon chapter, 130–31

Chronocentrism: avoiding, 280–82; and

backsh, 13, 237; identified, 235–36; of intelligentsia, 14, 278–79; and narrative sentences, 288. *See also* Temporal egotism

Chronotope, 3–4, 106, 250; Galilean consciousness of, 245; of historical novel, 110–11; of novel, 108–10; and polyphony, 113; of various genres, 107–10; wisdom of, 105–7

Cicero's tongue, 260

Clarissa (Richardson), 293

Classic, status of a, 299

Classification of organisms, 246–47

Closure, 7f, 12, 26, 41; and anticlosure, 12, 171–72, 284; and AK, 10, 79; and aperture, 12, 169–72; and art vs. life, 20, 38, 78; and detective fiction, 228; and D, 40–41, 162–63, 169; and George Eliot, 162, 197; and epilogue t, 191, 197; and essential surplus, 43–45; in Euripides, 299; and external vantage point, 18–19, 20; and foresh, 7, 117; and freedom, 43–44; life after, 153–54; and novel, 43–44, 169; and novel series, 153–54, 298; and polyphony, 100, 162–63; relative, 170; and temporal contradiction, 58; and vortex t, 162–63, 169

Clouds of story, 124

Cobb, John, and David Griffin, 291

Co-chronicler, 294

Coincidence, 160, 163–64, 231

Columbus, Christopher, 25, 28, 221f

Communal apartment, 201

Communism, 255; and backsh, 257–63 *passim*; and commemoration, 214; and end of history, 50, 53; fall of, 1, 201; and revolutionism, 204; now right-wing, 244

Compatibilism 4, 82–83, 285–86

Compatibility of truths, 269–73

Completions of novels, 298

Compromise: in evolution, 250, 283; and opinion, 269, 273

Compulsion: vs. determinism 285–86; to repeat and to surprise, 286

Conduct, 86

Cone of increasing diversity, 246–47

Confessions (Augustine), 45, 47, 50, 70

Consciousness of necessity, 24

Conservatives, 244–45

Conspiracy and its logic, 132, 148, 257

Constraints: and freedom, 223, 302; of history, 250

Contemplation (Kramskoy), 139–40

Contingency, 2f, 18, 26, 29, 71, 273; and art vs. life, 158–60; defined, 155, 158; dramatability of and difficulty of narrating, 76, 160; and evolution, 245–49 *passim*, 253f; and field of possibilities, 119, 156; and foresh, 187; and the "historic," 186; as illusion, 8; in multiple t, 232; and narcissism and paranoia, 78; and novels, 109, 197; and opinion, 261–64, 267–68, 273; and prediction, 197; and prosaics, 187; vs. providence, 164, 168–69; and sidesh, 6, 41, 267, 273; and sports t, 173–74; and structure or closure, 43, 158, 159–60; and suspense, 174; thought or transformed away, 157, 246; and T, 6, 155–62; and utopia, 261–64, 272; and Whiggism, 242–43
Continuations of works, 151–55
Continuous present, 293
Contrary-to-fact conditions (or counterfactuals), 118f, 228, 295, 303; in Chekhov, 214, 217–18, 222
Converging times, 231
Copernicus or "Copernican," 94, 118, 221, 233, 251–52, 260
Cosby Show, The, 175
Cossacks, The (T), 170
Costlow, Jane, 301
"Count no man's life happy . . ." 45
Craft, 25
Craving for certainty, 261
Creation, the, 297
Creative process, 23–27, 30, 98–105, 211; and agency, 285; and already written artifact, 103; and aperture, 171; criteria for, 285; vs. discovery, 9, 21, 24f; D's, 97, 105; and eventness, 23f, 98; and intentions, 80; and literary history, 24f; and novel, 42; and polyphony, 11, 98–100, 291; as "production," 23, 25; and the "ready-made," 23–24; "real present" of, 100; and suspense, 104–5; t of, 100–105
—theorists of: classical, 25–27, 98; Formalists, 24–26, 98, 285; Freud, 98; Poe, 98; romantic, 25, 26–27, 98; Shelley, 98
Crime and Punishment (D), 91, 93, 170, 204, 275, 290, 298; doubles in, 140; epilogue to, 163, 168, 191–92, 193, 299, 301; and future recollections, 294; and hypothetical or rehearsal t, 224–27; Raskolnikov's past in, 106;

and vortex t, 164, 167–68; writing of, 202
Crises and critical moments, 148, 157–58, 161, 163–65, 185; t of, 108, 110
Crooked Timber of Humanity, The (Berlin), 267, 269–70, 272–73, 306
"Cross section of a single moment," 105
Culler, Jonathan, 289
Cursor, 46
Cyberiad (Lem), 228
Cycle: of generations, 195; t as, 18f, 52, 194

D. Case, The (Fruterro et al.), 298
Dante Alighieri, 271
Danto, Arthur, 53–54, 288
Darwin, Charles, and Darwinism, 245–52 *passim*
Dating and outdating, 1, 110, 175, 255
David Copperfield (Dickens), 133
De Rougement, Denis, 72–73
Death, 79, 162, 229, 264; of the author, 23; B on, 38; by inertia, 219–20; instinct, 286; and love, 72; seal of, 62–63; and vortex t, 165
Debates as sports events, 176
Decisions. *See* Intentions and decisions
Declaration of Independence, 208
Decoy, 294
Defamiliarization, 277
"Defense of Poetry" (Shelley), 26–27
Déjà vécu, 69
Democracy and opinion, 262
"Demons" (Pushkin), 137, 299
De-novelization, 109
Descartes, René, 219
Desiccated present: defined, 188; and hypothetical t, 214; rhetoric of, 214
—kinds of: epic t, 189–90, 198; epilogue t, 12–13, 190–98, 214; repetition t (Alter), 301; utopian t, 198–201, 214
—and specific works or authors: AK, 191f; Brodsky, 201; C&P, 191–92, 193; *Cherry Orchard*, 192–93; *Fathers and Sons*, 193–97; S. Frank, 200–201; *From the Other Shore*, 199–200; Mayakovsky, 198, 201; *Middlemarch*, 197–98; *Signposts*, 200–201; Sinyavsky, 201; W&P epilogue, 197
Destiny, 73, 76; eluctable, 69–71; and foresh, 63–66; national, 51. *See also* Fate and fatalism
Destruction, 29, 33, 205

Detective fiction, 59, 141, 228, 298, 300; and sports t, 174; and suspense, 66

Determinism and indeterminism, 2ff, 33, 41, 49, 107, 155; and B, 82–113, 285; in BK, 147; and chance, 64, 85; and compatibilism, 82–83, 285–86; and fate or destiny, 63–67; and foresh, 49, 63–66; and ignorance, 6, 80; and isomorphism, 39; and James, 10, 82–86; and Lessing's curse, 8; multiple t, 13, 227, 232–33; and mutable past, 207, 211–12; no proof of, 4, 84; and NFU, 28–30, 34–37; and novels, 43–44, 162; and polyphony, 91–101; psychological vs. logical consequences of, 3f, 10, 66–67; resisting, 65, 286; senses of, 287; and temporal God, 95–97; and understanding = forgiveness, 80

"Development itself," 171

Devil's Dictionary, The (Bierce), 254

Dewey, John, 302

Dialogue, 93–100 *passim*, 190, 218; of character and author, 94; in D's creative process, 98–100; of Job and God, 96; and opinion, 271, 273, 280–82; with other times and cultures, 14, 211–12, 280–82; vs. relativism, 273; of sideshadows, 152–53

Dick Tracy, 150, 174

Dickens, Charles, 160, 257, 298; *A Christmas Carol*, 297; *David Copperfield*, 173; *Great Expectations*, 150, 159f, 301; *Edwin Drood*, 150, 298

Diderot, Madame, 54

"Dilemma of Determinism, The" (James), 4, 10, 82–87, 97, 168–69, 245, 284, 290, 304; on God, 95–96

"Discourse in the Novel" (B), 298

Diseases of presentness, 12–13, 188–233, 301, 303–4

—broad types: #1, desiccated present, 12–13, 188, 189–201; #2, isolated present, 13, 189, 201–14; #3, hypothetical t, 13, 189, 214–27; multiple t, 13, 189, 227–33, 303–4

—specific diseases: dream t, 214–22; epic t, 189–90, 198; epileptic t, 13, 166, 201–2, 205; epilogue t, 12–13, 190–98, 214; gambling t, 201–6; mutable past, 206–14; pure potential t, 222–23; rehearsal t, 224–27; repetition t (Alter), 301; revolutionism t, 203–6; utopian t, 198–201

—and specific works or authors: AK, 191f; Borges, 228–32, 233, 303; Brodsky, 201; C&P, 191–92, 193, 204, 224–27; *Cherry Orchard*, 192–93; *Fathers and Sons*, 193–97; S. Frank, 200–201, 204–5; *From the Other Shore*, 199–200; G, 203–4, *Gulag Archipelago*, 212; I, 201–2, 205; Lewis, 228, 232, 303–4; Mayakovsky, 198, 201; Mead, 206–14; *Middlemarch*, 197–98; *1984*, 206, 213; NFU, 223; P, 205–6; *Signposts*, 200–201, 204–5; Sinyavsky, 201; *Three Sisters*, 214–22; Wolf, 227f, 233, 303

"Do nothing" paradox, 223

Dobrolyubov, Nikolai, 56, 219

Doctors' plot, 263–64

Docudramas, 297

Documents and mutable past, 208, 213

Don Quixote (Cervantes), 12, 20, 152–53

Dostoevskian consolations, 20

Dostoevsky, Fyodor, 5–12 *passim*, 42, 80f, 133f, 209, 304; creative process of, 97, 98–100; and doubles, 140–41; and false confessions, 131; and Freud, 139, 145, 286; as gambler or epileptic, 201, 202–3, 302; on genre painting and representing past's presentness, 181–82, 183–87 *passim*; and intensified present, 11, 105–6, 205; and Lessing's curse, 8; and noncoincidence, 92–93; and polyphony, 11, 91–101; and process vs. product, 27–37, 40–41; and processual intentions, 142–45; and sidesh, 12, 120–48, 157–58, 161, 294–99 *passim*; and simultaneity, 100, 103–5; and socialist realism, 58; on types in transition, 179; uses chroniclers, 120–23, 294; uses hypotheticals, 138, 140, 296; and vortex t, 12, 162–69, 299

—critics and readers of, 91–92, 104, 131, 135f, 202; Belknap, 291, Bethea, 296; Catteau, 202, 302; J. Frank, 294–95, 296; Hollander, 296; Jackson, 287, 295; Katsenelinboigen, 286, 297; Katz, 295; Lunacharsky, 97; Miller, 296; Morson, 293, 299; Rahv, 301; Rice, 296; Wasiolek, 296

Dostoevsky, works

—AWD, 104–5, 179, 299, 301; "Apropos of the Exhibition," 181–82, 183–87 *passim*; "Dream of a Ridiculous Man," 144, 228; Kairova case, 142–45, 297;

Dostoevsky, works (cont'd)
Kornilova case, 105; "Meek One,"
295; "Peasant Marey," 294; spiritualism sketch, 32–33
—BK, 85, 93, 99, 113, 268, 286, 290f,
295–99 passim; devil chapter, 31–32,
52, 140–41, 146–47, 297; Grand Inquisitor chapter, 91, 261, 298; sidesh
in, 137–42, 244–47, 296, 299; vortex t,
164, 167f, 299
—C&P, 91, 93, 170, 204, 275, 290, 298;
doubles in, 140; epilogue to, 163, 168,
191–92, 193, 299, 301; and future recollections, 294; and hypothetical t,
224–27; Raskolnikov's past in, 106;
and vortex t, 164, 167–68; writing of,
202
—I, 13, 91, 93, 117, 290f; apocalypse
in, 299; D's views in, 98; and double
thoughts, 139, 296; and epileptic t, 13,
201–2; and life as process, 28; notebooks to, 132, 136–37; pseudo-foresh
in, 135–37; and vortex t, 163–67
—NFU, 23, 151, 139, 172; and determinism, 28–30, 64f, 285–86; double
determination, 36–37; and eventness,
9, 20–21; and logarithmic t, 117; and
pure potential t, 223; and process vs.
product, 28–30, 34–37, 40–41; vs.
utopia, 33, 261
—P, 91, 99, 128, 140, 204, 290f, 294f;
"At Tikhon's," 129–32, 295; epigraphs
to, 137, 167, 299; foresees totalitarianism, 306; and hundred million heads,
260; overcoming of t in, 205–6; and
sidesh, 120–38, 294; and vortex t,
163–65, 167
—other works: G, 203–4; House of the
Dead, 129, 158, 294–95; RY, 128, 179–
80, 300; Soviet 30-volume edition,
130ff
—notebooks and drafts: 98f, 134–35,
296; NI, 132, 136–37; NP, 122, 135
Dostoevsky and/vs. T, 92, 161; and
crises, 157–58; on memory, 180–
85; RY and AK, 179–80, 300; T on
Raskolnikov, 224; on representing
presentness of past, 12, 179–87
Double: agent, 127, 131; determination,
9, 36–38, 59; experience of readers,
43; explanation of events, 7; -feel,
230; perspective in art, 44–45, 50;
thoughts, 139, 296; of t, 118
Doubles of characters, 140–41, 146, 296
Doubling of stories: "At Tikhon's," 130–

32; by parody, 151; "Peasant Marey,"
294; P, 128–29, 130–32, 294
Drama, 18–19, 174–75
Dramatability, 176
Dream: B and Freud on, 89; as barome-
ter, 62; and field of possibilities, 146–
47; mythic, 192; prophetic, 75–77; and
hypothetical t, 224–27
"Dream of a Ridiculous Man" (D), 144,
228
Dumas, Alexandre, 153
Dunn, Francis, 299
Dyson, Freeman, 251
Dystopia. See Anti-utopia(nism)

Eagleton, Terry, 23
Eastern War, 171
Eclecticism and homogenization, 258–59
Ecstasy, 202–3
"Ecstatic Dissent" (Lerner), 306
Eden, 286
Edge of present, 105, 175f
Edited life, 214, 218–19
Effect (and V-diagram), 46–47
Egyptian Nights (Pushkin), 104
Einstein's Dreams (Lightman), 33, 67,
300
Eldredge, Niles, 293
Elections, 260–62
Elegy, 216
Eliot, George, 42, 106f
—Middlemarch, 12, 88, 109, 241, 287;
"Finale" to, 162, 197–98, 279; "that
imagined 'otherwise,'" 148
Eliot, T. S., 201
Embodiment, 89, 285
Embroidering, 73
Emerson, Caryl, 284, 290–91, 294, 298
Emma (Austen), 162
"Emotional-volitional field," 177
End of history, 1, 8, 14, 33, 53f, 58; and
foresh, 50–51; itself over, 258
"Endless church service," 31–32
"Engineer of human souls," 260
Enlightenment, 87–88, 152
Entelechy, 108
Enter into, 89
Entrails, 61
Epic, 112; t, 189–90, 198
Epileptic t, 13, 166, 201–2, 205
Epilogue t, 12–13, 190–98, 214; and
AK, 191f; and C&P, 191–92, 193; and
Cherry Orchard, 192–93; in current
theory, 279; and Fathers and Sons,
193–97; and nostalgia, 192–93; and

superannuation, 193f
Epilogues: to C&P, 163, 168, 191–92,
193, 299, 301; to *Middlemarch*, 162,
197–98, 279; to W&P, 197
Eschatology, 198; t, 13. *See also* Apocalypse; Revelation, Book of; Utopia(n)
ESP, 62
Essential surplus, 47, 88f, 97; in AK, 77–
78; and foresh, 45, 50, 287; vs. itself,
79–81; and process vs. product, 43–45
Eternal recurrence, 10, 51–52, 288
Ethics, 1f, 20, 74, 138, 278; and backsh,
284, 305; and B, 5, 86, 291, 294; and
blame, 303–4; and choice, 34, 232–
33; and crises or extremes, 108, 158,
291; and epileptic t, 202; and eventness, 21–22; and multiple t, 232–33,
303–4; and omniscient God, 95; and
pure potential t, 223; and rehearsal t,
227; and world's vulnerability, 304; as
zero-sum game, 232–33, 304
Ethiopia, 1
Eudemius of Rhodes, 51
Eugene Onegin (Pushkin), 25, 294
Eugénie Grandet (Balzac), 88
Eukaryotic cells, 248–49
Euripides, 173, 197, 299, 301
"Even web," 197, 279
"Eventless" history, 300
Eventness, 11, 27, 31–35 *passim*, 43, 90,
97; and creative process, 23ff, 98; ex-
plained, 20–22; and presentness, 22,
175; and process, 9; and sports, 175
Evil, 85–86, 217, 232–33, 303–4; "omen,"
(AK), 71
Evolution: and backsh, 13–14, 245–55;
and by-products, 2, 248, 251; and
compromises, 283; and contingency,
3, 13, 245–49 *passim*, 253f; fallacies
about, 248–50; as historical, 245, 249–
51; imaginary, 297; and progressivism,
2, 13, 246–49, 305; and sidesh, 13,
247, 249
Ex tempore, 14
Execution t, 165–66
Exorcism, 167
Ex-pression, 27
"Exquisite fit," 249
External open-endedness, 162
External vantage point, 51; and art vs.
life, 20, 38; and double perspective,
44–45, 50; and *Oedipus*, 59–61; and
testing fate, 68; and *Uncle Vanya*,
18–19; and utopia, 39–40
Extraction of square roots, 9, 23, 42

Extraordinary people, 275
Extreme situations, 99, 158, 291, 299

Fact: of the event, 184; -ion, 287; -oid,
222
Fading: epitaph, 222; memory, 215–16
Fahrenheit 451 (Bradbury), 256
Fallacies, 5–6; actual future, 300; bipolar, 183–87 *passim*, 234–40 *passim*;
chronocentrism and temporal egotism, 13f, 235–38, 241–43, 274–82,
288, 307; extreme situations, 158, 291,
299; hyperselectionism, 249–50; inferring history from current utility, 249,
251–53, 305; log-hauling, 239, 306;
nihilist's move, 301; Occam's vacuum cleaner, 303; plain man, 209–10,
302; probability of one case, 253–54,
306; prison house of perspective, 210–
12; reciprocity, 240; responsibility =
blameworthiness, 303–4; retrospection, 239–40; stencil work, 157, 171,
239; testing fate, 68; understanding is
forgiving, 80, 290; Whiggism, 241–42,
245f, 259, 279. *See also* Backshadowing; Progressive and progressivism
False: confession, 131; consciousness,
280; continuation, 153; impression of
necessity, 183; leads, 24
Fantasia (film), 292
Fascism as progressive, 244
Fate and fatalism, 18, 39, 41, 51, 107,
226; as choice, 68, 76, 230; and determinism, 63–67; eluctable, 69–71;
and essential surplus, 43–44; and fatal
person, 71; and foresh, 7, 63–66, 100;
and Lessing's curse, 8; psychological
vs. logical effects of, 3, 10, 66–69,
71; rhetoric of, 214; scroll or book
metaphors for, 63, 67; as vortex, 65
—in specific works or authors: AK, 75–
77; Aristotle, 36; Borges, 228, 230;
"The Fatalist," 10, 62–63, 67–69;
Oedipus, 59–61, 65, 100–101; *Three
Sisters*, 214–17
Fateful coincidence, 163–64
Fathers and Sons (Turgenev), 101, 109,
128, 268, 292; and epilogue t, 12,
193–97; and nihilist's move, 301; and
prosaics, 196–97
Field of possibilities, 106, 111, 145,
156, 164; and dreams, 146–47; and
middle realm, 12, 141–42; other world
as, 146–47; in P, 122, 124, 126; and
processual intentions, 143–45; and

Field of possibilities (cont'd)
sidesh, 119–20, 141–42, 155; and vor-
tex t, 164; and wishes, 141–42. *See also*
Possibilities; Unactualized possibilities
Fielding, Henry, 151
Figural interpretation, 54–56, 288
Filling in of character, 108
Final anthropic principle, 305–6
Finalization, 38, 89
Fisher, Robert, 296
Five-year plans, 263
Folklore, 148f
Footprints, 46
"For some reason," 155f
Foreknowledge of God, 97
"Foresee all contingencies," 156
Foreshadowing, 9–10, 42–81, 107, 111,
179; and accomplished future, 50–
52; and AK, 71–81; and art vs. life,
9–10, 45–47, 50–52; artifice of, 45,
50, 58, 61; and backsh, 234f, 238, 242;
and backward causation, 7, 47–50,
300; and bipolar fallacy, 183, 187; in
Borges, 229–30; and destiny or fate,
7, 63–66, 69–71; and essential surplus,
45, 47, 287; and evolution, 246f; history with, 50–52; identified, 47–50;
imposed by memory, 183; and *Oedipus*, 58–61, 100–101; and omens, 7,
10, 61–63; and presentness, 177–78,
188; and prosaics, 187; vs. pseudo-
foresh, 12, 134–37, 160–61; rarely
confirmed, 136–37; and sidesh, 11,
117–18, 134–37, 169; and storm, 47–
48; and structure or closure, 50, 117,
100–101, 159; and types, 54–57; of us,
246f; and vortex t, 166; W&P, 159,
169–72
Forever Flowing (Grossman), 263–64
"Forever simultaneous," 259
Forgery, 300
Forgetting, 215–16
Forgiveness, 80, 290
Fork asymmetry, 62
Formalism and Formalists, 21, 24–26,
95, 98, 285
"Forms of Time and of the Chronotope"
(B), 4–5, 105–10, 198, 284
Fossils, 46, 246
Fragment, 172, 306
Franciscans, 374
Frank, Joseph, 136, 294–95, 296
Frank, Semyon, 200–201, 204–5
Free speech, 262
Freedom as impure, 222–23

Freud, Sigmund, and Freudianism,
21, 89, 108–9, 139, 145; and creative
process, 26, 98; and death instinct, 286
From the Other Shore (Herzen), 14,
199–200, 301, 305
Fruterro, Carlo, et al., 298
Frye, Northrop, 293
Fusso, Susanne, 294
Future recollections, 294
Futurology, 197

Galilean, 3f, 8, 245, 252
Gambler, The (D), 202–4
Gambling t, 13, 201–6
Games, 148, 176. *See also* Sports t
Garbo, Greta, 71–72, 73
"Garden of the Forking Paths" (Borges),
13, 228–32, 233, 303
Gardner, John, 151
Garnett, Constance, 296, 299, 302
Ge, Nikolai, 182–83, 184, 187
General systems theory, 286
General vs. particular histories, 242–43
"Genotypically," 120
Genre painting, 181–82
Genres, 5, 152, 174, 186, 260, 300;
and major or minor characters, 93;
t and chronotopes of, 19, 88, 107–10,
120, 291
Geology, 110, 189, 247
Gestalt effect of memory, 178, 184
Giraffes, 251
Given vs. created, 23–24
Gleick, James, 290, 299
"Gnosticism," 85, 290
God, 18, 88, 188, 250, 302; all times
present for, 11, 49, 51, 55, 95, 97,
206; and author, 10–11, 44, 82, 88, 95;
bets, 96; historian as, 242; in *Master
and Margarita*, 262–63; and provi-
dence, 168–69; subjected to t, 11,
95–97, 98, 291
Goethe, Johann Wolfgang von, 96, 108,
189, 279
Golden Ass, The (Apuleius), 107–8
Golden Calf, The (Ilf and Petrov), 236
Gone with the Wind, 151
"Good night's sleep," 157
Goscilo, Helena, 290, 294
Gould, Stephen Jay, 13, 245–54, 272,
293; and T, 155, 245, 249; *Bully*, 251,
252–53; *Panda's Thumb*, 249–50;
Wonderful Life, 245–49, 253, 305
Grand Inquisitor legend (D), 91,
261, 298

Grandsons: generation, 275; "of those
heroes" (D phrase), 179
Great Expectations (Dickens), 150,
159f, 301
Greek romance, 107ff
Grendel (Gardner), 151
Grossman, Vasily, 263–64
Groys, Boris, 258–60
Guarantee, 1, 3, 66, 118, 197; of cer-
tainty, 255; that later is better, 244–45,
279; and presumed significance, 159–
60; of survival, 305–6
Guilt, 2, 52, 71, 74
Gulag, 201
Gulag Archipelago (Solzhenitsyn), 212
Gulliver's Travels (Swift), 297

H. (Haire-Sargeant), 151
Habit, 100
Halley's comet, 46, 54
Happiness, 72–73, 187–88
Harrington, John, 238
Harrowing of hell, 55
Hartshorne, Charles, 291
Harvey, W. J., 293, 295, 296
Haze: of possibilities, 118, 133; of
stories, 124
"He should have known," 236, 239
Hebrew Bible, 55, 96
Hedgehog and the Fox, The (Berlin), 271
Hegel, Georg Wilhelm Friedrich, 87,
155, 251, 271, 305
Henry IV, Part 2 (Shakespeare), 67
Hercule Poirot, 174
Herder, Johann Gottfried, 87, 270
Hero of Our Time, A (Lermontov),
62–63, 67–69
Herodotus, 45, 174
Herzen, Alexander, 99, 270; *From the
Other Shore*, 14, 199–200, 301, 305
Heteroverse, 94–95
"Higher liberalism," 128
Hill Street Blues, 174f
Historians, 20, 183, 185, 262; T on, 157,
276–77, 279. *See also* History
"Historic," 185–86
Historical: calculus, 185; drama, 292;
novel, 149, 179–80, 183
History, 49, 113, 176, 188, 270, 297;
and backsh, 234–45; in C&P, 167;
Communism's view on, 257–59; dia-
logue with, 280–82; direction to, 2,
244–45; eventless, 300; and evolu-
tion, 245, 249–51; with foresh, 50–52;
gambling with, 13, 203–6; general vs.

particular, 242–43; hypothetical, 119;
imitation of, 185–86; as improvisation,
14, 199, 281; inevitability in, 66–67;
inferring from current utility, 249,
251–53, 305; intellectual, 87–88; and
Last Judgment, 20, 51; and later =
better, 244–45, 274–77, 279; laws of,
21, 51, 54, 155–57, 162, 263; "looking
backward" on, 255–57; and mutable
past, 208–9, 211, 212–14; and novel, 5,
49, 51, 53, 101–2, 162; of other world,
146; post- or true, 255, 261, 272; and
presentness of past, 179–87; return to,
1, 33; and revolutionism t, 203–6; rewriting of, 213, 263; and rumor, 294;
and socialist realism, 57–58; scripted
beforehand, 263–64; stencil, 157; substantive philosophy of, 10, 53–54;
Whiggism and, 241–43, 279
—end of, 8, 14, 54, 255, 278; and Communism or socialist realism, 1, 53, 58;
ended, 1, 258; and foresh, 50–51; and
utopia or anti-utopia, 31, 33, 40
Hodgson, Ralph, 234
Hollander, Robert, 296, 299
Holocaust, 212–13, 283, 305; revision-
ism, 213
"Homogenization" of history, 258–59
Hope, 2; "-lessness" (B phrase), 90
Horwich, Paul, 46–47, 287
House of the Dead (D), 129, 158, 294–95
Humanity inevitable?, 247–49, 251–55
Humanness, 112–13
Humility, intellectual, 119, 267, 276
Hundred million: chances, 156; heads,
260
Hunger for: events, 286; meaning, 19,
71; possibilities, 12, 151–53, 297
Huxley, Aldous, 33, 261
Hyperselectionism, 249–50
Hypertime, 71, 289–90; hyper-, 71
Hypothetical, 96, 148; action at two
removes, 225; expressions in D, 138,
140; fiction as, 153; histories, 113
Hypothetical time, 13, 148, 214–27;
identified, 189, 214; and nonaction,
214–21; and rough draft, 218–19, 222
—types of: dream t (*Three Sisters*), 214–
22; pure potential t (NFU), 222–23;
rehearsal t (C&P), 224–27

Identifying with a character, 50, 104,
304; and AK, 10, 76, 80; vs. contemplating structure, 10, 61, 76; Oedipus,
61, 76

Idiot, The (D), 91, 93, 98, 164, 290f, 299; beginning and ending of, 135f, 296; and double thoughts, 139, 296; epileptic t in, 13, 201–2; and life as process, 28; notebooks to, 132, 136–37; pseudo-foresh in, 135–37; vortex t in, 163–67

"If only," 118, 217

Ignorance, 24, 80, 83, 249, 273; role of in determinism, 6, 8, 80, 155; and novel, 110, 268; = undetermined (suspense convention), 103–4, 175–76

Ilf, Ilya, and Eugene Petrov, 236

Imaginary evolutions, 297

Imperfect design, 250

Impostor, 130

Improvisation, 14, 24, 30, 74, 102, 104

Impurity of freedom, 222–23

"In the year 187-," 109

"Incalculably diffusive" (Eliot), 198

Incidentals of history, 243

"Incontestably necessary," 73

"Indefinitely prolonged present," 198

Indeterminate: equations, 147; length, 170

"Indistinct abstraction," 133, 296

Inertia: death by, 219–20, 227; of past, 119

Inevitability, 1, 10, 41, 111, 118, 183; and backsh, 236f; eluctable, 69–71; exemption from, 66–67; of humanity, 247–49, 251–55; and sidesh, 117ff; and T, 74, 161, 170, 183; and warnings, 69–71

Inferring history from utility, 249, 251–53, 305

Infinite: present, 202; temporal density, 201, 204–5

Infinitesimals, 185

"Information-bearing surplus," 97–98

Inner speech, 27, 285

Instantiation model, 49, 110

Insurance, 36, 46, 62

Intellectual: history, 87–88; models, 21–22; revolutions, 278

Intellectuals and intelligentsia, 8, 13, 66, 146; critics of, 14, 84–86, 200–201, 204–5, 275–77, 279; definition and criteria of, 274–75, 306; distinction between, 275; and progressivism, 274–77, 307; and revolutionism t, 199, 203–5

Intensely lived present, 188

Intensified present, 106, 110

Intentions and decisions, 80, 296; lin-

ear, 142f, 145; in rehearsal t, 224–27; processual, 12, 24, 142–45, 158, 285

Interim between adventures, 150

Intermediate: characters in historical fiction, 101; steps in fate, 65

Intermitted reading, 102–3, 292–93

Internal open-endedness, 162

Interquels, 151

Interrupting t to test fate, 68

Inverse temporality, 59

Irony, 180, 195, 216, 232, 236, 276; dramatic, 287; and foresh, 49; in historical novels, 111; of origins and outcomes, 268, 306; of series of utopias, 257–58; of stage directions, 215; unanticipated or unwanted, 43, 45

Irrelevancies, 7, 20, 121, 123, 178, 185

Irrevocability: and commemoration, 212–14; and mutable past, 207, 212–14; and remorse, 212; of future, 230

Isenberg, Charles, 295

Island, present as, 189, 201, 203, 282, 298

Isolated present, 13, 201–14; defined, 189; and vortex t, 201; —types of: epileptic t, 3, 201–2, 205; gambling t, 201–6; mutable past, 206–14; revolutionism t, 203–6; —in specific works and authors: C&P, 204; G, 203–4; *Gulag*, 212; I, 201–2, 205; Mead, 206–14; *1984*, 206, 213; P, 205–6; *Signposts*, 204–5

Isomorphic/anisomorphic, 11, 20, 39ff, 58; and bias of artifact, 8, 28–40; defined, 39; and essential surplus, 43–44; and *Oedipus*, 7, 60–61; and polyphony, 100–101

Isotropic/anisotropic, 45–47, 55, 287

It's a Wonderful Life (film), 148, 297

"It's all the same," 214, 219, 222

Jackson, Robert Louis, 287, 296

Jamais vu, 216, 302

James, Henry, 162, 299

James, William: "Dilemma of Determinism," 4, 10, 82–87, 95–97, 168–69, 245, 284, 290, 304; *Principles of Psychology*, 284; on probability argument, 253, 306

Jam-making, 73

Joachim of Fiore, 274

Job, 96

John, 168

Johnson, Samuel, 152, 201, 267, 286

Jolt: metaliterary, 103; metaphysical, 203; of times, 101
Jonah, 55
"Journey of the Mother of God," 298
Julian the Apostate, 297, 305

Kairova case and time, 142–45, 158
Kant, Immanuel, 23, 219, 267
Katsenelinboigen, Aron, 286, 291, 297
Katz, Michael, 295
Kellert, Stephen H., 287, 290, 297
Kelley, Kitty, 149
Kelly, Aileen, 301
Kermode, Frank, 284
Kharms, Daniil, 228
Kidnappers, 46
Kierkegaard, Søren, 100
Kieselhorst, John, 301
Kline, George, 300
Knots in time, 19, 108
Knowledge and asymmetry of t, 46–47, 48
Kornilova case, 105
Kramskoy, Ivan, 139–40

L. A. Law, 174
Ladder of life, 246, 247–48
"Lady Macbeth of Mtsensk" (Leskov), 294
Landscape painting, 177
Laocoön (Lessing), 8, 283–84
Last Chronicle of Barset (Trollope), 154, 298
Last Judgment, 8, 18, 20, 51, 222, 255
Last Supper (Ge), 182–83, 184, 187
Lateness of author, 88–90, 102f, 293
Law, 21, 263; and contingency, 155–57; and evolution, 3, 245; "and lawlessness," 10, 84; and history or literary history, 2, 24, 51, 54, 285; of nature, 28, 43, 185f; and novels' plots, 43, 162; of progress, 155–56, 195, 199, 244, 276
Layering of hypotheticals, 153
Leaps, 2
Left as automatically good, 244
Legibility of the future, 234
Leibniz, Gottfried Wilhelm von, 49f, 287, 302, 305
Lem, Stanislaw, 172; Cyberiad, 228
Length of works, 170, 292
Lenin, Vladimir, and Leninism, 1, 100, 214, 236, 272
Leningrad, 1
Leonov, Leonid, 58
Leontiev, Konstantin, 159

Lermontov, Mikhail, 10, 62–63, 67–69
Lerner, Robert, 274, 306
Leskov, Nikolai, 294
Lessing, Gotthold Ephraim, 8, 283–84
Lessing's curse, 8
Lewis, David, 228, 232, 303–4
Liberalism, 66, 74, 128, 200, 244
Libretto to history, 14, 281
Life: after closure, 153; lived over, 69
Lightman, Alan, 33, 67, 300
Light-years, 17
Lindenberger, Herbert, 292
Linear intentionality, 142f, 145
Linearity, 24, 64, 119, 183, 197; of t, 49, 65, 117, 120, 157, 162
Literary history, 24f, 258–59
Literature: as concrete philosophy, 4; vs. life (see Art and/vs. life); of middle realm, 149; of process, 293
"Little did they know," 118, 236
Lives (Plutarch), 2, 108, 250
Living: beyond the text, 82; "historically," 185–86; out vs. living, 51, 190; over, 69
Living Corpse, The (T), 154
"Loathsome literary salad," 58
Lobachevsky, Nikolai, 107
Logarithmic t, 34, 43, 107, 117
Log-hauling example, 239, 306
Looking Backward (Bellamy), 255–57
Loophole, 14, 90, 99, 113, 190
Loose: ends or threads, 39, 77–79, 169, 184, 236, 238; play, 10, 25, 82–86, 245
Lotman, Yuri, 285
Love, 72–73, 81, 219–20
Love, David, 301
Love in the Western World (de Rougement), 72–73
"Loyalty with the universe," 85
Lucian, 171, 297
Luke, 97
Lunacharsky, Anatoly, 97
Lyubimov (Sinyavsky), 33

Magnet: of vortex t, 164; of Whiggism, 242
Magnum, P. I., 173, 175
Mahomet's pitcher, 166
Major and minor characters, 93f, 112, 167, 197
Mandelstam, Nadezhda, 203
Maps of space and t, 17–18
Marella, 247
Marxism, 21, 50, 95, 113, 272, 288; and backsh, 236, 257–59; and creative

Marxism (cont'd)
  process, 23, 24–25; and inevitability,
  66–67; and prophetic history, 53–54;
  and socialist realism, 57–58
M*A*S*H, 150, 175
Master and Margarita, The (Bulgakov),
  14, 252–63
Masterplot of utopia, 306
"Material" (B's sense), 23
Matthew, Gospel of, 141
Mayakovsky, Vladimir, 198, 201
McLeod, Shannon, 290
Mead, George Herbert, 206–14, 302
"Mean directly," 94
Measurement of space and t, 17
Mechanical action, 224–27 *passim*
"Meek One, The" (D), 295
Meier-Graefe, Julius, 92
Memory, 17, 19, 45f, 106, 180, 203, 300,
  302; and future recollections, 294;
  and gambling t, 203; and happiness,
  100, 188; hole, 213; and intermitted
  reading, 102–3; and mutable past,
  208, 212–14; and presentness of past,
  178, 180–85; regularizes, 79, 178,
  182ff; and rereading, 77; and spe-
  cious present, 284; in *Three Sisters*,
  215–16, 302
Menippean satire, 297
Messiness of world, 184, 242, 250, 272
Metahistorical act, 1
Metahistory (White), 284
Metaliterature, 19, 61, 103, 284; and
  eternal recurrence, 52; in NFU, 9, 37
Metamorphosis, 107–8
Metaphysical: act, 1; elections as, 261;
  guarantee, 305–6; optimism, 272; as
  Mead's accusation, 207ff, 213
Metatime, 71
Meta-universe, 233, 303f
Meteorology, 157
Michener, James, 149
Mickey Mouse, 292
Middle realm, 11, 119, 131f, 228, 269;
  and BK, 139–42, 147; and field of
  possibilities, 141–42, 147; and hypo-
  thetical t, 214, 220; literature of,
  149–50; and opinion, 262, 269; and
  sidesh, 6, 141–42
Middlemarch (Eliot), 12, 88, 109, 148,
  287; "Finale" to, 162, 197–98, 279; on
  backsh, 241
Midrash, 149
Might-have-beens, 11, 118, 295
Miller, Robin Feuer, 284, 296

Milton, John, 279; *Paradise Lost*, 26, 41
Misanthropic principle, 253
Misreading, 80–81
Modal realism, 303
Modern Utopia, A (Wells), 283
"Modernization and distortion" (B), 111
Momentousness, 22f, 173, 175
Monologic, 87, 163, 270, 272
Montaigne, Michel Eyquem de, 271
More, Thomas, 152
More lives than one, 121, 149, 155
Morris, Simon Conway, 246
Morris, William, 256, 259, 306
Morson, Gary Saul: *Boundaries of Genre*,
  293, 297, 306; "D's Great Experi-
  ment," 299; "Genre and Hero," 306;
  Hidden in Plain View, 285, 299, 306;
  "Prosaic B," 301; "Prosaics," 298
Morson, Gary Saul, and Caryl Emerson:
  Mikhail Bakhtin, 290–91; *Rethinking
  Bakhtin*, 284, 290–91
Multiple plotting, 84
Multiple t, 13, 227–33; and blame,
  303–4; and Borges, 228–32, 233, 303;
  defined, 189; and determinism, 227,
  232–33; and Lewis, 228, 232, 303–4;
  and Wolf, 227f, 233, 303
Munchausen, Baron, 66
Murder by rehearsal t, 227
Mutable past, 206–14; and *Gulag*, 212;
  and hyper t, 290; and irrevocability,
  207, 212–14; and Mead, 206–14; and
  1984, 206, 213; and Soviet Union, 264
Mysteries of Paris (Sue), 103
Mysterious return, 133, 163, 295–96
Myth (-ification), 20, 100, 140, 186, 192

Naive (B's sense), 107, 281
Narcissism, 71–74, 78, 140
Narration by assertion, 190, 192
Narrative: predisposition (*see* Bias of the
  artifact); sentences, 33, 40–41
"Natural and agreeable," 277, 280
Natural selection, 247–51 *passim*
Necessity, 24, 36, 157, 183f; aesthetic,
  90, 160
Nechaev, Sergei, 99, 127
Needlessly prolonged transition, 12
Negative: age, 223; argument, 10, 87;
  definition, 223; discourses, 214; nar-
  ration, 80; providence, 164, 169;
  solution, 82
Nekhliudovs, 154–55, 298
Nekrasov, Nikolai, 152
Nemesius, 51–52

New Soviet man, 113, 259
News from Nowhere (Morris), 256,
    259, 306
Newton, Isaac, and Newtonian, 95,
    231, 278
Nick of time, 106, 120, 174
Nihilism, 193–97 *passim*
Nihilist's move, 195, 301
1984 (Orwell), 33, 152, 206, 213, 261
Nodes, historical, 156
Nonaction, 121–22, 124, 133, 193, 214–
    21
Nonadaptive change, 250
Noncoincidence, 92–93, 112–13
Non-Euclidian geometry, 107
Nostalgia, 192–93, 214
Notebooks and sideshadows, 150
Notes from Underground (D), 139, 151–
    52; and determinism, 28–30, 34–37,
    64f, 285–86; double determination in,
    9, 36–37; editor or ending of, 26–27,
    40–41, 172; and eventness, 20–21; and
    logarithmic t, 117; and pure poten-
    tial t, 223; and process vs. product, 9,
    28–30, 34–37, 40–41; punctuational
    pun in, 27; and square roots, 9, 23;
    and utopia, 33f, 261
"Notes of a Billiard Marker" (T), 154–55
"Nothing conclusive" (B phrase), 93, 282
Novel(s), 20, 82, 161, 169f, 250, 291f,
    296, 306; and anisomorphism, 100–
    101; and care, 304; and contingency,
    109, 197; continuations of, 151–55; de-
    novelizing, 109; and determinism or
    fatalism, 42, 43–44, 162; doubling of,
    128–29; and eternal recurrence, 52; vs.
    epic, 189–90; epilogues of, 190–98;
    -feuilleton, 103; as forms of thought,
    86–88; four times of, 100–105; histori-
    cal, 110–11, 179; and history, 49, 51,
    53; and irony of origins or outcomes,
    268, 306; of multiple plot, 210, 287–
    88; and noncoincidence, 92–93; 112f;
    as over, 174–75; and paraquels, 151–
    53; as parody, 151–53; and philosophy,
    42–43, 87–88, 107, 268; and prosaic
    choices, 9; as refuge, 42, 162; seri-
    alization of, 103, 149–50, 174; series
    of, 153–54, 298; and solitary reading,
    176; and structure or closure, 43–44,
    153–54, 169; suspense in, 42, 174–75;
    t and chronotope of, 88, 108–10, 112–
    13; and unfinalizability, 108, 110; and
    uniformitarianism, 189; and utopia,
    109, 256–57, 294

Novelistic: events, 159; truth, 42
Novelty, 285; Mead on, 207, 212
Nulliverse, 84

Occam's vacuum cleaner, 303
Oedipus (Sophocles), 65, 68f, 76, 117,
    176, 289; and foresh, 10, 58–61, 100–
    101; isomorphism of, 7, 100
Offense at laws of nature, 28, 285
Old Russian literature, 298
Old Testament, 55
Omens, 64, 67, 217; and AK, 71–81; and
    backward causation, 61–63; causes of,
    75–77; and foresh, 7, 10, 61–63; as
    warnings, 68–71
Omniscience, 44, 77, 95, 291
On Interpretation (Aristotle), 35–36
"On Socialist Realism" (Sinyavsky),
    57–58, 306
"On the same plane," 97
One of many possible: plots, 100, 113;
    realities, 112–13, 281
Opal Harbor, 184
Open, free discussions, 264
Operas, 298
Operator, t as, 145
Opinion, 1, 152, 267–82; and backsh,
    14, 280–82; and contingency, 261–64,
    267–68; and dialogue, 271, 273, 280–
    82; and "Philadelphians," 273–77; and
    pluralism, 14, 271–73; and possibili-
    ties, 267–82; and sidesh, 14, 267, 270,
    273, 280–82; and temporal egotism,
    278–82; and utopia or anti-utopia, 14,
    255–57, 261–64, 269–73
Oracles and oracular t, 59, 63f, 66,
    69, 117
Oral performance, 104
Ordinary moments, 157
Organ stops, 9, 34, 36
Orwell, George, 33, 152, 206, 213, 261
Orwin, Donna, 298
Other: novels in P, 132; possibilities,
    118, 120; world, 146–47, 297
Outliving one's life, 196
Outsideness, 38, 89, 94
Overdeterminism, 37
Overlap of temporalities, 50, 178
Oxford English Dictionary, 54–55, 57

Page proofs, 30
Palliser novels (Trollope), 12, 153–
    54, 292
Pamela (Richardson), 151
Panda's thumb, 250

Panda's Thumb (Gould), 249–50
Pangloss(ism), 85, 290
Paradise Lost (Milton), 26, 41
Paradox of creativity, 30
Parallel universes, 100, 227f, 233, 303
Parameter, t as, 2, 28, 145
Paranoia, 78
Paraquels, 12, 151–53
Parliament: British, 256, Soviet, 260
Parody, 151–53, 219, 298
Parricide, 128, 140f
Passive accomplice, 217
Past sidesh, 12, 119, 132–34, 303
Pastness, 182f, 209, 212, 239, 300
Paternity question in D, 128–29, 132
Patter, 142
Pearl Harbor, 184
"Peasant Marey, The" (D), 293
Penumbra of other possibilities, 151, 295f
Perfect: crime, 224f; design, 250
Periodization, 240
Perry Mason, 174
Pestle, 144–45, 164
"Phenotypically," 120
"Philadelphia," 273–77, 278
Philanthropy, 200
Philistine virtues, 85–86
Philosophical parable, 228
Philosophizing, 216, 220–21
"Philosophy of Composition" (Poe), 25–27
Photography, 46, 70, 176, 178, 185, 213
Phrenology, 194f
Phyla, 246ff
Physics, 2, 35, 245, 251, 278
Picaresque, 150
Pinter, Harold, 300
Plain man fallacy, 209f, 302
Planning, 252; and contingency, 157; hypothetical, 225; in rehearsal t, 224–25; for surprise, 98; for spontaneity, 264
Plato, 51, 152, 271; Cave allegory, 257, 306
Plausibility and genre, 106
Play-by-play, 178
Plot(s), 39, 42, 93, 228, 230; in AK, 79–81; and aperture, 169f; and choice or fate, 66, 106–7; and D, 99–100, 163; multiple, 287–88; one of many possible, 100, 112; and pseudo-foresh, 135–37; and T, 72, 75, 79–81, 160, 169; virtual or quasi-, 300

Pluralism, 14, 90; in James, 84–87, 95–96; and opinion, 271–73; vs. relativism, 269, 273
Pluriverse, 95
Plutarch, 2, 108, 250
Poe, Edgar Allan: "Philosophy of Composition," 25–27, 98; "Poetic Principle," 292; "Review of *Twice-Told Tales*," 292
Poetics, 93, 95, 97, 158, 284
Police agent, 127–28
Polyphony, 11, 41, 91–101; and closure, 100, 162–63; and creative process, 98–100, 291; and reader's time, 103–5; shortcomings of, 11, 105–6, 113; and temporal God, 95–97
Ponderosity of petty details, 159
Popper, Karl, 288
Popular culture, 12, 148–50, 173–77, 284
Possessed, The (D), 91, 99, 204, 290f, 294f; "At Tikhon's," 129–32, 295; chronicler of, 120–26, 130–31, 134; doubling in and of, 128–32, 140, 290f; epigraphs to, 137, 167, 299; foresees totalitarianism, 306; and hundred million heads, 260; and Narcissus, 140; and NP, 122, 125, 133; overcoming of t in, 205–6; and rumor, 123–24, 127–28; and sidesh, 120–38, 294; and vortex t, 163–65, 167
Possibilities, 70, 79, 83f, 120f, 137, 182; and aesthetic potentiality, 160; and anisomorphism, 38–39; and backsh, 234–43 *passim*, 277; and contingency, 18, 109, 155–56, 159, 160–61, 197; and creative process, 24, 26–27; and doubling of novels, 128–29; and eventness, 22; in evolution, 246–49; exceed actualities, 10, 83–84, 168, 304; vs. foresh, 49, 166, 177; and God, 95; haze of, 118, 133; hunger for, 12, 148–50, 151, 297; and hypothetical t, 189, 214, 220, 223–27; and James, 83–84; middle realm of, 11, 141–42, 132, 147, 269; and middle realm literature, 148–50; and multiple t, 189, 227–28, 231–33; and novels, 42, 109, 112, 119, 162, 295; and opinion, 14, 262, 267–82; and other world, 146–47; and parodies or paraquels, 151–53; and past sidesh, 133–34; and polyphony, 99; in P, 123–28, 133; of possibility, 1, 39, 117–19, 166; and psychology (BK), 138–39; ravelment of, 156, 240;

rebirth of, 1, 166, 264; and sports, 177; and utopia, 257, 272; vs. vortex t, 166, 168. *See also* Field of possibilities; Unactualized possibilities

Possible: other presents, 118; lives, 295; worlds, 248, 297, 305

Postepennoe, 168, 299

Postfigural interpretation, 56

Post- or true history, 255, 261, 272

Posthumous living, 13

Potential(s), 36, 112, 157, 162, 168f, 296; aesthetic, 158–62; audience, 177; in conflict, 270; in D, 99, 134, 137, 223; happiness, 188; hero, 177; of past, 181; and prison of perspective, 211; pure, 223; and sidesh, 118f

Pragmatism, 207–9

Pre-: cognition, 69; destination, 63–64, 67f; figuration, 10, 54–56; game show, 178; lapsarian sinfulness, 286; living one's life, 196; meditation, 143f; monition, 69, 229; parody, 151; quels, 151; reading, 151; recording devices (record future), 46, 48, 53, 57, 63, 70; sentiment, 140, 164

Prediction, 22, 44, 46, 93; and backsh, 239–40; and contingency, 157f; and evolution, 3, 245; and prosaics, 46; and pseudo-foresh, 136; vs. prophecy, 288; and sports t, 177

Present effect, 175

Presentness, 6–7, 12–13, 110–11, 117, 173–233; edge of, 175f; and eventness, 22, 175; and foresh, 177–78; and happiness, 187–88; and narrative sentences, 288; and novel, 42, 110; of past, 110–11, 178–87, 208–9; and sports t, 173–78; throb of, 191; trumped by memory, 178. *See also* Diseases of presentness

Preshadowing, 279

Presley, Elvis, 149, 297

Presumed significance, 159–60

Pretender, 118, 131, 152

Price, Martin, 287, 291

Prigogine, Ilya, 145, 297

Primary Chronicle, 65–66

Prime Minister, The (Trollope), 292

Principles of Psychology (James), 284

Prison house of perspective, 210–12

Private t, 101–2; 176–77

Probability argument, 253–54, 306

"Problem of the Text, The" (B), 23–24

Problems of D's Poetics (B), 91–101, 110,

282; B questions, 105–6; and closure, 162–63; vs. chronotope, 112–13; editions of, 96, 98; and pluralism, 272–73

Process theology, 291

Process vs. product, 9, 17–41; and (an)isomorphism, 20, 61; and aperture, 172; and bias of artifact, 61; and creative process, 23–27, 80; and death, 38; in D, 9, 27–37, 40–41; and essential surplus, 43–45; and eventness, 9, 21–22; and utopia, 30–33, 270

Processual intentions, 12, 24, 142–45, 158, 285

Production model of creativity, 23, 25

Professors, 307

Progress, 13, 194–95; changing criteria of, 199, 270; law of, 155–56, 195, 199, 244, 276; and single truth, 269–70

Progressive and progressivism, 39, 237; in evolution, 13, 246–49, 305; in *Fathers and Sons*, 194–95; of intelligentsia, 274–79, 307; and relativism, 244, 278–79; in Soviet art, 258–59; of spirituals, 274, 278; and time line, 244–45; T vs., 275–77; and Whiggism, 241–43. *See also* Chronocentrism; Temporal egotism

Prophecy, 229, 269; in dreams, 10, 75, 77f, 107; in history, 53–54; in *Oedipus*, 59–61; vs. prediction, 288; in Primary Chronicle, 65–66; socialist realism as, 57–58; and substantive philosophies of history (Marxism), 53–54

Prosaic(s), 25, 40, 190, 197, 200: and bipolar fallacy, 187; and choice, 19, 22, 157–58; and creative process, 25, 27; vs. crisis and revolutionism t, 161, 203, 205; in *Fathers and Sons*, 196–97; and love (AK), 72–74; in *Middlemarch*, 197–98; and presentness of past, 183–87; and sidesh, 157–58, 161, 197f; vs. vortex t, 167

Proust, Marcel, 102–3, 293

Providence, 164, 168–69

Provocation, 97–100, 291

Pseudo-foreshadowing, 12, 134–37, 160–61

Psychological vs. logical consequences of beliefs, 3, 10, 71, 63–64, 66–69, 228–29, 230, 290

Psychology, 1f, 138–39, 148, 167, 284

Ptolemaic, 94, 118f, 252

Public t, 101–2, 104, 176–77, 292

Publishers and revisions, 30
Pull of t and history, 50, 59, 62, 64, 164
Pun of creativity, 27–30, 31
Punctuated equilibrium, 293
Punctuational pun, 37
Pure potential t, 222–23
Pushkin, Alexander, 258, 271; "De-mons," 137, 299; "Egyptian Nights," 104; *Eugene Onegin*, 25, 294; "The Queen of Spades," 228
Pythagoreans, 51

Quantum physics, 228, 287
Quasi-: characters, plot, and events, 300; simultaneity, 228
'Queen of Spades, The" (Pushkin) 228

Rabelais, François, 297
Radical "democratic" critics, 7, 56–57
Rahv, Philip, 301
Ramifying t, 19, 22, 49, 156f; and Aristotle, 36, 70; and sidesh, 18, 117, 119, 281
Rasselas (Johnson), 201, 267, 286
Ravelment of possibilities, 156, 240
Raw material: present people as, 13, 199, 259–60; and creative process, 23
Raw Youth, The (D), 128, 179–80, 300
"Reaction in Germany, The" (Bakunin), 302
Reactionary, 237, 242–43, 258–59, 268
Read, Christopher, 301
Readability, 79, 157
Readers and reading, 51, 63, 89–90, 106, 190, 292f; of AK, 77, 80–81; and aperture, 164–71; and contingency, 159–62; of D, 91–94, 104, 123–24, 127, 136, 295; double perspective of, 43, 50; and essential surplus, 43–45; intermitted, 102–3, 292–93; and novel series, 153–54; of *Oedipus*, 59–61, 289; and rereading, 7, 44–45, 59, 103f, 299; and serialization, 299; solitary, 176; t of, 102–5; of utopia, 39–40; of W&P, 159–62, 184. *See also* Characters and reader; Rereading
"Ready-made," 23–24, 25, 112
Real historical t, 107–10 (B phrase), 176
"Real present of the creative process," 100
Real vs. actual, 83
"Reality in its revolutionary development," 57
Recessive gene, 120, 296
Reciprocity, fallacy of, 240

Recollection vs. repetition, 100
Recycling of characters, 153–55
Regret, 2, 18, 31, 52, 85, 233
Rehearsal: life as, 218–19; t, 224–27
Relative: closure, 170; independence of characters, 91, 96
Relativism, 244, 273, 278–79; vs. pluralism, 269, 273
Remembrance of Things Past (Proust), 102–3
Remorse, 212, 233
Repentance, 192
Repetition, 69, 100, 229, 302; t, 301
Replaceability, 109
Replay the tape, 148, 245–49 *passim*
Requiem, 90
Rereading, 51, 77, 100, 289, 299; and eternal recurrence, 52; first reading as, 44; and *Oedipus*, 59; and pseudo-foresh, 135f; and reading, 7, 59, 103f; and structure, 44–45, 104
Resolutions to resolve, 226
Resonance, 129
Responsibility, 2, 6, 9f, 87, 128, 227; B on, 86–87; and choice, 34, 63–64; and fate, 63–69 *passim*, 74–75; and (in)determinism, 63–64, 66, 87; and middle realm, 139–42; in multiple t, 304; and nonaction, 217; and omens, 71; for one's character, 108, 294; varies by genre, 107
Resurrection (T), 190
Resurrections of characters, 153–55
Retrodiction, 3, 46, 245
Retrospection, 157; fallacy of, 239–40
"Return the ticket," 85
Revelation, Book of, 1, 166, 205–6, 274, 295, 299
Reverse sentimentality, 139
Reversibility, 108f, 245
"Review of *Twice-Told Tales*" (Poe), 292
Revolution(ism), 13, 199–201, 214; intellectual, 278; t, 203–6
Rewriting history, 263
Rhys, Jean, 151
Rhythm, 90, 99
Rice, James L., 296
Richardson, Samuel, 151, 293
Ricoeur, Paul, 297, 300
Ripley, Alexandra, 151
Risk, 202–3, 225
Road not taken, 157
Robert of Liege, 274
Romanticization of the machine, 285
Rough draft, 13, 218–19, 222, 230

Roulette, 202–5
Rumor, 121–28 *passim*, 138, 148, 294, 297
Russia that did not happen, the, 148
Russian Herald, 179

Sacrifice, 31, 68
Salvation ex machina, 192
Sankovitch, Natasha, 300
Scandalous scenes, 163
Scarlett (Ripley), 151
Scene of the crime, 225
Schapiro, Leonard, 301
Science, 3, 42, 156, 162, 245–55, 278
Science fiction, 148
Scientific socialism, 257–58
Scott, Walter, 111
Scripted history, 263–64
Scroll, 63, 67, 208, 213
Seal of death, 62–63, 67
Self-laceration, 138, 296
Sensitive dependence on initial conditions, 156
Sentimentality, 80; reverse, 139
Sequels, 151
Serialization, 103f, 149–50, 170f, 295, 299; and aperture or presentness, 169–72, 174–75; and intermitted reading, 292–93
Sermon on the mount, 141
Shadow cabinet and history, 148
Shakespeare, William, 260, 271, 279; *Henry IV, Part 2*, 67
Shamela (Fielding), 151
"Shcherbatsky element," 73
Shelley, Percy, 26–27, 98
Shipwrecks, 109
Shklovsky, Victor, 98; *Third Factory*, 25
Shoehorning, 246
Sideshadowing, 5ff, 14, 113, 117–72, 284, 294–99 *passim*; and aperture, 169–72; and backsh, 211, 235, 237, 247, 249, 270, 277; and Bernstein, 6, 283; and Christmas stories, 297; and chronocentrism, 280–82; and contingency, 6, 41, 119, 155–62, 267, 273; and doubling of characters or novels, 128–29, 140–41; and evolution, 13, 247, 249; and fields of possibility, 141–42, 155; and hunger for possibilities, 148–50; identified, 11–12, 117–20; and memory, 179, 180–85; and middle realm, 6, 141–42; vs. multiple t, 13, 233, 303; and opinion, 267, 270, 273, 280–82; and paraquels or parodies, 151–53;

past, 12, 119, 132–34, 303; and presentness of past, 178–87; and processual intentions, 142–45; and prosaics, 157–58, 197f, 161; and pseudo-foresh, 134–37; and recycling of characters, 153–55; and responsibility (BK), 139–42; and rumors, 294, 297; vs. utopia, 120, 256–57; and vortex t, 12, 153–68 *passim*, 299; and W&P, 155–62, 169–72 —in D, 5, 11–12, 41; BK, 137–42, 144–47, 298f; C&P, 294; *House of the Dead*, 129; P, 120–38, 294
Sign, 7, 69–70, 257; vs. cause, 51, 60, 161, 300; and omens, 61, 76
Signposts, 66, 200–201, 204–5, 275, 301
Sigwart, Christoph, 284, 290
Simultaneity, 11, 100–105, 118, 206, 259, 290; and multiple t, 228; and sports t, 12, 176–77
"Singular singularity," 22
Sinyavsky, Andrei: *Lyubimov*, 33; "On Socialist Realism," 57–58, 306; *Soviet Civilization*, 201, 204, 255, 260
Skeptical Inquirer, The, 62
Skepticism, 64, 68–69, 110, 199–200, 278
Skinner, B. F., 294
Slander, 149
Smith, B. H., 284
"Smudge to smudge," 124
Smuggling meaning, 19
Soap operas, 150
Socialism, 51, 57–58, 199f, 249, 257–58
Socialist realism, 40, 57–58, 190, 259–60, 268
Society as artwork, 256, 259–60
Solipsism in the bleachers, 176
Solomon, 228
Solzhenitsyn, Alexander, 212
Something else, 7, 118f, 161, 277
Sophocles (*Oedipus*), 7, 10, 58–61, 65–69 *passim*, 100, 117, 176, 289
Soul vs. spirit, 90f
Soviet Civilization (Sinyavsky), 201, 204, 255, 260
Soviet Union, 7, 13, 23, 54, 57, 96, 283, 306; and backsh, 14, 236, 257–64; and B, 82, 96, 112–13, 190; and commemoration, 212–14; epic t and, 190; and new Soviet man, 113, 259; and previous art, 258–59; prosaic faults of, 201
Space and time, 47, 70; differences between, 17–18; and foresh, 48–49; and isotropy, 46
Specious present, 284

Speech zone, 294
Speed of time, 165, 289
Spiritual intelligence, 274–75, 278
Spite, 9
Sports time, 12, 173–78
Square roots, 9, 42
Stage directions, 215
Stalin, Joseph, and Stalinism, 57, 148, 259–64
Steiner, George, 171
Stellovsky, F. I., 202
Stencil work, 157, 171, 239
Stern tribunal, 276, 279
Sterne, Laurence, 102f, 292
Stewart, Jimmy, 297
Stoics, 51, 288
Stokowski, Leopold, 292
Storm, 47–48, 53, 63, 77
"Story of the Good Brahmin" (Voltaire), 228
"Story-line weight," 90
Strange: conjunctures, 143; synchronies, 11, 100–105
Structuralism, 21, 95, 285, 291
Structure, 10f, 18, 41, 58; and AK, 10, 76f, 79–80; and aperture, 171–72; and art vs. life, 38, 77–78; and contingency, 158, 159–60; escape from, 40–41; and essential surplus, 43–44; vs. event(ness), 93, 97, 104; and foresh, 7, 50, 100–101; of history, 20, 39; vs. identifying, 10, 43f, 61, 76; and isotropy, 40–41; in Oedipus, 59–61, 76; vs. polyphony, 97, 100
Substantive philosophy of history, 10, 53–54
Subtracting memories, 180, 295
Sue, Eugène, 103
Suffering in D, 129
Suicide: in AK, 78–79, 171, 191; Kirillov's, 205–6; Nekhliudov's, 154–55; Tuzenbach's, 219; and vortex t, 164
Superannuation, 54, 193f
Superfluous man, 69
Superman, 300
Superstitions, 75f, 146, 217
Surplus: of creativity, 23; of event, 9, 22; essential, 43–45, 47, 50, 77–81, 88f, 97, 287; of humanness, 112–13; information-bearing, 97–98; knowledge, 236; of possibilities, 84; of temporalities, 119–20
Surprise and surprisingness, 11, 29, 91, 160, 261, 263; and creative process,

25, 98–99, 285; and epilogue, 192, 198; and eventness, 21–22; to God, 96, 98; and historicity, 250; and loophole, 90; and prosaics, 22, 198
Surroundings vs. field of vision, 89
Survival beyond the vortex, 166
Suspense, 19, 22, 42, 45, 66, 104; and sports t, 174–76
Suspense convention, 104, 175–76
Swerve and fate, 70
Swift, Jonathan, 152, 197
Sylvie and Bruno (Carroll), 290
Symmetry/asymmetry, 39, 52, 60, 62, 78, 259, 261; of t, 45–47; and mutable past, 206–7; and totalitarianism, 264
Synchronies, 11, 100–105
Systems, 21–22, 271

Table of logarithms, 36, 42
Tabloid articles, 148f
Talmud, 228
Tannen, Deborah, 300
Tasting truth, 274
Teleology, 50, 58, 62, 66–67, 100, 254, 287; and history, 2, 199, 237, 279; vs. imperfect design, 250; and the progressive, 244, 279
Temporal: catastrophism, 212; collision, 59–60, 61; conflict, 111, 167; contradiction, 58, 66, 150, 292; density, 19; doubling (the "historic"), 185; humility, 119; illusion, 64, 185; incoherence, 238; layering, 178; sensitivity, 156; vacuum, 30–33; wisdom, 279–82
—egotism, 212, 235–38, 249, 278–82; avoiding, 280–82; of intelligentsia, 274–79, 307; and Whiggism, 241–43
Temporary closure, 154
Tenses, wisdom of, 119
Terras, Victor, 298
Terror(ism), 203ff, 225
Tests, 66–68, 99, 107, 210–11, 291
Theology, 2, 11, 49, 53, 57, 85–86; in BK, 138; James's, 10, 85–86; and literary structure, 44; process, 291; and temporal God, 95–97
Theoretism, 21, 285
Theory and literary criticism, 94–95, 273, 277; chronocentrism of, 278–79; and Marxism's appeal, 288; and plain man fallacy, 209; and prison of perspective, 211; purposes of, 4, 82
Thick description, 4, 190
Third Factory (Shklovsky), 25

Thought and Language (Vygotsky), 27
Three Sisters (Chekhov), 13, 214–22, 302
Threshold art, 297
Throb of presentness, 191
Time: "forges," 21; line, 18, 244–45; loops, 10, 70–71, 303; "no longer," 1, 166, 205
Timofeev, L. I., 57
"Tiny alterations," 157, 161, 298
Titles: *Forerunners*, 257–58; I, 137; of novel and series, 298
Todd, William Mills, 203, 300
Tolstoy, Leo, 5, 13, 41, 57f, 91, 106, 269–72 *passim*, 293, 306; and anisomorphism, 39; and aperture, 12, 169–72; and contingency, 155–62; critics of, 8, 191; describes fallacies, 13, 238–41, 249, 306; "for some reason," 155f; and Gould, 155, 244, 249; vs. intelligentsia, 14, 81, 275–77, 279; and Lessing's curse, 8; and length, 293; and prosaics, 73f, 185–87
—AK, 10, 88, 101, 103, 108f, 279, 299; aperture in, 169, 171; and contingency, 6, 78, 160; and epilogue t, 191f; and foresh, 71–81; and opinion, 268–69; and prefiguration, 55–56; criticized in RY, 179–80, 300
—W&P, 20, 93, 107, 111, 197, 292; and aperture, 169–72; and contingency, 6, 155–62; criticized by RY, 179–80; and happiness, 187–88; identifies fallacies, 238–42, 276–77; and intermitted reading, 102–3; and many truths, 271–72; and presentness of past, 179, 183–84, 185–87; public and private t in, 101–2
—other works: corrected Bible, 56; *The Cossacks*, 170; "The Devil," 150; *The Living Corpse*, 154; "Notes of a Billiard Marker," 154–55; *Resurrection*, 154–55; "Why Do Men Stupefy Themselves?" 224, 298; writings on W&P, 169–71, 184, 238–39; *Youth*, 154
Tolstoy and D. *See* Dostoevsky and/vs. T
"Too many facts," 121, 123
Torah, 55
Torture, 166f, 97–100
Total predictability, 287
Totalitarianism, 53, 259, 261, 264, 304; and opinion, 14, 269
Toulmin, Stephen, 273; and June Goodfield, *The Discovery of Time*, 283
Tour guides to utopia, 21–22

"Toward a Philosophy of the Act" (B), 21–22, 177, 285, 291
"Toward a Reworking of the D Book" (B), 38, 91, 96–97
Traces of unrealized possibilities, 84
Tragedy, 19, 71, 112, 187, 299; of anachronism, 194–95
Tragic necessity, 36
Transcription, 21–22, 87, 284
Treetop analogy, 185
"Trifles," 220, 225
Tristram Shandy (Sterne), 102f, 292
Triumph over time, 106
Trollope, Anthony: Barchester series, 12, 154, 298; *Barchester Towers*, 170; *Can You Forgive Her?* 288; *Last Chronicle of Barset*, 154, 298; Palliser series, 12, 153–54, 292; *Prime Minister*, 292; "Two Heroines of Plumplington," 298
Turgenev, Ivan, 42, 91, 99, 107; *Fathers and Sons*, 12, 101, 109, 128, 193–97, 268, 301
Twentieth century, 1, 14, 212, 269
"Twice two makes four," 28–29, 286
"Two Heroines of Plumplington" (Trollope), 298
Types, 7, 54–58, 179
Typical of the future, 58
Tyranny of the present instant, 282

Ultimate semantic authority, 94f
Unactualized possibilities, 220, 228; and James, 83–84; and hypothetical t, 223; and middle realm, 6, 118–20; and memory, 184; and multiple t, 189, 227–28, 231–33; and other world, 147; in P, 120–23; and self, 295; in W&P, 161. *See also* Field of possibilities; Middle realm; Possibilities
Unanimity, 260–61
Uncaused events, 290
Uncertainty, 96, 103–4, 148, 174–6, 197
Uncle Vanya (Chekhov), 18–19
Understanding: is forgiving, 80, 290; entails being, 210
Unfinalizability, 90, 92f, 97, 108, 110
Unfinished works, 150
Unfolding, 21, 34–35, 243, 246; vs. becoming, 2f, 5, 24, 28, 97, 110, 250
"Unhistoric acts" (Eliot), 198
Uniformitarianism, 110, 189
Unique evolution, 290, 297
Unity and polyphony, 94
Unknown and/vs. undetermined, 34;

Unknown and/vs. undeterm'd (cont'd)
and suspense convention, 103–4,
175–6
Unlikenesses and history, 242
"Unnecessary continuation," 198
Unnoticed causes, 62f
Unrecognized parody, 152
Unrepeatability, 22f, 245
"Unvisited tombs" (Eliot), 198
Unwelcome sideshadows, 151
Utopia(n), 19, 34, 58, 64, 74, 214;
and Archimedean thinking, 40; and
backsh, 14, 255–64; and certainty
or single truth, 31f, 255–56, 269–70;
eliminates possibility, 257, 272; literature, 31, 39–40, 255–57, 259, 306;
masterplot, 306; vs. novels, 109, 256–
57; and opinion, 14, 255–56, 272; as
product, 30–33; as sidesh, 120, 256–
57; Soviet Union as, 257–64; t, 13,
198–201, 214; and unanimity, 260–61

V-shaped diagram, 46–47, 48
Vagrant philosopher, 263
"Valorized temporal categories" (B), 189
Velleities, 214
Verificationism, 209
Victimization, 245, 280
Virgil, 3, 64–65, 66, 123
Virtual plot, 300
Vitalism, 194f
Voice-ideas, 98
Voltaire (François Marie Arouet), 270;
"Story of the Good Brahmin," 228
Vortex: fate as, 65; "of circumstances,"
167
Vortex time, 12, 162–69, 299; after, 166,
167–69; and coincidences, 163–64; and
isolated present, 201
Vortical expectations, 289
Voyeurism, 141
Vulgar formalism and Marxism, 24
"Vulnerability" of world, 86, 304
Vygotsky, Lev, 27, 285

Wachtel, Andrew, 144, 292, 298
Walcott, Charles Doolittle, 246–47, 305
Walden Two (Skinner), 294
Wallace, Alfred Russel, 249–50
War and Peace (T), 20, 107, 111, 160,
179; aperture of, 169–72; contingency
in, 6, 155–62; epilogue to, 197, 276–
77; on happiness, 187–88; length of,
102–3, 157–58, 170; and many truths,

271–72; and memory, 183–84; and
prosaics, 185–87; and RY, 179–80;
times of, 100–101; T on, 138–39,
169–71, 184
—episodes or characters: Czartoryski,
160–61; death of Pierre's father, 158–
59; Dolokhov, 170; Karataev, 93;
"Matryoshka," 186; opening scene,
292; Rostov's charge, 156–57, 187;
wolf hunt, 188
—analogies: historical calculus, 185;
log-hauling, 239, 306; perspective fallacies, 238–41; stencil work, 239, 257;
treetop, 185
Wasiolek, Edward, 296
Waste, 216, 223
Watt, Ian, 293
Wave of the future, 244
Waverley (Scott), 111
We (Zamyatin), 33, 256, 261, 286
Weather forecasting, 157
Weber, Max, 297
Wells, H. G., 152, 283
What Is to Be Done? (Chernyshevsky),
40, 56, 151–52
What may have been = what could
be, 148
Whig Interpretation of History (Butter-
field), 13, 241–43, 244, 239
Whiggism, 241–42, 279; and magnet,
242; scientific, 245f; squared, 259
Whirlwind motion, 106
White, Hayden, 284
Whittington, Harry, 246
Whole: of character's life, 90; seamless,
271; synchronic, 97; "ultimately," 271
"Why Do Men Stupefy Themselves?"
(T), 224, 298
Wide Sargasso Sea (Rhys), 151
Will: to destroy, 205; to will, 220
Williams, Julie, 290
Williams, Michael, 302
Windshield wipers, 48
Wisdom, 117, 269, 277; as coefficient
of history, 274–79; prosaic, 119, 158,
161, 196f
Wishes, 85, 141–42, 214–16, 296–97
Wolf, Fred Alan, 227f, 233, 303
Wonderful Life (Gould), 245–49, 253,
305
"World-in-the-making" (B), 110
Writer's Diary, A (D), 104–5, 179, 299,
301; "Apropos of the Exhibition,"
181–82, 183–87 passim; "Dream of a

Ridiculous Man," 144, 228; Kairova
case, 142–45, 297; Kornilova case,
105; "Meek One," 295; "Peasant
Marey," 294; spiritualism sketch,
32–33

"Yet-to-come" (B), 89f
You can't go home again, 17
Youth (T), 164

Zamyatin, Eugene, 33, 152, 256, 261, 286
Zero-sum game in ethics, 232–33, 304
Zone of familiar contact, 190

rebirth of, 1, 166, 264; and sports, 177; and utopia, 257, 272; vs. vortex t, 166, 168. *See also* Field of possibilities; Unactualized possibilities
Possible: other presents, 118; lives, 295; worlds, 248, 297, 305
Postepennoe, 168, 299
Postfigural interpretation, 56
Post- or true history, 255, 261, 272
Posthumous living, 13
Potential(s), 36, 112, 157, 162, 168f, 296; aesthetic, 158–62; audience, 177; in conflict, 270; in D, 99, 134, 137, 223; happiness, 188; hero, 177; of past, 181; and prison of perspective, 211; pure, 223; and sidesh, 118f
Pragmatism, 207–9
Pre-: cognition, 69; destination, 63–64, 67f; figuration, 10, 54–56; game show, 178; lapsarian sinfulness, 286; living one's life, 196; meditation, 143f; monition, 69, 229; parody, 151; quels, 151; reading, 151; recording devices (record future), 46, 48, 53, 57, 63, 70; sentiment, 140, 164
Prediction, 22, 44, 46, 93; and backsh, 239–40; and contingency, 157f; and evolution, 3, 245; and prosaics, 46; and pseudo-foresh, 136; vs. prophecy, 288; and sports t, 177
Present effect, 175
Presentness, 6–7, 12–13, 110–11, 117, 173–233; edge of, 175f; and eventness, 22, 175; and foresh, 177–78; and happiness, 187–88; and narrative sentences, 288; and novel, 42, 110; of past, 110–11, 178–87, 208–9; and sports t, 173–78; throb of, 191; trumped by memory, 178. *See also* Diseases of presentness
Preshadowing, 279
Presley, Elvis, 149, 297
Presumed significance, 159–60
Pretender, 118, 131, 152
Price, Martin, 287, 291
Prigogine, Ilya, 145, 297
Primary Chronicle, 65–66
Prime Minister, The (Trollope), 292
Principles of Psychology (James), 284
Prison house of perspective, 210–12
Private t, 101–2; 176–77
Probability argument, 253–54, 306
"Problem of the Text, The" (B), 23–24
Problems of D's Poetics (B), 91–101, 110,

282; B questions, 105–6; and closure, 162–63; vs. chronotope, 112–13; editions of, 96, 98; and pluralism, 272–73
Process theology, 291
Process vs. product, 9, 17–41; and (an)isomorphism, 20, 61; and aperture, 172; and bias of artifact, 61; and creative process, 23–27, 80; and death, 38; in D, 9, 27–37, 40–41; and essential surplus, 43–45; and eventness, 9, 21–22; and utopia, 30–33, 270
Processual intentions, 12, 24, 142–45, 158, 285
Production model of creativity, 23, 25
Professors, 307
Progress, 13, 194–95; changing criteria of, 199, 270; law of, 155–56, 195, 199, 244, 276; and single truth, 269–70
Progressive and progressivism, 39, 237; in evolution, 13, 246–49, 305; in *Fathers and Sons*, 194–95; of intelligentsia, 274–79, 307; and relativism, 244, 278–79; in Soviet art, 258–59; of spirituals, 274, 278; and time line, 244–45; T vs., 275–77; and Whiggism, 241–43. *See also* Chronocentrism; Temporal egotism
Prophecy, 229, 269; in dreams, 10, 75, 77f, 107; in history, 53–54; in *Oedipus*, 59–61; vs. prediction, 288; in Primary Chronicle, 65–66; socialist realism as, 57–58; and substantive philosophies of history (Marxism), 53–54
Prosaic(s), 25, 40, 190, 197, 200: and bipolar fallacy, 187; and choice, 19, 22, 157–58; and creative process, 25, 27; vs. crisis and revolutionism t, 161, 203, 205; in *Fathers and Sons*, 196–97; and love (AK), 72–74; in *Middlemarch*, 197–98; and presentness of past, 183–87; and sidesh, 157–58, 161, 197f; vs. vortex t, 167
Proust, Marcel, 102–3, 293
Providence, 164, 168–69
Provocation, 97–100, 291
Pseudo-foreshadowing, 12, 134–37, 160–61
Psychological vs. logical consequences of beliefs, 3, 10, 71, 63–64, 66–69, 228–29, 230, 290
Psychology, 1f, 138–39, 148, 167, 284
Ptolemaic, 94, 118f, 252
Public t, 101–2, 104, 176–77, 292

Publishers and revisions, 30
Pull of t and history, 50, 59, 62, 64, 164
Pun of creativity, 27–30, 31
Punctuated equilibrium, 293
Punctuational pun, 37
Pure potential t, 222–23
Pushkin, Alexander, 258, 271; "De-mons," 137, 299; "Egyptian Nights," 104; *Eugene Onegin*, 25, 294; "The Queen of Spades," 228
Pythagoreans, 51

Quantum physics, 228, 287
Quasi-: characters, plot, and events, 300; simultaneity, 228
'Queen of Spades, The" (Pushkin) 228

Rabelais, François, 297
Radical "democratic" critics, 7, 56–57
Rahv, Philip, 301
Ramifying t, 19, 22, 49, 156f; and Aris-totle, 36, 70; and sidesh, 18, 117, 119, 281
Rasselas (Johnson), 201, 267, 286
Ravelment of possibilities, 156, 240
Raw material: present people as, 13, 199, 259–60; and creative process, 23
Raw Youth, The (D), 128, 179–80, 300
"Reaction in Germany, The" (Baku-nin), 302
Reactionary, 237, 242–43, 258–59, 268
Read, Christopher, 301
Readability, 79, 157
Readers and reading, 51, 63, 89–90, 106, 190, 292f; of AK, 77, 80–81; and aperture, 164–71; and contingency, 159–62; of D, 91–94, 104, 123–24, 127, 136, 295; double perspective of, 43, 50; and essential surplus, 43–45; intermitted, 102–3, 292–93; and novel series, 153–54; of *Oedipus*, 59–61, 289; and rereading, 7, 44–45, 59, 103f, 299; and serialization, 299; solitary, 176; t of, 102–5; of utopia, 39–40; of W&P, 159–62, 184. *See also* Characters and reader; Rereading
"Ready-made," 23–24, 25, 112
Real historical t, 107–10 (B phrase), 176
"Real present of the creative pro-cess," 100
Real vs. actual, 83
"Reality in its revolutionary develop-ment," 57
Recessive gene, 120, 296
Reciprocity, fallacy of, 240

Recollection vs. repetition, 100
Recycling of characters, 153–55
Regret, 2, 18, 31, 52, 85, 233
Rehearsal: life as, 218–19; t, 224–27
Relative: closure, 170; independence of characters, 91, 96
Relativism, 244, 273, 278–79; vs. plural-ism, 269, 273
Remembrance of Things Past (Proust), 102–3
Remorse, 212, 233
Repentance, 192
Repetition, 69, 100, 229, 302; t, 301
Replaceability, 109
Replay the tape, 148, 245–49 *passim*
Requiem, 90
Rereading, 51, 77, 100, 289, 299; and eternal recurrence, 52; first reading as, 44; and *Oedipus*, 59; and pseudo-foresh, 135f; and reading, 7, 59, 103f; and structure, 44–45, 104
Resolutions to resolve, 226
Resonance, 129
Responsibility, 2, 6, 9f, 87, 128, 227; B on, 86–87; and choice, 34, 63–64; and fate, 63–69 *passim*, 74–75; and (in)determinism, 63–64, 66, 87; and middle realm, 139–42; in multiple t, 304; and nonaction, 217; and omens, 71; for one's character, 108, 294; varies by genre, 107
Resurrection (T), 190
Resurrections of characters, 153–55
Retrodiction, 3, 46, 245
Retrospection, 157; fallacy of, 239–40
"Return the ticket," 85
Revelation, Book of, 1, 166, 205–6, 274, 295, 299
Reverse sentimentality, 139
Reversibility, 108f, 245
"Review of *Twice-Told Tales*" (Poe), 292
Revolution(ism), 13, 199–201, 214; intellectual, 278; t, 203–6
Rewriting history, 263
Rhys, Jean, 151
Rhythm, 90, 99
Rice, James L., 296
Richardson, Samuel, 151, 293
Ricoeur, Paul, 297, 300
Ripley, Alexandra, 151
Risk, 202–3, 225
Road not taken, 157
Robert of Liege, 274
Romanticization of the machine, 285
Rough draft, 13, 218–19, 222, 230

Roulette, 202–5
Rumor, 121–28 *passim*, 138, 148, 294, 297
Russia that did not happen, the, 148
Russian Herald, 179

Sacrifice, 31, 68
Salvation ex machina, 192
Sankovitch, Natasha, 300
Scandalous scenes, 163
Scarlett (Ripley), 151
Scene of the crime, 225
Schapiro, Leonard, 301
Science, 3, 42, 156, 162, 245–55, 278
Science fiction, 148
Scientific socialism, 257–58
Scott, Walter, 111
Scripted history, 263–64
Scroll, 63, 67, 208, 213
Seal of death, 62–63, 67
Self-laceration, 138, 296
Sensitive dependence on initial conditions, 156
Sentimentality, 80; reverse, 139
Sequels, 151
Serialization, 103f, 149–50, 170f, 295, 299; and aperture or presentness, 169–72, 174–75; and intermitted reading, 292–93
Sermon on the mount, 141
Shadow cabinet and history, 148
Shakespeare, William, 260, 271, 279; *Henry IV, Part 2*, 67
Shamela (Fielding), 151
"Shcherbatsky element," 73
Shelley, Percy, 26–27, 98
Shipwrecks, 109
Shklovsky, Victor, 98; *Third Factory*, 25
Shoehorning, 246
Sideshadowing, 5ff, 14, 113, 117–72, 284, 294–99 *passim*; and aperture, 169–72; and backsh, 211, 235, 237, 247, 249, 270, 277; and Bernstein, 6, 283; and Christmas stories, 297; and chronocentrism, 280–82; and contingency, 6, 41, 119, 155–62, 267, 273; and doubling of characters or novels, 128–29, 140–41; and evolution, 13, 247, 249; and fields of possibility, 141–42, 155; and hunger for possibilities, 148–50; identified, 11–12, 117–20; and memory, 179, 180–85; and middle realm, 6, 141–42; vs. multiple t, 13, 233, 303; and opinion, 267, 270, 273, 280–82; and paraquels or parodies, 151–53;

past, 12, 119, 132–34, 303; and presentness of past, 178–87; and processual intentions, 142–45; and prosaics, 157–58, 197f, 161; and pseudo-foresh, 134–37; and recycling of characters, 153–55; and responsibility (BK), 139–42; and rumors, 294, 297; vs. utopia, 120, 256–57; and vortex t, 12, 153–68 *passim*, 299; and W&P, 155–62, 169–72 —in D, 5, 11–12, 41; BK, 137–42, 144–47, 298f; C&P, 294; *House of the Dead*, 129; P, 120–38, 294
Sign, 7, 69–70, 257; vs. cause, 51, 60, 161, 300; and omens, 61, 76
Signposts, 66, 200–201, 204–5, 275, 301
Sigwart, Christoph, 284, 290
Simultaneity, 11, 100–105, 118, 206, 259, 290; and multiple t, 228; and sports t, 12, 176–77
"Singular singularity," 22
Sinyavsky, Andrei: *Lyubimov*, 33; "On Socialist Realism," 57–58, 306; *Soviet Civilization*, 201, 204, 255, 260
Skeptical Inquirer, The, 62
Skepticism, 64, 68–69, 110, 199–200, 278
Skinner, B. F., 294
Slander, 149
Smith, B. H., 284
"Smudge to smudge," 124
Smuggling meaning, 19
Soap operas, 150
Socialism, 51, 57–58, 199f, 249, 257–58
Socialist realism, 40, 57–58, 190, 259–60, 268
Society as artwork, 256, 259–60
Solipsism in the bleachers, 176
Solomon, 228
Solzhenitsyn, Alexander, 212
Something else, 7, 118f, 161, 277
Sophocles (*Oedipus*), 7, 10, 58–61, 65–69 *passim*, 100, 117, 176, 289
Soul vs. spirit, 90f
Soviet Civilization (Sinyavsky), 201, 204, 255, 260
Soviet Union, 7, 13, 23, 54, 57, 96, 283, 306; and backsh, 14, 236, 257–64; and B, 82, 96, 112–13, 190; and commemoration, 212–14; epic t and, 190; and new Soviet man, 113, 259; and previous art, 258–59; prosaic faults of, 201
Space and time, 47, 70; differences between, 17–18; and foresh, 48–49; and isotropy, 46
Specious present, 284

Speech zone, 294
Speed of time, 165, 289
Spiritual intelligence, 274–75, 278
Spite, 9
Sports time, 12, 173–78
Square roots, 9, 42
Stage directions, 215
Stalin, Joseph, and Stalinism, 57, 148, 259–64
Steiner, George, 171
Stellovsky, F. I., 202
Stencil work, 157, 171, 239
Stern tribunal, 276, 279
Sterne, Laurence, 102f, 292
Stewart, Jimmy, 297
Stoics, 51, 288
Stokowski, Leopold, 292
Storm, 47–48, 53, 63, 77
"Story of the Good Brahmin" (Voltaire), 228
"Story-line weight," 90
Strange: conjunctures, 143; synchronies, 11, 100–105
Structuralism, 21, 95, 285, 291
Structure, 10f, 18, 41, 58; and AK, 10, 76f, 79–80; and aperture, 171–72; and art vs. life, 38, 77–78; and contingency, 158, 159–60; escape from, 40–41; and essential surplus, 43–44; vs. event(ness), 93, 97, 104; and foresh, 7, 50, 100–101; of history, 20, 39; vs. identifying, 10, 43f, 61, 76; and isotropy, 40–41; in *Oedipus*, 59–61, 76; vs. polyphony, 97, 100
Substantive philosophy of history, 10, 53–54
Subtracting memories, 180, 295
Sue, Eugène, 103
Suffering in D, 129
Suicide: in AK, 78–79, 171, 191; Kirillov's, 205–6; Nekhliudov's, 154–55; Tuzenbach's, 219; and vortex t, 164
Superannuation, 54, 193f
Superfluous man, 69
Superman, 300
Superstitions, 75f, 146, 217
Surplus: of creativity, 23; of event, 9, 22; essential, 43–45, 47, 50, 77–81, 88f, 97, 287; of humanness, 112–13; information-bearing, 97–98; knowledge, 236; of possibilities, 84; of temporalities, 119–20
Surprise and surprisingness, 11, 29, 91, 160, 261, 263; and creative process,

25, 98–99, 285; and epilogue, 192, 198; and eventness, 21–22; to God, 96, 98; and historicity, 250; and loophole, 90; and prosaics, 22, 198
Surroundings vs. field of vision, 89
Survival beyond the vortex, 166
Suspense, 19, 22, 42, 45, 66, 104; and sports t, 174–76
Suspense convention, 104, 175–76
Swerve and fate, 70
Swift, Jonathan, 152, 197
Sylvie and Bruno (Carroll), 290
Symmetry/asymmetry, 39, 52, 60, 62, 78, 259, 261; of t, 45–47; and mutable past, 206–7; and totalitarianism, 264
Synchronies, 11, 100–105
Systems, 21–22, 271

Table of logarithms, 36, 42
Tabloid articles, 148f
Talmud, 228
Tannen, Deborah, 300
Tasting truth, 274
Teleology, 50, 58, 62, 66–67, 100, 254, 287; and history, 2, 199, 237, 279; vs. imperfect design, 250; and the progressive, 244, 279
Temporal: catastrophism, 212; collision, 59–60, 61; conflict, 111, 167; contradiction, 58, 66, 150, 292; density, 19; doubling (the "historic"), 185; humility, 119; illusion, 64, 185; incoherence, 238; layering, 178; sensitivity, 156; vacuum, 30–33; wisdom, 279–82; —egotism, 212, 235–38, 249, 278–82; avoiding, 280–82; of intelligentsia, 274–79, 307; and Whiggism, 241–43
Temporary closure, 154
Tenses, wisdom of, 119
Terras, Victor, 298
Terror(ism), 203ff, 225
Tests, 66–68, 99, 107, 210–11, 291
Theology, 2, 11, 49, 53, 57, 85–86; in BK, 138; James's, 10, 85–86; and literary structure, 44; process, 291; and temporal God, 95–97
Theoretism, 21, 285
Theory and literary criticism, 94–95, 273, 277; chronocentrism of, 278–79; and Marxism's appeal, 288; and plain man fallacy, 209; and prison of perspective, 211; purposes of, 4, 82
Thick description, 4, 190
Third Factory (Shklovsky), 25

Thought and Language (Vygotsky), 27
Three Sisters (Chekhov), 13, 214–22, 302
Threshold art, 297
Throb of presentness, 191
Time: "forges," 21; line, 18, 244–45; loops, 10, 70–71, 303; "no longer," 1, 166, 205
Timofeev, L. I., 57
"Tiny alterations," 157, 161, 298
Titles: *Forerunners*, 257–58; I, 137; of novel and series, 298
Todd, William Mills, 203, 300
Tolstoy, Leo, 5, 13, 41, 57f, 91, 106, 269–72 *passim*, 293, 306; and an-isomorphism, 39; and aperture, 12, 169–72; and contingency, 155–62; crit-ics of, 8, 191; describes fallacies, 13, 238–41, 249, 306; "for some reason," 155f; and Gould, 155, 244, 249; vs. intelligentsia, 14, 81, 275–77, 279; and Lessing's curse, 8; and length, 293; and prosaics, 73f, 185–87
—AK, 10, 88, 101, 103, 108f, 279, 299; aperture in, 169, 171; and contin-gency, 6, 78, 160; and epilogue t, 191f; and foresh, 71–81; and opinion, 268–69; and prefiguration, 55–56; criticized in RY, 179–80, 300
—W&P, 20, 93, 107, 111, 197, 292; and aperture, 169–72; and contingency, 6, 155–62; criticized by RY, 179–80; and happiness, 187–88; identifies fallacies, 238–42, 276–77; and intermitted read-ing, 102–3; and many truths, 271–72; and presentness of past, 179, 183–84, 185–87; public and private t in, 101–2
—other works: corrected Bible, 56; *The Cossacks*, 170; "The Devil," 150; *The Living Corpse*, 154; "Notes of a Bil-liard Marker," 154–55; *Resurrection*, 154–55; "Why Do Men Stupefy Them-selves?" 224, 298; writings on W&P, 169–71, 184, 238–39; *Youth*, 154
Tolstoy and D. *See* Dostoevsky and/vs. T
"Too many facts," 121, 123
Torah, 55
Torture, 166f, 97–100
Total predictability, 287
Totalitarianism, 53, 259, 261, 264, 304; and opinion, 14, 269
Toulmin, Stephen, 273; and June Good-field, *The Discovery of Time*, 283
Tour guides to utopia, 21–22

"Toward a Philosophy of the Act" (B), 21–22, 177, 285, 291
"Toward a Reworking of the D Book" (B), 38, 91, 96–97
Traces of unrealized possibilities, 84
Tragedy, 19, 71, 112, 187, 299; of anach-ronism, 194–95
Tragic necessity, 36
Transcription, 21–22, 87, 284
Treetop analogy, 185
"Trifles," 220, 225
Tristram Shandy (Sterne), 102f, 292
Triumph over time, 106
Trollope, Anthony: Barchester series, 12, 154, 298; *Barchester Towers*, 170; *Can You Forgive Her?* 288; *Last Chronicle of Barset*, 154, 298; Palliser series, 12, 153–54, 292; *Prime Minister*, 292; "Two Heroines of Plumplington," 298
Turgenev, Ivan, 42, 91, 99, 107; *Fathers and Sons*, 12, 101, 109, 128, 193–97, 268, 301
Twentieth century, 1, 14, 212, 269
"Twice two makes four," 28–29, 286
"Two Heroines of Plumplington" (Trol-lope), 298
Types, 7, 54–58, 179
Typical of the future, 58
Tyranny of the present instant, 282

Ultimate semantic authority, 94f
Unactualized possibilities, 220, 228; and James, 83–84; and hypothetical t, 223; and middle realm, 6, 118–20; and memory, 184; and multiple t, 189, 227–28, 231–33; and other world, 147; in P, 120–23; and self, 295; in W&P, 161. *See also* Field of possibilities; Middle realm; Possibilities
Unanimity, 260–61
Uncaused events, 290
Uncertainty, 96, 103–4, 148, 174–6, 197
Uncle Vanya (Chekhov), 18–19
Understanding: is forgiving, 80, 290; entails being, 210
Unfinalizability, 90, 92f, 97, 108, 110
Unfinished works, 150
Unfolding, 21, 34–35, 243, 246; vs. becoming, 2f, 5, 24, 28, 97, 110, 250
"Unhistoric acts" (Eliot), 198
Uniformitarianism, 110, 189
Unique evolution, 290, 297
Unity and polyphony, 94
Unknown and/vs. undetermined, 34;

Unknown and/vs. underterm'd (cont'd)
  and suspense convention, 103–4,
  175–6
Unlikenesses and history, 242
"Unnecessary continuation," 198
Unnoticed causes, 62f
Unrecognized parody, 152
Unrepeatability, 22f, 245
"Unvisited tombs" (Eliot), 198
Unwelcome sideshadows, 151
Utopia(n), 19, 34, 58, 64, 74, 214;
  and Archimedean thinking, 40; and
  backsh, 14, 255–64; and certainty
  or single truth, 31f, 255–56, 269–70;
  eliminates possibility, 257, 272; literature, 31, 39–40, 255–57, 259, 306;
  masterplot, 306; vs. novels, 109, 256–
  57; and opinion, 14, 255–56, 272; as
  product, 30–33; as sidesh, 120, 256–
  57; Soviet Union as, 257–64; t, 13,
  198–201, 214; and unanimity, 260–61

V-shaped diagram, 46–47, 48
Vagrant philosopher, 263
"Valorized temporal categories" (B), 189
Velleities, 214
Verificationism, 209
Victimization, 245, 280
Virgil, 3, 64–65, 66, 123
Virtual plot, 300
Vitalism, 194f
Voice-ideas, 98
Voltaire (François Marie Arouet), 270;
  "Story of the Good Brahmin," 228
Vortex: fate as, 65; "of circumstances,"
  167
Vortex time, 12, 162–69, 299; after, 166,
  167–69; and coincidences, 163–64; and
  isolated present, 201
Vortical expectations, 289
Voyeurism, 141
Vulgar formalism and Marxism, 24
"Vulnerability" of world, 86, 304
Vygotsky, Lev, 27, 285

Wachtel, Andrew, 144, 292, 298
Walcott, Charles Doolittle, 246–47, 305
Walden Two (Skinner), 294
Wallace, Alfred Russel, 249–50
War and Peace (T), 20, 107, 111, 160,
  179; aperture of, 169–72; contingency
  in, 6, 155–62; epilogue to, 197, 276–
  77; on happiness, 187–88; length of,
  102–3, 157–58, 170; and many truths,

271–72; and memory, 183–84; and
  prosaics, 185–87; and RY, 179–80;
  times of, 100–101; T on, 138–39,
  169–71, 184
—episodes or characters: Czartoryski,
  160–61; death of Pierre's father, 158–
  59; Dolokhov, 170; Karataev, 93;
  "Matryoshka," 186; opening scene,
  292; Rostov's charge, 156–57, 187;
  wolf hunt, 188
—analogies: historical calculus, 185;
  log-hauling, 239, 306; perspectival fallacies, 238–41; stencil work, 239, 257;
  treetop, 185
Wasiolek, Edward, 296
Waste, 216, 223
Watt, Ian, 293
Wave of the future, 244
Waverley (Scott), 111
We (Zamyatin), 33, 256, 261, 286
Weather forecasting, 157
Weber, Max, 297
Wells, H. G., 152, 283
What Is to Be Done? (Chernyshevsky),
  40, 56, 151–52
What may have been = what could
  be, 148
Whig Interpretation of History (Butter-
  field), 13, 241–43, 244, 239
Whiggism, 241–42, 279; and magnet,
  242; scientific, 245f; squared, 259
Whirlwind motion, 106
White, Hayden, 284
Whittington, Harry, 246
Whole: of character's life, 90; seamless,
  271; synchronic, 97; "ultimately," 271
"Why Do Men Stupefy Themselves?"
  (T), 224, 298
Wide Sargasso Sea (Rhys), 151
Will: to destroy, 205; to will, 220
Williams, Julie, 290
Williams, Michael, 302
Windshield wipers, 48
Wisdom, 117, 269, 277; as coefficient
  of history, 274–79; prosaic, 119, 158,
  161, 196f
Wishes, 85, 141–42, 214–16, 296–97
Wolf, Fred Alan, 227f, 233, 303
Wonderful Life (Gould), 245–49, 253,
  305
"World-in-the-making" (B), 110
Writer's Diary, A (D), 104–5, 179, 299,
  301; "Apropos of the Exhibition,"
  181–82, 183–87 passim; "Dream of a

Ridiculous Man," 144, 228; Kairova
case, 142–45, 297; Kornilova case,
105; "Meek One," 295; "Peasant
Marey," 294; spiritualism sketch,
32–33

"Yet-to-come" (B), 89f
You can't go home again, 17
Youth (T), 164

Zamyatin, Eugene, 33, 152, 256, 261, 286
Zero-sum game in ethics, 232–33, 304
Zone of familiar contact, 190